If This Is Love, Why Do I Feel So Insecure?

If This Is Love, Why Do I Feel So Insecure?

CARL G. HINDY, PH.D.

J. CONRAD SCHWARZ, PH.D.

ARCHIE BRODSKY

THE ATLANTIC MONTHLY PRESS
NEW YORK

Published simultaneously in Canada
Printed in the United States of America

Library of Congress Cataloging-in-Publication Data
Hindy, Carl G.
  If this is love, why do I feel so insecure? / Carl G. Hindy,
  J. Conrad Schwarz, Archie Brodsky. — 1st ed.
   ISBN 0-87113-310-5
   1. Love.   2. Security (Psychology)   I. Schwarz, J. Conrad.
II. Brodsky, Archie.   III. Title.
BF575.L8H57   1989   152.4—dc19   88-27112

The Atlantic Monthly Press
19 Union Square West
New York, NY 10003

First Printing

Design and composition by The Sarabande Press

To our parents

and to our teacher,

Julian B. Rotter

ACKNOWLEDGMENTS

First, we wish to thank our participants, the hundreds of men and women, parents and siblings, friends and roommates who shared their feelings, experiences, observations, and opinions. As they read our book, we hope that the insights it contains will reward them in some measure for their care and courage. Likewise, we thank our many clients, who have taught us so much over the years; we hope that we have helped them along the way.

We are especially indebted to a number of psychologists, both teachers and colleagues—some for their invaluable input into the design of the study, others for their hours of reflection and discussion on theoretical, clinical, and methodological issues. They include Julian B. Rotter, Jeffrey D. Fisher, George J. Allen, L. Eugene Thomas, David Kenny, Herbert Getter, Minor Chamblin, and Jerzy Karylowski.

We are grateful to the University of Connecticut Research Foundation for grants to Carl Hindy (35-613), Conrad Schwarz (35-460), and Dena McLerran (35-584), which aided us in gathering information on the love relationships of young men and women at the end of their college experience. We are also grateful to the National Institutes of Health (R01 MH31750-01-06 and R01 01AA06754-01-03) and the UConn Research Foundation (35-544, 35-634), whose grants to Conrad Schwarz supported the initial recruitment and assessment of families that participated in the Family Dynamics Study. These funds also assisted with the development and maintenance of the extensive data base employed in this research.

A research effort of this magnitude requires the cooperative effort of many individuals playing diverse roles. The soldiers in this small army of researchers were the numerous undergraduate psychology majors who over the years have assisted in various aspects of data collection, coding, and checking. We thank them and hope that the benefits they derived from their voluntary participation equal the high value we placed upon their contribution. The lieutenants were the graduate students in psychology at the University of Connecticut who helped organize and supervise the initial data collection and data coding for the Family Dynamics Study. Listed in chronological order from their initial participation, they are: Marty Krugman, Bronwen Williams, Marianne Barton-Henry, Tom Pruzinsky, and Dena McLerran. Each has gone on to receive the doctoral degree in clinical psychology.

Many talented people labored at the tasks of computer scoring the coded questionnaire data and building the integrated computer data base. In addition to the graduate students listed above, important contributions were also made in the areas of data-base management and statistical analysis by George Goldsmith, Sterling Green, Robert Upson, Jack Mearns, Sharla Rausch, and David Wheeler. David Wheeler deserves special thanks, first, because he was the person most involved with the computer analysis of our data on love relationships and second, because his patience, ingenuity, perseverance, and even temper contributed so much to the successful solution of the problems we encountered along the way. We are also grateful to Yola Harrison and Shelley Mackaman, who were involved in the ancillary studies discussed in Chapter 7.

We thank Ann Merritt, who has served as the executive secretary of the Family Dynamics Project from its inception in 1978 to the present. She prepared many of the questionnaire forms, monitored the progress of the initial data collection, assisted with the preparation of grant proposals and requests, and reviewed earlier drafts of portions of this book manuscript. Her support has been unflagging and her good humor uplifting.

Our thanks to Mary Arnold, Wendy Goble, Carolina Herfkens, Joy Kosta, Stanton Peele, Samantha Shane, and Ilene Whitacre for comments on portions of the manuscript. One of our loyal readers, Kathleen Lomatoski, also brought together a wide range of resource listings that we hope will be useful to those seeking such assistance. Special thanks are due to Susan Vonderheide for her numerous stylistic contributions throughout the entire manuscript.

Ann Godoff and Nancy Lewin, a sensitive editorial team, set high standards and encouraged us to write the book we wanted to write, even if that meant breaking out of commercial publishing formulas. John Brockman and Katinka Matson showed imagination and faith in envisioning and supporting the project. Finally, we thank Sara Bailis and Evans Research Associates of San Francisco, as well as Michael L. Commons and PC Genius of Woburn, Massachusetts, for the logistical support they provided at crucial moments.

Carl Hindy and Conrad Schwarz give warm-hearted thanks to their wives, Susan Vonderheide and Carolina Herfkens, for their personal support. They lent their encouragement at every step—from the first thought of a book through the editing of the last page; on many occasions, they gave sustenance and cheer to three hungry authors.

Here the source of a man's strength lies not in himself but in his relation to other people. No matter how close to them he may be, if his center of gravity depends on them, he is inevitably tossed to and fro between joy and sorrow. Rejoicing to high heaven, then sad unto death—this is the fate of those who depend upon an inner accord with other persons whom they love. Here we have only the statement of the law that this is so. Whether this condition is felt to be an affliction or the supreme happiness of love, is left to the subjective verdict of the person concerned.

—Lao Tsu, *Tao Te Ching* (Richard Wilhelm, trans.)
Bollingen Series 19, 3rd ed.
Princeton University Press, 1967, p. 238.
(circa sixth century B.C.)

CONTENTS

I

Why Passion Turns to Pain:

The Riddle of Insecure Love

Elaine, a thirty-six-year-old ballet dancer, began therapy after an emotionally draining episode. After fifteen years of an amiable, childless marriage, she had fallen in love with her mentor, a prominent choreographer. Although she knew little of Peter outside of their artistic and professional activities, in her mind their shared dedication to dance became a romantic bond. She often dreamed about Peter; she thought of him every time she began to dance, and eventually as she lay awake at night after silent, perfunctory lovemaking with her husband, Steve.

For quite a long time she said nothing to Peter, until finally she wrote him a long, unrestrained letter weaving together her love of dance with her love for him. When she saw him next, Peter, a quiet, formal man, reacted with discomfort. He complimented her work and expressed pleasure in their professional relationship, but disclaimed any romantic interest in her. One remark he made stuck in her mind. "This doesn't seem to have much to do with me," he said.

Elaine was shaken by this remark. For several weeks she agonized over how she had made a fool of herself. He was right — this didn't have much to do with him. How could it? She didn't even know him well enough to say anything really personal to him in her letter, much less talk about being soul-mates. Painful as it was, Elaine had to admit that her letter was not so much a message to another person as a transcript of a private obsession.

This insight led her to think back to the other men she had approached during the past several years, for this was not the first time she had lost her head this way. There had been other infatuations, other letters, other anguished declarations, and other rebuffs. Elaine was an attractive, intelligent woman, yet all these men had rejected her—some at the outset; others after a one-night affair. Now Peter, her mentor in this as in other areas, had told her why. Her letters and impassioned pleas, so full of longing, of suppressed energy, *weren't at all about the recipients.* All too plainly, they expressed her own needs outside the context of an actual relationship. Her desires were too intense and her demands too great for these men to handle comfortably.

A thoughtful, self-conscious person, Elaine found this a troubling insight. What made her act so "crazy"? She had a decent home life; she didn't need to go out looking for a relationship. Why did these intense feelings arise? What were they about? What needs was she seeking to satisfy?

Since her feelings about ballet had figured so strongly in her romantic attraction to Peter, she began to explore with her therapist what ballet meant to her. As a child Elaine had worked hard to free herself from her domineering mother and to get closer to her cold and distant father. Elaine's mother apparently had preferred that her husband be alienated from the children, so that he could not interfere with her influence over them. Elaine could barely remember spending any time alone with her father. From her earliest years, the one thing that had won Elaine her parents' unqualified approval (though not affection) was her dancing. Still, despite her parents' penchant for displaying her as a prodigy, dance had become for Elaine a deeply personal refuge, the one outlet she had for expressing feelings safely. She danced to please not only her parents, but herself.

Soon after her arrival on the state college campus, she met Steve, a man with whom she remained continuously involved; upon graduation they were married. Elaine had struggled hard to break away from her family and go off to school, and her independence was still tentative and uncertain. Steve seemed self-assured and talked a confident line, not so much about conquering the world as insulating himself from it in spiritual self-sufficiency. He, too, had a distant father and an overwhelming mother, and this similarity of backgrounds may have contributed to the compatibility he and Elaine felt with each other. However, Steve's style, like his father's, was to set limits, erect barriers, and stay at arm's length—a tendency Elaine found increasingly frustrating as the years went on.

The overriding social and cultural preoccupations of college life in the late 1960s could obscure large differences in personal preferences and temperaments. Indeed, Elaine and Steve had less in common than they thought at the time. She a serious performing artist, he a philosophy major headed for a professorship, they thought themselves the perfect match. Actually, though, Steve used philosophy to tame life and distance himself emotionally, while Elaine danced with self-absorbed reverence.

By the time Elaine entered therapy, she was actively discontented with her marriage. Most of her complaints centered on Steve's emotional un-availability. "He's a good husband, but there's nothing to grab on to. He's not very affectionate physically. I love him, but I don't feel connected to him. It's like we're running on parallel tracks." Feeling blocked in her intimate life, Elaine had poured herself more and more into artistic performance. It was as if she were dancing again and again the steps that had made her feel valued and appreciated as a child.

Her therapist told her, "Sometimes the things people complain about in their spouses are things they don't really wish to change. People choose complaints they can live with, even if they don't like them. If they didn't have those complaints, they wouldn't know what to do next—and they might get really frightened. Ideally, you might want Steve to be different, but then you might have to change yourself to meet him on different ground." It appeared that Elaine had set herself up with an impassive man, like her father, whose defensive shell she needed to break through, while Steve had set himself up with an emotionally demanding woman like his mother to fend off. Marriage had liberated Elaine from the impasse of being unable to get close to her father for fear of rejection by her mother, yet it simultaneously had welcomed her back into a familiar prison of emotional neglect.

Had she wanted simply to gain the affection she felt she had been denied, she might well have obtained it either in or outside of marriage. Instead, she re-created (both in her marriage and in her attempts at love affairs) the struggle for acceptance that had been so frustrating for her as a child and that she had never resolved. It was as if what she found rewarding was reliving the struggle itself, rather than reaching the goal. In adulthood as in childhood, dance was both her magic potion to beguile others and her magic carpet of escape. Her fantasy about Peter, her admired colleague and teacher, was so seductive because Peter personified her unconscious belief that love could be won through performance. For a time after he spurned her advances she worried that he would stop teaching and advising her; this unfounded fear stemmed from interpreting her failure to win his affection as equivalent to being panned by critics after a performance.

Had she been able to form an intimate relationship with Peter, the lifelong association Elaine had drawn between acceptance-as-approval and acceptance-as-affection would have been put to the test. The outcome likely would have been more deeply disorienting than fulfilling. But in reality Elaine did not run that risk, since she declared her love in a way that assured that Peter would not reciprocate. She wouldn't have known what to do if he had reciprocated, for she unconsciously assumed that he would reject her. Rejection put her in the familiar—and, in that sense, less threatening—position of worrying about whether he would even teach or work with her again. One day she made a grand appeal for love; the next day she felt compelled to salvage any scrap of attention, as she had with her father.

As she began to understand the kinds of choices she had been making all her life, Elaine was better able to separate her marriage from the fantasies that had surrounded it. From week to week she wavered between wanting a divorce and resolving to work on her marriage. Her therapist suggested that she take steps in both directions simultaneously, in order to test out how it might feel to go down either path. He encouraged her to speak with an attorney about what getting a divorce would entail, and at the same time to be more assertive with her husband and clearer about her needs. She had, after all, been stuck in inaction for years. If she experienced her marriage as a charade, it was not only because Steve was not emotionally present, but also because she had let his withdrawal from her go unchallenged. Instead of testing the limits of their relationship, she had played by its implicit rules (in which she, too, had invested) while simultaneously imagining herself living with Peter as his wife and lover, dance partner and protégée.

Perhaps she should not take for granted that Steve did not want intimacy, or was incapable of expressing it. Perhaps he wanted closeness, but was afraid to initiate it. He, too, might have painted himself into a corner by settling into rigid, limiting roles with her. When two people have been making love silently for fifteen years, it can be hard for either to break out of the pattern and be as uninhibited in their marriage as they might be in a new love affair. Could Elaine and Steve still transform their marriage? Although it was not Elaine's job to make her husband over, she could at least take responsibility for her end of the relationship and try to bring out Steve's capacity for expressing affection by expressing the affection she still felt for him.

Her first effort to communicate more deeply with Steve was tentative. Hesitantly, she ventured that she was struggling to find meaning in her life. Steve easily assimilated this into his philosophical framework, and a discussion of the meaning of life ensued. If she didn't go far enough the first time, she went perhaps too far the second time, when she blurted out, "I'm thinking of leaving you." This revelation was more precipitous than her therapist had advised; he would have preferred to see her build up to it. It was understandable, however, that a woman who was used to escaping into romantic fantasies rather than asserting herself, even about household matters, would have difficulty moderating weightier communications. For a few years Elaine had wanted to have their house repainted, but she had not said so to Steve. She had not mastered the middle ground between silent compliance and angry defiance.

Despite these rough edges in communication, Elaine was impressed with the vigor and tenacity with which Steve reacted. He proved surprisingly willing to do whatever was needed to save their marriage. Thus, her initiative opened up serious discussion between them in many previously untouched areas. Still, the outcome remained in doubt. "I don't know if I really want to work on the marriage, or if I'm doing it out of guilt," she said. "The feeling may be gone by now." Her mood and his shifted from day to day between optimism and pessimism, giddy excitement at the possibility of recapturing their youthful romance and resignation that it was not to be. Elaine felt better when she assumed a share of control. As she asserted herself more both in and out of the marriage (for example, by discussing divorce procedures with a lawyer), she felt less trapped, and more comfortable remaining married by choice. But when she felt that Steve was reasserting control, she wanted to leave him.

Steve wanted Elaine to commit herself to the marriage prior to working out the issues. He mobilized friends and relatives to prevail on her to stay. It seemed as if he was uncomfortable with the uncertainty she had introduced and wanted to restore the predictability of their relationship. He did not understand that the more he struggled to do so, the more he risked losing her. She wondered whether, once reassured of her loyalty, he would simply revert to his old ways. For herself, she would reserve judgment and would explore both paths—marriage and divorce—until she was reasonably sure that she was making the right choice.

Elaine's embarrassing romantic fantasy about Peter had revealed an insecurity that had many roots—in her background, in her husband's, in their relationship, and in other aspects of her life. No one answer could explain it all, and no one solution could set things right. But there were explanations, and there might be solutions. With this acknowledgment of complexity, and of hopeful possibilities as well, we will examine the experience (the symptoms, the feelings, the varieties, the causes, and the cures) of insecure love.

This book is based on the first major research project about insecure romantic love. This subject has been talked and written about a great deal in recent years: the desperate longing that many people feel for an intimate connection, the repeated and often futile efforts to find that connection, the emotional turmoil and the jealousy that occur along the way, and the painful experience of depression that may follow. What we have not seen previously are reliable explanations about how and why this happens: what early experiences contribute to creating a person who is prone to insecure romantic love, and what other personality traits this person is likely to display.

Six centuries before Christ, the Greeks called it *theia mania,* meaning "the madness from the gods." The poet Sappho described this condition as an overwhelming desire to be in a loved one's presence, to make physical contact, to be approved of and cared for, to possess and be fulfilled by another. *Theia mania* had symptoms familiar to us today: agitation, sleeplessness, fever, loss of appetite, and heartache. The Roman poet Ovid wrote *The Art of Love,* a literary version of today's comprehensive guide to wooing and winning the person of your dreams. In a final chapter, entitled "The Remedies for Love," Ovid advised:

> So now listen to me, young people who have been so deluded,
> Whom, for all of your pains, love has completely betrayed,
> I have taught you to love—
> Do you want to know how to recover?

Almost two thousand years later, the word *mania* has returned to the literature in the words of sociologist John Lee, who described the manic lover as "consumed by thoughts of the beloved," with an "insatiable" need for attention and affection. Lee noted that "the slightest lack of enthusiasm from the partner brings anxiety and pain; each tiny sign of warmth brings instant relief, but no lasting satisfaction."

Our notion of insecure love is similar to what Dorothy Tennov, in her book

Love and Limerence, labeled *limerence*—that is, a state of continually or repeatedly being "in love" as opposed to loving. To define the look and feel of this insecure love, we have borrowed from the literature of psychoanalysis and other branches of psychology as well as poetry, music, and drama, and focused on the following experiences:

- the unrealistic pursuit of a glamorous, elusive love object, one who keeps you perpetually up in the air or treats you with downright cruelty or disdain
- the sensation of having "fallen in love at first sight"
- the goose bumps of nervous arousal you feel in the presence of—or just thinking about—your beloved
- the obsessive preoccupation with the romantic infatuation, to the exclusion of work, school, family, friends
- the belief that all your happiness—indeed, your whole life—is wrapped up in whether this one person returns your affections
- the wish to live on an island of emotional isolation with your partner, with neither of you having emotional ties (or even much contact) with anyone else
- the continual demands for confirmation of love as, never satiated, you plead for ever more evidence of the devotion you feel is your due
- the agony and ecstasy of roller-coaster mood swings as your partner fails to meet your demands for consistent affection or avoids that ultimate commitment
- the feeling that your passion is all the more intense when you are least sure it is being reciprocated.

Tennov described these sensations, feelings, thoughts, and behaviors, but did not measure them. We have sought to capture them on a questionnaire that begins the next chapter. Some related experiences fill out the picture of insecure love:

- the insane jealousy that rages within you regardless of whether your partner is actually unfaithful
- the agonizing, cataclysmic, and often vindictive breakup
- the depressed aftermath, when you feel empty, devastated, as if the core of your being has been taken away.

Extreme jealousy, which becomes increasingly intense as the relationship unravels, and depression after the relationship ends are part of the course of insecure love and will be discussed in later chapters.

"Love hurts," sang the Everly Brothers, like many others before and since. But why does it hurt some of us more than others? What leads some of us to search for love in a self-defeating way that sets us up to be hurt again and again? What makes otherwise accomplished, confident people anxious, fearful, and insecure in their romantic involvements? Do they repeatedly choose the wrong people to fall in love with? If so, why? Do childhood experiences hold the key? Most important, what are some realistic steps we can take to do something about the problem? Can understanding lead to change and growth?

To answer these questions, we (psychologists Carl Hindy and Conrad Schwarz) conducted a nearly decade-long research project at the University of Connecticut. In the first stage of the study, 360 students in their freshman year (half women and half men) answered an exhaustive set of questionnaires (six to eight hours' worth) about their personalities and family backgrounds, as well as their dating habits, sexual experience, sexual fantasies, and alcohol and drug use. In addition, each student's parents, a sister or brother, and a college roommate or best friend filled out questionnaires concerning their observations of the student and the student's family. All family respondents contributed their perspectives on such issues as the mother's and the father's child-rearing styles, the parents' marital adjustment, and the degree to which either parent exerted a dominant influence over the child. The student and the sister or brother also rated the closeness of the student's relationship with each parent, and the two parents rated their own and each other's personalities. This in-depth survey provided a very full picture of a young person's life, seen from a number of different angles. It is a picture of how personality develops, how a person comes to be what he or she is, in a context of family relationships.

A few years later, when they were finishing college or had recently graduated, most of the same research participants filled out questionnaires about each of the four romantic relationships they considered most important in their lives thus far. For each relationship they answered thirty-three questions (reprinted at the beginning of the next chapter) about the experience of insecure love, or "anxious romantic attachment." Other questions included how long the relationship lasted, whether or not it was exclusive (i.e., monogamous), how intensely the partners felt about each other, and how much time they spent together. Each participant was asked to rate his or her romantic partners on certain key characteristics (for example, physical attractiveness, trustworthiness, and emotional consistency). Additional questionnaires explored how intensely she or he experienced a wide range of emotions in the course of each relationship, as well as jealousy toward the partner and depression after the relationship ended.

Altogether, nearly 1750 people spent about 7500 hours taking a number of well-established, reliable psychological tests. Counting several related studies, the total number of participants was close to 2500. From this large-scale study of the romantic involvements of young men and women, we believe we have learned some useful facts about how people's backgrounds and life histories lead them to form strong romantic attachments in anxious, insecure ways. We will share our findings here for what they may contribute to self-awareness and personal growth.

We were especially encouraged to find that if you look at enough information about a person, you can discern more clearly the person's temperament and consistent patterns of behavior. That is why we had family members and friends fill out questionnaires. It is also why we asked people to answer questions about four relationships rather than just one. People's lives make sense if you look at them from enough angles. If a person filled out a questionnaire about one love affair, we might just learn about an extreme situation in that person's life, a relationship that was unusually passionate or frustrating. But by asking about four relationships, we could average out a person's answers and get a better idea of what that person's romantic involvements typically were like.

In this way we identified people who were especially prone to insecurity in their love relationships and others who were not. We also identified certain kinds of childhood experiences that appear to put a person more at risk for insecure love relationships later on. Finally, we identified tangible, observable characteristics of insecure relationships. All of this information can help you determine whether a relationship that you are or were involved in might be characterized as insecure.

Starting with the test at the beginning of the next chapter, you will be able to answer many of the same questions about your relationships that our study participants answered. You can also give these questionnaires to your partner, or else answer them about your partner as well as yourself, to get a sense of what the experience is like on both sides. In addition, throughout the book the formal research findings are supplemented by fictionalized vignettes based on clinical experience as well as interviews with people who wanted to share their experiences. By interweaving these clinical and personal accounts with our data, we will paint a composite portrait of the person troubled by insecure love.

The experience of insecure love, which we also refer to as anxious romantic attachment, has two main components. One is *anxiety.* This is the "he loves me, he loves me not" sensation of being kept constantly on edge by a fickle lover. Anxious lovers feel as volatile as the stock market—up one day, down the next. Their passion rages all the more intensely when they are least sure that it is reciprocated.

The second component of insecure love is *obsession* with the loved one. Love at first sight, longing to see the loved one every day, wanting to go off and live on a deserted island together—these are signs of a romantic obsession. To the obsessed lover, the possibility of rejection feels like the end of the world.

A person who experiences romantic insecurity tends to be both anxious and obsessed. For such a person, love is a tempestuous experience, involving a range of emotions: on the one hand, excitement, joy, and sexual arousal; on the other, distress, fear, shame, anger, contempt, and disgust. Everyone feels these emotions sometimes, but the person who is insecure in love feels them especially intensely and often goes quickly from one extreme to the other.

You may recognize some of these feelings from your own (or a friend's or lover's) experience. You may recognize, too, some other signs of insecure romantic love: dating many different people, falling in love (and declaring love) frequently, feeling love more quickly and more intensely than one's partner does; and, sadly, having one's love go unrequited.

There is another side to insecure love. Some people always seem to be between relationships. They tend to pass up the highs of romance in order to avoid risking the lows of rejection. While this *detachment* looks very different from anxiety, it may in fact be closely related. Those who avoid romantic involvements may be anxious, too—so much so that they prefer not to expose themselves to experiences that might arouse their anxiety.

A person's *choice of partners* also reveals something about the kinds of relationships the person seeks. People tend to be obsessed when they find their partners particularly attractive. They tend to be anxious when they find their partners inconsistent in their behavior. You can, of course, look at the cause-and-effect relationships from either or both directions. An inconsistent partner can make you feel anxious; conversely, feelings of anxiety can lead you to perceive your partner as inconsistent and even provoke your partner to act inconsistently. Then, in a vicious cycle, you may end up feeling more anxious. Either way, information about your partner can provide useful insight into your insecure relationship.

Insecure love takes on different colorations as a relationship evolves. At the beginning there are the pounding heart and sweaty palms, the goose bumps of nervous arousal at the mere thought of the beloved, and the frequent, sometimes frantic phone calls. Later, when the insecure lover has invested more emotionally in the relationship and has more to lose, insecure love can show itself as *jealousy.* Many people at one time or another have been either on the giving or receiving end of intense jealousy: the obsessive preoccupation with the lover's whereabouts, the accusing questions, the compulsion to search dresser drawers for incriminating evidence or to cruise the streets to locate a certain person's car. The aura of romance and the excitement of infatuation—let alone trust and mutual respect—may be shattered by the destructive symptoms of romantic insecurity.

Finally, when the relationship ends, it is usually the insecure lover who is jilted. This person may be left feeling that life has lost its zest, that there is hardly energy left to get out of bed in the morning. There is a hollow, empty feeling, as if the core of one's being has been cut out. One may alternate between cursing the ex-lover and longing, even pleading, for his or her return. These are feelings of *depression,* and, like jealousy, they are commonly found in the same people who earlier manifested the feelings, thoughts, and behavior of insecure love.

Anxious attachment (or detachment), jealousy, and depression are all pieces of the jigsaw puzzle of insecure love. They are like barometers registering at key intervals in the history of a love affair or marriage, all of them measuring the same thing—the quality of a person's emotional connections with others. The character of a relationship is revealed when the relationship begins, when it is threatened, and when it ends. By looking at each of these stages in turn, we can trace the typical course of a relationship driven by one or both partners' insecurity.

Although our research has confirmed many of these descriptive features of insecure love, its most original contribution, we believe, lies in shedding some light on prior family relationships that contribute to a person's later susceptibility to insecure love. In the introductory case, both Elaine and Steve had domineering, intrusive mothers and aloof, withdrawn fathers. This background was important in shaping both partners' later development, although it had different implications for Elaine as a woman than for Steve as a man. It represents one, but far from the only, type of family pattern that may later lead to anxious romantic attachment in adulthood.

A person is (in varying degrees) more likely to feel insecure in love if one or both parents are rejecting, indifferent, or inconsistent in their demonstrations of affection. There is a clear contrast between the parents who are remote disciplinarians and those who establish a warm, nurturing relationship with a child. Parents who provide a model of an emotionally secure relationship can help a child avoid anxious attachments.

Among the families of female and male victims of insecure love, there are similarities as well as polar opposites; these will be highlighted throughout the book. Yet the *experience* of insecure love remains the same for both sexes, making mutual understanding an easier task. If insecure romantic love has been a part of your experience, you will be able to gain insight into both your own and your partner's feelings and behavior.

The roots of our study lie primarily in the work of psychoanalyst John Bowlby and psychologist Mary Ainsworth, who studied the different kinds of emotional attachments that infants form with their mothers. They observed that infants whose mothers respond reliably and sensitively to their needs tend to form secure attachments. When the mother is not reliably responsive, the infant may become anxious, noisily demanding contact with the mother while often avoiding actual contact. When the mother abuses or regularly overstimulates, the infant may turn away when in the greatest need. These patterns of attachment, if reinforced in early childhood and adolescence, may persist throughout life. In the three styles of infant behavior just described, there are similarities to three habitual approaches to adult romantic love: secure, anxiously attached, and detached.

The emotional relationships you form as an adult cannot, of course, be explained completely by the way your mother treated you when you were an infant. On the contrary, as you grew up you experienced many different kinds of attachments that may have played a part in your learning to feel secure or insecure in your connections with people. Our study explores a number of dimensions of mother-child, father-child, and even mother-father relationships as they affect later emotional attachments. It is important to understand what these relationships were like in your own life because, if you do not, you may be doomed to repeat them.

People who are habitually insecure in love relationships would say they are looking for acceptance, nurturance, and unconditional love. Yet they typically repeat destructive patterns over and over again, reexperiencing the rejection and the struggle against it. This sounds like such a painful way of life; why would people choose it? Perhaps because the struggle, having begun in infancy or childhood, is so familiar that it has become easier than more risky alternatives. Perhaps because, fearing the worst, people often see evidence to support it, which confirms repeatedly their negative view of themselves and their experience. Or perhaps there is some promise of ultimate resolution and mastery that the never-ending struggle falsely holds out.

To stop handicapping oneself in these ways, self-understanding and pattern-breaking experiences (which offer different rewards) are required. Therapy can help by bringing the sources of self-defeating behavior to conscious understanding and mastery. We hope that our findings about the childhood origins of insecure love, together with case histories of self-discovery and personal growth, will prove similarly helpful. If so, all of us will be better able not only to overcome any limitations of our personal histories, but also to serve as models of emotional security for our children and to prepare them to enter into love relationships more confidently and successfully.

2

THE LOOK AND FEEL

OF ANXIOUS LOVE

Think of a romantic relationship that is, or was, especially important to you. Better yet, think of three or four people to whom you have been strongly attracted or with whom you have felt emotionally involved. These can be people you dated for a long time or only briefly, or even just felt infatuated with—as long as the person meant a lot to you at the time. For each of these relationships or romantic interests (called A to D, or however many you wish to think about), place a number from 0 to 8 in the space beside each statement to indicate how true that statement was for you in that relationship. (Mentally fill the blank in each sentence with the name of the particular partner you are thinking of.) The higher the number, the more true the statement. That is, 0 means "not at all true; it didn't happen that way," while 8 means "definitely true; that's just the way it was."

STATEMENT   PARTNER (WRITE IN NAMES)

A   B   C   D

1. "S/he loves me, s/he loves me not;" It seemed
   that _____'s feelings for me changed very
   frequently and unpredictably.   ___ ___ ___ ___

2. I often wished that _____'s feelings for me
   were as strong as my feelings for him/her.   ___ ___ ___ ___

3. _____ seemed very capable of *both* hurting
   and comforting me.   ___ ___ ___ ___

4. Sometimes I felt that I was forcing _____ to
   show more feeling, more commitment.   ___ ___ ___ ___

5. As a girlfriend/boyfriend, _____ was
   certainly temperamental.   ___ ___ ___ ___

6. "Uncertain" is a word that well captures the
   nature of my relationship with _____.   ___ ___ ___ ___

7. I often felt that I was giving more than I was
   receiving in my relationship with _____.   ___ ___ ___ ___

8. _____ made me *both* very happy *and* very
   sad.   ___ ___ ___ ___

9. It annoyed me when _____ seemed unsure
   of her/his feelings for me.   ___ ___ ___ ___

10. I knew that _____ didn't care for me as
    much as I had hoped s/he would, but I
    couldn't accept it.   ___ ___ ___ ___

11. Things might have worked out better if
    _____'s feelings were as strong as mine
    were.   ___ ___ ___ ___

STATEMENT   PARTNER

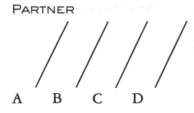

A   B   C   D

12. _____ said or implied that s/he felt
"suffocated" or "smothered" by the attention
and affection I was giving her/him.   ___   ___   ___   ___

13. I was unable really to believe in _____'s
feelings for me.   ___   ___   ___   ___

These statements express one major component of the experience of insecure love, *romantic anxiety*. It consists of feelings of uncertainty and fear, a sense that you are never on sure ground with your lover. A person who scores high on romantic anxiety will go through tumultuous feelings and sharp mood swings in the course of a relationship, often alternating between the heights of euphoria and the depths of despair. If you wrote in high numbers like 6, 7, or 8 for many of these questions concerning just one relationship, there may have been something about that person or that relationship that made you anxious. But if you have a lot of 6s, 7s, and 8s for several partners, then it seems likely that you regularly feel anxious about intimate relationships.

A typical anxious lover is Charlie, who scrubs his girlfriend's kitchen floor and gets up early to take her children to school, as if to say, "How can you not love me after all I do for you?" Forever seeking confirmation of her love, he laments, "I send her flowers, I cook her meals, I wash her car. But the more I do, the further behind I get. I guess I'm losing her respect." Charlie feels driven to have sex as frequently as possible, not for pleasure but for tangible reassurance that he is in contact with his beloved. Haunted by fears of rejection, he alienates her by searching through her letters and photos, anguished at the thought of what he might find. Not coincidentally, he has chosen a women who withholds the tokens of affection that he craves. "I want to stop doing this to myself," he muses, "but part of me loves the madness I'm living."

Now here is another set of statements that focus on a different aspect of the experience. Fill these out the same way for each of the same partners.

Remember, 0 means "not at all true; it didn't happen that way," while 8 means "definitely true; that's just the way it was."

STATEMENT   PARTNER

                                      A   B   C   D

14. I felt that if _____ rejected me, I might
    never get over it.   __   __   __   __

15. I spent much time analyzing my relationship
    with _____, weighing it in my mind. __   __   __   __

16. While I was dating _____, I had little
    desire to see other women/men.   __   __   __   __

17. From the beginning, I was eager to see
    _____ almost every day.   __   __   __   __

18. I would often lie awake at night thinking
    about being with _____.   __   __   __   __

19. After just a few dates, I felt that I might be
    in love with _____.   __   __   __   __

20. I spent a lot of time daydreaming about love,
    romance, and sex with _____.   __   __   __   __

21. The ending of my relationship with _____
    was long and drawn out, rather than sudden. __   __   __   __

22. When my relationship with _____ was
    definitely over, I felt that I had "hung on" too
    long.   __   __   __   __

23. During my relationship with _____, my
    friends and work (or schoolwork) got much
    less attention.   __   __   __   __

24. "Exciting" is a word that captures the nature
    of my relationship with _____.   __   __   __   __

STATEMENT   PARTNER

A   B   C   D

25. I wanted to spend more and more time with
    _____, feeling that I just couldn't see her/
    him often enough.   ___   ___   ___   ___

26. I felt preoccupied with feelings about _____.   ___   ___   ___   ___

27. _____ and I talked very frequently about
    our relationship.   ___   ___   ___   ___

These statements fill in the other half of the picture of insecure love, the part
that we call *romantic obsession*. This is a consuming preoccupation with the
object of your love, even to the neglect of the other people, interests, and
responsibilities that make up your life. As with the first group of statements,
high scores (6, 7, 8) on many of these items for just one relationship may mean
only that you lost your head in the grip of an unusually strong passion. But
high scores for several relationships suggest that you have a habit of losing
yourself in passionate involvements.

Kate is a woman in her thirties whose husband left her a year ago after ten
years of marriage. Unable to let go of him even now, she frequently drives past
his current lover's house to see if his car is there. She describes her plight in
terms that suggest she is living inside a glass dome of obsession: "I idealized
this man. He helped me grow up; he taught me so much. I constantly told
him how much I loved him, but still it wasn't enough. I don't care about what
he's done—all the affairs he's had. If he called up tomorrow, I don't think I'd
even play hard to get. I still love him and want him back. I probably still
idealize him, too. He's the only person who understands me totally."

Romantic anxiety and obsession go together; each contributes to making
the other what we observe it to be. In the presence of anxiety, attachment can
turn into obsession, and, with a passionate obsessive attachment, there is
often the fear of losing or failing to gain a relationship. It can be useful to look
at anxiety and obsession separately because some people feel one more strongly
than the other. But most often it is the same people who experience both to

some degree. If you are anxious in love, you are likely to be obsessed, and vice versa. Therefore, we will speak mainly of insecure love as a total experience consisting of both anxiety and obsession.

Statements illustrating the general phenomenon of insecure love are listed below. Again, 0 means "not at all true; it didn't happen that way," while 8 means "definitely true; that's just the way it was."

STATEMENT   PARTNER

                                          A   B   C   D

28. I made a bold attempt to win _____'s favor.   ___   ___   ___   ___

29. My feelings for _____ seemed to grow
    stronger when s/he expressed uncertainty
    about our relationship.   ___   ___   ___   ___

30. I am not usually as "moody" as I was during
    my relationship with _____.   ___   ___   ___   ___

31. I was afraid that _____ would stop loving
    me.   ___   ___   ___   ___

32. I saw "warning signs" of trouble in my
    relationship with _____ but tried to ignore
    them.   ___   ___   ___   ___

33. I felt an aching of the "heart" (a region in the
    center front of the chest) when I wasn't sure
    how _____ felt about me.   ___   ___   ___   ___

When we looked at how people answered them, we found that these six questions did not fit in specifically with either the anxiety statements or the obsession statements. Instead, they fit in about equally well with both groups, because they aren't about anxiety or obsession in isolation. Rather, they describe an experience of anxious attachment, or insecure love, that includes both components. So if you or your spouse or lover scores high on many of these six statements plus the twenty-seven that preceded them, you may be especially interested in what insecure love is, how it comes about, and what you can do about it.

Having answered these thirty-three items, you have taken the key portion of the Hindy Anxious Attachment Test, the same questionnaire that hundreds of experimental subjects have answered. We believe that this survey is the best test psychologists have yet devised for capturing what poets, playwrights, and novelists for thousands of years have called lovesickness and what in this book is called insecure romantic love or anxious romantic attachment — some of the main characteristics of which are illustrated here in two case vignettes.

JULIE AND MIKE: MY HUSBAND, MY RORSCHACH

Julie's days have a sameness that might be considered either soothing or terrifying. Although her husband, Mike, has suggested that she get a job if that would make her happy, she stays home with their two-year-old daughter and keeps house because she senses that this is what Mike *really* wants her to do. She keeps the house spotless — not that he ever required her to do so, but she may as well play safe. Once or twice a week she sends Mike a greeting card or a gift; indeed, she can hardly walk into a store without buying him something. And whenever he asks her to join him for coffee or lunch, she fixes her hair and puts on a fancy dress.

Julie has been married to Mike for three years, but she feels she hardly knows him. "I wish he'd communicate more," she says, meaning that she wishes he would let her know exactly what he wants — not so that she can have more to share with him, but so that he will not leave her. A pleasant, inarticulate man, Mike seems satisfied enough, and he has a way of letting things slide. So Julie leaves nothing to chance. When they got married, Mike's father expressed concern about continuing the family line, so she had a baby as soon as possible. And since Mike can get a little lax in his business affairs, Julie occasionally goes to the office and makes sure things are in order. She is intent on securing everything in the harbor so that her husband will not drift out. Nothing is going to disturb the precarious peace she has, in her late thirties, found for herself.

Why does Julie fuss over Mike this way? Perhaps she is grateful to have found such a good, or at least inoffensive, husband on her second try. For ten years she put up with an alcoholic who abused her, flaunted his love affairs, and didn't earn a steady living. After that hell, Mike's mildly patronizing air and glancing criticisms should be easy enough to live with, especially when Julie finds him generally accepting and understanding of her. Yet what is striking about Julie is that she treated her first husband, almost until she left him, with the same care and devotion she shows Mike. Moreover, even now her placid domestic life is occasionally shattered by her own unexpected outbursts of temper. Sitting alone in her perfectly ordered home, from which she has taken such care to remove all external threats, she broods about the chanciness of life with Mike. Maybe he didn't wave goodbye as she stood at the window watching him leave for work. Maybe he didn't show enough appreciation of her latest gift. Later, on his return home, Julie throws a loud and angry tantrum, lashing out at her husband's insensitivity. Stepping outside her submissive skin, she screams hysterically, "Just leave me; just leave me if you don't love me"—the last thing she would ever want. When the storm passes she is exhausted and depressed, but Mike will make it all right by showing her extra consideration.

It almost doesn't matter how Mike responds—or what he did or didn't do to deserve it. In these interchanges he seems little more than a blank piece of paper on which Julie superimposes her inner life like a Rorschach ink blot. Who is Julie screaming at? Her second husband? Her first? Someone earlier still in her life? Although her situation (which she has helped set up) contributes to her susceptibility to tantrums by allowing her too many moments of idleness and brooding isolation, the issue seems to have more to do with her personality than any one situation. To understand Julie's deep-seated anxiety about her marriage, we must go further back in her life. We will return to Julie in a later chapter.

BARBARA AND LEN: NOWHERE TO TURN

Barbara was a tall, well-groomed, well-dressed woman in her early twenties. "Why won't he leave her?" she blurted out repeatedly, as much to herself as to the therapist she was seeing for the first time. She spoke rapid-fire: "That marriage is miserable, it's miserable, it's all over. She can't hold him. She can't just hold him, can she?" In the course of the hour she went back and forth between laughter and tears. It took time and a calm, comforting demeanor for the therapist to get the whole story.

Barbara had first met Len as one of her teachers in college. Twice her age, he had responded patiently to her appeals for guidance and had become her most valued mentor. Len was married, and he and Barbara were not romantically involved while she was still an undergraduate under his tutelage. But when she graduated and went off to a prestigious graduate school for which he had groomed her, they began a long-distance affair that was highly charged with excitement. Len would jet in for a professional meeting, or else he would send Barbara tickets for a weekend rendezvous on neutral ground, sometimes in Europe or the Bahamas.

This exciting romance lasted for two years. Meanwhile, though, Barbara was not thriving in graduate school. She was doing well academically, but in the cold, busy, competitive environment of a large campus she did not make new friends. For the first time she was far away from her family and the kids she grew up with—and Len. Every weekend she spent with him made her realize all over again that her heart wasn't in her work. When he was with her she experienced renewed spunk and vigor. When he flew off she became depressed and went into semihibernation until his next visit.

Without consulting Len, Barbara left school, returned home, and took a job in a convenience store. She tried to persuade Len to leave his wife, about whom he had complained a lot during their long liaison. But Len was uncomfortable having Barbara so close to his door. This was not what he had had in mind. Although evasive, Len was concerned as he saw Barbara grow increasingly discontented and desperate. Gently he guided her toward therapy as he had once guided her toward graduate school.

Outwardly, Barbara was a young, healthy, energetic person with high intelligence, but this was not how she experienced herself. She felt lonely living by herself in an apartment, was weighed down with uncertainty about her life, and hated her job behind the counter. Unable to relate to her school environment, she had returned home in order to cling to Len, but found she felt just as restless, alienated, and up in the air when she was unable to claim her lover's exclusive devotion. Obsessed with Len for several years, she became all the more obsessed as she felt the consequences of not having created a full life for herself. Nervously pacing around her therapist's office, she had little left to hope for except divine intervention. "We were careless last weekend," she mused. "Maybe I'm pregnant." Actually, though, she would need to reconnect herself with the everyday realities of life she had lost sight of in her overwhelming passion for Len.

IS ROMANTIC OBSESSION ALWAYS SUCH A BAD THING?

Is it necessarily good to score low on anxiety? Or on obsession? Might a person with very low anxiety be lacking in empathy, in conscience? Could a 0 on obsession signify an utter lack of attraction to one's lover, or perhaps a failure to form a bond of emotional commitment? Would it be better to score in the middle on these items than at the bottom? These are important questions whose answers will become increasingly apparent, especially in Chapter 4, on the aloof, detached version of insecure love.

Bear in mind that the thirty-three statements are worded to convey a notion of excess rather than healthy involvement. The kind of attachment described is obsessive, not caring. Therefore, an answer of "not true" to the statements on the questionnaire means that the person simply did not experience the excesses described; it does not mean he or she was aloof in the relationship. Feelings, thoughts, or behavior may become unhealthy if taken to the extreme. Some of the statements in the questionnaire could, in isolation, depict the start of either a beautiful or a desperate relationship. Still, a person who scores high on the questionnaire as a whole, including *both* anxiety and obsession, is likely to be involved in a pattern of insecure love.

These conclusions are borne out by the total picture of people's lives that unfolds throughout this book. We have compared people's scores on anxious romantic attachment with how intensely they have felt jealousy and depression, what kinds of partners they choose, how they were brought up, and what their personalities are like. A many-sided portrait of the person who suffers from insecurity in love is carefully created chapter by chapter. We will explore the different arenas in which people live and the many ways they express—and become—who they are.

This in-depth analysis of insecure love will be like peeling off, one by one, the layers of an onion. The analogy with an activity that elicits tears seems apt, in that the process of exposing the secrets of our lives must necessarily stir up difficult feelings and awaken painful experiences. To relive our suffering in order to understand better why we have suffered is to risk realizing how much we have lost. We take that risk in the hope that we can further reduce pain and find greater fulfillment for ourselves and our children.

Later chapters will reveal some causes of—and possible cures for—insecure love. For now, we'll concentrate on the look and feel of insecure love: in particular, the feelings you are likely to have and the kinds of relationships in which you are likely to get involved if you or your partners are anxiously attached. Except where we specify differences between women and men, our findings apply to both sexes. We found that women and men score high on our questionnaire in about the same proportions. Surprisingly, given the way popular books on this subject are directed exclusively toward women, psychological research has shown that, if anything, men may be more strongly disposed than women to fall into the excesses of romantic attachment. Some typical differences, however, between the feelings and behavior of men and women in response to romantic insecurity are illustrated by the following vignette.

MARTY AND FRAN: THE BALANCE OF POWER

When Marty, age thirty-four, came in for therapy following a distraught phone call the day before, he looked as if he might need to be hospitalized. Tearful and shaking, he drummed his fingers and tugged at his beard as he told his story. His wife had left him two months earlier after ten years of marriage. Since then he had made himself miserable by following her around, pleading with her, and provoking confrontations when he found her with her new boyfriend.

Marty described the waves of bad feelings that had come over him since the separation. Sometimes, especially when he had some hope of persuading Fran to come back, he felt fairly stable and able to work. At other times, especially when he saw her arm in arm with her boyfriend, he felt weak, shaky, and increasingly tense. With each cycle of hope followed by disappointment, he suffered from increasing loss of sleep and appetite. By now he had noticeably lost weight and was obsessed with terrible fears of being alone. "All I want is to feel her holding me again, and to feel that it will last," he said in a childlike way.

With the help of supportive therapy and medications, Marty was able to stay out of the hospital, although he did have to take a leave of absence from his job. One Sunday he managed to coax Fran to come over to the house. Crying and shaking hysterically, he pleaded with her to come back to him. She agreed to a trial reconciliation—with the warning that she would leave again if he didn't continue to work on the problems that had stalemated their marriage.

Marty clearly knew the source of some of their marital problems. He lamented about all the time he had spent bowling, hunting, and going to the track with his buddies. Gently his therapist pictured for him the life of quiet desperation his wife must have led all those years when he was out with his friends so much of the time, while showing her little affection at home. Marty described frequent fights when Fran became irrational while he remained cool and logical. Uncomfortable with conflict, he found in sports and male camaraderie a refuge from her outpourings of emotion. Yet his habitual withdrawal left her unfulfilled, so she finally turned the tables on him and exposed his own emotional vulnerability.

Marty agreed that he had habitually ignored his wife, but now that he had been shocked to his senses, he was really trying to "do that romantic stuff" that she seemed to crave. He bought her flowers and surprised her with an evening of dinner and dance that they both enjoyed. But despite the lip service Marty paid to "the romantic stuff," he still sounded emotionally distant from Fran, and the couple did not appear to be communicating intimately. For example, Marty didn't know for sure whether Fran had stopped seeing her boyfriend.

Before long Marty was able to return to work. As his situation stabilized, his therapist began to worry that Marty might be recovering *too* quickly. The more comfortable Marty felt with Fran back home, the less motivated he would be to work on their marriage. Then Fran might walk out a second time, and the cycle would begin all over again. Week by week Marty's therapist watched him settle back into his old routine.

Finally, the therapist suggested marital counseling for the couple. Instead, Marty cancelled his next session, leaving the message that he was going to the auto races. The therapist called to see how he was doing.

"Oh," the therapist remarked, "so you and Fran are into auto racing."

"Fran? No," said Marty. "I went with my buddies."

Many men experience romantic insecurity the way Marty did. After being oblivious for years to essential emotional issues in a relationship, they are flustered and dismayed when their partner suddenly threatens to leave. The disorientation such a man shows when his partner does walk out is heightened by the fact that he experiences her departure as a sudden and unexpected event. The loss of his loved object means that he is now deprived of what was a fixture in his life. But if the immediate crisis is resolved and the valued object is restored to his possession, he may bounce back quickly and resume his prior habit of ignoring her.

Women less often experience such acute distress because they tend to be more aware of the problems in their relationships all along. They therefore suffer less dramatically if the relationship enters a crisis period, though if it ends, they suffer longer than men. Likewise, once a woman has asserted herself sufficiently to change long-standing inequities in a relationship, she may for some time remain unmoved by her partner's protestations that he is reformed. Fran, like Elaine in Chapter 1, reacted noncommittally when her husband pleaded for a renewed commitment to their marriage. She knew all too well that she needed to maintain some leverage in order to bring about lasting readjustments in the relationship. During such transitions, therapists often hold the husband accountable while restraining him from pressuring his wife for a commitment that she does not feel ready to make.

THE FIRST ENCOUNTER

In a preliminary study we gave our questionnaire *only* to men. This study yielded essentially the same findings as the later, more ambitious study of both women and men. In addition, subjects went through a dramatic, lifelike experiment that registered their feelings before and after they met an eligible (or so they thought) woman. This experiment showed how a man feels and what he expects when he is about to meet an attractive woman—and how his feelings and expectations change once he does meet her.

A young man walks into a waiting room and is greeted by a serious, deadpan experimenter. The student has been there once before to fill out two hours' worth of questionnaires, which included answering the questions at the beginning of this chapter (called the anxious-attachment scale) about two previous romantic relationships. He also answered questions about his dating habits in general, what he thought of himself, and how his parents raised him. This time the experimenter says, "Thank you for coming; have a seat. We're studying the way people get to know each other when they first meet as strangers. You will be meeting, in turn, two women who, like you, have volunteered for this study. They are in the rooms over there." He points to a corridor lined with doors leading to small rooms. "Before you meet them," he goes on, "I'd like you to fill out a questionnaire."

"What? Again?" the student asks.

"This one's different," replies the experimenter. He hands the student a clipboard with a questionnaire and, clipped to it, a Polaroid photo of the first woman he is to meet. There is a camera on the table, and the photo looks as if it was just taken when the volunteer waiting across the hall came in. The student can't help but look at the attractive face in the photo as he checks off how strongly he feels certain emotions at this moment (for example, "I feel affectionate," "I feel sad," "I feel warmhearted," "I feel overjoyed," "I feel nonchalant"). He also indicates what he expects from this encounter with a stranger by answering the following series of questions:

How strongly do you expect that the woman you are about to "get acquainted with" will
    (1) find you very interesting to talk with?
    (2) find you very attractive?
    (3) respond very warmly to you?
    (4) like you very much?
    (5) desire to get further acquainted with you at some future time?

Actually, the two women he is about to meet are not volunteer participants like himself. They are in on the experiment, "accomplices" chosen for their attractive appearance as well as their social skills and flexibility in enacting different roles. The first woman has been instructed to treat him *either* warmly or coldly. In the warm role, the woman shows considerable interest in the man, expresses much enthusiasm, and engages in a good deal of eye contact. In the cold role, she shows little interest, avoids eye contact, and sits in a defensive posture. The second woman has been told to act toward the subject in a normal, neutral manner. (That way, if the first woman has treated him coldly, he won't be depressed when he leaves.) After each of the two encounters he comes back out into the waiting room and answers the same series of questions he answered previously about his moods and about his expectations concerning the woman's attitude toward him. Now, however, the latter questions apply to the woman he has just met. Having been treated warmly, coldly, or neutrally by a new female acquaintance, he is asked:

How strongly do you expect that in a future interaction with the woman whom you have just "gotten acquainted with," she will
    (1) find you very interesting to talk with?
    (2) find you very attractive?
    (3) respond very warmly to you?
    (4) like you very much?
    (5) desire to get further acquainted with you at some future time?

He is also asked how attractive he finds this woman, how warm and friendly he finds her, how much he likes her, and how much he would like to get further acquainted with her. In turn, the two women and the experimenter rate how attractive and how warm they find him to be.

This simulated first encounter with a potential date reveals the first signs of insecure love. Those who felt insecure in their romantic attachments—that is, those who scored high on the anxious-attachment scale at the beginning of this chapter—reacted differently from others to the prospect of meeting an attractive stranger, the promise of a new relationship, and the reality of acceptance or rejection.

For one thing, they had different feelings while they awaited the encounter. Those with a history of anxious romantic attachments felt four kinds of emotions more intensely. First, they were more likely to show a mood of *concentration*. That is, they checked off statements like "I feel earnest"; "I feel attentive"; "I feel intent"; "I feel engaged." Second, they were more *excitable*. That is, they felt "carefree," "witty," "talkative," "playful," "lively." Third, they experienced more *anxiety* ("clutched up," "jittery," "fearful"). Fourth, and by a big margin, they were full of *aggression* ("rebellious," "defiant," "annoyed," "angry," "fed up," "grouchy").

Together, these feelings make up a fight-or-flight state of arousal. The anxious lover-to-be is keyed up, at high energy, extra-sensitive to stimulation, and ready to react angrily. More of him than of the average person is at stake in such an encounter, since more of his sense of himself, and whether or not others will accept him, depends on the approval of a prospective lover. It is as if he sees himself in the mirror of others' impressions of him. And, on balance, his feelings in this situation are more negative than those of the person who is not so insecure in love. He finds uncertainty—i.e., fear of rejection—especially stressful.

Despite being more emotionally aroused, those who scored high on anxious attachment did not (on the average) expect any more—or less—of the woman they were about to meet than did those who scored low. Their expectations did, however, vary more widely. This finding points to our anxious lovers' lack of self-confidence about their own acceptability as an intimate partner. Because they had not developed stable expectations for love and affection, their expectations in this situation were strongly influenced by the outcome of their most recent romantic experiences, whether those happened to be positive or negative.

After they met the woman, however, some revealing differences occurred.

As would be expected, those who did not score high on the anxious-attachment scale experienced a better mood and had higher expectations after being treated warmly. Naturally, when they were treated coldly, their mood worsened and their expectations declined by about the same amount. Meanwhile, those who *did* score high on anxious attachment, when they were treated warmly, became even *more* elated and developed even *higher* expectations than our other subjects. This fits our common-sense image of the insecure lover as excitable, dependent on acceptance by others (particularly a prospective lover), and subject to widely varying moods.

Was it the case, then, that our anxious lovers suffered a deeper plunge in their moods and expectations when they ran up against the cold woman? Surprisingly, it was not. Their expectations about a relationship with this woman did indeed go down, which showed that they knew they were being given the cold shoulder. But their mood stayed at an even keel! Emotionally, they reacted positively to warm treatment, but did not react negatively to cold treatment. Perhaps the aloof response they received served to relieve them of any pressure, and thus anxiety, about an attempt to foster yet another insecure love relationship. They could just write the woman off as "not interested in anyone, including me." In interpreting the lack of emotional reaction to cold treatment, we must also bear in mind that an experiment may not arouse all of the same feelings that an actual date would.

KURT AND HELEN: ONE-SIDED LOVE

The story of Kurt and Helen illustrates the behavior and thought patterns of a typical male insecure lover. Shortly after the ending of a brief but emotionally charged romance, and while he was still experiencing intense feelings of abandonment and injustice, Kurt met and began to date Helen. By their second date, Kurt had once again fallen in love, and he said so to Helen. Helen was attracted to Kurt and told him that the feeling was mutual, but she began to have second thoughts when he broached the subject of marriage on their fourth date. Feeling threatened by Kurt's ardor, she began to pull away even though she liked him very much. Kurt's response to Helen's new coolness was to increase his pleas for reciprocation. He called her twice a day and sent flowers, candygrams, and greeting cards with sentimental verses.

Still flattered by all this attention, Helen sometimes allowed herself to enjoy it, but she began to feel smothered. "I do really like you, Kurt," she told him, "but we have to slow down. I'm feeling overwhelmed." Kurt was delighted to hear Helen say she liked him. Indeed, he didn't seem to hear anything else. But he did notice the growing discrepancy between this statement and the way she acted. He began to think, "If she really likes me so much, why won't she go out with me this week? I wonder what she's really up to." Increasingly preoccupied with her, he began making surprise visits to her apartment.

Helen finally decided to call it quits. This, however, was easier said than done. Kurt kept pursuing. In the same breath he would express both undying love for Helen and rage that she didn't appreciate him. Kurt's confused feelings of "love," anger, and anguish led him to seek psychotherapy. "I know it's not Helen," he confessed. "This is what happens all the time. The more I love a woman, the less she wants to do with me."

Like the men in our study who were ecstatic at the least sign of positive feedback from a woman, Kurt heard only Helen's encouragement, not her distancing. Men like this are hard to shake. It seems that women must be perfectly consistent in rejecting them, or else they will hang on to any grain of hope. One must be extremely firm to break up with such a man, and that can be hard for a sensitive woman to do.

THE EMOTIONAL EXPERIENCE OF INSECURE LOVE

A good way to tell whether you are in the grip of insecure love is by the way you feel in the course of a relationship. A person who is insecure in a relationship typically experiences certain emotions more intensely in that relationship than does a person who feels more secure. These are the emotions you might experience strongly if you are in an insecure love relationship:

- interest
- joy
- sexual arousal
- distress
- fear
- shame
- anger
- contempt
- disgust

By looking more closely at each of these, we begin to form a picture of the inner experience of insecure love.

To start with the positive feelings, *interest, joy,* and *sexual arousal* all have more to do with romantic obsession than with romantic anxiety. If you are obsessively attached to your lover, you are likely to experience these feelings intensely. On our questionnaire, *interest* was expressed by the words "alert," "attentive," "interested," and "concentrating." The terms used to express *joy* were "ecstatic," "delighted," "happy," and "joyful." Do these describe how you feel, or felt, in the presence of your lover? They certainly describe how Celeste felt at the height of her love affair with Doug (who was married at the time).

> It was the most wildly crazy relationship in the world. I was teaching him about romantic love, which he had never felt. I'd wait on his phone calls—he could be anywhere in the country, and he'd excuse himself and call me. He'd hop across a fence in the middle of the night to meet me; he'd walk backwards in the snow. It was crazy—racing up and down the road in our cars, making love in a playhouse, drinking beer out of our shoes—nutsy, crazy stuff, but wildly good, romantic. It was good sex, good fun. I was never as creative, never as beautiful. I painted better, wrote better. I wrote him poetry every day. I couldn't believe I had written it; I could never do it again.

If you felt strong *sexual arousal,* you would have checked "sensuous," "turned on," and "sexually excited." Dorothy, for example, would have checked off these words to describe her relationship with Mark, a man to whom she felt obsessively attached.

> This looked like the winning ticket for me. This match would take care of my whole life. But first I had to check out the sex. It was my initiative, and it was great, better than great. He was a very experienced lover.

Although *interest, joy,* and *sexual arousal* are strongly associated with romantic obsession, sexual arousal is reported more frequently by women who are romantically obsessed than by men who are romantically obsessed. It is also reported by women—but not by men—who are high in romantic anxiety. In men, sexual feelings in a relationship are more of a constant; these feelings have relatively little to do with whether a man is insecure in love. But for women, sexual feelings are tied up with the strength of their emotional attachment and with their anxiety about losing it. Being sexually aroused in a relationship may represent a larger emotional investment for a woman than for a man.

Of all the feelings polled, *distress* is by far the most prominent in the emotional life of people who experience insecure love, whether their primary symptom is anxiety or obsession. In their different ways, Julie, Barbara, and Marty (in the case studies earlier in this chapter) went through periods of deep distress. The words used to indicate distress ("downhearted," "sad," "miserable," "discouraged") graphically describe the downhill slide from the peak of joy described above. More than anything else, distress sums up the emotional lot of the insecure lover. Here, from our interviews, are a few examples of the intensity it can reach:

> *Lynne:* It's really bad on Sundays. It's always been like that. When I was a kid, Sundays were depressing because of school being the next day. That's when it hits me hardest now. But I wake up every single morning thinking of him. I really have to fight to get out of bed sometimes. It's heavy; it's a really heavy feeling.

> *Carol:* After he moved out we spent a few weekends together. At first I'd be so thrilled to be with him, but by the end it would be clear that nothing had changed. When I came home from those weekends, it was like the day he moved out all over again. The pain, the knot in my stomach, the tightness in the chest—and I just couldn't stop crying. I felt that if he'd just give me another chance, we could make this relationship work. That's the way I feel still. I'm so desperate to have this relationship that I can't go on with my life.

> *Joe:* I've been beaten almost to death in fights. I've been in intensive care. But I've never felt pain like this.

Such distress may also be what those high in anxious attachment have to *fear* (when they check off "scared," "fearful," "afraid," and "frightened"). Although fear more closely resembles anxiety than obsession, it is more strongly associated with obsession, especially for women. Why? Perhaps because our study asked people to rate their strongest experience of each feeling in a particular relationship, not how often or how consistently they had that feeling. Anxious lovers may be chronically fearful, but obsessed lovers may experience deathly fright all at once—namely, when they sense that they are about to lose the partner to whom they feel so attached.

Those who are insecure in love express *shame* by reporting that they have felt "humiliated," "ashamed," "disgraced," and "degraded." Ray, for example, reveals his anguish in these words:

> I've always been so dependent on other people—I can't stand it! I don't want to be sick like this. It's devastating; it's horrible; it's humiliating!

Unlike the positive feelings described earlier, shame is much more a part of romantic anxiety than of romantic obsession, both for men and for women. Perhaps a fear of having one's shame discovered contributes to the anxiety. On the other hand, one who is anxiously attached may expect rejection, and its anticipation may bring feelings of shame, humiliation, and degradation. Later we will see how childhood experiences can induce feelings of shame along with a susceptibility to insecure love.

Shame is altogether a more prominent emotion in insecure love than *guilt* ("conscience-stricken," "guilty," "repentant," "blameworthy"), except for women who are romantically obsessed, who tend to feel mildly guilty as well as mildly ashamed. Lynne is an example of a person who feels guilty about being insecure, and whose guilt is magnified and manipulated by an ex-lover:

> If I end a relationship, I usually end it quickly, and I don't feel guilty or depressed. But if the man ends the relationship, then I go through a lot of depression and guilt, as if I were the wrongdoer. Scott broke up with me, but he tells me that it was all my fault. He says he really wanted to get married, but I was just too insecure, too impatient for him. I can really get hooked on thinking, "Did I act so crazy that I drove him away?" When I let myself (which is often), I get consumed with these thoughts, and then I have to call a friend to talk me out of them.

A different set of feelings is identified by those who find themselves intensely "angry," "annoyed," "enraged," and "mad" at their lovers. Those for whom *anger* figures prominently in the experience of romantic love may well suffer from romantic anxiety—as did Julie, whose mysterious explosions of temper at her husband were described earlier. In her own words Julie gives some insight into the connection between insecurity and anger:

> I told Mike I had missed him and asked if he had missed me, but he brushed me off. I wanted to talk to him in bed, but he was too tired. He sometimes acts as though I'm just a piece of furniture. When we make love I feel like I'm the most important person alive, but other times I feel as if I'm in his way. When things are fine, he never calls me during the day. But when I finally blow up at him, he calls two or three times and comes home early. Sometimes I just don't want to see him. I want to make him hurt inside like he hurts me. But when this feeling blows over, I'll feel guilty.

People (especially men) who are anxious in their love lives tend to feel more anger toward their partners. In the simulated first date described earlier, anger was simmering before the partners even met! Anxiety can be painful, and it is natural to be angry at a lover who makes you anxious. As Chapter 5 will show, people with high romantic anxiety tend to see their partners as behaving inconsistently. It is at this inconsistency (particularly unfaithfulness) that the anger is directed. Gail, for example, indulges in bitter thoughts toward the man who had recently been her lover:

> I saw him in my mind every day. I was just dying inside. I imagined myself seeing him out with someone else, and I started to hate him. It was bad enough that he dumped me like he did, but to go out with an old girlfriend that he said he didn't care about anymore! I started to doubt everything he had ever told me. No, he had never loved me, never cared about me.

Anger can shade into feelings of contempt and disgust. For instance, Ray alternates from one moment to the next between pleas for his ex-wife's return and sour reflections on her unworthiness:

> If I let myself think about all the ugly things, it would wipe out the love. The way I had to go and confront her about that money after we split up, I was so *furious* at her. I thought, "What kind of marriage partner is she? She can't even be trusted! Why would I want to be married to her?" Okay, so I loved her, so sex was wonderful with her, so we held hands and walked along the river, and we went to the Bahamas, and it was all very romantic. So what? There were all those bad things that I shoved aside to concentrate on the good things, which I lost anyway.

Contempt ("contemptuous," "sneering," "scornful," "disdainful") is as strongly related to romantic anxiety as anger, particularly for men. But while anger also is present with romantic obsession, contempt is not reported by obsessive lovers. Evidently it is hard to feel "sneering" or "scornful" toward a lover who inspires obsessive attachment. Likewise, *disgust,* expressed in words like "disgusted," "feeling of revulsion," "nauseated," and "feeling of distaste," is found in men high in romantic anxiety, but is not associated with romantic obsession.

Generally, men more often direct their insecure feelings outward, targeting their partners with anger, contempt, or disgust, while women are somewhat more likely to direct it inward, reporting feelings of fear and guilt. These differences between the genders are, however, only differences of degree. There are more similarities than differences in the way men and women react to the experience of insecure love.

In a study involving *only* men, we obtained similar results with differently worded questions. The higher a man scored on anxious attachment, the more he described (in the same relationships) feelings of:

- euphoria and elation
- depression and anxiety
- personal fulfillment
- emotional instability
- a heightened sense of personal worth

From euphoria and elation to depression and anxiety—a virtual emotional rollercoaster! It sums up what we learned from the larger study of women and men—that the same people can experience great extremes of positive and negative emotion, "joy" as well as "distress," in the same relationships. No wonder they also reported "emotional instability." Yet still they described these stormy relationships as personally fulfilling. As for the "heightened sense of personal worth," that is an alluring trap to be avoided. For if you get your sense of personal worth from a relationship, what happens when the relationship is taken away from you?

WHAT AN INSECURE RELATIONSHIP LOOKS LIKE

Another way to gauge your susceptibility to insecure love is to look at the kinds of relationships that draw you in. Relationships in which one or both partners are insecure look different (let alone *feel* different) from more secure relationships. That is, they tend to take a somewhat different course and have certain identifiable characteristics.

People who score high in insecure romantic love generally date many different people in a given year, even though they do not (on the average) go out on more dates than the average person. It seems, then, that they have trouble finding relationships that last. Feeling love or infatuation for many different people and expressing it by *saying* "I love you" to many of them can also be signs of insecure love. Interestingly, the two do not always go together. Sometimes people feel love without declaring it, and sometimes people declare love without feeling it—perhaps as a way of testing the waters, hoping to elicit a similar declaration in return. Despite falling in love more often, people who are insecure in love do not (on the average) enjoy dating any more or less than other people do. Apparently the agony and the ecstasy cancel each other out!

A long-lasting relationship may be a sign of romantic obsession, although it may simply indicate attachment to an attractive partner. The same is true when one spends many hours each week with one's partner: there is a statistical association between romantic obsession and excessive time spent together. Neither duration of the relationship nor amount of contact is associated with romantic anxiety. If the two variables are combined into one, called intensity of contact (hours per week multiplied by duration of relationship), that figure predicts obsessive attachment, though not anxiety. One young man spent so much time with his girlfriend over a period of years that he thought of her family as his own. When she broke up with him during their sophomore year in college, he was devastated:

> I just got so attached to her and her family. I kind of grew up with them. I thought we'd be together forever. I still don't believe this happened; I don't want to believe it. Now I have panic attacks at night, breathing heavy and not sleeping. I feel like I'm going to feel this way for the rest of my life. I'm afraid of going through life alone.

The more sexually active a relationship is (compared with other relationships one has had), the more obsessed with it one is likely to be. This is especially true for women—another sign that sex represents a greater emotional investment for a woman than for a man.

Although people who are high on anxious attachment (that is, both anxiety and obsession) do not necessarily spend more time with their partners than other people do, they do spend more time talking with them on the telephone. This discrepancy suggests that insecure lovers may be more engaged in the unrequited pursuit of elusive partners, as they incessantly dial their lovers' numbers. Other findings support this conclusion.

For example, let us take a hypothetical couple, Cathy and Phil. The more intense Cathy's feelings of love and infatuation for Phil are, the more romantically obsessed with him she is likely to be. This sounds obvious, and indeed the correlation is one of the strongest among all of our findings. Similarly, the more intense Cathy's love, the greater her feelings of romantic anxiety, although this correlation is not nearly so strong. Still, the two components (obsession and anxiety) together make for a strong correlation between the intensity of her love and her overall anxious attachment score.

What is the effect of the intensity of Phil's love for Cathy on her susceptibility to anxious attachment? In itself, not a great deal. The more Phil loves Cathy, the more obsessed she is likely to be with him, but only to a modest degree. Understandably, the more he loves her, the *less* anxious she is likely to be about him, again only to a modest degree. Putting the two components together, if Phil's loving her more makes her more obsessed but less anxious, her overall score on anxious attachment is hardly affected. Thus, the intensity of the *partner's* love has little to do with the extent to which one experiences insecure romantic love.

But now let's look at the anxiety component by itself. The more Cathy loves Phil, the more likely she is to feel anxious about her relationship with him. The *less* Phil loves her, the more likely she is to feel anxious about it. What if she loves him more *and* he loves her less? Then she is likely to experience the most anxiety.

In fact, among all the characteristics of relationships we examined, the one that best predicts anxiety is the *difference* between the intensity of one's own love and the intensity of the partner's love. The greater your own love than your partner's love, the more anxious you are likely to feel. This was the case with Barbara (in the story in this chapter), whose passion was not reciprocated by the older married man with whom she was involved. This love-inequality factor also is associated with romantic obsession and with anxious attachment as a whole, although not quite as strongly as is the *intensity* of one's own love alone.

The importance of unrequited love as a key sign (and perhaps source) of romantic insecurity is confirmed by some additional questions that reveal more of the nature of a relationship as it unfolds. You can ask yourself these questions about a relationship that is or was important to you:

How intense were your feelings for [*your partner*] after the first date?

How intense did your feelings for _____ become, at their strongest point?

At what point would you say that you first felt love for _____?

By a big margin, those who feel insecure in love have more intense feelings after the first date *and* more intense feelings at their strongest point than those who do not feel so insecure. They also experience love sooner in the course of the relationship. Apparently, love develops less intensely and more slowly for those who are less anxious in their attachments.

How fully is this extraordinary passion returned? Is it mutual? Ask yourself these additional questions:

How intense did you feel _____'s feelings for you were after the first date?

How intense did you feel _____'s feelings for you became, at their strongest point?

Who would you say finally terminated the relationship?

We found that the degree to which a person is anxiously attached has no bearing on the perceived intensity of the *partner's* feelings after the first date. The more anxiously attached one is, the more intense one finds the partner's feelings to be at their strongest point—but the partner's feelings still fall considerably short of one's own. We get a picture here of the insecure lover's feelings running far ahead of the partner's on the first date. Sometimes the partner catches up, but usually not. Finally, the relationship is more often terminated by the partner. The insecure lover is usually jilted, rarely being the one to end the affair.

All of these findings indicate that the intensity of passion displayed by a person who feels anxiously attached is primarily a private, inner experience, with no assurance of reciprocity. At best, there is an imperfect match between what this person feels and what his or her chosen love objects express in return. In the story of Kurt and Helen, told earlier in this chapter, Helen became suspicious—and finally disenchanted—when she sensed the indiscriminate nature of Kurt's extravagant attentions. She felt as if she had been handed a role in a romantic script Kurt had written long before he met her.

Another question that may have a bearing on insecure love is whether or not one or both partners date other people at the same time. This aspect of a relationship has little to do with romantic obsession, but does have some effect on anxiety. If you and your partner are both seeing other people, you are likely to feel less anxious about the relationship and perhaps less attached to your partner as well (presumably because the relationship has been defined, by mutual agreement, as an open rather than exclusive one). But if your partner is seeing other people and you are not, you are likely to feel *more* anxious. We will consider the impact of your partner's behavior more fully in Chapter 5. Meanwhile, let us look at some typically complex stories of insecure love.

3

EXPERIENCES OF

INSECURE LOVE

The stories that follow show how three people have experienced the characteristics of anxious romantic attachment outlined in the previous chapter. The first is Donna, a bright, attractive student who enjoyed a passionate love affair with an admired professor until she and he had to decide how seriously they wanted to take their relationship. The second is Ray, an impressive salesman whose self-assurance melted when his wife began to demand the independence he previously had said he wanted her to have. The third is Carol, who lifted herself out of a financially and emotionally impoverished family, but remained uncertain about when to commit herself fully to a man.

These cases dramatize how the emotions associated with romantic anxiety and romantic obsession are felt and expressed—how they come about, how they go together, and how the same person can experience widely varying emotions in quick succession. The three stories also introduce other major themes to be picked up in later chapters: the close connection between anxious attachment and its apparent opposite, detachment; the effect of one's choice of partners on the experience of insecure romantic love (and vice versa); the tactics of the anxiously attached lover; the searing experiences of jealousy and postrelationship depression; and the roots of anxious romantic attachment in childhood experience and family relationships.

DONNA: TAKING SECOND PLACE

Donna is a tall, attractive woman in her late twenties who takes considerable care with both her appearance and her speech. The impression she gives is one of beauty, intelligence, composure, and an articulate manner of expression; it does not bespeak insecurity. Yet when asked if she had ever felt anxious and insecure in a love relationship, Donna replied, "Yes, in fact, I had two relationships like that. For a while I had them both at the same time, since I was still seeing Jack after I met Bob."

When Donna met Jack she was a sophomore at an Ivy League college in New England. "I was standing in line at a bar, and whenever I turned around here was this face like Bruce Springsteen—you know, the working-class hero—smiling at me. Finally, he started talking to me." Jack, who did a late-night show on the college radio station, was funny and entertaining as well as kind and considerate. Unfortunately, he didn't seem to be available much, and then only on the run, since he was tied up at the station five nights a week and also did preparatory work there during the day. He and Donna enjoyed their time alone together, but they didn't get to be alone much. Jack spent most of his free evenings at social functions with local celebrities. He would bring Donna and then lose track of her while he was busy making contacts. "I guess I'm trying to forget a lot of this," Donna said as she tried to recall these stories, but she remembered nonetheless:

> It was so perfunctory. It was like we were there just to be there. I wasn't having a good time. Jack would go off to talk to people, and I'd be left on my own. When I think back now I just think, "What a fool I was." I used to sit at the bar and get plastered by myself. It was better than following him around or just sitting with the women, and besides, it was the only way I could get a rise out of him. When guys would come up wondering who this woman was sitting alone, Jack would come over and blow his stack. Then we'd get in a huge fight on the way home.

Donna was not by nature a wallflower, and it angered her to be placed in that position. She was an assertive, achievement-oriented young woman who chose men for some of the same attractive qualities she herself displayed: competence, poise, personal magnetism. The men she fell in love with tended to be older than she and highly accomplished in their fields. Unsure of her ability to hold such a man's affection, she was afraid to challenge him. She did not risk asserting herself for fear of losing a relationship that meant so much to her. As a result, she sold herself short, denying herself the impact she might have had as an equal—and highly valued—partner in the relationship. That was how she ended up at the bar, seething with anger as she waited for Jack to return to her side.

This submerged conflict exploded into the open one New Year's Eve.

> Of course, Jack celebrated New Year's with his listeners, and we went out after he got off the air at 1:00 A.M. I always took second place to the radio show and whoever he wanted to impress. We went to an all-night bar that a friend of his owned. Half the people Jack knew were there, and they were all drinking. I passed out all these party favors, and by 5:00 A.M. I was tired and wanted to go home. Jack said, "I'm not ready to go home." "Fine," I said, "I'll call myself a cab." But he wouldn't let me call a cab and go home alone. We were both drinking all night. When we finally did go home, I remember—this was so amazing—I didn't say a word to him the whole way back to his place. Then in his apartment we had a huge flareup. I was so loaded I don't remember what happened next. I remember him belittling me, and I remember him slapping me in the face. I don't remember whether he slapped me because of something I said or to shake me to my senses. I was crying, crying, crying. When he slapped me I just stared at him and tried to swing back at him, and he grabbed my arms. It was so unlike me. Maybe it was the liquor; maybe it was all the stuff between us coming out. All I remember is going to sleep—it was already light out—and then waking up before he did and leaving.

This scene shows how three of the emotions found to be associated with anxious romantic attachment—*anger, fear,* and *distress*—can go together. Donna was angry at Jack's neglect and mistreatment of her, but she was too obsessively attached to him to let go. For fear of losing him she would hold her anger in until the provocation became so extreme that she would explode. Once having expressed her anger, however, she would become distressed and remorseful, fearing that she had stepped out of line, "blown it," and was about to lose the man she loved. In this way, anxious romantic attachment can override a person's sense of fairness, equality, and even self-respect.

Donna was still seeing Jack when she met the man who became the great passion of her life. Bob, a political science professor ten years her senior, was faculty advisor of a campus club to which Donna belonged. In that role he had to be discreet about any romantic inclinations toward students, but Donna "caught little signs" of interest from him. One day in his office she asked him out. Her initial impressions of him illustrate the high level of *interest* that the romantically obsessed lover tends to experience:

I liked his looks—not handsome, but very distinctive. Bob didn't see himself as attractive, and the other girls in the World Affairs Club didn't find him attractive either, just different, interesting looking. But to me he looked like Richard Dreyfuss, and he fit the image intellectually. I loved to listen to him. He could carry on eloquently about anything. Maybe that's what started me fantasizing about him.

With regard to her feelings in this relationship, Donna surely would have checked off words like "alert," "attentive," "interested," and "concentrating" on the emotions questionnaire, as do subjects who score high on romantic obsession. Her account of the early development of their relationship also fits the picture of insecure romantic love presented in Chapter 2:

Bob was shocked when I asked him out, but he also told me that he was flattered. That surprised me and made me feel kind of strange. Here I was a little undergraduate student, and he was a Ph.D., and he was flattered? The first few times we were together, I was uneasy. I felt very insecure about it. For me it was love from the first time we were physically intimate. I told him right away that I loved him; I didn't hold back. He looked at me like he was shocked, because he was seeing somebody else at the same time. He answered that he cared about me and had feelings for me, and that this was a nice little thing we had because I was seeing somebody else just as he was. It took a long time, about two months, before he said, "I love you." Then he blurted it out one night after a lot of champagne. It made me feel really good, though. I was dying to hear those words. After that I didn't feel so all alone, so vulnerable. Before, it was as if this guy had power over me, like he could do anything he wanted and I would think he was just neat. Now he didn't have the upper hand anymore.

As in our study, the person who identified herself as an anxious lover experienced love more quickly and declared her love first. Her partner was slower to reach a level of passionate involvement and probably never came to love her as intensely as she loved him. The last sentences in this passage show that Donna experienced love as a kind of vulnerability. By giving herself without full reciprocation, she felt that she put herself at a disadvantage. Because her love for Bob was greater than his for her, she did not challenge his control of their relationship. For example, she disclosed more about the other person she was seeing than did Bob.

I didn't know the woman Bob was seeing, and he made it a point never to mention her name. He always referred to her as "this other person." He'd

sometimes compare us, like he'd say, "This other person is statuesque, too."
That was the one thing I ever learned about her—that she was "statuesque"
like me. It drove me crazy. I'd say, "Look, it's no big deal. You know who
Jack is." But he'd just become cross and say, "I don't rub it in your face; I wish
you wouldn't rub it in mine." But he did rub it in my face, and it gnawed at
me all the time. I'd lie awake and wonder who she was.

Donna never found out how much control she could have exercised in her
relationship with Bob because she never put it to the test. If she had, she
might have surprised herself. What kept her from taking the risk was her
growing obsession with her lover.

> I lived and thought Bob. I dreamed about us being together in the future
> even though I knew it never really could happen, because he was so far
> ahead of me in everything. I dreamed of being married to him. That was a
> dream, believe me, because he had never married and never intended to.
> He was admired in his circle, and I dreamed of going to social functions
> with him, like when he spoke in public.

In an eerie echo of Jack's disregard for her at his social functions, Donna
reconciled herself to utter anonymity at Bob's.

> I'd go with him to forums and colloquia, but we'd always have to go
> incognito or run from place to place because he'd been escorting "this
> certain person" for so long. I dreamed of going with him to functions and
> public events and really being with him instead of having to wait in the
> wings. I dreamed of showing him off to my friends. But those were all
> dreams. I never came out and told him I wished we could go places openly
> together, but I told him I wished we could be together more often. He'd
> say, "You're letting this get out of hand." I'd say, "Yeah, I know."

Donna's longing to be with her lover all the time is part of the pattern of
anxious romantic attachment.

In her relationship with Bob, Donna also experienced heightened *sexual
arousal,* which carries added vulnerability for the romantically obsessed
woman.

> The relationship was *very* passionate. We used to kid around about him
> being so macho, so sexy to me; he was really great. During school we had
> to be very careful. I'd run to his office, and we'd act like student and
> advisor until we shut the door behind us. As time went on we spent more

time together; we'd meet after school and go to a local bar or whatever. It
was fun having to be really careful. We were so sexual with each other, it
was like *all* the time. We went at it like rabbits.

The passion Donna enjoyed with Bob was clearly mutual, but it probably
involved less emotional risk for him than for her. A woman more typically
becomes sexually aroused as she grows to love someone who, she believes,
cares for her in return. If this expectation is disappointed, she may be
susceptible to feelings of depression and guilt for having risked herself both
emotionally and sexually.

In Donna's case these feelings were precipitated by the stress of becoming
pregnant and the impact it had on her relationship with Bob.

> Because we were so sexually active, it didn't surprise either of us when I
> became pregnant. It was almost as if we were expecting it. But when I told
> him I was pregnant, as soon as the words left my mouth I knew the
> relationship was over. We used to play at the idea of becoming pregnant
> when we made love, but when it happened, even though he wasn't upset
> about it, I sensed that things wouldn't be the same. It was something
> neither one of us had wanted to happen, and even though it didn't surprise
> us, it was a real turning point. It kind of killed something between us.

Outwardly, Donna and Bob accepted the choice of an abortion as a given.
Neither of them was ready to support a child financially or emotionally. Donna
was still in school, and Bob said that he did not intend to marry. "I've never had
misgivings or second thoughts about it," says Donna. Nonetheless, she must
have experienced inner conflict about giving up the potential for a child that
might have bonded her to the man she loved. Although she felt she could not
share her feelings with him, she might have wished that Bob would at last leave
the other woman for her and give her the role of wife and mother of his child.

Donna found the abortion procedure physically very painful, and one can
only imagine the unspoken emotional pain for her. It must have been especially
painful to her to go through it alone, without Bob there to support her.

When she came back to Bob's apartment afterward, the reception she got
confirmed her foreboding that their relationship would not survive this crisis.

> I don't know why, but I pretty well knew what he would say when I came
> back after the abortion: "I think we need to put some time between us
> now." He was very melancholy that night. He said, "You need to sort out
> your feelings, and I need to sort out mine." I don't know what was actually

bothering him, but I think that the pregnancy and abortion made him think more about how he was doing wrong to the other woman; it made that really concrete for him.

In fact, his behavior that night showed considerable distress on his part and contributed to Donna's anguish as well.

> He was watching some sports event on TV, and we didn't say a lot at first. Then he had the nerve to put his arms around me and tell me that he was unbelievably sexually excited. I thought he had to be kidding. I had just been through one of the worst things in my life, and he actually wanted to have intercourse. I thought he was out of his mind. Normally he'd never say anything so direct. He's so intellectual, he'd just say something like, "I'm aroused." I said, "You've got to be kidding. I can barely walk." But he was very persistent; there was no telling him no. I was shocked, and I felt very mad. At that point I felt that I was definitely being used. He didn't succeed; that was one time I didn't feel like it. I just got up and pushed his hands off me and walked across the room and said, "Why don't you fix me one of those—whatever you're drinking." I was so tired, so thirsty, so drained; I'd had it. We didn't say a whole lot else.
>
> Finally I said, "Maybe I'd better go. I have to work tomorrow." He said a perfunctory "yes" and reminded me about how we should put some time between us. I was so drained, I didn't know what to say. I tried to act like "Yeah, it's no big deal." But it was very painful for me to leave that night.

Although Donna was able to assert herself in the above scene by saying "no" to Bob's sexual advances, she could not ask him to give her any emotional support. Still unwilling to do anything that he might interpret as a burden, she bore the heaviness of her grief alone.

> It was August, and I remember just going and parking in this field and crying my eyes out until the sun went down—which was a couple of hours, since the sun was still high in the sky when I got there. I kept playing the same tape over and over again in the car. Then I went to this bar and practically drank myself to death. I stayed and cried for another couple of hours and then fixed myself up before I went home. I didn't want anyone asking any questions, because it wasn't too cool to be dating a professor.

From beginning to end, she accepted Bob's terms and allowed him to structure the situation. She never found out what might have happened if she had challenged the other woman's primary position in his life.

Despite Bob's coolness and apparent insensitivity, Donna desired him enough to hold on. She also realized that he was in pain, too. She continued to call and ask to see him, "even for one last time," but he kept her at arm's length without severing contact altogether. "I don't think we should do that right now," he would say. "I don't think it would be healthy."

Although Donna occasionally ran into Bob on campus and later did get together with him a few times, for the most part she kept her anguish to herself. "I never broke down and cried in front of him," she recalls. "I never told him that I wanted to stay together and that he was the greatest love of my life." Instead, Donna experienced privately her *distress*—the predominant emotion in the experience of insecure love.

Her distress lasted for some time. "It was still killing me two months later, when I cried after I went to see him." The remnants of her romantic obsession with Bob lasted much longer. Two years later, when asked, "How long did it take you to get over Bob?" Donna hesitated and then laughed. "Maybe I'm not over him yet," she replied. "At least that's how I feel today. There's a part of it that's still alive for me."

A few years later, when Donna was about to marry a man she had met in the interim, she contacted Bob and asked to see him. They went out together two nights before her wedding. She describes the encounter.

> We went out to dinner and then had a few drinks. It was very platonic. I had wondered in the back of my mind if he was going to ask me to go home with him. Maybe I wanted him to ask. I wouldn't have done it, though. Even though I would have wanted to with all my heart, I wouldn't have said yes. I don't know why. But we just had dinner and drinks and talked about school.

Donna measures her maturity by her ability to acknowledge and resist this persistent romantic obsession.

> I still think of him. The other night I remembered it was his birthday, and I almost went to the phone to call him. Then I said no, I wouldn't be able to live with myself. I thought, I'll send him a card. But I couldn't do it. I wouldn't be able to live with myself, because I had made these marriage vows. I feel great that I could tell myself no. I think about Bob occasionally, but not in the sense that "I wish I had Bob again." I feel good that I'm over that. I learned a lot from it.

If Bob really was the great love of Donna's life, she may have missed an opportunity by never trying to extend the limits he defined for their relationship. Donna was able to attract the dynamic, confident, accomplished men she desired, but once involved with such men, she seemed to become intimidated. With characteristic insight she provides some background that reveals how this pattern may have arisen in her early life:

My mother is very domineering; I call her a nag. She's very critical and often speaks before she thinks. She's intelligent and a good problem-solver, but in personal matters she lashes out blindly and is ruled by her emotions. To this day she and I have never gotten along. I never had a birds-and-bees talk with her and never really was close to her at all. What I got at home was the belt; every time I stayed out late I got an inch cut off my hair.

My mother is still as narrow-minded as she always was. She wears her hair the same and thinks the same way. But my dad has grown and blossomed out, learning new ways and accepting different viewpoints. I'm the same way; I'm open-minded, and I'll try anything at least once. My dad is really a neat guy. Even as an adolescent I wanted to be close to him, and I know he wanted to be close, too. But it was an awkward time, because we kids were a bunch of wild Indians. He and I are so close now. I cry every time I hear his voice. His voice is so soft and sweet, and he's even-tempered and rational. He's not henpecked, because he lets my mother's nagging go in one ear and out the other. He'll just let things slide to keep her off his back. He's much more worldly than she is, and they've grown apart a lot in recent years. I don't know how they've managed to stay together this long.

In Donna's aspiration to win the love of impressive men who were often older than she, one can recognize her close emotional identification with a beloved, respected father. Her lack of confidence in her capacity to be loved by such desirable men may have come from the competitive relationship she had with her mother. Perhaps her unwillingness to challenge Bob's girlfriend's place in his life originated in her unresolved relationship with her mother. Perhaps, too, the sight of her father patronizingly dismissing her mother's complaints contributed to her feeling that she had no choice but to walk out of Bob's apartment, and out of his life, without protest. Whatever the specific connections, Donna's personal strengths as well as limitations seem closely tied to the way she experienced those first relationships that taught her what subsequent relationships would be like.

RAY: ANGUISH OR ANGER?

"Nobody ever told me they loved me until after I turned forty," recalls Ray, who earns an excellent living selling medical instruments to hospital chains. To hear him talk just weeks after the breakup of his marriage, it would be hard to recognize the successful man beneath his grief and disorientation. He speaks sadly and somewhat quizzically of his childhood as an emotional wasteland.

> My parents were "nice" people who provided for me and did not abuse me. But I wasn't close to either one of them and didn't really like them very much, especially my father. (I get along better with my mother now.) They weren't very affectionate. They were very disciplined; you had to do your homework and whatever else you were supposed to do. I see people who have wonderful lives, who love their children and do things with them. I didn't get that from my parents. They never showed me how to feel love and express it.

His life, he says, was transformed in his early forties, when he met his wife, Jennifer:

> It was only then that I learned how to love and to express love. Before that I had some concept of what love was about, but not really being with people and being able to touch them and communicate. To know that it was all okay, that it was really nice to be with someone, to love them and share with them — that was new to me. That was what I had with Jennifer, and when it was wonderful, it was really wonderful.

The first years of their marriage were characterized by the ecstatic *joy* that is the positive side of the emotional experience of romantic obsession.

> It seemed that everything started changing in my life around the time we got married. I had a whole new awareness. I never experienced with another woman what I did with Jennifer. I remember once walking by the river with her in Paris, and it was wonderfully beautiful. That's why I needed her — to experience that love and union. When I had that connection with her, it was everything I'd ever dreamed love was about.

As we found to be typical in our study of anxious romantic relationships, part of the joy was sexual. "We experienced a lot of love, a lot of intimacy, and we had a wonderful sex life," Ray reminisced. "But there was a lot of conflict, too," he added, "and we couldn't maintain the love for any length of time."

Despite Ray's idealized, "touchy-feely" evocations of his early years with Jennifer, the seeds of the conflict were there at the outset.

> When we got married, I knew we would have a problem with our lifestyle. She decided to make a contribution to our joint finances that matched my salary, even though she made more than I did. But that wasn't enough for us. We went to Hawaii; we went out to dinner four or five times a week; we did all the great things you can do in the city. There just wasn't enough money, and I felt she ought to come across with more, since she had more. I was shocked when we did a joint income-tax return for the first time, and I found out she had put fifteen thousand dollars into her own trust fund. She never discussed or shared that with me. I thought, "If she loved me, she wouldn't do things like this." Maybe it had something to do with love, and maybe it didn't; I don't know. But that was the connection I made in my mind, and I was hurt by it.

As Ray admits, he was hurt as much by his interpretation of his wife's behavior as by what she did. He interpreted her material withholding as meaning that she did not love him, which caused him emotional distress. Yet he was also aware of—and was capable of sympathizing with her about—some early losses she had suffered that made her financial decisions more understandable.

> I used to think that she didn't share the money because she didn't love me. But as I began to put the pieces together in counseling, I realized how afraid she was. Her family was rich and lived in the best places. Her father died when she was still a child, and her mother took all the money and spent it. Her mother remarried, and Jennifer loved her stepfather. Then one night he woke her up in the middle of the night to tell her good-bye.
>
> Her mother dragged her around, living in all these different places, and was so extravagant, accumulating diamonds and furs, that sometimes Jennifer felt like she didn't know where her next meal was coming from. Toward the end, in counseling, I realized that the stuff she pulled didn't have to do with not loving me; it was just her fears. Once I really felt that compassion for her, it didn't bother me anymore, but I had to go through pain to get there.

This background helps explain Jennifer's role in the conflicts that Ray characterizes as "the silly little pettiness over all the junk." Coffee cups, for example:

> I remember when she asked me, "How many coffee cups do you have in your car?" Here we had this beautiful home, and together we made over a hundred thousand dollars a year, and she was worried about a few dollars' worth of coffee cups. I said, "I don't know. I'll go see"—even though I was in my pajamas at the time. So I walked down from the third floor, put on a coat over my pajamas, and went out and found two coffee cups in my car. We both kept tossing these issues back and forth, back and forth.

What were they fighting about? In this incident, so clearly symbolic rather than substantial, we see Jennifer through Ray's eyes as a rigidly orderly person who maintained a sense of security by insisting that everything in her environment be just so. To Ray, this was not the same woman who had unlocked for him the mysteries of love. He wanted her to love and accept him, perhaps even look up to him. Instead, he experienced her as demanding and critical. It was vital to him to have recognition, respect, and status in his household. Instead, he felt that his wife had reduced him to an errant schoolboy. Ray was left feeling that he had to dig in his heels (going out in his pajamas, as if to say, "Here, take your goddamn coffee cups!") or withdraw from her.

A similar incident, trivial but charged with emotion, gives a glimpse of how Ray's unfinished business from childhood clashed with Jennifer's to create a hostile standoff.

> One time I had a strange visual illusion. Jennifer, who couldn't stand it when I would move her things in the house, drove up while I was taking out the trash. As she stepped out of the car I knew she was going to ask me about the trash. I just knew she was going to ask me what I was throwing away. Isn't that sick? She got out of the car, and when I saw her, it was as if I saw my mother. I saw her as my mother in a pale green silk dress.
> She came up and asked me what I was throwing away.
> "Trash."
> "Is there anything of mine in there?"
> My eyes filled with tears. "Why would you say that to me? Why would you think I would throw away something of value?"
> She just looked at me and walked into the house. I felt funny because I felt as if I had encountered my mother, and I thought it was a little kooky.

When Ray met Jennifer he had envisioned her as the personification of warmth and love. Yet he came to see her as a woman like his mother, withholding affection while strictly monitoring his activities and ready with a scolding whenever the occasion arose.

For Ray, and undoubtedly for Jennifer, these conflicts made for a life of extreme emotional turmoil.

> A lot of times I would lose my temper, and I would say things to her that would shock me, because my image of myself was that I was a very nice person. I realize that nice people get angry, and I guess it's okay to be angry; it's part of living. Still, I was shocked by my own behavior, like when I told her that she was the most selfish, self-centered bitch I had ever seen. I simply could not imagine anybody being the way she was about money and possessions—this woman who was very feminine, very loving, and all that. I loved this lady. Yet here I was all at once going crazy, and she was, too. We were both acting like wild animals. It wasn't the way I wanted it to be, but when I got angry I couldn't do anything about it. It upset her, of course, and it would hurt me later. I would feel guilty about it because she was so soft and feminine. I loved that about her, and I'd be so devastated after I hurt her. I discussed my anger one time with my minister. He explained that I was saving it up too much. I wasn't really communicating with my wife. Instead, I was blowing up like a balloon, and then when it burst I'd let out all my anger. And she did the same thing to me. It got pretty ugly sometimes.

It is not only the particular emotions of *anger* and *guilt* and *distress,* rage and remorse and hurt, that typify the experience of insecure love; it is also their being felt so intensely in combination with one another in a compressed time span. Ray sums up this tempestuous emotional experience in these words: "There were enough bad things to remember about that marriage, but there were also beautiful things. A lot of it was awful, but when it was good, it was supergood." Earlier, Ray said that his capacity for intimacy, joy, and emotional attachment expanded dramatically when he married Jennifer. Yet he also said, "I never felt all this pain until I got married. When I got married, everything magnified." As we saw in Chapter 2, it is often the same people— those most susceptible to anxious romantic attachment—who experience the greatest extremes of both euphoria/elation and depression/anxiety within one relationship. Together, these two states add up to the condition of emotional instability.

Recoiling from this turmoil, Ray left Jennifer three times in the course of their marriage. "I just couldn't do it," he explained. "I couldn't stand it— couldn't stand the conflict. What I thought I wanted in life was a lot of peace and love." Like others caught in the throes of insecure love, Ray felt intense *disgust* with his partner and himself. He interpreted this feeling as a revulsion toward Jennifer's dependency on him and, as he came to realize, his dependency on her.

> I was very aware of her great need for me. In the end that was why I could not go back to her, even though I wanted to with all my heart; I wanted to be with her. We were going to counseling, working on the marriage, waiting for one or both of us to be healed. In our last counseling session she demanded that I come back, otherwise the marriage was totally over. I told her that I could not do that. I really felt that somewhere we got lost in our marriage. If we could start over and rebuild our relationship, give me two or three months and I felt that I would feel safe enough to go home. But I saw this desperation in her, and it horrified me. It was like it was immoral; it just repelled me. What I really felt was that she was sick. And then I realized that we were both sick, and that what I was waiting for by not going back was that one of us was going to get well. We were working on it; we had some goals; and I really thought we could make it.

We might wonder, however, whether the real object of Ray's revulsion was something very different from dependency. Jennifer was security conscious, but she dealt with her insecurity by arranging to have financial independence and by controlling her own resources. She criticized Ray's laxity in handling material possessions and probably reminded him that she earned more money than he did. Her independent and relatively successful quest for security was an affront to a man who wanted to be looked up to as an authority, worthy of respect, not to be belittled and disdained. He had hoped that she would come to him for guidance about important decisions. Instead, she implied that he could not be trusted to manage anything, large or small. Thus, Ray may have been angry and disgusted, not because Jennifer was *too* dependent, but rather because she was *not as* dependent on him as he would have liked.

Having discovered love only as he entered middle age, Ray held onto a naive image of love made up of idyllic word pictures. He lacked experience in the continual give-and-take that complicates love, but need not detract from it. With Jennifer the give-and-take was especially tense. Ray, who wanted admiration and deference, may have been morally offended because his wife had the gall to criticize him. Still, the deterioration of their relationship was not his doing alone.

Ray and Jennifer appear to have been one of the many couples who start out by fulfilling each other's needs, but then fall into a cycle of mutual disappointment and withdrawal. Typically, the man's greatest need is for recognition and status, while the woman's greatest need is for intimacy and affection.

Jennifer, finding Ray either too emotionally remote or unworthy of the respect he sought as provider and head of the household, denied him her trust and withheld her generosity. His self-esteem wounded, Ray increasingly withdrew his affection from Jennifer, which led her to carp at him all the more.

No one person starts these destructive cycles, but both partners suffer from them. Couples such as Ray and Jennifer lock themselves into a pattern of escalating suspicion and mistrust in part by thinking and speaking of each other in harsh rather than sympathetic language. Jennifer thought of Ray as "controlling," when she might instead have accepted that he needed respect. Ray might not have been so resentful of Jennifer's "demanding" attitude if he had understood her to be wanting love and affection. A couple can take a first step toward breaking the negative cycle by reframing their thoughts about each other in more positive language, so that they will want to meet each other's needs rather than resist each other's demands. In this way they can learn to view not only each other, but also themselves more sympathetically, instead of through the distorting mirror of negative images they convey to each other. Such therapeutic insight and guidance were not available to Ray and Jennifer, however, and they became less and less able to give each other the benefit of the doubt.

The separations that Ray repeatedly initiated—he moved out three times—may have been motivated by feelings of anger and humiliation. Perhaps he was trying to call Jennifer's bluff, as if to say, "You'll see how much you'll need me!" Perhaps he hoped to enforce the respect that Jennifer did not grant him of her own accord. He apparently could tolerate being separated from his wife as long as he felt he was in control and could move back if he chose. While he missed Jennifer, he seemed to have been willing to forgo intimacy to maintain (as he saw it) his status. Jennifer, though, may well have experienced him as pulling away from her and further frustrating her needs.

Thus the couple's disengagement proceeded. They filed for a separation while they were sorting out their marital problems in counseling. Both were traveling a great deal, doing business in different cities, but they kept in touch and continued to negotiate their differences.

While they were thus poised between marriage and divorce, Jennifer bought a house without consulting Ray. Once he had moved out of their former house, she understandably began to take care of herself and plan for her own future (which she had tended to do anyway). Equally understandably, Ray found her action alienating—"bizarre," he called it. He then began looking for a house of his own.

I couldn't relate to her going ahead with the house while we were still trying to make things work out, but I guess that's the way it was. It looked like it was all over. I started thinking that if I was going to be single again, I'd better get my act together and start planning my own investments. But given the way I felt when she sprang that house deal on me, I thought it only fair, if there was any possibility that we'd get back together, that I call my wife and tell her I was considering buying a house, too. First she was upset about it, but then she called me back and told me she thought it was a wonderful idea.

Both partners' ambivalence is evident here. Ray didn't know whether to act as if he were married or single. Jennifer, seeing clearly the significance of the separate purchases, initially protested. Then, apparently deciding that her sadness was only nostalgia and not protest, she called back and blessed Ray's independent initiative.

A week later came Valentine's Day. Ray, in one of his more confident moods, sent Jennifer flowers. He called her the following day, only to be greeted with these words: "I have to tell you that I've found someone else." As in so many other tales of the anxiously attached, it was the partner who finally called it quits.

After the initial shock of hearing this announcement, Ray managed to buoy himself up with a desperate feat of wishful thinking. But it only bought him a short reprieve.

Of course, I was stunned when she said that. But after I hung up the phone, I sat with it for a couple of hours and saw it differently. I called her back and said, "Jennifer, don't you realize what's going on? If you have really reached the point where you can wipe me out of your life, then you're healed, you're well, and I can come home." It really set me free—the idea that I could come home because her dependency was healed.

She said, "I don't want you to come home. I told you I'm seeing this guy."

It didn't bother me at all. "Get rid of him. Get him out of there. I'm coming home."

We went back and forth about it, but she didn't budge. We had been through so much pain and suffering, but whatever happened to her, it was so quick, so swift, and it was final for her. And that didn't make sense to me.

Ray's gambit might have been inspired by prior conversations in which Jennifer had remarked, "I need to be more independent." Thus, he could conjure up the hope that if she were now able to feel more independent, she would once again be contented with their marriage. Mainly, however, his extraordinary denial of his impending doom testifies to the depth of the pain, confusion, and rage he could not bring himself to face. Here he relates the agonizing *distress* he felt when the truth came home to him, together with the *fear* that his despair might lead him to harm himself.

> I started going crazy. And then I just fell apart, and I called my counselor five hundred miles away. My phone bill must have been . . . I don't know how much. But thank God he was there for me, and I was able to get him, because I thought I was going to kill myself. I couldn't believe it. Like right now, I felt all this emotion in my body. I live in a condo at the beach, and I thought, "I'm going to walk in the ocean and drown myself." It terrified me. I had had suicidal thoughts back when I was in school, but that's years and years and years, and it shocked me to feel that way again. I thought, "How could I do this? How could I even think about doing it?" But I couldn't control it. It was crazy. It's like if I believed in a devil or something like that. None of it made sense. Thank goodness I had my counselor. I couldn't sleep at night. I was sick. Sick sick sick. I cried and cried and cried for days and days and days. I've been crying for two months. All that over trying to hold on to another human being.
>
> It just lingers and lingers and lingers, but some days I don't cry. It's crazy, being a man and crying all the time—and you don't know why you're crying. It's bizarre. I'm getting tired of thinking about it, talking about it. I want to get rid of it. I don't even talk to my friends about it anymore—it's boring. It's time for me to get on with my life. There's got to be a secret; if I only knew what it is.

In a calmer moment, Ray reflects:

> I've gone through an emotional trauma that is beyond any pain I've ever experienced. It was totally irrational. It didn't make sense to me, because I'm an intelligent person, and I'd had a lot of training about love relationships, marriage, that sort of thing. I realized, of course, that on a rational level you can't understand it. Why should you even try?

"I've cried, I've been angry—I've done it all," Ray concludes. He ran the gamut of emotions from joy to grief to rage to yet another feeling associated with anxious romantic attachment—namely, *shame*.

> I would call her on the phone, and it was like she wouldn't have anything to do with me. Then I felt like I had done something wrong. I felt very childish, like I was a little boy. I wanted to say, "What did I do wrong? I tried so hard!"

Whether or not he had tried to call Jennifer's bluff by moving out, she had now called his. When she made the decisive choice to leave him, she challenged both his control of their relationship and his sense of self-sufficiency, leaving him with feelings of humiliation and inadequacy. He really did not know what he had done wrong.

Yet he could also turn the blame on her, expressing *disgust* and *contempt* for her flaunting her love affair and embarrassing him.

> When I finally did get to see her, I said, "I'm morally offended by the way you ended our marriage." She met this guy and brought him into our home. When I called, he was there. She took him to our church and introduced him to our friends. Maybe I'm a little old-fashioned, but so is she, or so I thought. It's so unlike her to do that; she's so prim and proper. It would have been easy to carry on that relationship away from everything connected with me. I was hurt that she brought my friends into it, because they knew how hurt I was, and it made them uncomfortable. She was very selfish.

In Ray's anguish, sexual jealousy was entangled with the possessiveness about material property that Ray felt had poisoned the marriage.

> After the wonderful sex life we had had, I couldn't stand the thought of her being with someone else. I could see them in our house, making love, and my mind would conjure up all these things. That was the worst of all. It was like she had the world by the tail. Here I was like a big sissy, begging this woman on the phone to take me back. I wrote myself a note saying, "Wait a minute; this doesn't make sense," and put it on my desk. So I called and told her, "If you want a divorce, if you want this guy, fine, but I want my things out of the house." She asked me to leave everything there until I figured out where I was going to live. But I said, "Jennifer, it's very simple. I don't want my wife's lover sitting in my chair." I loved her, and I didn't want him holding her hand in my chair. I tried not to get ugly about it, but that was the way I felt. So I took out the furniture that had belonged to me before we got married, and it devastated her home.
>
> She told me that was a terrible thing to do. She said I should be happy for her, that she's found someone who loves her. That really upset me, but I calmly said to her, "You know, that's a real nice way to feel. I really wish that I could love you so much that I could be happy that you found someone else to love you. That's the way Jesus loved. I'm not there yet, Jennifer, but give me time. I might get there."

One incident in particular illustrates vividly the pain of the jealousy that Ray felt.

I had a plant in our bedroom, and some paintings on the wall that were so beautiful I had tears in my eyes when I bought them. Every time I thought about this man and my wife making love in front of my plant and my pictures, it was like being there myself, watching. I had to get my things out. It seemed so childish, but that was how I felt. So I went and got them out. That was the worst part of it. I was obsessed with her sleeping with him.

She couldn't understand why I wouldn't give or even sell her my things. I told her, "All these things are part of my consciousness, part of me." One time I laughed and said, "It's a package deal, you know. I go with it."

This was Ray's final retaliation—to take away the tokens of physical security that mattered so much to Jennifer, but for which she was unwilling or unable to give reciprocal tokens of her love.

Torn apart by his bitterness and his anguish, Ray notes the irony of his situation.

What's all this crap about remorse and sadness? There were so many bad things about the marriage that I really should have told her to go kiss up a rope.

Still, his obsession has continued unabated.

I want to let go of her, let her find her own life. But I can't. It's like I'm chained; I can't get out of it; I can't get released from these thoughts. Like my thoughts have me; I don't have them. Why am I doing this? This woman isn't Cleopatra. I know there are other people to love.

My counselor kept saying that it wasn't Jennifer; it was something else. What did she represent for me? What am I trying to hold on to? That longing for love, that connection, that wonder? Somewhere that has to be available for me. Jennifer's not the only source of love in my life. If I could really see that, see beyond Jennifer, I could be free.

I don't ever want to feel this way again. This isn't love. It's something here inside me. I wish I could just chuck it up. It's awful. Whatever it is, I feel that a lot of people are bound by it. I'm sure it must keep people in marriages that are very unhappy. There's got to be a way out. There's an answer somewhere, and the answer is simple, but I haven't found it yet.

We are working toward answers, though not simple ones, for Ray and others in his plight. Ray's admission that "it wasn't Jennifer; it was something else," which he calls "something here inside me," recalls the story of Kurt and Helen in Chapter 2. Helen came to feel that Kurt's ardor for her had little to do with her as an individual. On the contrary, she felt as if she were being asked to act out a prepared script in Kurt's private romantic drama. The intense passion felt by the anxiously attached lover thrives even in the absence of a reciprocal attachment. It does not take its character or energy from one particular partner. Instead, it is a kind of inner drive that may be directed at a succession of partners in turn. Devastated as he is, Ray might go through a period of detachment to allow his wounds to heal. Or he might recover surprisingly quickly if he again finds a suitable object for "that longing for love, that connection, that wonder."

CAROL: TOO MUCH, TOO LATE

Carol, thirty-seven years old and employed as a secretary, had "nothing to show" for two long-term relationships that had lasted a total of thirteen years. Both men left her for reasons that were unclear to her. Carol's story differs from those we have seen thus far because it is not a case of full-blown anxious romantic attachment in the early stages of a relationship. On the contrary, with both men Carol hesitated to commit herself emotionally until it was too late. Yet when these relationships ended, she was as devastated as was Ray. Her story shows, therefore, how *detachment* can be the obverse of *attachment*.

Carol "fell into" the first of her two significant relationships when she was an unwed mother in her early twenties. Bruce, a friend of her roommate's boyfriend, hung around their apartment long enough to strike up a friendship with both Carol and her four-year-old daughter. As Carol tells it,

> After just being there together for a while, we began to have fun. He was somebody to be with, and he was entertaining. He made me laugh, and he always had things planned. My life was fulfilled.

This low-key beginning is not typical of anxiously attached lovers. On the contrary, it might seem to have been a promising start for a secure relationship. Why, though, at the end of this restrained description, does Carol use a strong word like *fulfilled?* Part of what drew her to Bruce was that he had a large family and many friends.

> He's the kind who invites fifteen people over on a Saturday night without having anything particular in mind: "We'll figure out what we want to do." That was the part of him that satisfied me. There were a lot of caring people that I became attached to because I was living with him.

This gregarious lifestyle meant so much to Carol because she felt she had never really had a family life prior to meeting Bruce. A child of middle-aged parents, she saw her brother and sister grow up and leave home while she was still an adolescent. Her parents, too, seemed to have retired from active childrearing by the time she came along.

> My father didn't care, and my mother, who was more or less subservient to him, was too old (almost two generations removed from me) to understand how to help me through adolescence.

Her father, a strict disciplinarian, did nothing to help her overcome the social isolation imposed on her by living far from school. Without a reliable means of transportation, she either passed up dances and movies or risked being stranded without a ride home, in which case she would be punished for staying out too late.

Her parents' remoteness and her lack of social experience early in life denied Carol not only the experience of family love and closeness, but also pragmatic guidance for living her life. She was on her own, both emotionally and in learning to make important decisions. As a result, she was susceptible to strong emotional attachments, and, without the security of strong family ties, she may have been too needy to exercise her best judgment in choosing the people with whom she became involved. Leaving home at the age of seventeen after a clash with her father, she became involved shortly thereafter with a man several years older than she, whom she describes as "an alcoholic who had quit school at sixteen. He was good-looking, but he had nothing else." This man fathered her child. When he proved unreliable, unfaithful, and physically abusive, she left him, accepting the financial and emotional burdens of raising a child alone—a child who soon became very important to her.

From this background, Bruce, the next man in Carol's life, was a step up. Bruce provided her with emotional, but unfortunately not financial support, since he did not work regularly. The easy informality of Bruce's life went with a lack of ambition that did not match Carol's aspiration to a middle-class standard of living. "I just don't want to live this way," thought Carol. With a child to support, Carol may have put pressures on Bruce that led him to seek refuge elsewhere. Or he may simply have been expressing his own freewheeling, hedonistic tendencies by enjoying the company of other women. In either case, based on numerous clues, Carol became "obsessed with the thought that he was seeing other women. It drove me crazy."

Carol and Bruce decided to move out West to get a new start. By the time Carol arrived to join him, however, Bruce had already established new social contacts and was going out alone in the evenings. For Carol, the move had changed nothing.

> I'd sit home crying, not knowing where he was, and think, "My God, what did he bring me out here for, if he doesn't really want to be with me? I think I'm going crazy."

Carol moved back East, and Bruce promised to follow in a few months. Carol describes the final straw that ended the relationship:

> I knew in the back of my head that he wasn't coming back, that something was wrong. But I couldn't give up on it, and I'd cry and cry and cry. Finally, a mutual friend called me and said, "He's living with another woman out here, and he was seeing her before you came out." I was devastated, but angry, too.
>
> I had a job and my daughter to take care of, and I decided to go back to school and get my life back together. But I was very lonely, and I wasn't enjoying dating. I wasn't enjoying going out with somebody when it wasn't really right and we were just having dinner. I'd think, "I'd rather be home watching the Saturday night movie than pretending to have this conversation with these people."

Carol experienced a mixture of *distress* and *anger* as her six-year relationship with Bruce came to an end. Still, while she had found with Bruce the warmth that had been lacking in her parents' home, she was looking for something different.

She found it when she met Stan on a blind date. "We were attracted to each other from the beginning," she recalls. For Carol, the attraction was neither intense nor primarily physical; there were strong elements of status that perhaps served to repair her damaged self-esteem.

> He dressed well and could talk with anybody. He had middle-class friends, and we all got along. I felt like a middle-class person when I was with him, and I felt as if we were a middle-class couple going places. I grew up at the poverty level, and I've always felt like a second-class citizen.

She also liked Stan's "truthful, aggressive personality," by which she meant that he expressed his feelings and desires clearly. "He was an honest, direct person—sometimes to a fault, where he rubbed people the wrong way. But at least I knew what I was dealing with."

Again, however, it was not love at first sight, at least for Carol. She seemed to hold back, because "once burned, twice shy."

> He was the one who initiated and created a nice relationship. He wanted us to go out together and spend a lot of time together. He built up the relationship; I was standoffish. I was dating him, I liked him, I thought he was nice, but it was he who put the effort into making us a couple.

Within two months Stan proposed marriage. Carol replied, "Well, I really don't know. I'm still cutting my ties with Bruce, and I still care about him. It doesn't seem to be the right thing to do just yet." Here, with an attractive man who professed strong love at the outset, Carol hesitated to commit herself. Superficially, this would not appear to be the response of an anxious, romantically attached lover.

Although she put off the question of marriage, Carol before long was swayed by Stan's attentions.

> He constantly wanted to be with me. He always told me how nice I looked. He was so open, and he made me feel so secure. He'd say, "I want to tell you every day how much I care about you and how much I love you." I thought, "Gosh, this is so pleasant."
>
> When we went out, he was so demonstrative. He let everybody know he was with me. We'd go to a party, and he'd just want to sit in the corner with me and talk. I said to myself, "God, this is a relief. With Bruce, toward the end I was so insanely jealous it was making me sick. I can't go through that again."

"With the home, the middle-class life, and all of Stan's consideration," Carol concludes, "I felt I was probably the happiest I've ever been." As with Bruce in their early days together, she was experiencing the *joy* that is especially intense when one is romantically obsessed. For Carol, though, this joy (which she calls "relief" in the above passage) had a special character. Starting with so few advantages in life, she found in each successive relationship a new set of satisfactions. Her first relationship gave her a rudimentary connection with someone outside her family. More important for the long run, it left her with a child that she could love. Bruce exposed her to good feelings and social companionship. Stan offered even more substantial benefits: financial security, social status, and (at the beginning) the promise of exclusive devotion.

For Carol, a relationship with this man was not simply a matter of personal feelings; it meant putting together the ingredients of a comfortable, middle-class life:

> With Stan I got closer to my ideal expectations in life. He had a good job, and we bought a house—the first one I had ever lived in. We both had decent cars; you didn't have to worry whether they'd pass inspection. I learned water-skiing and golf; all I could afford to do before that was play cards. I felt so comfortable with the whole situation.

Still, with all that she valued in this relationship, Carol allowed the seeds of its destruction to take root. Her daughter, now an adolescent, irritated Stan from the beginning with her demands and impositions. Openly disapproving of Stan, she kept in touch with Bruce, Carol's previous boyfriend, who was her psychological if not biological father. Meanwhile, Stan's marriage proposal went begging. Stan may have resented the fact that Carol, instead of reciprocating the unconditional love he initially offered, gave her daughter's needs priority. Carol lent credence to this interpretation by explicitly linking the question of marriage to considerations of her daughter's well-being.

> He really wanted to get married, but I kept saying, "Oh, wait a while. The kid's giving us a hard time. Once she's settled, fine. What difference does it make? Why can't we wait just one more year?" Finally, when my daughter moved out to go to an out-of-state boarding school, I said, "Maybe now it's time." But his response was, "Well, I don't know. We've gone this far without getting married. Maybe we should leave well enough alone."

Boarding school brought her daughter in contact with her biological father, and Carol spent time and money on long-distance telephone calls to both of them to protect her child from abuse. Her love for her daughter was genuine and deep. So far was she from being a self-seeking opportunist that she allowed this maternal bond to interfere with her own prospects for an advantageous marriage. In this respect she was like many other unwed mothers who become intensely involved with their children in the absence of other close relationships and then, for that very reason, find it difficult to form such relationships. On the other hand, Carol might have been more willing to marry Stan if he had more strongly identified with and supported her love for her daughter and included the girl more fully in his vision of their life together.

Over the next few years, Stan increasingly detached himself from Carol. He no longer wanted to go to her office parties or visit her friends and family. Like Bruce, he socialized more and more on his own. Again, Carol was consumed by obsessive feelings of jealousy.

> I acted like a detective, making excuses to go down to a club he belonged to, just to check up on what was going on. There were women around there, but there was nothing going on. There was just something inside me saying, "Something's wrong. Check up. Find out. Is he running around on you?"

Carol's uncontrollable jealousy, initially groundless, was fueled by her experiences in her previous relationship and served to hasten the deterioration of her present relationship. By the next Christmas, their last together, the relationship had become so alienated that Carol stayed home from her office Christmas party rather than go without Stan, who insisted on going to his own party without her.

When Carol's daughter graduated from high school, she came home with a menagerie of pets, and Carol took her in "until she could get on her feet." A month later Stan decided to leave. Carol wanted him to go into counseling with her. "Look," he said, "we've been together so long. Why don't we go our separate ways and try to find something we like better? I'm almost forty now. I'm halfway through this life, and I'm not happy."

Years earlier, he had been eager to make a permanent commitment, but Carol had not been ready. As a result, the sexual bond that united them was not reinforced by the bonds of marriage and children. When Stan's passion waned, there were no formal ties and no major shared emotional investments to keep him involved. Carol's error, if it can be called one, was not to see the crucial importance of timing. In her eagerness to meet her daughter's emotional needs, she forfeited her own future contentment.

After Stan moved out, Carol went through a period in which feelings of distress mingled with fear and guilt in an obsessive preoccupation with her lost love. Her pain was intensified and prolonged by Stan's inconsistent behavior, which repeatedly reawakened fantasies that he might return to her.

> For three months I was crying all the time. Riding to and from work, any time I had to think, it was constantly on my mind—how lonely I felt without him, how I hadn't wanted this to happen. What did I do wrong? Maybe I shouldn't have let my daughter interfere. Maybe if we had

married, it would have bonded us together. Why did he suddenly leave? The only answer I could come up with was that this was a midlife crisis, and that once he had thought things over he might change his mind.

Although Stan was now dating a younger woman, he and Carol went away together for a few weekends. Each time she felt tormented by the inconsistency she perceived in him.

> It felt like such a reprieve to be with him, but I was hurt because I could feel the distance he was trying to keep between us. The first night would be really nice. We'd go out to dinner and have a nice conversation and go to bed. But by the next day he was having second thoughts, like "Maybe I shouldn't be here" or "Do I want to sever this or don't I?" In the course of the weekend he would pretty much decide that he did.

One might infer from this story that Stan was incredibly cruel to keep Carol dangling on a string. On the other hand, a seven-year relationship does not end in a day for a man any more than for a woman. Weekend ambivalence is common among reunited ex-lovers. They feel a rush of emotion on seeing each other again, but then draw apart when the problems that compromised the relationship reappear. Carol's naivete, together with the intensity of her desire, prevented her from seeing the mounting evidence that her long love affair with Stan was ending.

After a period of irregular contacts, she stopped hearing from him. Several weeks later, she learned that he was about to marry a woman he had recently met. Understandably, she felt crushed by this revelation.

> God, how could he do this? How could he make love with me and then decide a month or two later to marry somebody else? I was sure we were going to get back together. And then to find this out—I can't describe how hurt I felt. To think that we spent all those years together, and I don't even know why he left. And then to go through a whole year of hoping and anticipating we'd get back together, and crying and carrying on and not being able to do anything except work, work, work—and here we go again. Another year of this? I can't go on like this. And now he's in the area, and I've got to hear about it from everybody I see. I don't dare leave my house. I don't want to run into him with her.

"Each time it gets worse," says Carol, referring to the endings of her relationships with men. She lists the now familiar, but increasingly intense symptoms of her grief:

I felt bad when Bruce and I broke up. I felt miserable last year when Stan left me. When I found out he was getting married, it was just like it was happening all over again. There's a great big knot in my stomach, and my chest is tight most of the time. I can't even contain myself from crying when I'm on the phone talking business. My mind wanders off, tears come to my eyes, and there I am blattin' all over the place.

Carol finds it difficult to maintain any kind of social life because her consciousness is so absorbed by regrets and longings.

I'm not very sociable because I don't have anything to talk about except how miserable I feel. I'll go out with a female friend to a movie, which keeps my mind occupied, and then have a drink or coffee with her, sometimes even dinner. But I have to limit the time, because dinner leaves me too much time to think. We can be having a nice conversation, and then all of a sudden these thoughts come over me, and I'm talking about him and crying. And my friend is sitting there feeling so bad, but she can't do anything for me.

If anything, I feel worse on a date with a man because I don't really want to be with this man when there's somebody I'd rather be enjoying myself with. I think, "Why am I doing this? Why can't it be the way it was?" I get obsessed with that, and then I go home and cry myself to sleep, and then I get up and it's another day. It's a vicious cycle that I can't break out of.

Carol's fears about the future are expressed in a dread of isolation and a feeling of personal insufficiency.

The thought of being alone is the worst thing that crosses my mind. I've got three bedrooms for me and my daughter, and what good is it having her living here when she's never around? So I'm all by myself in this big house. I hate being all by myself. There's only so many things you can do by yourself. Even going for a walk isn't any fun by yourself, but almost anything is fun if there are two of you.

She gets close to the source of these concerns when she relates how she wanted to attach herself to Stan's family as she had to Bruce's:

I have a very hard time cutting ties. I still have friends from grammar school. I used to tell Stan how obsessed I was with having ties. He's got a large, wonderful family with lots of brothers and sisters and aunts and uncles. My family are all dead or scattered in different places. I once said to Stan, "I wouldn't even mind moving closer to your parents, just so we could have some family life with them." I want to be part of a family; I want to be close. I want to have all that around me—that security, I guess.

When it came to love and intimacy, Carol grew up "on the outside looking in." Her desperate search for close personal ties originated in response to parents who were harsh and distant and a brother and sister who were too old for her to relate to emotionally. Growing up in that environment, she yearned for love, yet dreaded the risks it entailed. She shows considerable insight into her ambivalence about romantic attachments as she summarizes the course of her relationships.

> With Bruce and Stan, and others as well, I did not initiate. They were attracted to me, they wanted to take me out, and I just thought it was okay. I have a hard time letting go and saying, "I really care about this guy, and I'm going to give him my all." Instead, I keep a distance, as if I'm saying, "I'm only going to give him so much," while I get comfortable enough to feel that I really care. Then, when I finally do give it my all and leave myself wide open, it starts going the other way. That's when they start backing off.

Carol begins a relationship cautiously, protecting the emotional vulnerability she senses in herself. Once she finally lets down her guard, she becomes doubly vulnerable to obsessive romantic attachments, despite the fact that she does not show the typical signs of intense passion and amorous pursuit of the partner at the outset—what is commonly called love at first sight. Instead, her intensely felt need for love is initially masked by *detachment,* and her story therefore looks forward to Chapter 4.

When she does become attached, she appears to attach herself to a fantasy as much as to an actual person. So far, she has not been able to find a man to fulfill the fantasy. Inexperienced in love, untrained in how to protect herself in a difficult world, she may have made more than one unfortunate choice of partners. In particular, she may have felt drawn toward Bruce's and Stan's outward self-assurance while failing to recognize the deeper uncertainties these men felt. On the other hand, her caution and hesitation may have brought out the inconsistency in men who initially wanted a committed relationship. These are examples of how one's choice of partners affects, and is affected by, one's susceptibility to anxious romantic attachment, which is the subject of Chapter 5.

Donna, Ray, and Carol, who have dramatized the look and feel of insecure romantic love, will appear again in later chapters as they illustrate the ideas explored there. Among other things, Donna exemplifies *compliance,* one of the tactics of the anxiously attached. Ray's saga is a classic case of both *jealousy* during and after a relationship and *depression* when the relationship ends. Carol, who also suffered from intense feelings of depression, shows how *detachment* can be the flip side of excessive attachment. Her story points as well to the need to look at the *partner* of the romantically insecure lover in order to understand the dynamics of the relationship. Finally, all three cases demonstrate the importance of *family history* in the development of anxious romantic attachment. Together, these themes will fill out the picture of the past and present circumstances that contribute to intimate dilemmas.

4

THE SMOKESCREEN

OF DETACHMENT

When we compared people's scores on the anxious-attachment scale with their answers to questions about their family backgrounds, we came upon an intriguing finding. Many of the people who scored *lowest* on anxious romantic attachment reported childhood experiences similar to those of the people who scored *highest*. For example, compared with the great majority of participants who scored closer to the middle on anxious attachment, those at *both* extremes much more frequently had parents who were rejecting or inconsistent in their affection.

This discovery showed that insecurity about making intimate connections does not always take the form of anxious or obsessive romantic attachment. On the contrary, people can experience insecure romantic love in more than one way. People who are insecure about romantic attachments have had past experiences (whether in childhood or in romantic involvements) that have led them to fear rejection intensely. To cope with that fear, they adopt different strategies, depending on what has worked for them in relating to past lovers or family members. Some people try to reduce their anxiety by increasing the security they feel in their relationships. These are the anxiously attached individuals described in Chapters 2 and 3. They cling to their partners or declare their passion in dramatic terms in an effort to elicit a reciprocal commitment. Others cope with their insecurity in what seems the opposite way—by acting detached and self-sufficient in their relationships or even turning away from romance altogether. They avoid what for them are the large risks of emotional involvement by not getting involved.

These strategies are comparable to the different ways investors might cope with the uncertainties of the stock market in an unstable period. One person might monitor her or his investment closely by reading the stock prices in the daily newspaper and speaking frequently with a stockbroker. Another might stay out of the market altogether. Both of these individuals are seeking to reduce uncertainty. Likewise, when it comes to love relationships, some people show a deeply ingrained pattern of anxious attachment, while others have an equally long-standing habit of avoidance.

There are even those who alternate between detachment and anxious attachment, trying to cope with feelings of insecurity. One such person was Carol, in the previous chapter. With each of the two men with whom she had long-term romantic involvements, Bruce and Stan, Carol initially held herself aloof from emotional involvement. If you observed Carol at the beginning of a relationship, you might describe her as a cool, emotionally secure, even self-contained person. Yet in retrospect Carol realized that she had hesitated for fear of exposing the emotional vulnerability she knew she felt. By the end, she had waited too long, and she suffered greatly when the bonds that had by then come to mean so much to her were severed.

If Carol had been given our anxious-attachment questionnaire to fill out at the beginning of one of those relationships, she might have checked off low scores (0 through 2) on most of the items, indicating that she did not feel very involved in the relationship or very anxious about whether the man would be a secure presence in her life. As she said, "I have a hard time letting go and saying, 'I really care about this guy, and I'm going to give him my all.' Instead, I keep a distance." In time, as she let down those barriers and risked greater vulnerability (in her words, "when I finally do give it my all and leave myself wide open"), her scores would have gone up. Like a person pouring money into the stock market in the hope of making up for recent losses, Carol would have become more anxious as she increased her emotional investment. By the end, if asked to rate the strength of her obsessive attachment after Stan was gone, she might have checked off 8, the highest score, on many of the items.

This example helps explain why some people who scored low (or detached) on the anxious-attachment items had backgrounds similar to those who scored high. (Again, bear in mind that both groups were quite small compared to the vast majority who fell somewhere in the middle.) These two groups at the extremes of the scale might have included some people with consistent lifelong habits of responding in either an anxiously attached or detached way to the same childhood experiences of uncertain acceptance by parents. On the other hand, some of our research participants might have scored at opposite extremes of the scale at different moments in their lives. Had they been excited about the relationship they were involved in when they took part in the survey, they might have filled out a lot of high scores. If, however, they had just begun to venture a new and perhaps frightening emotional investment after a painful breakup, they might have checked off low scores.

Look back at the questionnaire you filled out at the beginning of Chapter 2. If you scored consistently low on the statements pertaining to romantic anxiety, romantic obsession, or both, this chapter will be especially relevant to you. The same will be true if you imagine scoring low on these items at some other time in your life, or in some other phase of your current relationship. Even if you yourself do not fit the picture of detachment that such scores signify, you may know someone who would, perhaps a spouse or lover. The self-assessment questionnaire can thus help you identify what may be needlessly stopping you from enjoying the satisfactions of intimacy.

People who appear detached often have as much desire for intimacy as anyone else. They may yearn for closeness, but fear exposing themselves to possible loss and to the grieving and despair that would result. Although they may have a great deal to offer in love relationships, they are afraid to show their true warmth. They are lonely souls who feel that they dare not take what they want, need, and deserve. Greater awareness of the roots of detachment may give such individuals the insight needed to venture the risks and rewards of love.

As some of our cases will illustrate, the detached stance is especially common among men. It can be an evident source of frustration for the woman who wants her partner to be emotionally available. It can be, as well, a less readily identifiable source of frustration for the man engaged in an endless pursuit of achievement, power, and recognition in place of intimacy. Today many men and, increasingly, women substitute outward accomplishment and the admiration of others for the satisfaction of the basic human need to form close relationships. Since this deeper need for intimacy remains unrecognized and unsatisfied, the quest is likely to prove futile, whatever gratifications it provides along the way. This is one form of detachment we observe in this chapter.

To understand better how detachment can be an expression of romantic insecurity, let us break down the anxious-attachment scale into its two components—romantic anxiety and romantic obsession—and consider what it may mean to score high or low on each in combination with the other. In the diagram on page 72, the higher a person scores on romantic obsession, the farther to the right that person would be. The higher a person scores on romantic anxiety, the closer to the top of the chart that person would be.

Since most people score fairly close to the middle on both romantic obsession and romantic anxiety, most people would appear in the circle in the center, labeled Invested-Concerned. Does this mean that there is an optimal middle range of romantic anxiety or romantic obsession that is beneficial? It seems logical to assume that there is an adaptive and beneficial level. In performance tests and athletic competitions, the people who do best are those who score in the mid-range of anxiety. Love is not a performance, but the effects of anxiety still would seem similar. Too much anxiety is obviously disabling. Too little, on the other hand, might leave one insufficiently motivated to make contact and adjust to another person's wishes, as well as insufficiently concerned about what happens to oneself or one's partner. Similarly, some degree of attachment is essential to a mature, committed love relationship. It is reasonable to think often about a loved one and to feel bound to that person's fate, but not to be so driven by obsessive fantasies or dependency needs as to be incapable of approaching life independently. A person who feels some degree of romantic anxiety and obsession, but can keep these feelings in balance, is more capable of forming enduring, satisfying love relationships.

What about the people who are closer to the extremes on either dimension? First, recall from Chapter 2 that romantic anxiety and romantic obsession tend to go together. More often than not, people experience similar degrees of anxiety and obsession. This is not always the case: some people are very anxious but not very obsessed (upper left), while others are very obsessed but not very anxious (lower right). However, more people can be found in the upper right extreme (Obsessed-Anxious) and the lower left extreme (Nonobsessed-Nonanxious) than in the other two.

The fact that romantic anxiety is associated so strongly with romantic obsession indicates that the items that signify romantic obsession on the questionnaire really do convey an intense preoccupation—to the point of being excessive—rather than a normal involvement with a romantic partner. Romantic obsession is associated with some of the same alienating childhood

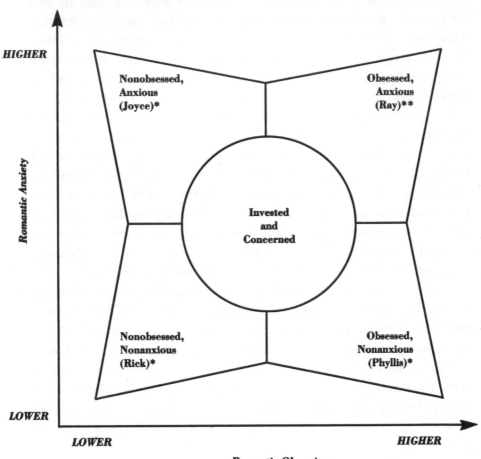

**TWO MAJOR COMPONENTS OF INSECURITY
IN LOVE RELATIONSHIPS**

* This Chapter
** Chapter 3

experiences as romantic anxiety and sometimes leads to troubled interpersonal relationships. One illustration is the 1987 movie *Fatal Attraction*, starring Michael Douglas and Glenn Close. Romantic anxiety and romantic obsession together make up an overall pattern of feelings and behavior that we call anxious romantic attachment, which is represented by the upper right corner of the diagram (Obsessed-Anxious). The romantically insecure, or anxiously attached, individuals presented in the previous two chapters fall into this quadrant.

We cannot say whether this extreme, or any of the other three extremes, is necessarily unhealthy. Everyone has different ways of handling anxiety and attachment, and many different personal styles can be part of a satisfying life, provided that a person maintains some balance and perspective. You probably know people who exhibit endearing idiosyncracies in their relationships, suggesting either excessive anxiety or obsessive attachment, but who clearly have a loving marriage and family life.

You might find yourself in the lower right extreme (Obsessed-Nonanxious) if you are somewhat romantically obsessed, and yet you don't feel much anxiety because you are an emotionally secure person with a consistently loving partner. Some of the people in this group are blessed with partners who are equally obsessed with them! As well-matched couples, they can have healthy relationships if their mutual obsession is not so extreme that it cuts them off from the rest of the world. Likewise, some people in the lower left extreme (Nonobsessed-Nonanxious) are undemonstrative, even matter-of-fact about their love, but their love is still genuine and mutual.

Nonetheless, in a study in which people are rating their four most important love relationships, those who score *lowest* on attachment, and perhaps also on anxiety, may be detached to a degree that denies them or their partners the satisfactions of intimacy and emotional security. To have many 0s, 1s, and 2s across the board for one's four most important relationships indicates a lack of engagement in romantic love. This interpretation is supported by the fact that those who scored lowest on the anxious-attachment scale, like those who scored highest, frequently experienced disruptive family problems or a lack of nurturance in childhood. Such backgrounds appear to lead some people to be overinvolved in romantic feelings while others close themselves off to those very same feelings. A person who was not well cared for as a child may not understand how to care for others. That person's partner may in turn feel insecure because the affection he or she shows is not reciprocated openly by the detached person.

People have different degrees of awareness of their own detachment. Some may consciously long for intimacy, but be afraid to reveal such wishes to others. By not acting on their desires, they avoid rejection and disappointment, but remain painfully aware that something very important is lacking in their lives. How can they avoid that awareness? By suppressing the wish altogether. If you don't know that you desire love, then you don't miss it. That is why some people who appear to be detached admit to wishing that they had some intimacy in their lives, while others insist that they do not need it. Some in the latter group might once have said that they did yearn for love, but they have found it easier to forget this wish than to grieve forever the loss of its fulfillment.

At its most extreme, detachment can take troubling, sometimes destructive forms. In the lower right quadrant, a maladaptive way of being Obsessed-Nonanxious is to have intense feelings of attachment to a relationship that is very distant or even a fantasy. One may be secretly in love with a person one sees every day. Or, like Phyllis in this chapter, one may channel romantic longings into a crush on a famous person who is not aware of one's existence. Two people who live far away from each other may say that they are in love, but never test the relationship with the demands of frequent contact. Or one may carry the torch for a deceased spouse or an ex-lover one hasn't seen for years. These are examples of obsessive attachment without anxiety. To love someone who is not in a position to reject you is to choose the predictability of fantasy.

There is a parallel extreme in the lower left quadrant. Some of those who are Nonobsessed-Nonanxious may have been so wounded as children by insensitive care that they now are largely incapable of normal relationships. Unable to trust even their parents to take care of them, they seek to protect themselves by obtaining what they feel they must have for survival, even if they end up hurting others along the way. These individuals, who have been labeled "psychopathic" or "antisocial" personalities, are capable of great deception and sometimes commit criminal acts without remorse. They treat people, including lovers, as property to be stolen, exploited, and abandoned at will. Lacking the usual experiences of human attachment and vulnerability, they feel little or no anxiety or love.

Such people may form what appear to be strong attachments, but these are mainly with people who feed their egos by reflecting in a positive way their images of themselves. If you are loyal to them, they will love you, and the relationship will seem close and warm. But they do not appreciate you as an individual, only as an extension of themselves. If you challenge them or appear to betray them, they will turn on you. This pattern of low or absent anxiety and obsession is somewhat more common among males than among females. Rick, to be described later in this chapter, comes close to exemplifying this type of detached person.

By no means, however, does a person who scores low on romantic obsession, or even on both romantic obsession and romantic anxiety, necessarily fit this picture of extreme and constant emotional detachment, with its antisocial overtones. There is a more typical form of fluctuating detachment that is a primary focus because it is part of the experience of so many people. These individuals do want to have relationships of mutuality. However, they, too, are emotionally self-protective as a result of having been hurt either in childhood or in previous adult relationships. They seek to avoid romantic attachments to spare themselves the pain of anxiety that arises from the anticipation or actuality of rejection and disappointment. Since they experience considerable anxiety about relationships, one might expect to find them among the Nonobsessed-Anxious in the upper left quadrant. Consider, however, that these are people who stay out of romantic relationships, or characterize their relationships as unromantic, so that they will not have to feel anxious. To the extent that this strategy is successful, they may not feel much anxiety as long as they do not acknowledge to themselves that a particular relationship is very important. Moreover, since anxiety is so unpleasant for them, they may select "safe" partners, individuals who love them, but in whom they have only a weak interest. If so, they will appear as Nonobsessed-Nonanxious in the lower left portion of the diagram.

Whether such anxiously avoidant people fall into the upper left or the lower left region depends on how fully they acknowledge their underlying anxiety. But it really makes little difference. Either way, if they are drawn in by the possibility of a romantic involvement, they may suddenly find themselves in the upper right (Obsessed-Anxious) quadrant, along with the anxiously attached lovers with whom they have so much else in common. People who fear involvement may require more evidence, more reassurance, before they allow themselves to become committed. Once they let their defenses down, however, they are very vulnerable to feelings of romantic obsession as well as romantic anxiety—feelings that sometimes are expressed only after the relationship ends. A person such as this may flip back and forth between the left and right sides of our diagram, periodically venturing out into the dangerous territory of anxious romantic attachment and then scurrying back to the refuge of detachment when a relationship does not work out. This pattern is typified by Joyce, our first case history, but it also appears in the stories of Deborah, Alex, Larry and Jan, and Anna.

JOYCE: THE SILENT ANGUISH OF DETACHMENT

In movies from the 1940s and 1950s we see a recurrent character type, the hard-boiled woman, whose first reaction to all men is "Kiss off, buster." Wearing a tough exterior, she fights off what she simultaneously most wants and most fears—until the kindness and persistence of her suitor convince her that it is safe to relax her defenses. A contemporary variant is the hardened veteran of the dating circuit. Burned once too often, knowing all the tricks, she shows no affection until she is thoroughly convinced that she has found someone special.

These images may help us understand Joyce, a woman who projects great self-assurance and appears to keep tight control over her emotional involvements. Unaccountably, this worldly, confident woman suffered a breakdown when she felt betrayed and abandoned by a man with whom she had not been intimately involved and to whom she had never declared her love. She was devastated by the loss of a "love" that was never made public. Her story illustrates how anxious romantic attachment and detachment can be two sides of the same coin.

Joyce is an engaging, vivacious woman in her early thirties who speaks energetically, but in an emotionally unrevealing way. "I'm very open about what I want in relationships," she says. "If I'm not interested, I say so right away. I guess I want to be in control. It's hard for me to be the subservient female, waiting for a man to call me."

Joyce presents herself as forceful and in control in this account of a recent relationship.

> This was a very nice guy that I met at a public meeting. I called him—in fact, I called a bunch of places to get his number; he never knew that! We hit it off easily, but we'd both been through some tough times, and everything just blew up in our faces. I brought out the insecurities in him because I'm a strong, assertive woman. His ex-wife was weak, and I was just too much for him. We ended up not speaking to each other.
>
> Some weeks later I called him on a whim. Referring to a wonderful experience we had had together, I said, "Do you want to go out to the beach again and see the eclipse of the moon? That's a once-in-a-lifetime experience, too." I expected it might irritate him, but he jumped at the

chance and thanked me for opening things up again. My feeling was, if anything happens, fine; if not, no loss.

But he's scared to death of me. It was two in the morning, and real dark. We were coming across the dunes at the crossroads, and it was scary out there. I reached over to grab his arm, and he said, "Oh, God, don't touch me," as if he'd melt if I did. It was a strange reaction, but I let it go.

Although she can play the assertive role in a relationship, Joyce is wary of revealing her feelings.

> I've met men and fallen in love with them, but I've never verbalized it to them. I've always sat back and thought about it. I don't say "I love you" easily. That comes out long and hard. So therefore I haven't said "I love you" to too many people.

This is the opposite of what we find with anxiously attached lovers, who tend to declare love before their partners do. It is a picture of detachment, and in it we can sense Joyce's emotional reserve as well as the vulnerability that lies beneath it.

This vulnerability was exposed, if only briefly, when Joyce was hospitalized for an overdose of tranquilizers following an incident involving her supervisor at work. This was a man to whom she feared revealing the love she had carried for him for over a year.

> My boss was caught embezzling—from my account, yet! I had the police bothering me, and I might have ended up in jail myself. It was very tough for me, and I just fell apart and had to leave work. I felt that this man that I had looked up to for a year, whom I felt closer to than I ever felt to my Dad, had betrayed me. He lied to me.
>
> They put me on a tranquilizer, and I ended up in the hospital after I took too many. It was not a deliberate suicide attempt. It was a deep-rooted pain. I have never felt that pain before or since. It was an almost physical pain of feeling so alone, so isolated, that all you want to do is make the pain go away. You'll do anything to make the pain go away. I took a few tranquilizers, and I felt better, but the pain started coming back, so I took a few more. I don't think it was a conscious wish to die. It was a wish not to feel so bad.

Where did the pain come from? What did it mean for her? Joyce relates her experience with her duplicitous boss to her memories of her father.

That guy—oh, he was a doll! When I was out sick he sent me a dozen red roses. He was one of those men who—I don't know if he was a con artist, but he knew exactly the right thing to say to make me feel very vulnerable. I never had an affair with him, yet I felt very close to him. He was like a dad, or my perception of what a dad should be.

My real Dad and I never really had a relationship. We never went on vacations with him, and I cannot even recall a whole week when we saw each other regularly. I don't think I ever really knew him. My boss was like a daddy to me. I felt safe with him for the year that I knew him. Then when he was exposed, I didn't feel safe anymore. I have never regained the trust I placed in him.

Here is a woman who in most circumstances is self-assured and assertive, but who suffered an emotional collapse after the ending of a relationship that was in fact unshared and unreciprocated. She had formed a private emotional attachment to a man with whom she was never sexually intimate, but who was able to make her feel, in her own words, both vulnerable and safe. That combination evoked powerful feelings in her, which she attributes to the incompleteness of her relationship with her father. Inside the mature woman was a little girl longing for a father to love her. She wanted someone who could engage her need to be loved while allowing her to feel safe enough to take off the armor she wore in her dealings with men. She had found such a man in her supervisor, but was afraid to tell him so. Her emotional connection with him remained in the realm of hope and fantasy, but its loss was no less real to her when she was suddenly deprived of the comfort it had given her.

Continuing her story, she reveals another childhood source of her emotional vulnerability—namely, her mother's indifference toward her.

When I got out of the intensive-care unit, my Mom called and said, "I can't come." Now if your daughter had just got out of the ICU, and if they had just pumped charcoal out of her stomach for six hours, and if you were five hundred miles away, you'd be on your way up there, right? Here I had almost died. But she said, "We're busy. I can't get away." I said, "Fine, fine." I figured, "I'm not going to die to get her attention."

Yet even (or perhaps especially) at this moment of intense anguish, with long-repressed feelings laid bare, Joyce quickly regained her outward self-assurance and showed herself in all her polish.

I spent a couple of weeks in the hospital, and it was great. People thought I was one of the hospital staff.

"No," I'd tell them, "I'm a patient here."
"You don't look like one."

As she gives a glimpse of her past relationships, Joyce reveals that her detachment has had another side to it.

> I try to be strong, and on the outside I really am. Inside, when it comes to a one-to-one relationship, forget it. The insecurities are real hard unless you have that daddy or someone else you can go to. When I do get into a relationship and let it ripen for a while, I become very dependent. A guy I lived with once asked me to move out because I was too dependent. He felt I could never make a go of it. I didn't work; I couldn't. My life functioned around him. Whatever he wanted to do, I'd do. I never said "Boo" to him. Now I do! I'm coming out of that dependency now.
>
> Recently I started up with a guy I dated years ago. I could have him back, but I don't want him now that I'm more independent. I was very dependent on this man. But in the last couple of years I've become very independent. So I guess I'm saying, "I don't need you now."

Joyce's present independence probably represents a mixture of real personal growth and a brave facade of detachment. In any case, she clearly has expressed her unresolved feelings about her parents and her somewhat brittle self-esteem both through periods of strong dependency and through periods of invulnerability and detachment. "I have never felt special to any one person," she concludes. "No, I have never felt real." The same might be said by an anxiously attached lover.

RICK: ANTISOCIAL DETACHMENT

As compared with Joyce, detachment means something different when applied to Rick, a flashily dressed man engaged in a wholesale business. Rick comes close to fitting the pattern of extreme, "antisocial" detachment described earlier. He came into therapy a year after he and his wife, Maria, separated. He stated that he felt agitated and suicidal because he could not stand to see his wife with a new boyfriend, who was about to move into what Rick called "our" house. He had not previously sought therapy over the separation, but had been in treatment recently for alcoholism.

Rick spoke the language that he expected a therapist might want to hear. He acknowledged himself to be "immature" and "dependent," even though he seemed generally self-sufficient and outwardly in control of his life. He cited feelings of pain and regret at losing his wife and related intimations of spiritual peace he had experienced at Alcoholics Anonymous meetings. It was difficult, however, to tell just what Rick was thinking and feeling because his speech had an inconsistent, moment-by-moment quality. He seemed to say what he felt would give the right impression at the time, without regard to whether it squared with something he had said half an hour earlier.

Although Rick proved a frustrating client for his therapist, he was actually rather likable. A "self-made man," he loved to recount how he had been "a raggedy-assed kid who grew up on the city streets" and "climbed my way to the top." He had, indeed, had a difficult childhood, with poverty, neglect, and abuse at home and danger on the streets. To survive in that environment he had had to act tough and associate with powerful people of his own age, i.e., adolescent gang leaders.

As an adult he kept up the same pattern. Weighed down with gold jewelry, he was preoccupied with impressing people by picking up the tab in restaurants and sending bottles of champagne to any table where he recognized people. Identifying with friends and associates who in his eyes were powerful and glamorous, he overextended himself financially to keep up with them and then had to borrow money from them. Gambling, drinking, and extreme indebtedness "went with the territory."

In his beguiling way Rick sought to envelop the therapist in a benign version of this collusion. Calling him "Doc," he put the therapist on the same pedestal he claimed for himself and tried to make him feel like one of the powerful people Rick exalted. Feeling flattered himself, the therapist could easily see how Rick drew people into relationships.

On the other hand, in his relationship with his estranged wife, Maria, Rick showed how he reacted to someone who challenged him and refused to play his game. Concerned about his suicide threats, Maria agreed to come in with him for joint therapy sessions. She explained her decision to leave him by saying, "I'm climbing out of the box he's kept me in." Rick agreed that he was strong-willed and volunteered that he had learned to think of women as weak. Maria, however, was not weak. She fought and argued with him incessantly during the sessions; indeed, they had not a positive thing to say to each other. When the therapist pointed out the inconsistency between his expressed attitude toward his wife and his expressed desire to have her back, Rick explained, "You can't say anything positive to her. If you compliment her on anything, like if you say, 'I like your necklace,' all of a sudden she'll get it into her head that she's an expert in jewelry, and she'll want to open up a jewelry store. Crazy. That's the way she is." Maria retorted, "You could have been nicer about it, instead of telling me in front of everybody to shut up."

For her part, Maria picked at Rick for making bad business decisions and getting them into debt. She gave the impression that she had encouraged Rick in his big deals as long as he was winning, and then turned on him when he came up a loser. Had she flattered Rick and bolstered his self-image, he probably would have killed for her. Instead, she cut him down as he cut her down. Rick chose a woman who frustrated his most evident desire—namely, to impress people—and he found himself endlessly dueling with her.

We can only conjecture about Rick's motives, because he did not stay in therapy very long and was not aware enough of his feelings to articulate them. He asserted that he did not want to lose his wife because "she's as close to a trusting friend as I've ever had," but he could not explain what he meant by trust. "Why did it take seeing me with someone else to make you change your mind?" Maria responded. She reported that he had shown no interest in working out their problems until he saw her with another man. Rick had come to therapy saying that he was having difficulty separating from his wife because he felt attached to her. He had tolerated the separation quite well, however, until she asserted her independence more fully by seeing another man. The concrete image of this other man basking in Maria's company brought home to Rick that he no longer held possession of her.

It would be unfair and inaccurate to say that Rick did not have feelings. But his feelings were so obscured by a lifetime of defensive evasions (concealing who knows what wounds) that they were not accessible to him, his wife, or the therapist he saw for several sessions. In an effort to give him some real feedback, the therapist reminded him of the histrionics he had displayed when he first came in. "Maybe you wanted Maria to see how much you were suffering," the therapist suggested. "Well," Rick replied, "I *am* a very manipulative person." This last gambit closed off the dialogue, since it seemed to say, in essence, "You're not one up on me; I'm one up on you. I could have told you that I'm manipulative."

Rick falls into our Nonobsessed-Nonanxious extreme because there is little in his experience that we can identify as either romantic anxiety or romantic attachment. In a sense, he is the opposite of Joyce. Whereas Joyce hid her feelings beneath a veneer of hard-boiled self-sufficiency and worldliness, Rick made a show of feelings that neither he nor his therapist could be sure were truly his own. All the while he remained encased in an emotional invulnerability that Joyce might well have envied, but that she probably was fortunate not to share.

Rick is an extreme case, but not an uninformative one. On close examination, one can see his image reflected in the behavior of many other men, far more refined and responsible than he, who do not express much emotion in their relationships and whom women experience as self-absorbed and controlling. Some of these men, like Ray in Chapter 3, do experience a period of emotional upset when a relationship ends. Others move on to the next relationship in the same self-contained way. It is of interest that the finding cited at the beginning of this chapter—i.e., that individuals who score very low on the anxious-attachment scale are similar in other ways to those who score very high—shows up more prominently among men than among women. There appears to be a more clearly identifiable group of detached men than detached women. Detachment is more available as an emotional strategy to men than to women because women, as a rule, are more openly aware of their need for emotional connections.

DEBORAH: LOVE IS A JOB

Just as some people have difficulty reentering the job market after spending a number of years in a homemaking role, so a professional person may not be able to readjust smoothly to the "relationship market" after years of exclusive dedication to a career. This is especially true when a person who was uneasy with intimate relationships to begin with has found in work a convenient distraction from the risks and complications of love. The case of Deborah illustrates this style of detachment.

At the age of thirty-three, Deborah gave up a high-level job in public administration "because the rat race was really getting to me. I had no time to myself and no time to find a relationship with a man, either." She left her job with plans to do free-lance consulting work, as well as find time for her personal life.

After a few weeks spent recovering from exhaustion, Deborah began in earnest to pursue the elusive intimacy she lacked. Besides seeking introductions from friends, she applied herself to mastering the intricacies of the personal classified ads in an upscale magazine. With a discriminating eye for detail she scrutinized the wording of each ad for clues to the qualities she looked for in a man. Was he sensitive? Was he comfortable with his feelings?

Did he admit to imperfection, and could he accept it in someone else? Was he ready for a committed relationship?

Deborah undertook her quest for a relationship with the same serious attitude, concentrated effort, and analytical approach that had been successful for her in other arenas.

> I think I've followed up every relationship that's made itself available. I'm committed to having a relationship, and I'm working my head off to make it happen. At some point I may have to think about having a child on my own, but before I'll consider such a serious decision I at least ought to put the same kind of effort and energy I've put into my professional career into trying to generate a significant relationship. I have always been self-aware and have worked hard at growing and changing. Now I'm very consciously going about attempting to date. I'm working very hard at forming relationships, and at learning what it is that works for me and what doesn't work.

Thus far, nothing has worked in a lasting way. As this quote suggests, Deborah has conceived of her search for a man in the studied language she brings from years of goal-directed activity. It does take work for a single adult to find a relationship, but Deborah has had trouble bringing this work to fruition. She has made herself extremely knowledgeable about the singles scene in her area, with files full of listings of singles bars, clubs, and magazines. Yet she rarely goes to the places where singles meet, and she has not answered very many ads. She energetically accumulates information, but hesitates to use it. As a result, she has met too few men to get beyond the unfavorable odds the singles scene holds out.

In part, Deborah is experiencing what psychologists call an approach-avoidance conflict. If you have mixed feelings about reaching a particular goal, it is easier to work toward it when you are still far away from it. As you get closer, fear and doubt begin to take over. Reading ads and cataloguing listings can be done at a safe distance from the fray; actually going to a club and meeting people is another matter. With her self-image at stake as well as a real possibility of a painful outcome, Deborah might well have preferred to stay at a distance from the action, organizing and strategizing as if she were planning someone else's social life.

Deborah has shied away from close personal relationships through much of her adult life. She believes that this was a choice she made early on.

> At the beginning I was so involved with my profession that I felt no need for relationships. My working life and my personal isolation went very

well together, since the demands of the agency could be overwhelming. Those were years when I wanted to be a professional woman even if it meant never having children—which I wasn't sure I wanted to do anyway.

What made her unsure that she wanted to have children were her memories of her own childhood.

> Emotionally I had a lot to work through from my own family, and I decided that I wouldn't have children until I felt confident that I wouldn't do to them what my parents had done to me. I wanted to get to the point where I'd be struggling with the same ordinary issues every other parent does, like "Can I do a decent job of raising my kids?"

What were the childhood traumas she alludes to? "Part of me," she explains, "is a little girl who never got taken care of and will always want to be taken care of." She feels that her mother, whom she describes as withdrawn and self-absorbed, was too wrapped up in her own wants and needs to nurture her properly. Her father, a brilliant, dynamic architect, reacted to his wife's self-centered behavior by adopting Deborah almost as a mate from an early age (though not in a sexual sense). In her teens she accompanied him on public tours and presentations while her mother stayed home with a series of vague illnesses.

Deborah's being placed in this role reinforced her mother's view of her as a competitor and may have exacerbated her mother's emotional withholding. "I never really connected with my mother," she concludes, "so I couldn't completely separate from her." Her father's premature elevation of her to adult status also, she believes, deprived her of the benefits of normal childhood experience. In other words, Deborah was what psychologists refer to as a parental child.

> As a child, I was a great adult. I took responsibility for the household when my parents were away, and I went with my father when my mother stayed home. I got a lot of reinforcement for being that kind of super-responsible child. But you don't get reinforced as an adult when you've missed a lot of what you should have learned from being a child.

Although her parents live far from her now, Deborah's father remains a large presence in her consciousness.

> He is very demanding and has very high expectations. But he is also nurturing, and he passed on to me his terrific appreciation and love of life.

I think my standards were so high when I started dating because my father is such a classy guy. For a long time I probably was in love with him and looked for men who would meet that high standard.

But there was also a dark side to her father: his demands, his disapproval, his tantrums. He could be rough with Deborah when she did not act like the adult he expected her to be. Moreover, traveling with him as his official escort and assistant had its threatening as well as its thrilling side. She feared him even as she admired him.

Throughout her college years Deborah dated a fellow student who never made a sexual advance toward her. She describes the ambivalence she felt about the prospect of being intimate with him.

Did I want physical intimacy? I did and I didn't. I think I was still struggling with it. I was always wondering why he didn't want to be sexual and not quite figuring it out. Was it him or was it me? In retrospect I think he may have been gay, but didn't know it. But at the time I personalized it onto myself. It felt as if I was being rejected all the time. I was involved with lots of other things in college, but this unresolved relationship was always a painful thread running through it.

The same thread of ambivalence and irresolution continued to run through Deborah's romantic relationships after college: choosing a man who at some level avoided intimacy, wondering whether she herself was to blame, letting the situation remain unresolved, and busying herself with external activity as a buffer against the pain she felt. For several years she was involved with a man who taught at a university in a different part of the country. They commuted back and forth for occasional weekends and spent a summer together, but the geographical distance between them enabled them to avoid the issue of commitment. When they finally put the relationship to the test, it broke up.

Having hemmed and hawed for a long time, I finally moved to Ann Arbor to be with him, and within a few months we split up. So I had to come back home, and that was a huge drama that required rebuilding my life. That was several years gone right there.

Intimacy has not come easily for Deborah. As much as she longs for a romantic attachment, those she has had have felt like a heavy weight on her shoulders. With this experience, she shows an understandable wariness ("hemming and hawing") of new involvements. "Every time I've broken up from a relationship," she remarks, "it's taken me a couple of years to recover before I'm ready to deal with another one." The hesitation beneath her expressed eagerness to follow up every lead may help explain her inability to find a long-term relationship, which is frustrating to her and puzzling to others.

> People always seem to think there are men knocking down my door all the time. All my life people have thought that. But it's just not true. Whether I'm not as attractive as people think, or whether I've been putting out something negative, who knows?

"I don't see myself as not engaging with men," Deborah says. "If anything, I'm afraid that I engage too quickly, that I get sucked up and have unrealistic expectations about the man. If I let myself, I probably could get all excited after the second date and think, 'This is terrific. This is the man of my dreams.'" She recognizes that her detachment arises at least in part from her fear of losing her identity in a relationship.

> I'm so deliberate because I'm aware how in the past I'd get sucked up and then lose my sense of myself. If everything you are is based on a relationship and that relationship falls apart, you lose everything. The pain of being involved with someone for a long time and then disengaging and not quite having a sense of yourself left is awful. That's why it would take me so long to rebuild.

For Deborah, the stakes involved in risking an attachment are high. She dreads the submergence of her identity in that of another person. Fearing attachment even as she desires it, she struggles to keep a safe distance. The results of this dilemma can be seen in the way she has approached the urgent issue of finding the right partner while there is still time left on her biological clock.

Deborah fully recognizes her need for intimacy, but struggles with the emotional vulnerability that stands between her and romantic love. She has, however, learned from her experience. As she puts her childhood traumas and past relationships in perspective, she is better able to avoid the extremes of detachment and anxious attachment. Currently, she strives for balance in her attitude toward men.

> There was a time when I would have been more likely to say, "This guy's a klutz," or "A-plus on the ad!" or "He's the world's expert on everything." Now I'm able to have more empathy and at the same time not set my

expectations too high. I say to myself, "Let's suspend judgment here. Everybody's going to have their pluses and minuses. Let's go out with him for a while and then see, and try not to readjust things in my head so that I'll fall in love and distort things."

ALEX: THREE'S COMPANY, TWO'S A CROWD

Alex is a mild, friendly man more interested in fencing off a peaceful preserve for himself than in bringing others under his sway. In fact, he is himself a refugee from high-pressure environments both in work and in love. Formerly an engineer, he dropped out to teach mathematics in a small-town high school, where he coaches the basketball team. "I wanted to be more of a 'people person,'" he explains. At about the same time, his wife, always more attuned than he to success and material rewards, came to aspire to even greater professional advancement. This incompatibility of goals led the couple to divorce.

Alex is a hyperconscientious man who sets needless deadlines for himself and fears being caught unprepared. In industrial engineering, where "everything has to get done yesterday," external pressures combined with internal ones, which made life unacceptably stressful. As a teacher, too, Alex worries about having his lesson plans prepared weeks in advance. "I have to be ahead all the time, never behind," he says. Even so, he describes himself as blissfully contented with his job.

With regard to the breakup of his marriage he seems to feel relief combined with a sense of failure.

> My wife and I grew apart quietly; we were happy until near the end. We married during the hippie era, when you canned vegetables and made your own clothes. But even when we were growing our food, my wife had her eye on the main chance. She became more and more image-conscious and had to have all the name brands: first a Volvo, then a BMW. Her ambitions shot up just when I opted back to the simple life. The divorce was quick and amicable. Everyone was shocked; they thought we were the perfect upwardly mobile couple. For my part, I made no attempt to stop her from leaving, but I had a hard time accepting that the marriage didn't work. I'm not used to failing.

Alex didn't want to fail at marriage, yet he did nothing to stop the drift toward divorce. He simply went underground emotionally, as if to deny that the marriage had existed. That way, the divorce, which he equated with failure, could be covered over as well, and Alex could pretend that all was well in his personal life.

After the divorce Alex wanted to keep himself emotionally protected in his personal life. However, he began to miss the connection with his wife and her family, together with the social network they had shared. To fill this gap he has become involved with two women. One of them, Betty, is a fellow teacher at the high school. The other, Shirley, lives in a rural region where he spends his summers. He describes these relationships as companionate rather than passionate. Both women are undemanding and slow to criticize, in contrast to his ex-wife. They listen to him, laugh with him, and do not pressure him for commitment. He characterizes each as "just a friend, no more than that." About both relationships he says, "Something's missing. They give me security, but that intangible quality is lacking."

Reluctant to risk another emotional involvement, Alex conducts his current relationships with studied detachment. When he feels some passion developing for Betty, he deliberately pulls back.

> If I feel my barrier coming down, I put it back up. She'd say I'm holding back by not depending on her for anything, as well as by not showing much emotion. But it just doesn't feel right to me.

"Something's missing" is Alex's rationale for not getting more involved with either woman. Yet these same words also express his uneasy sense that he is missing a deeper engagement with life. At forty he teeters on the edge, unable to let go of the habits and routines with which he is so contented, yet puzzled by intimations that there might be more to life than that. He wonders what it would be like to experience "that special feeling."

These issues came to a head for Alex when Betty was seriously injured in an automobile accident. Unwilling to abandon her during her long hospitalization and convalescence, he was drawn into demonstrations of loyalty, such as making extended visits to her parents' house, which he had previously avoided. Feeling trapped and anxious, he spoke with her more openly about Shirley, his summer companion, with whom he was, if anything, more comfortable. Thinking he was letting Betty down gently, he confessed to feelings of guilt about having dated Shirley without telling her. This display of conscience only endeared him further to Betty and raised her expectations of him. Whether out of obligation, an unconscious desire for closeness, or a reluctance to give up the social network he shared with Betty (in place of the one he had had with his wife), he felt himself marching unwillingly into greater commitment. But just when the anxiety was becoming troubling, he was saved, for the time being at least, by the calendar. The school year ended, and, with Betty's family now actively disapproving, he headed for his summer house and his annual reunion with Shirley. "She just lets me be," he says. "She's quite content with me as I am. When I'm away, she doesn't come after me. She just waits for me to come back."

The phrase, "Something's missing," is what Deborah (above) calls "a typical line" men use to disengage themselves after a brief affair. In Alex's case, is that something missing in the woman or in himself? Possibly both. After the way his marriage ended, Alex understandably might shy away from involvement with a dynamic woman like his wife. Once burned, he might be inclined to play it safe and minimize the risk of another painful rejection by choosing women who would not have such attractive alternatives as his wife had found for herself. Yet by choosing women who would be less demanding of him and less likely to leave him than his wife, he may also have chosen women who would not engage his interest as fully as she had.

Alex's inability to give himself completely to either woman is similar to his inability to show love in his marriage. Even though there are two women who might gladly share his life with him, he declines to pursue a stable, permanent relationship with either. Instead, he has diffused the intensity of his romantic feelings by seeing Betty and Shirley simultaneously. Since each knows about the other, each knows that her relationship with him is limited, and neither can be fully secure with him. In addition, he has allowed a geographical barrier to stand between him and the woman to whom he feels closer—or perhaps he simply allows himself to feel closer to the woman who is off at a safe distance. Although from time to time he feels stirrings of discontent, he is so set in his ways and so successful in managing his life on his own terms that he seems unlikely to experience any dramatic upheaval.

PHYLLIS: PLEASE, MR. POSTMAN

One way to reduce the discomfort of romantic anxiety is to be involved with someone who lives far away. Letters, long-distance phone calls, and occasional weekends together can make for a less stressful relationship than daily contact. One couple who decided to get married on the basis of a long-distance romance came in for counseling because they felt they didn't really know each other! "It's like getting a mail-order husband," the woman remarked. Among the cases in this chapter, Deborah had a postal relationship lasting several years that broke up when she moved in with the man, and Alex kept his local girlfriend at arm's length by maintaining a summer affair with a woman in another state. Phyllis, a thirty-six-year-old housewife, carries on a more extreme variation of the postal romance. She writes to a man who takes no notice of her existence.

Every week Phyllis would send a card, a letter, and sometimes a gift to a television soap-opera idol with whom she fell in love when she attended a performance in the studio. She would buy some inexpensive, sentimental trinket and send it certified mail, return receipt requested, so that she would get an acknowledgment. After a while she began to receive "personal" thank-you notes, which thrilled her—until one day she was sent two identical ones by mistake. Seeing her idol's fabricated signature and realizing that the notes were not from him, she was temporarily devastated. But then she convinced herself that someday her idol might actually open one of her gifts in person, or read one of her letters himself. So she steadfastly continued to send cards and gifts.

Phyllis's absorption in this fantasy is unusual for a person of her age. Her background likewise was unusual in the extreme degree to which it failed to equip her to deal with love and romance—indeed, with life. Her mother was extremely inconsistent in her affection, and her father was so distant that he hardly noticed her. Thus it is no surprise that Phyllis grew up with little self-confidence and without a clear sense of herself. In her parents she saw a marriage of convenience; they were emotionally aloof and lacking in affection. So in Phyllis's mind, any man would do for a spouse, since a husband just sires children and earns a living.

When she was twenty, Phyllis married the first man who proposed to her, thinking that another might never come along. From the beginning she never felt that she was in love with him. In any case, she now believes, she had no idea what love was. She needed a man to make her life with, but felt cut off from her husband, especially after he began to spend more and more time out drinking with his friends. Never close, the marriage at least had some rationale during the first few years when the children were born. As the years went by, however, the marriage came to be a farce. At first Phyllis blew up at her husband when he went out drinking, which only led him to stay away from home all the more. Eventually, though, they settled into mutual indifference. He expected nothing of her except that she stay home and take care of the children. He had lost interest in her sexually, although he did not appear to be interested in other women. For her, he was a provider. She did not seek a divorce because she could not bear to risk losing her children, who represented her only real emotional grounding, and did not believe she could support them or herself on her own.

Coming from a bleak childhood and a loveless marriage, Phyllis had an outsized reaction to the television actor's good looks and sensuous manner. In her fantasy relationship with him, she found an attachment without anxiety. She enjoys the feelings of romantic obsession in a safe space of private dreams, where they do not threaten the bread-and-butter security of her marriage.

Phyllis's secret fantasy is not so different from the self-absorbed experience of the anxiously attached lover who is insensitive to anything but the most positive feedback from his or her partner. Phyllis just goes one step further by choosing a partner from whom there will be no feedback at all. She gives her love totally to someone who cannot reciprocate, and who therefore will not reject her.

While expressing her need for a fulfilling romantic relationship through this fantasy, Phyllis also has had occasional anonymous sexual liaisons with men she meets at out-of-town discotheques. Lonely and disconnected, spurned by her husband, she finds it difficult not to respond when a man looks her way. Rather than do entirely without affection from men, she chooses to accept the momentary passion provided by these physical encounters, pretending that they will lead to close emotional relationships. But if she allowed a relationship with a real-life man to take on any meaning for her, it would threaten the accommodation she has reached with her husband. This is a risk she will not take as long as she lacks confidence in herself to gain and securely hold a man's affection. The few men who *have* taken an interest in her she has managed to frighten away by not allowing them to call her or even take her out to dinner.

Obsessively attached to a fantasy, Phyllis is detached not only with her husband, but also with other men who might represent a real hope of emotional fulfillment. The relationship that is most real in Phyllis's inner experience, the one with the daytime television star, does not exist in reality. Her relationship with her husband is the one that is most real insofar as she depends on it for survival, but it does not exist in her inner experience.

JAN AND LARRY: DETACHMENT CAN BE MUTUAL

Larry awoke in the middle of the night feeling extreme physical distress, including a racing heartbeat, perspiration, difficulty in breathing, and tightness in his chest. He had an uncanny feeling of impending catastrophe and feared that he was losing his mind. After several such episodes, he went to the hospital, but no organic cause was found. For months Larry had been suffering from headaches, fatigue, muscle aches and stiffness, and frequent colds and viruses. These symptoms disappeared when he went alone to the Caribbean for a week's vacation, but returned when he came home.

His first nocturnal panic attack occurred when he visited his parents, who live several hundred miles away, for his brother's bar mitzvah. The second attack came when he was about to fly back. It was as if he didn't want to come home to where there was no one with whom he felt completely comfortable and where he faced problematic relationships with his girlfriend and a close friend from childhood.

Larry is a tall, lanky, good-humored twenty-nine-year-old man who comes across as friendly and mellow. He speaks frequently of his need for independence, of "not wanting to be tied down" and "wanting to be able to do the things I want to do." Unfortunately, he went into a business deal with his childhood friend, whose ineptitude ruined the enterprise and, with it, Larry's financial independence. Larry was forced to take a regular full-time job—the last thing he wanted to do. Still, he continued to play chess every week with his friend, as if nothing had happened, and never expressed the anger he must have felt toward him. Larry never talks about his feelings. He always smiles and smooths things over. His physical symptoms are the only visible clue to the conflicts he feels.

Larry and his girlfriend, Jan, have kept each other at arm's length for several years. Each insinuates that it is the other who is not serious; somehow they are never both serious at the same time. Jan is a somewhat reserved person who was deeply hurt as a child by her father's neglect and then abandonment of the family. She acts as if she's waiting for the perfect man, who, of course, is not Larry. Nonetheless, she depends on Larry for many small favors that help her handle the minute responsibilities of daily life.

For a time Larry was seeing another woman besides Jan. Jan appealed to everyone who knew him for help. "You know who really cares for him; I do," she would say. Yet she could not express her feelings directly to Larry, and when his other affair ended she again became aloof and undemonstrative.

Larry probably preferred it that way, given his own avoidance of emotional expression. He has said, "It's not impossible that we might live together." But he shies away from that commitment, fearing that he would be taking on another difficult partner, who, like his chess and erstwhile business partner, would tie him down and not pull her own weight. It would be just like with his friend, Larry imagines: you get tied up with somebody; you're taken advantage of; you have to smooth over the other person's anger and swallow your own; and you can't get out of the relationship because angry recriminations will confront you at the exit gate. The key for Larry is always to side-step any angry confrontations, as he did with his friend when their business failed. Larry stands aside from a full involvement with Jan because he anticipates discomfort. He would be putting too much of himself on the line by engaging in the conflict needed to assert his values and to have Jan be more responsive to his concerns. As time passes, however, it becomes more and more difficult to end the relationship without bringing down on himself a mountain of unpleasantness. He is trapped.

Several weeks after his troubled visit with his family, Larry arranged for his company to transfer him from California to Missouri. He left Jan his one-year-old car as a token of their connection. He did not leave her his new telephone number, but after a few months she extracted it from his family. She called, and he was surprisingly receptive. Having pulled up stakes "to find myself," he found himself rather lonely without Jan. Before long the two of them were in almost daily telephone contact, often initiated by Larry.

It seems that Larry and Jan probably were uncomfortable with continual close contact and turned their relationship into a telephone relationship, reducing their anxiety to a tolerable level. They have found a way to be distanced and yet connected, which both seem to want. Linked together in their ambivalence, they shield each other from other eligible partners who might demand more of them.

This equilibrium, however, is not necessarily permanent. As long as Larry continues in his detached stance, he takes the risk that Jan will meet the perfect prince of her fantasies—one who will sweep her off her feet as Larry never could. This dream represents Jan's wish to be reunited with the father who abandoned her at an early age. If she finds some plausible embodiment of it, Larry will be left to face the consequences of his inability to acknowledge his own feelings.

The nocturnal panics Larry experienced before returning from his family's home were a sign that he is not as independent as he insists. He had difficulty breaking away from his family because he still felt strongly his earliest emotional attachments and had not developed any comparably close ties in the places he called home as an adult. When Larry is with his family he feels a wholeness of connection that he finds tantalizing, disorienting, and perhaps threatening. Similarly, his ambivalence toward Jan reflects his fear of the kind of intimate attachment by which, however unconsciously, he feels bound. Were he to lose her, he would likely find that she matters to him more than he now realizes.

THE PAIN OF ATTACHMENT
AND THE RELIEF OF DETACHMENT

A person like Larry, who assumes a detached stance because he experiences romantic attachment as threatening, is not so different from an anxiously attached person. Both anxious attachment and detachment are ways people compensate for a lack of secure attachments early in life. Both are rooted in experiences of insecurity, uncertainty about being accepted by others, and fear of rejection. Understandably, a person who has been badly hurt in one relationship may enter into the next with caution. Individuals such as Carol (in Chapter 3) and Joyce and Alex (in this chapter) oscillate between intense attachments and periods of emotional disengagement.

This does not mean that individuals do not develop stable, even lifelong patterns of anxious attachment or detachment. People have experiences that set them up to respond habitually in one way or the other. Some people are predominantly anxiously attached, however much they may wish for respite. Others are predominantly detached, their fear blocking the active and realistic pursuit of love. What is striking, though, is that detached individuals *do* reach out for attachment, and vice versa. In this chapter we have seen detached personalities—Deborah, for example, or Larry—struggling to break out of their defenses and take emotional risks. Similarly, many who are caught up in romantic anxiety and obsession yearn for the safe haven of emotional isolation. Anxious romantic attachment and detachment are like mirror images, each leaning toward the other.

Shortly after her grandfather's death, Julie, who appeared as a case example of anxious romantic attachment in Chapter 2, wrote this note in her diary concerning her feelings about her husband, Mike:

The evening was wonderful. We came home, watched a movie, made love, and held each other almost all night. I lay awake for a while, thinking about how much I want to be good for Mike. Now that Gramps is gone, there is no one else I want to please except him. My child means the world to me, but my love for her isn't scary like my love for Mike.

Attachment can be painful—"scary," as Julie puts it. It is what she wants most, but it is also what she most fears losing. Sometimes it feels as if it would be better not to have it so that she doesn't have to fear losing it. By analogy, a poor person might take solace from the fact that there is a lot you don't have to worry about if you don't have a million dollars.

Elizabeth, another woman struggling with the same dilemma, expressed similar sentiments in her diary.

I love attention—caring, unconditional attention. I wish a friend would visit or call today, but I know no one will, so I won't get my hopes up. If anyone does, it will be a pleasant surprise.

I wonder why I get so attached to anyone, even the dog—anyone who pays attention to me—even when the feelings I get from the relationship are more painful than pleasant. Am I that insecure and afraid of rejection?

"More painful than pleasant"—this is the paradox of anxious attachment. For all her great needs for attention and affection, Elizabeth is reluctant to leave the house to look for a job or expand her social life. She fears rejection so much that she is willing to forgo the positive rewards of involvement with people. She has very limited emotional energy for attachment because, for her, any kind of attachment brings with it great anxiety. Only with her husband does her need for attachment overrule her wish to avoid pain. Even there, in her primary relationship, she sometimes questions whether the connection is worth all the obsessing.

It bothers me that I felt so much at ease and contented while my husband was away. As soon as he came home I felt cornered, as if my private space were being trespassed upon. I ought to be happy to see him come home. I do love him very much, but I guess I need more space.

I feel as if I'd like to go away for a week or two by myself—maybe to the shore or the mountains. It even occurred to me that it would be nice if I got sick and had to go to the hospital. Then I wouldn't feel guilty that I should be taking care of things at home.

Her obsession with the marriage can be so draining that Elizabeth wishes she could just go away, be alone, and not have to think about it. She wants a vacation from the thoughts and feelings connected with her husband; she also wants unconditional caring, which her husband may not be able to provide.

Detachment also lurks in the shadows of anxious romantic attachment in the case of Jim, a young man whose outward behavior clearly puts him among the anxiously attached. Jim is so concerned that his fiancée will leave him for someone else that he becomes extremely insecure when she is out of his sight and questions her about her whereabouts when she returns. He takes such an intrusive, proprietary interest in how she spends her time that he risks driving her away. He gave her an engagement ring so that he would feel more secure about her loyalty. This strategy backfired, however. By increasing his investment in the relationship he unwittingly intensified his feelings of insecurity.

By now these feelings have become so hard to bear that he feels a need to disengage emotionally. "I just have to learn not to care about her so much," he vows. This is not the same as saying, "I just have to learn to trust her and not be anxious." Attachment and anxiety are so thoroughly fused for Jim that he feels he needs to discard the one with the other. If he didn't care about his fiancée, he would not be anxious, but at the price of no longer being attached to her.

In fact, that is the direction in which he seems to be moving. "Maybe I shouldn't marry her," he muses. "What if I find someone I like better?" In a kind of anticipatory sour-grapes rationalization, Jim is trying to reduce his invest-ment, and with it his insecurity. He wants to give himself a way out in the event that the woman leaves him. Although—indeed, *because*—he is so anxiously attached, he is preparing a strategic withdrawal. That is, his anxiety has risen to such a high pitch that he contemplates giving up the object of his obsession rather than continuing to bear the anxiety indefinitely. Jim would score at the high end of the anxious-attachment scale, but he seems to be looking wistfully at the low end. The disengagement he maps out hypothetically is the choice that others, the ones we call detached, actually make.

Ironically, anxiously attached individuals often give more insight into the motives for detachment than detached people themselves do. Someone like Larry, who keeps his emotions to himself and from himself, is not about to speak openly about the pain he feels. Detachment is, after all, a way of avoiding the pain. It takes Julie, Elizabeth, and Jim, who experience the pain directly, to give clues about how and why others turn away from it.

ANNA: BREAKING THROUGH DETACHMENT

Detachment can be challenging for a therapist to treat, since a detached person, while appearing intact and outwardly cooperative, typically resists disclosing his or her feelings. A person who avoids emotional relationships is likely to have difficulty forming—or acknowledging—a therapeutic relationship as well. One role of the therapist is to draw the person out (with adequate assurance of safety) into an openness that he or she will learn to enjoy and wish to replicate in his or her life. If nothing else, therapy can be an experience of a less detached relationship than the person is accustomed to, an experience that desensitizes and encourages the person to take further steps in that direction.

Even without therapy, people's lives are not static. Growth can occur through fortuitous circumstances as well as personal resolve. An example is Anna, a magazine editor in her late twenties who would not speak about her feelings with a therapist—or with anyone, for that matter—but who found a partner who could disarm her defenses.

Anna had no role models to teach her how to show emotion. Both her parents possessed a stoic quality that seemed to show emotional strength, but was actually an indication of their fear of emotional displays. Her father used humor as a way of distancing himself from others, including Anna. The only way Anna could relate to him was by joking. Her mother, perpetually surrounded by seemingly close relatives, always was too involved with various activities to get close to her. She viewed Anna as strong, independent, and autonomous, and not in need of warm maternal support. In turn, Anna viewed herself as more identified with her father, and so did not pursue a closer relationship with her mother. In sum, Anna's relationships with both parents were distant.

When Anna became involved in a long-term relationship with a man, she found herself unable to express her love for him. Lacking sufficient self-confidence to believe that he really was in love with her, Anna felt too insecure to show him how much she loved him. She went so far as to put him off when he proposed marriage. So unsure was Anna of his commitment to her (in spite of the evidence) that to avoid making herself vulnerable she convinced herself that she was unsure of her commitment to him. Subsequently he left her to marry a much more demonstrative woman.

Anna would have scored very low on the anxious-attachment scale, since she did not acknowledge even to herself how attached she felt to this man. Nonetheless, she was devastated by the loss and remained so for a few years. Putting off the marriage was a test of the man's love, and he failed the test. Subsequently, she looked at all men with mistrust. If a man was one minute late to meet her, she immediately concluded that he was not going to come at all. Evidently, she thought, he did not care enough either to go through with the date or to let her know otherwise. When he did show up, she was genuinely surprised. She suffered greatly from assuming the worst about herself and others.

A few years after her previous relationship ended, she met Jon, a friendly, jovial man who pursued her in a concentrated, yet unthreatening way. It took weeks for him to get to have lunch with her, but he would not be denied. As their relationship developed, her friends would remark that he seemed very much in love with her. "Oh, I don't know," she would say. Did he really drive all day just to see her for a weekend? "Oh, he probably has nothing else to do."

Anna bore Jon's pursuit stoically. Always needing to show a strong face to the world, she displayed a nonchalant, take-him-or-leave-him attitude. Unlike her previous boyfriend, though, Jon was unperturbed by such barriers. Either he saw that underneath her facade she did love him, or he was confident that his love would be strong enough for both of them until she had time to warm up to him. In either case, he was right. After more than a year he proposed marriage, and she accepted. Since then, Anna has kept her reserved manner; she is not outwardly much different from the person she was before. Occasionally, though, she smiles openly when she speaks with her friends about Jon.

Jon was the ideal partner for a person who distanced herself emotionally from prospective suitors. He expressed his feelings directly and went to great lengths to prove again and again how much he loved Anna. Instead of engaging in mutual distancing, he wore down her defenses with the openness and simplicity of his appeal.

Anna's meeting Jon was a fortunate accident, leading to a happy marriage. As the following chapter will show, both the characteristics for which one chooses a partner and the characteristics one happens to find in a partner have a great deal of bearing on the experience of insecure love.

5

PARTNER

GRIDLOCK

Whether one feels secure or insecure in a love relationship depends in part on the behavior, and even the physical characteristics, of the person with whom one is romantically involved. To round out our understanding of romantic anxiety and romantic obsession, we need to look at how one chooses one's partners, acts toward them, and reacts to their behavior. This chapter will focus on how your partners may have contributed to your experiences in love relationships, as well as what your ideal partner's image may say about the kind of relationship you want to have.

In our research we selected ten qualities of a partner and asked the following questions to determine which ones have the greatest impact on how strongly (if at all) a person experiences romantic insecurity. You can answer these ten questions with regard to each of the partners you had in mind when you filled out the anxious-attachment scale in Chapter 2. Then compare your answers here with the ones you gave in Chapter 2 about the way you experienced your relationships with those individuals. As in Chapter 2, there are four columns for rating four partners, labeled A through D.

Please rate each partner on a scale of 1 to 10 on each of the following ten qualities. As you might expect, 1 means "extremely low" (for example, extremely unattractive), while 10 means "extremely high" (for example, extremely attractive).

CHARACTERISTIC   PARTNER (WRITE IN NAMES)

                                        A   B   C   D

1. Physical attractiveness   —   —   —   —

2. Socioeconomic status   —   —   —   —

3. Trustworthiness   —   —   —   —

4. Popularity with others   —   —   —   —

5. Prospects for success in life   —   —   —   —

6. Intelligence   —   —   —   —

7. Self-assurance   —   —   —   —

8. Generosity   —   —   —   —

9. Warmth   —   —   —   —

10. How consistent or stable was _____ in her/
    his feelings for you?   —   —   —   —
(1 = totally inconsistent; 10 = extremely consistent)

Now go back to Chapter 2 and match up what these partners were like with how insecure you felt in your relationships with them. Suppose you felt the greatest romantic anxiety with Partner A. On which traits in the list above did you rate Partner A highest? On which traits did you rate this partner lowest? Some of these characteristics probably influenced the degree of anxiety you felt about him or her. Let's say you scored highest on romantic obsession with Partner B. Did any of the characteristics on which this partner rated very high or very low contribute to your obsession with him or her?

Think of the partner with whom you felt the greatest anxious romantic attachment. Your assessment of your partner's characteristics will give you clues as to why you felt insecure with this particular person. Some people react very negatively to a partner who is inconsistent, while others are less disturbed by this trait. Some especially value a physically attractive partner, whereas warmth and friendliness are more important to others. These personal preferences will probably contribute to the impact of the partner's qualities on one's emotional reactions.

We asked these same questions of approximately 250 participants in our research about their four most important relationships, a total of roughly one thousand relationships. When you match up your scores on the anxious-attachment scale in Chapter 2 with the ten characteristics of your partners, you are doing what we did by computer to see what general patterns might occur in the experience of men and women.

Interestingly, our findings fail to support some commonsense notions of what makes people anxious in love relationships. For example, we had thought that the "market value" of each of the two partners in the competitive dating marketplace might have something to do with anxious romantic attachment. More specifically, we thought that a person who was of low market value relative to his or her partner would feel more anxious and insecure than one whose market value was higher than that of their partner.

Other researchers have observed that, in dating and married couples, the man and the woman are usually of approximately equal physical attractiveness and social class. This may happen either because men and women find such matings suitable or because those are the matings available to them on the open market. Following from this, one might reason that people would not feel satisfied with partners who are much less socially desirable than they (that is, less physically attractive, less intelligent, less wealthy, less successful). But more relevant here, might one not feel quite insecure with a partner who was much *more* socially desirable than oneself, and who therefore might have more options available? Indeed, a person who experiences strong feelings of insecurity might be especially motivated to find a partner who possesses characteristics valued highly by our culture (for example, one who was good-looking, bright, and wealthy), but might then feel doubly insecure about the prospect of losing such a highly valued partner.

But we were up a blind alley: there was no connection between insecure love and mismatch of partners. Relative market value was no better at predicting anxious romantic attachment than was the partner's attractiveness by itself. Thus, either the idea of market value is of little use in understanding anxious romantic attachment, or else a simple, objective assessment of oneself or one's partner fails to capture the many considerations that influence what makes a person valuable to us. As we will see later in this chapter, "market" value is in the eye of the beholder. How attractive or desirable you and your partner happen to be may matter less than your subjective experience of your own and your partner's value—that is, how attractive or desirable you *feel* you are, relative to your partner. Many people who are considered highly attractive lack confidence in themselves and take it for granted that it is their partner who has all the options.

Although some explanations that sounded plausible were not confirmed by the data, those that *were* confirmed made intuitive sense as well. Participants' responses reveal that the ten characteristics of partners listed above actually coalesce into three clusters, and that these clusters differ in their relevance to anxious romantic attachment. The first cluster is related to the promise of external achievement and success: *socioeconomic status, prospects for success, intelligence.* The second focuses on superficial appeal, or what one might call first impressions or social impact: *physical attractiveness, popularity with others, self-assurance.* The third concerns the partner's behavior toward the person with whom she or he is romantically involved or who views her or him as a romantic object: *consistency, trustworthiness, generosity, warmth.* A partner who scores high on this "nonfickle factor" is one who can be counted on to be emotionally available and to take the other person's feelings into consideration.

You can see whether the characteristics of your partners tend to be high or low on any one cluster by adding up their scores within each of the three clusters. For each partner you are rating, fill in the scores you assigned that partner on the ten characteristics listed at the beginning of this chapter and add them up as follows:

CHARACTERISTIC   PARTNER

                                                    A   B   C   D

Socioeconomic status   ——   ——   ——   ——

Prospects for success in life   ——   ——   ——   ——

Intelligence   ——   ——   ——   ——

TOTAL (External Success cluster)   ——   ——   ——   ——

CHARACTERISTIC	PARTNER			
	A	B	C	D
Physical attractiveness	—	—	—	—
Popularity with others	—	—	—	—
Self-assurance	—	—	—	—
TOTAL (First Impressions cluster)	—	—	—	—
Consistency	—	—	—	—
Trustworthiness	—	—	—	—
Generosity	—	—	—	—
Warmth	—	—	—	—
TOTAL (Emotional Loyalty cluster)	—	—	—	—

On which cluster or clusters do your partners get the highest scores? Do you see a consistent pattern in the partners you choose?

We found that the cluster of partner characteristics most related to romantic obsession is the one we labeled First Impressions. Within this cluster, *physical attractiveness* is, by far, the partner characteristic that best predicts romantic obsession. The more attractive the partner, the more likely one is to be romantically obsessed with that partner. On the other hand, the cluster most strongly associated with romantic anxiety is the one we labeled Emotional Loyalty. Within this cluster, the partner's *consistency* is the characteristic that tells the most about whether a person experiences romantic anxiety. The more consistent the partner's feelings toward one are, the less anxious about that partner one is likely to be.

Together, then, the highly physically attractive but emotionally fickle partner is likely to have the greatest power to wreak havoc with your love life. Before the separate effects of these two characteristics are presented, here is the story of a woman who regularly chose the sort of partner who combined the two.

PAT: FORMULA FOR HEARTACHE

Pat always approached the most attractive men she saw at social functions. At one of these, one man stood out as handsome and a sharp dresser, although a friend whispered to her that he had "a one-track mind—only interested in sex." Hearing this, Pat was not deterred. She walked right up to him and, with a dramatic flourish, said, "Hi, nice to meet you. I hear you like to get laid. Well, I don't!" With that she turned around and marched off. Pat would not have said that she was coming on to this man; rather, she might have explained that she was reflecting back to him an image of what she perceived to be his shallow, hedonistic way of life, giving him a proverbial slap in the face. Naturally, though, he responded to her challenge by making inquiries about her and pursuing her, and the two began dating. As her friend had predicted, he not only was very interested in sex, but had an uncontrollable habit of pursuing every woman he found attractive. Yet he seemed not to notice that every woman, including Pat, eventually left him because of his infidelity.

Another involvement began for Pat in a strikingly similar way. Upon entering a nightclub she saw a man ignoring the woman with whom he ostensibly was dancing. Like Narcissus, he was entranced by his reflection in a full-length mirror. He seemed captivated by his image, bumping and grinding, and appeared to be dancing with himself rather than his partner. Pat couldn't resist; she stepped between this man and the mirror and danced face to face with him at his own frenetic pace, trying to break through his self-absorption and force him to make contact with another human being. Once again she entered into what became a relationship of mistrust and lies, as this man, too, leapfrogged from one woman to the next.

In laying down the gauntlet for each of these very attractive, but obviously vain men, Pat could hardly have chosen more difficult partners. In both cases she was drawn in by first impressions—their physical attributes, their outward allure and social polish, and their air of sensuality and charisma. But along with these qualities came their relentless self-preoccupation and need to demonstrate machismo through sexual conquests. In each man, the combination of high physical attractiveness and low emotional loyalty proved a deadly combination for Pat. Mesmerized by the former, she was tortured by the latter.

In choosing men who displayed rather clear signs that they had great difficulties with emotional loyalty and intimacy, Pat had found a formula for intense emotional involvement, often culminating in disappointment. Perhaps the short interval before she became disappointed made it all worthwhile for her. Perhaps she derived satisfaction from the uncertainties of her quest. Clearly, Pat relished a challenge. Why was the challenge of bringing attractive men under her sway so important to her? Did the excitement of pursuing such dangerous prizes outweigh the unlikelihood of lasting success? Did she have something to prove, something to make up for? Was she angry at someone who had once left her? Did she seek out unpredictable situations in the hope of making them predictable?

ATTRACTIVENESS AND OBSESSION

Of all the partner characteristics listed, *physical attractiveness* is the one most strongly associated with romantic obsession for both men and women, but the association is stronger for men. It is commonly assumed that men place a higher priority than women on physical beauty in choosing partners, and indeed we find that the partner's attractiveness is a source of greater obsession for men than for women. For men, none of the remaining nine attributes has any reliable connection with romantic obsession. For women, in addition to the association with the man's attractiveness, there is some positive association between obsession and the partner's *warmth, popularity,* and *self-assurance.* Given partners of equally high attractiveness, a woman is more likely to obsess over that partner who is also warm, popular, and/or self-assured.

Pat, the woman in the story above who is attracted to handsome, flashy, self-centered men, comments, "All the guys I've been involved with are superattractive. Maybe that's the problem." Many of the people we interviewed, women as well as men, have said the same thing in different words. Donna, in Chapter 3, compared one boyfriend to Bruce Springsteen, "the working-class hero," and another beau to Richard Dreyfuss ("I liked his looks—not handsome, but very distinctive"). A male interviewee links his pursuit of attractive women with motivations that leave him open to romantic obsession:

> I was fortunate in that I usually managed to be the guy who got to go out with the prettiest girl in town. To this day it amazes me. The average Joe will not ask the glamor girl out because "there's just no way." I didn't have that attitude; I jumped right in.
>
> I didn't have very high self-esteem; I had a lot to overcome. I was told that my appearance, my facial features, would scare people, men and women alike. I'd be told, "You know, the first time I met you, you scared the hell out of me. I thought you were going to rip my face open." Well, whether it was in spite of this or because of it, more often than not I'd end up with the prettiest girl in town.

The other two partner characteristics having to do with superficial appeal or first impressions—popularity with others and self-assurance—also figure prominently in the opening lines of stories that end in romantic obsession. Recall Carol, in Chapter 3, saying of Stan, her lover, "He dressed well and could talk with anybody." Lynne (who appears later in this chapter) said of her boyfriend Scott, "He was so calm and in control—I thought he was wonderful." One may be obsessed with a highly attractive person who is also stable and emotionally committed. But if the attractive partner is fickle, as Pat's lovers turned out to be, then the romantic obsession is likely to be compounded by intense feelings of anxiety.

INCONSISTENCY AND ANXIETY

Romantic anxiety is most affected not by what the partner looks like, but by the way the partner acts. The trait of the partner that best predicts whether one experiences romantic anxiety in a relationship with that partner is the *consistency* of that partner's feelings. The less consistent the partner, the more anxious one tends to be. The related qualities of *trustworthiness, warmth,* and *generosity* also are associated with less anxiety.

Anxiety in romantic relationships seems to be brought forth somewhat differently for men and for women. The anxiety level of women is strongly affected by the partner's inconsistency and is *not* affected by the partner's physical attractiveness. The anxiety level of men also is affected primarily by the partner's inconsistency, but it tends to be related to the partner's attractiveness as well.

Inconsistent behavior and romantic anxiety go hand in hand. Out of the many things discovered in this study, this one seems to say something especially important about insecure love. We place such confidence in this finding because it is consistent with two things learned near the end of Chapter 2, where the same question was asked in two ways.

First, we found in Chapter 2 that the romantic anxiety a person felt in a relationship was affected by whether or not the relationship was exclusive. If two people who were romantically involved with each other were both dating other people at the same time, they reported less anxiety about the relationship and were less attached to it as well. In essence, they defined their relationship as something less than consuming for both of them. However, if only one of the lovers was seeing other people, the other was likely to feel more anxious.

This fits our finding that the partner's inconsistency is a major source of romantic anxiety; infidelity is, after all, a form of inconsistency. Although someone like Alex in Chapter 4, who was involved with two women, may be consistent in the feelings he displays toward either woman, both of them probably would experience his nonexclusiveness as a form of inconsistency. From Betty's perspective, the attention Alex gave to Shirley belied his love for Betty, and vice versa. Many of us have said, "I can love more than one person at a time." But it sounds less convincing when we share the honor of being on the receiving end!

Not surprisingly, when one's partner is unfaithful, this is a tremendous source of anxiety. In Chapter 3, Carol was driven to intense anxiety by her perception that each of her boyfriends, first Bruce and then Stan, was playing around. Donna, on the other hand, was involved in a mutually nonexclusive relationship with Bob, the professor, in which they both acknowledged that they were seeing someone else. Still, Donna's anxiety about the relationship was heightened by tormenting thoughts about Bob's other girlfriend. Although this example would seem to contradict our data, the story makes clear that Donna felt more involved with Bob than Bob did with her, and that she probably would have willingly given up her other boyfriend if Bob had committed himself exclusively to her.

Recall, too, from Chapter 2 that one of the best ways to predict a person's anxiety in a relationship is with the "love difference," that is, how much the person loves the partner and how much the person is loved in return. The more Donna loves Bob *and* the less she thinks he loves her—in other words, the greater the disparity between her emotional investment in the relationship and his—the more anxious she is likely to feel. If she perceives him to be inconsistent in his feelings toward her, she probably will feel that he is not very invested in the relationship, and therefore will feel anxious if she herself does feel strongly invested. This illustrates what sociologist Willard Waller, writing in 1937, called "the principle of least interest"—namely, that the partner in a romantic relationship who has less interest in the other person has more power than the one whose interest is greater.

Here is where we find a link between romantic anxiety and romantic obsession, as well as between the characteristics of the partner most closely associated with each. How intensely one feels romantic anxiety depends not just on the strength of one's love or the weakness of the partner's love, but on both together. As noted in Chapter 2, the strength of one's love is very closely associated with romantic obsession. (The two are almost the same thing in different words.) Therefore, a person who is deeply in love and obsessed with his or her partner is more likely to experience intense romantic anxiety. After all, if you don't care very much about someone, you probably will not care too much if that person acts inconsistently toward you.

Psychologist Gregory White found that the belief that one's partner is more physically attractive than oneself is associated with the belief that this partner is relatively less involved in the relationship. Thus, the very qualities that lead one to be romantically obsessed with someone carry with them the seeds of romantic anxiety as well. The more of a prize you think you have, the more likely you are to feel that you may lose it, and the more painful the loss will be. If someone is very attractive to you, you may infer that this person will be attractive to others as well, and that you can therefore expect competition. If, in addition, the person's love is not consistent, you may lose her or him.

Does this sound suspiciously like the "market value" idea that our research did not support? Not quite. Comparing people's value with their partners' in the dating marketplace failed to predict how anxious they felt about losing their partners because we used *objective* measures of people's desirability—for example, how *others* rated their attractiveness. Actually, people think, feel, and act on the basis of *their own* sense of how attractive and desirable they themselves are, which is based as much on their self-esteem as on any objective characteristics they have. Some very attractive people see themselves through a filter of insecurity and therefore think that they are at a disadvantage with respect to almost any partner. And when we find that romantic anxiety is predicted by the difference one perceives between the strength of one's own love and that of the partner's love, we are in the realm of a person's *subjective* experience—something that is not captured by objective estimates of that person's market value.

We have seen, then, that a partner's attractiveness is linked with romantic obsession, which in turn predisposes one to stronger feelings of romantic anxiety, especially if that partner acts in an anxiety-provoking way. For example, Melissa often received compliments from other women about how handsome Roy, her boyfriend, was. These compliments gave her little comfort; indeed, she felt them to be double-edged. She was sure that a rival for Roy's affection, probably more attractive than she, lurked wherever he went—perhaps under her very eyes. "I have to work twice as hard to keep up his interest as he does to keep up mine," she would say. "I have to *do* things; he just has to *be* there." After a while Roy began to tease her about these worries and made a point of calling attention to attractive women in Melissa's presence. It was hard for Melissa to tell whether he was just expressing annoyance at her doubting his loyalty or whether he wanted to keep the upper hand by feeding her insecurity.

Even though the partner's attractiveness is mainly associated with romantic obsession while the partner's inconsistency is mainly associated with romantic anxiety, it makes sense that these are also the two partner characteristics most strongly associated with the overall experience of anxious romantic attachment. It would be a mistake to think of romantic obsession and romantic anxiety as two entirely separate states. Although they can be experienced separately, there is an underlying logic that, more often than not, ties them together.

LYNNE AND SCOTT: NEVER A SECURE MOMENT

Lynne was twenty-five, with a good job as a field supervisor for a state board of education. Her previous relationships had been essentially normal, with no great extremes of passionate involvement, conflict, or jealousy. Usually she had been the one to break things off. She explains, "I know what I want and what I don't want. If I'm not interested, I don't stay involved."

She was unable to maintain this even-tempered outlook when she met Scott, who radiated a physical and intellectual attraction that she had not experienced before. He was confident and assertive at the outset, which added to his appeal. For the first few months Lynne and Scott enjoyed their relationship in what seemed an uncomplicated and mutual way. Then they reached a turning point, as Lynne explains:

Things went fine as long as circumstances limited us to a normal dating schedule. But the first time we had an opportunity to go away together, Scott and I both realized we were crazy about each other. At that time we still had a lot of chemistry, a great deal of attraction. But he immediately withdrew and said, "I can't get too close because I just came off a heavy relationship, and I don't feel I can get into something deep just yet."

When he pulled back, that's when I found I wanted more. I think the fact that he was unattainable made me want him more and more.

Scott proved to be a maddeningly noncommittal lover, and Lynne was drawn into an emotional whirlpool by his inconsistency, which seemed to attract her even as it frustrated her.

At that point we went back to weekly dating, but I wanted to see him more. There was constant turmoil—conflict and maybe tension— between us. I was patient with him until I couldn't take it anymore. I pressured him for a decision about getting married. He said, "No, I don't want you," and broke up with me and started going out with someone else. That was when he finally decided to move to New York to take a better job. He had been talking about it ever since I met him, but he had always said he didn't want to go away and lose me.

A month before he left, he called me and said he couldn't stand being without me. We got back together, and when I went away on a field trip he called me like crazy. Meanwhile, I found out later, his ex-lover was pursuing him. I also found out that he had had an affair with someone else while he was involved with her, which may have brought about the breakup. Once his ex came back into the picture my friends started telling me I should end the relationship because it was too much, too crazy, too many things going on.

One week I was getting calls and cards saying how much he loved me. The next week I'd find out that he was seen with his ex-girlfriend, or he went out with this one, or that one slept over. But I hung in there. I was hoping he would ask me to move to New York with him. He hinted at it, but he never said it.

It would be difficult to sort out the ambivalent feelings about both Lynne and his previous lover that had contributed to Scott's vacillation about moving to New York. Contrary to Lynne's expectations, the situation did not become untangled when he did move and later asked her to join him. If anything, it became more enmeshed.

Finally, when I visited him, he asked me to move there to live with him. I asked him for a commitment leading to marriage, but he said he wasn't ready. I said to myself, "All right, I'll make him see that this is a good thing between us. At least he doesn't want his ex-lover back, or he wouldn't have moved." So I gave up my job, my apartment, everything, and moved to New York with no commitment from this man.

While I was living there he concealed things from me and got very defensive when I confronted him. There were secret phone calls, and when I'd catch him on the phone and ask who it was, he'd say, "None of your business. I don't have to tell you everything." And then I'd find out it was his ex. She called our house a great deal. He said, "It's okay. She's my friend. She can call whenever she wants." Then I read a letter she had written him, saying, "You can't let go of your past. You shouldn't be with Lynne there." I never knew the whole story. I was going crazy not knowing what was going on.

Here Lynne draws a direct connection between Scott's inconsistent behavior and her growing anxiety. Her vulnerability was heightened by her having separated herself from her home, her job, and her family and friends.

Now I was completely dependent on Scott, financially and emotionally. But I felt it was worth giving up all those things for the chance to marry him. I thought he needed to get away from his family and his ex-lover, who was calling him all the time. As it turns out, that's not what he wanted. He still wanted her in his life. But he also wanted me. And I made it easy for him to have it both ways.

The inconsistency of Scott's feelings toward Lynne reflected a substantial disparity between Lynne's emotional investment in the relationship and his. That was indeed how Lynne experienced it.

I was in love with him. He indicated he was in love with me—at times. He would tell me he was, anyway. I don't know if he really was.

By Lynne's account, Scott may have played upon her anxiety by calling attention to the fact that his love for her was not equal to hers for him.

Somehow I put him on a pedestal. I gave him some sort of special status— that I'd never find anyone better than he was, and that I was lucky to be involved with him. He made me feel that way, at least before we lived together, by always telling me when there were other women in his life.

"Oh, yes, there's so-and-so, and she calls me all the time," he would say. Even when we lived together he kept doing that with his ex-lover. I suspect he kept her on the string to make me jealous.

Lynne's experience corroborates our finding, explained in the previous section, that the partner's perceived attractiveness contributes to romantic anxiety by increasing both the partner's value and the likelihood of competition for the partner's affection.

The relationship ended in the same cloud of uncertainty that had hung over it almost from the beginning. As Lynne vented her anxiety with increasing frequency in outbursts of frustration and jealousy, Scott withdrew from her. He would tell her, "One more outburst and you're gone. I can't live like this anymore." Lynne looks back on her displays of temper as "my way of leaving. I think in my heart I knew it had to end, but I didn't have the strength to end it, so I let him throw me out." Finally Scott told her, "You are gone. You will leave by the end of the week." But after she left New York he gave her one last set of mixed messages.

When he took me to the train we had a tearful, emotional scene. A week later we spoke on the phone, and he said, "I miss you terribly. I'm sorry we can't live together. I will always love you." A few weeks later his ex-lover was out there, and he was saying rotten things to me. Then he sent me a letter declaring a cease-fire and saying it was all my fault anyway. It was so characteristic of him—hot and cold, night and day, back and forth.

Yet while Scott's inconsistency caused Lynne great misery and eventually contributed to ending the relationship, it never deterred Lynne from trying to win the love of this man whom she valued so highly. As she summed it up, "I stayed in that relationship because there was always that thrill, that challenge of not being able to get this guy to marry me."

WHICH IS THE CAUSE AND WHICH IS THE EFFECT?

Common sense would have it that the partner's traits are a cause of a person's insecurity in love relationships and are not themselves strongly affected by that insecurity. When one enters into a relationship, one cannot know everything one would like to know about one's chosen partner. Especially when competing with an established rival for this person's affection, one may not know whether one will win the person's affection and loyalty until one is well into the relationship. In the first place, it would be difficult to choose a partner every time out who would disappoint one's hopes, even if one had some unconscious reason to want that outcome. In the second place, even if one's partners were selected by a random lottery, one would meet some who would elicit the kinds of reactions we call romantic obsession and romantic anxiety. Thus, while individuals may tend to be more or less anxious or obsessed in their relationships, the kinds of romantic partners they encounter will also have a marked effect on the extent of anxiety or obsession they experience within a particular relationship.

But there is another side to the story, too—that people who tend to be anxiously attached might perceive, choose, or act toward their partners in a way that brings out the partners' inconsistency. In this research the participants were reporting about past partners who were not on hand to be observed directly by the researchers. Rather, we had to rely on the perceptions of the person filling out the questionnaire—i.e., the person who was or had once been in love with that partner. Physical attractiveness, like all of the other traits listed, is in the eye of the beholder. An anxiously attached person may rate a partner highly attractive as a way of rationalizing the attachment or may learn over time to see that partner as attractive. For example, facial features that at first sight seem plain or odd may come to be endearing as one becomes emotionally invested in the partner.

Similarly, when someone rates a partner as inconsistent, it may mean that the partner really was inconsistent. Or it may mean that the person doing the rating, being insecure to begin with, expected the partner to be inconsistent and looked for evidence to confirm this belief. Seeing in the partner the image of a rejecting parent or a duplicitous lover from the past, an anxiously attached person may find rejection or betrayal when it is not really there. That is, the person may project onto the present situation feelings whose true basis lies somewhere in the person's past.

This was the case with Paula, who had married in her late teens only to find that her husband was an abusive alcoholic. For several years after her divorce she looked at all men mistrustfully. When she met Ken, an older man whose sharp witticisms belied his gentle manner, she reserved judgment for some time before she agreed to marry him. After their marriage she continued to feel uneasy about a certain flirtatious flair he exhibited, together with the fact that his ex-girlfriends seemed to pop up all over town. Coming from a history of broken relationships, she found it natural to mistrust him. Ken's response was one of frustration. "Why am I getting all this crap from you?" he exploded. "I've got twenty years on you, and I'm not supposed to have a past?

And why do I constantly have to hear about your ex-husband? He dumped all over you, and you throw him up to me at least once a day!"

Ironically, Ken, too, had felt insecure as a result of past experiences, but he had had longer to work through them. In his words,

> A long time ago a woman I really loved left me cold, and I built up an incredible resentment toward women. I'd go out and tell them anything they wanted to hear, do anything they wanted to do, and then I'd drop them like that, just to get even for the hurt I felt. Finally, one woman said to me, "What are you doing? These women didn't do that to you." It snapped something in my head, and I said, "That's right." But it took a long time before I did anything about it. I spent years getting back at that old girlfriend.

Since Ken had, in his own view, "mellowed out," he found Paula's accusations frustrating and unfair. He was very considerate toward Paula, and she could find no evidence that he was unfaithful.

Paula, however, was becoming friendly with Ken's ex-wife, whom she would see whenever she picked up Ken's children. She began asking questions and was told that Ken had not told her the truth about his previous marriage. His ex-wife claimed that he had cheated on her almost from the start, not just when the marriage was breaking up.

When Paula confronted Ken with this testimony, he reacted with predictable outrage.

> There was nothing to it. My flirtations got out of hand the last year of that marriage, but it was over by then anyway. Before that, it was like a lot of other couples: she heard a lot of stories, believed them all, and got bent out of shape. But I heard a lot of stories about her, too, and they started before I ever did anything wrong.
>
> I'm upset that Paula even talked to her about it. What aggravates me most is Paula's comparing that marriage—which I had doubts about from the beginning and didn't even want to go through with—with this one. There's no comparison. I was not in love with my previous wife, and that was also umpteen years ago. I was a different person then.

Feeling fated by her own past, Paula unwittingly sought to lock Ken into his. "He denied it to her; why shouldn't he deny it to me?" she reasoned. "After I heard what she told me, I felt I had no choice. How could I believe anything he said? Why should he be any different now?"

Ken felt stymied. If Paula was going to deny not only what he said, but what he *did*—that is, the current evidence of his feelings and behavior toward her—how was he to reassure her? Feeling wronged and attacked, he lapsed into *his* old resentments. "It's all so crazy," he remarked, "that I'm saying to myself, 'What's she doing this for? Is she saying all this to cover up something *she's* doing?'" In this atmosphere of suspicion, the personal growth to which both Paula and Ken had committed themselves in marrying each other was, for the time being, stalled by the conflicts each brought with them from past relationships.

Another way of "creating" an inconsistent partner—and an all too common one—is to give so much of oneself that one is inevitably disappointed with what the partner gives in return. One feels a lack of reciprocity, not because the partner gives too little, but because one's own level of commitment is so unrealistically high as to leave one open to frustration and feelings of rejection. One's perception of the partner as inconsistent thus stems from a need for very strong and clear expressions of affection that no partner can consistently provide.

Frequently, a woman may love someone "too much," see that the partner does not love her as much, and then reject the partner before he rejects her. In a sense, this is what Paula did in the story just above. Feeling herself unworthy of love, she could not bear the vulnerable position she was in with Ken, and so she found reasons to disqualify him and disbelieve his love for her.

Betsy is another person who compensates for her fear of rejection by giving more than she receives. "I don't really know what a normal relationship is," she says. "I can't get close to people; it's too painful." Actually, she does get close, but then is so devastated by the slightest hint of indifference from a man that, feeling dangerously vulnerable, she pulls away. Her ambivalence about her therapist typifies her relationships with men. One week she expresses a fear of losing him; the next week she says, "Maybe I shouldn't come here anymore." It is as if the most important people in her life are the ones from whom she most needs to distance herself.

Betsy appears to teeter on the edge of detachment. Love seems so exhausting and painful for her that one might wonder (as she often does) why she gets involved with men at all. In fact, the detached person hypothetically goes through the same cycle of emotions that Betsy lives out. The detached person's rationale—"I'm bound to get hurt anyway, so I won't love at all"—is the broken record Betsy plays each time she begins a new relationship. However, she feels empty and lonely if she stays away from intimate contact for long, and so she jumps back into the water, only to swim desperately for shore again. Unable to be reassured of any man's love, she finds all men too inconsistent to suit her.

Finally, the anxiously attached individual may be so emotionally caught up that he or she actually creates the partner's inconsistency. In a vignette in Chapter 2, Kurt showered Helen (a woman he had been dating only briefly) with flowers, candy, frequent phone calls, and even proposals of marriage. Interpreting the normal caution she showed as though it were disloyalty and rejection, he became so overbearing with her that she finally broke up with him. Helen did not behave at all inconsistently toward Kurt until he put so much pressure on her that she came to feel alienated from him. In this way, an anxiously attached person may create inconsistency in the partner's feelings and behavior, either by perceiving it or by provoking it.

WHY DOES A PERSON
CHOOSE AN INCONSISTENT PARTNER?

As noted above, it would be unfair and surely too all-knowing to claim that if an individual gets involved with an unworthy partner, he or she must harbor an unconscious wish to be disappointed and hurt. Such a sweeping interpretation does not allow for bad luck, or for the fact that one is not omniscient when one enters into relationships, or that some people act in a misleading way with the masks they wear. Nonetheless, people do make choices that are harmful to them, varying in degree from relatively minor to what some might call self-defeating or even masochistic. These choices can come about in several ways.

Most commonly, perhaps, people simply choose partners on the basis of availability, propinquity, and opportunity. Sometimes these accidental couplings produce suitable partners for long-term relationships; sometimes they do not. At the outset, sexual attraction and the boost to one's self-esteem may overwhelm all other considerations, but as time passes it becomes more crucial for a couple to be compatible in other ways. You may become involved with someone because that person is strongly attracted to *you*, even if you otherwise would not have been attracted to that person. It is not so easy to turn away affection, even from a less than ideal source, and especially when there are no attractive alternatives on the horizon.

Rather than be alone, people accept relationships that are not always a good match. If the present partner satisfies some very important needs of the moment, it may be hard to evaluate objectively how well she or he will satisfy all of one's important needs in the future. Rather than be selective and hold out for a suitable partner, people often go for the bird in the hand, hope for the best, and face the consequences later. The consequences may include having a partner with whom one feels perpetually insecure, or spending years in a relationship that never yields commitment and then facing the anxiety of being alone again, like Carol in Chapter 3.

A person who tends toward anxious romantic attachment is especially vulnerable to such errors of the heart. Wishes and hopes color the lenses through which anxiously attached individuals view their partners. As described in Chapter 2, these individuals are attuned to their intense inner experience of love rather than to a logical analysis of how a prospective partner may behave in a variety of future circumstances. As one rushes blindly into an emotional involvement with a partner who happens to engage one's attention, one often assumes that good things go together, that the partner who is beautiful and loving will be ideal in all other respects. The anxiously attached lover risks going to either extreme: on the one hand, being too critical and suspicious and failing to appreciate the partner's consistency; on the other hand, being too accepting and failing to notice the partner's inconsistency until it is too late. Thus, we have stories of the anxiously attached lover as perpetrator, alienating his or her partner with undue pressure, as well as stories of the anxiously attached lover as victim, grievously wounded by an unfaithful partner.

Laurie is an example of a person who closed her eyes to her partner's inconsistency under the pressure of her need to feel loved and connected. Laurie felt grateful to Jeff, her husband of two years, for having broken through her emotional reserve with his assertive, self-confident air. Jeff was a handsome man who presented himself well and made a good impression on people. These qualities made him a desirable partner for Laurie, who since childhood had been a prized showpiece for her parents in the town where they lived. Jeff fit so well into the image of perfection Laurie had been trained to project that she overlooked his flirtations, his tantrums, and his general unreliability. However much he provoked her, she held to her fantasy of him as an ideal husband with an appealing combination of passion and tenderness. Yet when confronted with undeniable evidence that he was having an extra-marital affair, she became utterly disillusioned and moved back in with her parents, who systematically removed all pictures and other traces of Jeff from their house. For months Jeff tried in vain to win Laurie back, but found her completely closed off emotionally. Then she could see nothing positive in him. "It's over," she insisted.

Finally, their marriage counselor said, "Maybe it really *is* over." The counselor stated that Jeff might be incapable of changing in some fundamental ways, and that Laurie might have to make some choices on the basis of that realization. Thus challenged, Laurie did another turnaround, moved back in with Jeff, and resumed idealizing him. She said that he had been punished enough and had sincerely repented.

To the counselor, however, it was not clear how much Jeff had changed. The movement that had occurred was more on Laurie's side, and it seemed more a cyclical than a progressive movement. If Laurie could not believe totally in Jeff, she felt she had to reject him, since nothing less than perfection was good enough for her, or for her family. Forced to choose between these extremes, she felt drawn irresistibly to close ranks with Jeff, since she needed a fairy-tale marriage to avoid embarrassing her parents and feeling that she had failed them.

A person may choose partners for certain desirable characteristics while either ignoring their undesirable characteristics or accepting the latter as a price that must be paid for the desirable ones. Physical beauty is immediately apparent and captivating; a pattern of inconsistent feelings and behavior may be less evident at the outset, or it may be easily dismissed by a person who would wish that it not be there. Early in a relationship, one may not care that a woman of great beauty and polish may be self-centered and aloof, that a lover's attractiveness and charm may come at the price of ceaseless competition with other suitors, or that a partner who lives in the fast lane may only rarely slow down long enough to enjoy a moment of mutual affection and never stop to raise a family.

As we noted earlier, people who appear to choose a series of inconsistent partners may in fact be acting toward each of their partners in an alienating way. Or they may have such great need for affection and loyalty that any partner seems inconsistent to them. Is it possible, though, that some people gravitate toward inconsistent partners because they find the inconsistency itself somehow alluring? Possible, but not likely. At least, there are other ways to explain people's repeated involvement in uncertain, stressful romantic quests besides assuming that people deliberately seek pain.

Anxiety is the down side of being emotionally aroused. There is an up side as well, for arousal can also be experienced as positive excitement and anticipation. Arousal can fuel passion, as exemplified by the emotional bonds formed by people who together go through an intensely stressful situation such as combat, fraternity hazing, or a demanding academic curriculum. A dating couple may find their emotional bond strengthened when they have their first sexual experience together or, as in *Romeo and Juliet,* when their families stand opposed to their involvement.

The emotions one feels while pursuing an attractive partner with uncertain prospects of success can have a double-edged quality, flipping back and forth between anxiety and pleasurable arousal. Anxiety tends to be high in such situations because the degree of anxiety one experiences in a given relationship is influenced both by the value of the prospective partner and by the likelihood of acceptance or rejection by that partner. Some people are so afraid to fail that they choose an impossible task, a highly valued person who is hopelessly out of reach, so as to make sure that any approach will inevitably lead to rejection. By removing any chance of acceptance, they spare themselves the anxiety that would accompany approaching a potentially attainable partner. At the other extreme, some people choose partners who, although relatively unattractive, are safely available. Here the anxiety level is low, both because the partner is not highly valued and because the risk of rejection is small. Romantic anxiety is greater when the partner is of relatively high value and there is a chance of either acceptance or rejection. A person's estimate of the probability of rejection is, of course, influenced by past experience as well as by the consistency of the partner's behavior.

Passionate love, like anxiety, often is identified in our culture by physical signs of emotional and sexual arousal: sweaty palms, thumping heartbeat, and sexual desire in the presence of the beloved. There is a strong temptation to label these sensations as "falling in love," since it looks and feels a lot better to be in love than to be insecure. Actually, though, a person in pursuit of an attractive romantic partner is likely to feel a mixture of enthusiasm and anxiety, since either success or failure is possible. There is something to lose, but there is also something to gain, and both possibilities contribute to the person's excitement.

AMY: PARADOXICAL CHOICES

Anxiously attached individuals seem repeatedly to seek the excitement of an uncertain quest. What brings them to this peak of energy again and again? Why do they persist in what is often a fruitless search? The story of Amy crystallizes these questions and points to possible answers.

Amy, a bright, attractive woman of thirty-two who has never been married, echoes a word used by Lynne (in the previous case) when she characterizes herself as "going for the unattainable" in her selection of partners. She meets many "nice, average guys" who often become her "buddies." With these men, she explains, "it just isn't there for them or for me, but we like each other as people. We can trust each other, go to movies together, bring each other medicine when we're sick, and just be there to talk to." Once in a while Amy does fall in love—invariably with a man who is too domineering, too popular with other women, or too career-oriented and ambitious to be a satisfying companion. She wants a man who projects an image of ambition and success, which means her spending many hours alone "wondering whether to be jealous of his work or some other woman."

Amy's account of her friendships with her male buddies makes for a very positive description of what an intimate relationship might be like: trust, companionship, support, communication. She appreciates the value of a partner who is warm, accepting, faithful, and reliable. But the captivating, overpowering men she chooses as lovers are the ones least likely to be there for her when she needs them. In fact, when a man seems ready to make a commitment, she finds that her ardor for him cools.

> Once a relationship is attainable, I don't want it. Maybe it's just the conquest I want. It's as if I'm saying, "I can have him; I don't want him. I'll find somebody else I can't have."

Amy says that she is looking for the comfort and security of a stable relationship, yet she has not actually experienced the long-term rewards such a relationship would offer. Perhaps that is why she is still drawn to the repeated pursuit of a glamorous lover who either lies just out of reach or slips from her grasp after a brief period of intense romantic fulfillment. It is a heady experience to feel that she might be able to win the affections of a highly desirable man who can bathe her in the reflected glow of his special allure. Amy does know *these* rewards, fleeting though they may be.

We can imagine different beginnings for Amy's story. She might, for instance, have experienced rejection at the hands of a stereotypically masculine, domineering father. As a result, she is motivated to approach men who resemble him and thus to master the anxiety such men arouse in her. By taking up this challenge, she repeatedly overcomes her fear of rejection and proves her own adequacy. These rewards may be very satisfying to her even if the relationships that result are not so satisfying. Then again, Amy may have had a good father, one more like the men she calls buddies. In this scenario, her sexual response to these men is inhibited because they remind her of the warm, loving father whom she was not allowed to love sexually. With "good" men declared off limits, she can fall in love only with "bad" men.

You can imagine different beginnings for Amy based on your own experiences and observations. Just as there can be more than one way to explain how Amy came to be where she is today, so there are different ways of understanding how anxiously attached lovers return again and again to situations to which they react with such intense mixed feelings. Here, briefly, are two such explanations. They are not incompatible with each other; indeed, both may well apply to the same person.

One explanation begins with the infant or young child who does not develop a confident, reliable expectation of love and affection from others. Lacking experiences of consistent love and affection from which to generalize, this person is unable to feel comfortable with the possibility that his or her love and affection will be returned by others. Feeling unable to count on people as stable, secure sources of emotional gratification, he or she is made anxious by the uncertainty. Whereas the detached person avoids the uncertainty, and with it the anxiety, the anxiously attached person seeks to win love and affection in spite of the anxiety. Finding oneself reliving painful experiences of inconsistency and rejection, one may be motivated to try to gain mastery over them, so that they will have a different outcome in the future. One may struggle with irrational fears, knowing that they have more to do with the past than the present, while still feeling anxious in the process. Psychologists have observed that people retain a strong memory of problems they could not solve, in the hope that they can "go back and do it right this time." In that hope of mastery may lie one reward that fuels the anxiously attached person's quest.

Looked at from another angle, the anxiously attached person's seeming attraction to inconsistent partners actually is based on the partner's physical attractiveness and other measures of social desirability. According to this explanation, people who (for whatever reason) are low in self-esteem place especially high value on partners who are outwardly attractive. To win, even temporarily, the affection of someone whom many find highly desirable is most rewarding to those in greatest need of a boost to the ego. This is a high-stakes game, with much excitement and hopeful anticipation; even sporadic victories can make the risks seem worthwhile. Although the attractive partner may also have other desirable options and may soon move on to them, it is the attractiveness, not the inconsistency, that makes the earliest and strongest impression. At the outset one may easily overlook the faults of a partner whose good looks and self-assurance one longs to appropriate for oneself. Thus, like a gambler going deeper and deeper into debt, but occasionally winning a jackpot, the anxiously attached person keeps playing the game, even though the investment of time does not pay off in an enduring emotional commitment.

It is unlikely that either of these explanations, or any other, will ever be proved definitively correct or incorrect. Rather, strands from a number of interpretations may be simultaneously relevant to your self-understanding. The value of such accounts lies in offering you alternate paths to self-knowledge and insight. A coherent, plausible story of your life can be a valuable tool for recovering your past and giving direction to your future.

HOW SIMILAR ARE A PERSON'S PARTNERS?

We have also examined whether people repeatedly choose partners who are similar in terms of the ten characteristics discussed in this chapter. If we know what a person's last partner was like, can we predict what the next one will be like? Does a person choose successive partners who are attractive or unattractive, trustworthy or untrustworthy, warm or cold? Do people keep repeating the same mistakes in their choice of partners after a series of unhappy relationships? Not necessarily.

The young adults (college seniors and recent graduates) in our sample had partners in their four most important relationships who differed considerably from one another. Interestingly, among the variables that showed the least similarity across the four partners were the two that are the most important determinants of anxious romantic attachment: physical attractiveness and emotional consistency. (Men did show somewhat more consistency than women in the physical attractiveness of their partners.) Perhaps these young adults had not yet had enough relationships for their four most important ones to reflect reliably their personal preferences, as opposed to the accidents of their still brief life histories. Perhaps they tended to look each time for something different from the last relationship—for example, to follow an exciting, but painfully disappointing, relationship with a safe, but dull, one. Perhaps, after engaging in a tense pursuit of a highly desirable partner, only to lose in the end, they were more ready to accept someone who was pursuing *them*. Perhaps their choices varied in response to the state of their self-esteem;

for example, one might react to a traumatic relationship by retreating to a more secure one, or build on a gratifying experience by next taking on even greater risks. The greatest similarity among partners occurred with respect to socioeconomic status; these young people tended to find their partners within a particular social class. All told, there is little evidence that they felt driven always to choose partners who displayed the same set of characteristics.

These young adults did show a stable pattern with respect to one characteristic, not of partners, but of relationships: namely, the number of hours per week they spent together with their partners. Even with different kinds of partners, individuals seem to have a set way of carrying on a relationship, with a given number of contact hours per week that carries over from partner to partner. As indicated in Chapter 2, the more time they spend, the more romantically obsessed they are likely to be.

We learned two useful things about the similarity among partners. First, the participants apparently searched their memories carefully, since they took the trouble to give very discriminating answers about the different people with whom they had been romantically involved. Given this highly individualized, nonstereotyped description of each partner, it would seem that we can trust the ratings they assigned those partners.

Second, if people typically get involved with different types of partners, then even those who have made some unfortunate choices have a reasonable hope of doing better. The more potential partners to whom you are exposed, the more likely you are to find one who satisfies you. The advantages of greater exposure can be defeated, however, if you let yourself be diverted into an involvement with the wrong person simply because that person shows a strong and persistent interest in you. To get the benefits of acquaintance with a wider range of prospective partners, one needs to screen out unsuitable partners and learn more about the remaining prospects without going through a year-long relationship with each person. And to do that one needs to be well aware of one's own wants and needs.

You cannot change the family into which you were born, but you can choose to become intimately involved with different sorts of partners, in order to be less susceptible to anxious romantic attachments. First, you need to know what characteristics of a partner matter most to you and what kind of partner would make a good choice for you. The questionnaire that follows is designed to help you clarify these choices. If you look honestly at where you have been in your relationships and where you want to go, you are taking a first step toward more realistic, fulfilling choices.

YOUR IDEAL PARTNER

The previous self-assessment questionnaires in this book take stock of your experiences in love relationships, including the partners with whom you have been involved. This one gives you a chance to think about what your *ideal* spouse or lover would be like. Please take a moment to imagine this ideal partner. Next, skim the following list of statements before you rate any of them, so that you can have a general idea of what descriptive characteristics are included. Then, keeping your overall priorities in mind (since you can't have everything!), write a number from 1 to 7 on the line printed next to each statement to indicate how important that feature is to your personal vision of an ideal partner. The higher the number, the more important the characteristic is to you. That is, 1 means "not at all important," 4 means "somewhat important," and 7 means "very important," as in the following scale:

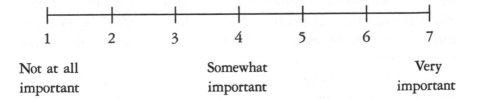

| 1 | 2 | 3 | 4 | 5 | 6 | 7 |

Not at all important   Somewhat important   Very important

Remember, no one person can combine every desirable trait, so resist the temptation to write in many 6s and 7s!

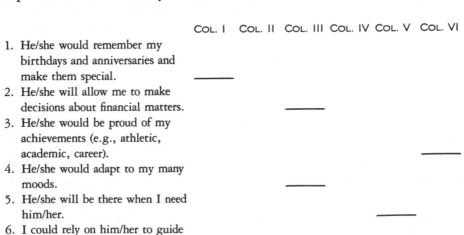

COL. I   COL. II   COL. III   COL. IV   COL. V   COL. VI

1. He/she would remember my birthdays and anniversaries and make them special. _____

2. He/she will allow me to make decisions about financial matters. _____

3. He/she would be proud of my achievements (e.g., athletic, academic, career). _____

4. He/she would adapt to my many moods. _____

5. He/she will be there when I need him/her. _____

6. I could rely on him/her to guide my decisions. _____

	COL. I	COL. II	COL. III	COL. IV	COL. V	COL. VI
7. He/she would try to make me comfortable when I am sick.				_____		
8. He/she would be very affectionate.	_____					
9. He/she could be persuaded to see things my way during an argument.			_____			
10. He/she would recognize that I am a very good parent.						_____
11. He/she would see me through hard times.					_____	
12. He/she will accept and like me the way I am.	_____					
13. He/she would allow me freedom to pursue my interests and hobbies.		_____				
14. He/she would work hard at making our home comfortable.				_____		
15. He/she would act as if our honeymoon had no end.	_____					
16. He/she would admire me for my social ease.						_____
17. He/she would recognize my authority in the household.			_____			
18. He/she would be responsive to my sexual needs.				_____		
19. He/she would want to take care of me.					_____	
20. He/she will always be pleased to see me after work.	_____					
21. He/she would take my advice about major purchases.			_____			
22. He/she would be proud to be seen with me.						_____
23. He/she would want to have romantic evenings.	_____					
24. He/she will give me recognition when I do something well.						_____
25. He/she would want me to make my own decisions.		_____				
26. He/she would be quite willing to change jobs and move with me wherever my career advancement takes me.			_____			

	Col. I	Col. II	Col. III	Col. IV	Col. V	Col. VI
27. He/she would be "in love" with me.	———					
28. He/she would appreciate the fact that I have much insight into human nature.						———
29. He/she will speak up on my behalf when my attributes are questioned.					———	
30. He/she would prefer to furnish the house according to my taste.		———				
31. He/she would be strong in areas in which I am weak.					———	
32. He/she would encourage me to go out by myself.		———				
33. His/her caring attitude and concern would make me feel loved and accepted.	———					
34. He/she will take charge of family matters.					———	
35. He/she will see me as quite intelligent.						———
36. He/she would never leave me stranded.					———	
37. He/she would respect my need for occasional separate leisure time.		———				
38. He/she would be someone who excites me sexually.				———		
39. It would be clear to him/her that I am a separate person and can take care of myself.		———				
40. He/she would rather have it my way than argue.			———			
41. He/she would make me feel thoroughly loved and adored.	———					
42. He/she would respect my need for an occasional separate vacation.		———				
43. He/she would feel that I need no protection, that I can rely on myself.		———				
44. He/she would physically satisfy me.				———		

	COL. I	COL. II	COL. III	COL. IV	COL. V	COL. VI
45. He/she will strongly encourage and help me to achieve my career goals.					___	
46. He/she would respect my desire to do some things on my own.		___				
47. He/she would show me affection always, not just in bed.	___					
48. He/she would help me solve my unresolved problems.					___	
49. He/she will recognize that I have the final say in many decisions.			___			
50. He/she would come close to being the best lover imaginable.				___		
51. It would be okay with him/her if I spent some evenings out without him/her.		___				
52. He/she would be very attentive to me when I am tired.				___		
53. He/she would see me as witty and charming.						___
54. He/she will provide a nice house.				___		
55. He/she would brag about me to others.						___
56. He/she would generally take my suggestions or advice.			___			
57. He/she would appreciate my desire to pursue a career.		___				
58. He/she would tell me how attractive I am.						___
59. He/she would frequently cook for me.				___		
60. He/she would not make noise in the morning, so I can enjoy an extra hour in bed.				___		
61. Understanding my feelings would be important to him/her.	___					
62. He/she would see me as competent and worthy in my chosen field.						___
63. He/she would expect me to make my own career decisions.		___				
64. He/she will respect and admire me.						___
65. He/she will try to ease my pain.				___		

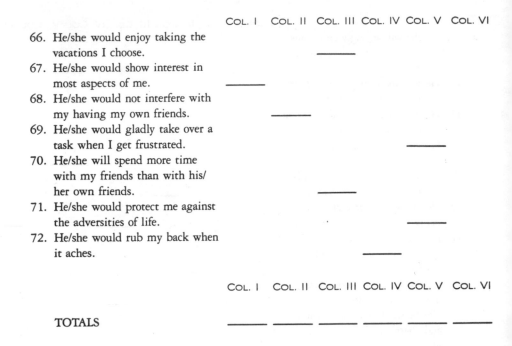

	COL. I	COL. II	COL. III	COL. IV	COL. V	COL. VI
66. He/she would enjoy taking the vacations I choose.			———			
67. He/she would show interest in most aspects of me.	———					
68. He/she would not interfere with my having my own friends.		———				
69. He/she would gladly take over a task when I get frustrated.					———	
70. He/she will spend more time with my friends than with his/ her own friends.		———				
71. He/she would protect me against the adversities of life.					———	
72. He/she would rub my back when it aches.				———		
	COL. I	COL. II	COL. III	COL. IV	COL. V	COL. VI
TOTALS	———	———	———	———	———	———

We have many different needs that we seek to meet in our relationships with people. Even in romantic relationships, love and affection represent only one of the needs we may be trying to meet. This questionnaire was developed very carefully to show how we go about meeting the six basic psychological needs (listed below) in love relationships. Many people were polled to arrive at a broad range of opinions about what desirable traits best express each of those six needs. In deciding what an ideal spouse or lover would be like for you, you are really saying a great deal about the needs you would want your partner to meet. What is ideal for you would not be ideal for someone else.

Now that you have filled in all the items, you can find out which needs are most important to you by adding up your answers to the items in each of the six columns. First, go down Column I and add up all the numbers you have written there. Write the total in the space provided at the bottom of Column I. Then do the same for Columns II, III, IV, V, and VI. The higher the total in each column, the more important the need represented by that column is to you. Those needs (with definitions adapted from Julian B. Rotter's social learning theory) are as follows:

Column I shows your score on the *Need for Love and Affection.* This is the need to be accepted unconditionally, to be well liked, and to have the devoted interest, concern, and affection of your partner and others.

Column II shows your score on the *Need for Independence.* This is the need to make your own decisions, to be self-reliant, and to achieve goals on your own merit.

Column III shows your score on the *Need for Dominance.* This is the need to exercise power and influence over your partner or others.

Column IV shows your score on the *Need for Physical Comfort.* This is the need to be in an aesthetically pleasing environment, to avoid pain, and to experience bodily pleasure.

Column V shows your score on the *Need for Protection and Dependency.* This is the need to have your partner or others shelter you from frustrations, provide emotional security, and help you achieve valued goals.

Column VI shows your score on the *Need for Recognition and Status.* This is the need to excel and be viewed as better than others in school, occupation, athletics, social standing, attractiveness, or whatever is important to you.

When this questionnaire was given to several hundred college students, approximately equal numbers of them scored highest on each of the six needs. Even though the questionnaire is concerned with romantic love relationships, the need for *love and affection* did not predominate over other needs. About the same number of people, for example, scored highest on the need for *independence,* which, at its extreme, indicates a strong tendency toward detachment. These findings show that people enter into love relationships for a variety of reasons and to fulfill a variety of needs. There is room for many needs to be satisfied in an intimate relationship, provided that the partners understand and support each other's needs.

The students who filled out this Ideal Partner Questionnaire also rated their overall happiness in their current relationship. The ones who described themselves as happiest were those who could admit that they had needs more commonly attributed to the opposite sex: for men, needs for *love and affection* and for *protection and dependency;* for women, needs for *independence* and for *dominance.* Married couples and individuals in marriage and divorce groups attest to this as well—that men with "feminine" needs and women with "masculine" needs have the best chance for fulfillment in marriage. Presumably, those who express such a range of needs not only are more likely to have needs compatible with those of their partners; they are also better prepared to be aware of and sensitive to similar needs in their partners, and to cooperate in fulfilling them. Ray and his wife Jennifer (in Chapter 3) might have benefited greatly if they could have clarified their needs from this perspective. Both had great needs for love and affection as well as for recognition and status, but they could not empathize with, let alone satisfy, those needs in each other.

Unmet needs cause friction in love relationships. Looking at a couple from the viewpoint of the partners' respective needs reveals the following potential sources of strain to the couple's emotional bond:

1. *Noncomplementarity of needs.* How well do your needs mesh with your partner's needs? Try to think of examples, using the six basic needs listed above, of ways in which partners might be out of synchrony with each other's needs. It is very demoralizing to have a partner who ignores or ridicules your needs. In that case your partner becomes an obstacle, rather than a source of support, in satisfying those needs.

One couple experienced a conflict between the husband's absorption in solitary work and the wife's desire for an active social life. The wife felt a need for her husband's approval, but instead he actively squelched her social needs. Here the wife's need for love and affection from others, as well as from her husband, was blocked by her husband's disapproving attitude. Her social aspirations also may have symbolized needs for independence and for recognition and status outside the home. Her husband, meanwhile, apparently felt that his needs both for independence and for recognition and status (through his work) were threatened by his wife's social needs. He also may have interpreted her giving time and attention to others as a withdrawal of love from him, leaving his need for affection not fully satisfied.

2. *Imbalance of needs.* An imbalance of needs occurs when you or your partner attach far greater importance to one of the six needs than to the other five. For example, a person who has a very high need in one area—say, for love and affection—probably would try to satisfy that need in a wide range of situations, even ones in which that need was not easily met. In the words of an old saying, "If all you have is a hammer, everything looks like a nail." Intense need in one area may be difficult for even the most devoted partner to satisfy and may therefore cause great strain in a relationship.

One man felt such a lack of acceptance and nurturance from his parents that his life seemed a perpetual quest for the Holy Grail of love and affection. His first attempt at marriage was with a woman who replicated his parents' indifference, yet after their divorce he made several attempts at reconciliation, "just to see if she would love me, to get some kind of assurance that she did." Later he married a woman who was warm and loving toward him, but he felt almost as dissatisfied with her as with his first wife. His second wife, while wanting to satisfy him, felt drained by his constant need for reassurance. When she tried to keep up normal, diversified contacts with people, he felt threatened. When she cut back to appease him, she felt confined. "No normal amount of affection will ever satisfy him," she concluded. "He wants something bigger than life."

3. *Needs all met in one place.* In our mobile culture, where many couples float freely, detached from the larger social networks in which they once were embedded, they depend too often on a spouse or lover to provide for most or all of their psychological needs. This is a really precarious position to be in, since no one relationship can satisfy all of a person's needs.

A woman in her late twenties who grew up in a nomadic family felt that she never had established firm moorings in life. She worked irregularly at clerical jobs after high school and had little motivation to continue working once she was married. She began to suffer disabling complications of the diabetes that she felt had always retarded her progress in life, and it grieved her that she would not be able to bear children. Without a vocation, close friends, or much of a future, she lived through her daily interactions with her husband. She found odd jobs she could do at his place of business so that she could be with him during the day. He, however, felt that she sometimes interfered with his business interactions; moreover, the sheer amount of time they spent together came to be a source of friction between them. As her isolation and vulnerability grew, her needs for love and affection and for protection and dependency became burdensome to him. "She won't let me work, and when I get home she won't let me watch TV," he complained. "There's no reason she can't learn to amuse herself sometimes—then we'd both be better off."

4. *Strong needs coupled with low expectations for satisfying them.* You may have powerful needs, but little hope of meeting them in a particular relationship. You may feel trapped in a relationship that is unsatisfying and feel frustrated because you do not see a better alternative available to you. In this situation, sometimes referred to as "low freedom of movement," a person may turn to fantasy to satisfy his or her needs. An example is Phyllis, the housewife in Chapter 4 who compensated for a loveless marriage by absorbing herself in an imaginary romance with a television actor.

A parallel example is a woman who, as a child, was frozen out of her family circle by her father, who seemed to have questioned her paternity. "He couldn't wait to get me married so he could wash his hands of me," she said. Denigrated and rejected, she approached adulthood with a very limited view of her options. She dated little and was never intimate with anyone but her husband-to-be, of whom she said, "I was shocked that he even liked me when we met." She was so grateful to have a husband at all, let alone one who was clever and accomplished, that she disregarded his cold, unloving attitude toward her and followed his orders unquestioningly. After a number of years he became so abusive that she left him, but she felt terrified to face life alone and worried that she would always "fail" at intimacy and marriage. At this juncture her thoughts returned to a man with whom she had had an extended telephone romance (but had never met) before she was married. The calls would have been labeled crank calls by almost anyone else. Yet she began to dream that this man would reappear and reveal himself to her in the flesh. When she started receiving telephone calls from a stranger, she felt sure that it was the same person. However, she never did meet him, as she never had in the past. Because all her experience had set her up to believe that she had little freedom of movement, this woman resorted to fantasy to satisfy her long-suppressed need for love and affection.

5. *Exceptionally high minimal goal levels.* Your criteria for the satisfaction of your needs may be unrealistically high. By analogy, consider the student who feels that he or she is a failure for getting a B + in a course instead of an A. By comparison, other students are delighted to get a B +. A person for whom obtaining love and affection is important should ask what specifically she or he needs from the partner to feel that this need is being satisfied. Are these criteria realistically attainable? Some people ask for so much that they end up feeling frustrated. By asking more than the partner can really give, they may cause the partner to feel inadequate, and the partner may then become even less able to satisfy their needs.

A woman who had spent her childhood in the midst of constant financial struggle ("We didn't have to worry where the next meal was coming from, but we always wondered how we were going to pay the next bill") was left with a high need for physical comfort. She undertook a professional career and looked to marriage as a further bulwark against financial need. For her, a husband was a breadwinner before anything else. She became involved with a bright, talented attorney who was determined to establish a private practice in a competitive market. After two years together they began to talk of marriage, but it troubled her that his practice was still struggling. Although they lived in modest comfort on their combined income, she wanted to see her husband (if he was to become that) established in a salaried position with a large law firm. She was especially concerned that he be in a position to provide adequately for the family if she were to give up full-time work to have children. Her partner, however, was not ready to give up his dream. "I need more time to establish myself," he insisted. "If it comes to the point where I have to throw in the towel and take a job for the good of our family, I'll do it then, but not before. I want to see this thing through." This commitment did not satisfy her, since she expected him to give unquestioned priority to satisfying her need for physical comfort, and the couple went their separate ways.

6. *Conflict of needs within the individual.* How well do your needs mesh with one another, both in general and in your present relationship? You might have two strong needs (say, for independence and for protection and dependency) that would be difficult to fulfill simultaneously with any partner. In that case, you might have to clarify your personal priorities. If you felt forced by a partner's needs to choose between two strong needs of your own, you might have to decide whether the relationship was important enough to try to negotiate the conflict.

A woman who had spent the years since her divorce as a single, working parent married a man from a traditional Greek background who expected his wife to sit on a ceremonial pedestal and let him make the decisions. From her perspective, "We fight all the time. The problem is my independence. I have to give it up to make him happy." Because she loved her husband she tried to conform to his expectations, but found it difficult to unlearn lifelong habits of assertiveness. Here, her need for independence was in conflict not only with her husband's need for dominance, but also with her simultaneous need for love and affection. Likewise, the husband's need for love and affection was in conflict with his need for dominance. Both had needs that conflicted in their relationship with each other, as well as within themselves. Each spouse had three options: to decide which of the two needs was more important; to try to expand the limited potential their marriage offered for satisfying their needs together; or to find a more suitable partner with whom both needs could more readily be satisfied.

Understanding insecure love in terms of needs requires clarification of both partners' priorities. By using the Ideal Partner Questionnaire, you can get a sense of how well your needs are being fulfilled in your present relationship as well as in past relationships. A particular relationship may or may not offer a realistic prospect for fulfilling your strongest needs. On the other hand, you might decide to encourage your partner to be more sensitive to your needs.

Since a relationship is a two-way street, try to have your partner fill out the

Ideal Partner Questionnaire, too. Or you can fill it out on your partner's behalf, predicting his or her responses based on what you know about him or her. This exercise can help you be more sensitive to your partner's needs; it can also show you whether the needs you believe your partner feels most strongly are needs that you can and want to satisfy. Although you cannot and should not mold yourself into the image your partner desires, it makes sense to be involved with someone whose needs are compatible, rather than in conflict, with yours.

If you believe that your own or your partner's needs are not being fulfilled satisfactorily for whatever reason, you may feel prompted to reassess the way you handle intimate relationships. You might consider (a) working on your current relationship so that your needs or your partner's will be better fulfilled; (b) compromising on needs, so that both of you will have some needs met much of the time; (c) arranging to take turns satisfying incompatible needs; (d) dividing up spheres of interest, so that each of you will have your needs met in the areas most important to you; (e) choosing a different partner, or a different kind of partner, who can better satisfy your needs; or (f) questioning whether your needs are really unchangeable and whether you might grow in ways that would enable you to build your relationships around a different set of needs.

Your security in a relationship lies in your ability to satisfy your partner's needs, and vice versa. But the exchange of need satisfactions in a thriving relationship is not a matter of keeping a tally and giving only in order to receive, for it is gratifying as well to identify with someone else's needs and to satisfy them as if they were your own. Empathic concern and trust lead to mutually cooperative interaction, directed toward meeting both partners' needs.

TACTICS OF

INSECURE LOVE

People who are anxiously attached in a romantic involvement have a strong desire to feel that their love is reciprocated and that the relationship will be secure. At the same time, they fear that this will not be the case — that is, that rejection and loss are imminent. This gap between need and expectation is a source of considerable pain. To avoid the pain, people find ways to try to obtain reassuring information that will reduce their uncertainty and feelings of insecurity.

Most people want to be reassured that they are loved. They learn to do things that worked in the past — perhaps with their parents or with previous partners — to reduce the anxiety associated with the prospect of rejection. These strategies are implemented by tactics designed to keep a relationship alive and to elicit signs of a partner's love.

The tactics illustrated in this chapter include *domination,* which involves the use of demands and threats to coerce the partner into demonstrations of loyalty and affection. The person who uses the tactic of *compliance* refrains from making any such demands, preferring instead to believe that no news is good news. The compliant lover hopes to keep the partner's loyalty by placating and appeasing the partner. Finally, there is *ingratiation,* the tactic of offering gifts or services in exchange for love, as if to say, "Look at all I did for you; now here's what I want from you."

Whereas these are all tactics of *attachment, detachment* is expressed in techniques for making sure the partner is close enough but not *too* close. The tactics of measured detachment entail subtle adjustments of the emotional distance between partners, so that a relationship is still possible for those who become anxious when they take too great an emotional risk.

TACTICS OF ATTACHMENT: DOMINATION AND COMPLIANCE

A person who uses *domination* as a tactic of anxious romantic attachment makes demands and backs them up with threats—of punishment, of retaliation, of withdrawal of affection. These threats, which may be explicit or implicit, are intended to keep the partner on the defensive and maintain the upper hand. This tactic works as long as the partner values the attachment and fears the threatened retribution. It is less effective if the partner has attractive options available.

At the other extreme, the tactic of *compliance* involves avoiding any offense to the partner, taking care not to make unpleasant or excessive demands, and pleasing and indulging the partner in any way possible. Subordinating his or her own needs to those of the partner, the compliant lover is always attuned to the partner's needs so as to accommodate them before they are actually expressed.

This strategy of accommodation can make life easy for the partner, even one who is very demanding. Superficially, at least, the dominating and compliant styles complement each other well. For this reason, dominant and compliant individuals often are drawn to each other, as our cases in this section will show.

That does not mean, however, that this kind of pairing is workable in a long-term relationship. The sacrifices involved in compliance may come easily to a person in the early stages of passionate love. People who adopt this strategy, especially if they question their own attractiveness, may readily make those sacrifices to win and hold on to an attractive, highly valued partner. But with the exception of those who are so insecure that they will subordinate their needs permanently in order to maintain a relationship, compliant lovers are likely to become less accommodating as passionate love evolves into companionate love. It is increasingly hard to keep giving without taking as the years and decades go by. Typically, a viable, long-term relationship requires greater equality. Equality, however, may be difficult to achieve once a pattern of inequality has been established.

Consider how the partner is likely to react to a compliant lover. At the outset, even a person who is not especially demanding may enjoy being an object of deference. Most people are susceptible to being flattered, catered to, and pampered. After a while, though, a normally secure person is likely to lose respect for, and lose interest in, one who is always acquiescent. One who suppresses one's true self to fit the partner's demands may come to seem nondescript and lacking in character. Without expressed wishes, desires, and values, a person may come across not only as wishy-washy, but also as difficult to please, since the partner will not have cues as to how to go about pleasing such a person. For a partner who wants to please, that can be frustrating. Thus, the very tactic a person uses to preserve a relationship may prove its undoing.

People who *will* stay involved with a compliant lover are likely to be relatively self-centered and domineering. They are also most resistant to demands for greater equality later on. Those who act as if they are not entitled to much consideration are likely to get and keep partners who feel entitled to have everything for themselves, rather than partners who are amenable to the adjustments needed to sustain a long-term relationship.

While it may be tempting to accommodate a dominating lover as a strategy to gain initial acceptance, you might question whether that is the type of relationship you would want to have for the rest of your life, and whether you would want to spend a lifetime with a partner who is content with such a relationship. Settling for a relationship of dominance and compliance is putting off what may be a painful, but probably inevitable test of the soundness of the relationship. For if a partner does not value you enough to accept an equitable relationship, then the prospects for a long and happy relationship with that partner are questionable.

The cases that follow show several pairings of dominating and compliant partners, either or both of whom are anxiously attached to some degree. Sometimes it is the compliant partner who is clearly insecure in the relationship; sometimes it is the dominant lover. Often the partners are trying to meet complementary needs by playing on each other's insecurities.

DONNA AND BOB: THE FUTILITY OF SELF-EFFACEMENT

A classic case of compliance is that of Donna in Chapter 3. She was the student who was romantically involved with her professor, Bob. Her clandestine relationship with Bob consisted of a long series of compliant acts on her part. Donna accepted that Bob had a primary relationship with another woman, about whom she reluctantly suppressed her curiosity. She went out with him incognito and stayed in the background when she accompanied him to public events. She made love when he wanted to, even if she didn't always share his desire at the time. She agreed to have an abortion when she became pregnant by him. Finally, she accepted the distance he imposed in the awkward aftermath of the abortion. The role she had assumed was typified by this encounter, which occurred some weeks after they broke up:

> I stayed away from him on campus because I knew that's what he wanted me to do. I never made a scene with him. I never dropped by his place, because that was a no-no. I did call him periodically to get together, but he was always busy. Then one night he returned my call, and we went out drinking, talking, fooling around. I didn't mention that I was seeing somebody else because I knew that would send him through the roof. I could feel that I was trying to act like I was getting along, like it didn't bother me, like I could go home with him or not, take it or leave it. We went home together and went to bed, just like I knew we would, and it was a mechanical, in-and-out thing. I knew he didn't feel for me the same way I felt for him that night. I think he was doing it basically as a release, while I was doing it to be close to him again. I just wanted to be close to him, and if it meant maybe allowing myself to be used a little, okay. In a sense I enjoyed it, in that it was satisfying to be close to someone I wanted so much. I didn't feel bad about it. It wasn't that different from some times we had had when we were together, when we would go out and have a good time and then go right home and go to bed.

All along Donna had taken a back seat and made herself and her desires inconspicuous. She feared that if she challenged Bob, she would lose him. Yet in the end these strategies failed. Donna lost Bob as much because of her diffidence as in spite of it, since she never really asserted herself as a contender for a central place in his life.

What if Donna had taken the risk of demanding that Bob take her seriously and accord her equality in their relationship? She might have gained his respect, changed the way they related to each other, and perhaps displaced her rival for his affections. On the other hand, she might have lost him sooner, as she feared she would. In that event, she would have discovered unmistakably, and with less investment of time and emotion, that this relationship held little future potential for her, since Bob's involvement with her was predicated on her taking a compliant role. Had she tested the limits of the relationship and lost, she would have emerged not only free to try other involvements, but also strengthened psychologically by her assertion of self-respect.

JUDY AND FRANK: ECHOES OF COMPLIANCE PAST

When Judy met Frank at the beach where she regularly hung out with her girlfriends, she was seventeen and had never been seriously involved with a man. She saw Frank's swarthy, handsome face, his slim, trim build, his skill with a surfboard, and the charm and polish he had developed by the age of twenty-three. She did not see his quick temper, his tendency toward violence, or his history of irregular employment and minor scrapes with the law. All of her well-to-do friends were impressed with Frank, but he only had eyes for Judy, a tall, blonde California girl with a beautiful complexion and an open, inviting expression. He pursued her, and they began dating.

Early on, Judy began to see signs of Frank's possessive, domineering nature. When he worked he would call her at scheduled breaks in his workday, and if he could not reach her he would confront her with intrusive questions. He began to show this jealous side after he and Judy became sexually intimate. Although Judy had never had sex with anyone before, she thought of sex as a normal, healthy activity. Frank seemed a suitable first sexual partner because he was so attractive and self-confident. To her surprise, the experience itself was a letdown. It was all intercourse, no foreplay. "Is that all there is?" she thought, but she couldn't really be sure, since she had no other experiences with which to compare it.

Judy acceded to Frank's demands. She accepted a relationship in which he defined the terms and controlled their interactions.

> Sex wasn't for my pleasure; it was mostly for his. After a while I felt like he was using me as an exercise board. Since he was always angry at me, I would use sex as one way to please him. "If that's what keeps him happy . . . ," I thought. Since I hadn't had a sexual relationship before, I thought that was what it was supposed to be.
>
> He told me what was good and bad. Like he said you never did the F-word; you "made love." To hear him tell it, he always made love. But I know now that he didn't know what making love was. It wasn't even close to what it could be.

There is an echo here of Donna, who accommodated Bob sexually so as to be able to feel close to him. But Frank exercised a coercive and at times brutal domination of Judy that had no counterpart in the more sophisticated world of Donna and Bob. As Frank took up more of Judy's time, prohibited her from going to the beach, and monopolized her attention at the weekend dances where she used to socialize with others, Judy felt increasingly isolated from her friends. "We'd spend days just sitting around the house," she recollects. "I'd always be with him, and I couldn't go anywhere by myself." Once when she went to visit a close friend, Frank demanded that she be back home in an hour so that he could reach her by phone. Even her relationship with her parents was not safe from his attacks.

> Once on the spur of the moment my Dad took me out to get something I needed. I left a message for Frank in case he called. He did call, and when I got back he was real mad at me. He yelled, "Why didn't you tell me? Who said you could go?" My God, I was with my Dad! I couldn't believe Frank did that. It was a sign that things were getting out of control.

Frank's insecurity, so evident even with regard to Judy's family and friends, veered toward the extreme when another man came into view. Judy, from a more mature perspective, recalls his behavior—and hers—with some disbelief:

> Frank had an attractive male friend who always used to pop up when we went dancing. To Frank, it was as if I was always looking at this guy. It got to the point where I'd have to look at the floor when we danced rather than look around and by coincidence make eye contact with the guy. Even when we weren't dancing, there was the chance that I'd happen to see him if I let my eyes wander—which made things hard for me when I wanted to look for my friends! It got to the point where I'd have to look straight ahead when I was driving with Frank, because if I looked to the side he'd say I was looking for this other guy. "Who are you looking at over there?" he'd scream.

Frank was romantically obsessed with Judy and was anxious and afraid of losing her. With his questionable past, his criminal associations, and his uncertain prospects, he did not feel confident that he could hold the affection of a woman who came from respectable society. In Judy he found a woman who was not only respectable, but also very attractive—a real prize in his and his friends' eyes. Realizing, perhaps, that his initial success with her was due to her being young and impressionable, he felt that he could keep her only if he monopolized her completely. He isolated her from other people because he feared that he would not look good in comparison with anyone else—whether his friend, her friend, or her father. He did not want her to be exposed to people who might lead her to question her involvement with him. He controlled his romantic anxiety by holding her almost as a prisoner, believing that he could thereby remain her sole source of value, meaning, and satisfaction.

He even tried to persuade her not to go to college—a desperate tactic which made sense from his perspective. The only way he felt he could hold on to her was to keep her from growing up, to preserve her as the seventeen-year-old who had fallen for him when they first met. But he was unsuccessful, as Judy relates:

> Here's this man telling me my lifelong dream wasn't going to be, just because he said so. I said I was going to do it anyway. There weren't a lot of things I put my foot down about, but that was one. I sometimes think, though, that he could have talked me out of it if I had gone out with him longer before I started college. That would have been a big regret for me.

Judy put her foot down about one other issue as well. That was birth control, which she made a condition of having sex with Frank. She explains that "I cared about him and all, but I knew there was no way I would have a kid with him." Limited as her experience was, Judy nonetheless realized that this was not the man she wanted to marry. She thereby managed to maintain a degree of psychological, if not physical, independence. In this respect, her experience contrasts with that of Donna, who aborted an unplanned, but perhaps not totally unwished for pregnancy. Judy believes that she was not anxiously attached to Frank, as Donna was to Bob. "I just liked him and liked dating him," she says matter-of-factly. It was Frank's dominating role, rather than her compliant one, that more clearly represented a tactic of anxious romantic attachment. By issuing threatening orders that Judy obeyed, Frank reassured himself of her devotion and thus reduced his anxiety.

Why, then, did Judy comply with what, in retrospect, appear as arbitrary, irrational, and demeaning demands? In part, Frank elicited from her a reaction of sympathy. "I cared about him, and I cared what happened to him, because he'd supposedly been through so much," she explains. "It was always 'Poor Frank—he's been wronged.'" Although Frank was unable in the end to isolate Judy from the opinions and values of others, for a time he prevailed on her to understand and accept him on his own terms.

> He openly admitted to me that he used to hit his previous girlfriend, who came from his part of town. Yet he had never hit me. There were times when he got so angry and frustrated, I'm sure he would have hit somebody else in my place. Maybe that was his way of showing he loved me. Love to

him meant never hitting your girlfriend. It was kind of sick, but I think that's how he showed his love.

Judy's acceptance of Frank also stemmed from inexperience. Having no other models of what a romantic relationship was, she took a while to discover that she wanted—and could demand—more than Frank offered. Coming from an intact, loving family, she could draw on a reserve of emotional security that protected her from being completely enmeshed in her attachment to Frank. At the same time, her family was one that exemplified and taught conventional sex roles. Her brother strongly identified with his father, while Judy stayed close to her mother and took the same passive, submissive role that she saw her mother play. This background left her vulnerable to Frank's overbearing demands.

For the year or so that she was involved with Frank, Judy attempted to conceal his excesses from her family and friends. She was embarrassed to let them see how he was treating her, and she did not want them to pressure her to give him up. The relationship fell apart, however, when Frank openly violated her family's standards, which were also her own.

> I bore these things pretty much alone. My best friend knew some of what was going on, but she didn't really understand until one night toward the end. We all went out to go dancing, and Frank was a little drunk; he always turned into a jerk when he was drinking. For the first time he got rough with me, pulling my arm hard as he said, "Get in the car! Get in the car!" So we went, a bunch of us piled into my friend's little car, and I was sitting on his lap. He was berating me, like yelling in whispers, and I was crying, and he was grabbing my chin and turning my face. My friend saw him doing this and said, "I saw that!" She pulled over to kick him out of the car, but he apologized and swore he hadn't hurt me.
>
> We stopped at a liquor store on the way to the dance pavilion. By that time he was threatening everyone in the car without their knowing it. He was telling me that if I behaved, my friends would be okay. Then he went into the store and started a fight with the cashier. I took off and ran up on the dunes. He came out and was real mad that I was gone. He couldn't see me in the dark, and he kept calling me while my best friend was upset and crying and yelling at him. It was a real big scene, and I just sat there on the dunes watching everybody. I was torn between worrying about how he'd abuse me if I was there and how he'd abuse everybody else if I wasn't there. Finally he just punched a trash barrel. My friends were really scared.
>
> Eventually we went up on the dance pavilion. When we left it was pretty obvious that I wasn't happy and that he was just dragging me away. A girl I didn't know said to him, "If you hurt her, I'm going to get you."

He took me to the parking lot and yelled at me and shook me by the arms for I don't know how long. It left bruises on the back of my arms. It was so embarrassing to have my friends waiting for us while he was doing this to me. They were waiting to leave, but he wouldn't let me go. I felt hopeless. All I could do was let him yell and shake me until he was done. It was like "Oh, well, what else can I do? Maybe he'll shut up soon, so we can all leave."

With the help of her parents, Judy extricated herself from the relationship after the following incident:

I went to pick him up to go to a movie, and he came in a car with some guys I considered bad, that I didn't want him hanging around with. He had been drinking. He got in the car and told me to move over because he was going to drive. He knew I didn't let people drive my car, but there was no fighting with him when he'd been drinking. So I moved over. Then a man walked past, a harmless guy I knew from the store where I worked. He must have looked the wrong way, because Frank started yelling at him, "What are you looking at?" The guy showed some sign of sticking up for himself, so Frank got out and started walking toward him. I got freaked out and took off in my car. I came home crying and upset. I told my parents about how he'd been acting. I was sure he was going to come up there and threaten my family—and he had the connections to get some-body killed. He did come, and my Mom gave him back all the things he had given me and told him off, like he was a big bully.

When I ran off I didn't think I was ending the relationship; it was just an instinctive reaction to get out of there. When things calmed down I told my parents I knew it was pretty much over, and I told Frank to leave me alone.

But she still had one more intimidating experience to go through:

Afterward I'd see him around, and he'd act like he wanted to get back together. One night when I got out of work he showed up and grabbed me behind a building. He had a good hold on me—I couldn't get out of it—and he gave me a lot of verbal abuse. It was the first time I'd tried to get away from him. I tried punching him, a knee in the groin, but it didn't work. Finally, when I didn't come home for dinner, my Dad came looking for me and saw my car. I yelled when I saw him, and Frank let me go. That night I registered a complaint with the police. At first they didn't take me seriously because I wasn't bruised or bleeding, but when they looked up Frank's record of woman battering they sent two police cars just to talk to him.

After that Frank never again confronted Judy directly. But he would still show up when she left work and smile and wave to her from across the street, which sent chills up her spine. Judy was left suffering with symptoms of post-traumatic-stress syndrome:

> I was afraid to go anywhere by myself. Everywhere I went, I'd think he'd be there, and I'd be scared. I felt weak emotionally, and I was shocked that I'd been physically unable to get away from him. I'd had the cocky attitude that if any guy tried to hit me, I'd get him, but it doesn't work that way unless you know how.
>
>   When I did see him, it was real hard to talk to him. Eventually I was able to say, "You don't scare me," but it took a year to get there, and even then it was hard to move my lips because they were shaking. It was a big step for me to come across like that even when inside I was feeling, "Oh, my God, what am I doing?"

After more than a year of emotional recuperation, Judy became involved with Allan, a somewhat younger man whom she met while working at a summer job in a college laboratory. She welcomed the different tone and spirit of this relationship.

> I've always had this big thing about hugging, like with my mother. It made me mad that Frank couldn't hug me without having his hands wander. Allan is the best hugger. He'll always hug me, even when he's mad at me. We're very physical, sexual, not in an actual intercourse way, but with a lot of touching and nonverbal communication. I need that; I love it; I thrive on it.

Her introduction to a more full experience of sex was a revelation.

> I was real surprised when I was introduced to foreplay. It was like "Wow!" There was so much more to it than I had known—a reciprocal giving rather than taking. We don't have sex often—which is not like with Frank, where the relationship was based on sex. That's important to me. I'm always testing Allan. We'll be playing around, and then I'll say, "No," and wait for the angry reaction I'd get from Frank. But Allan says, "Okay," and hugs me, and I love that. If I refused Frank, he'd push me away and not want to have anything to do with me until I agreed to have sex. A friend of mine had a boyfriend who would kick her out of bed if she refused him. He'd tell her to go find someplace else to sleep. What makes these people think they can act like that toward another human being? I can't comprehend it.

Here Judy not only reacts to and describes her sexual relationship with Allan by contrasting it with her relationship with Frank, but even deliberately tests the relationship so as to assure herself that it really is different. Her concern to repudiate her involvement with Frank extends even to the language in which she and her boyfriend speak to each other.

> Frank always called me "stupid," so now if Allan uses that word, even in an innocently joking way, it gets me upset. Frank would also say, "You're mine, and I own you"; he had this conception that he owned my body. So when Allan would say, "You're mine," I'd say, "No, I'm mine." It would frustrate him because he didn't mean it the same way; with him it was just something cute and harmless. So we worked on a compromise, where I "share myself" with him. People don't understand why these little things hang on, now that it's been a few years since I was with Frank. It's really strange. It's the incredible power he had over me.

The ghost of Frank is very much present in Judy's life. The compliant role he taught (or reinforced in) her is hard to unlearn.

> In sex the only goal was to please him—which still hangs on with me, as if that's still the goal. It's like the foreplay is for me, and the intercourse is for the man. This causes a conflict because Allan feels that he's not pleasing me. He can sense that I'm doing it just to please him, and he's not like that. He'd rather suit me than himself.

In some ways, in spite of herself, Judy persists in complying, as if she were still involved with Frank and not Allan. In other ways she reacts especially strongly against any reminders of Frank in her current relationship. She reacts not only by asserting her independence, but also by reversing roles and exerting control herself.

> I find myself demanding a lot from Allan, like "This is how I want this done," and "You'd better do this." Like when I get sick, he'll pamper me and baby me, but when he gets sick I'll tell him off for not taking care of himself. It's mean of me, because he's so good to me. I get the feeling that I'm not nice enough to Allan, but I want to make sure things are right. I want to have things my way a lot, and yet I'm trying to talk him out of letting me have my way all the time. I know how it feels to be on the short end of the stick, and I don't want it to be like that.
>
> I control the amount of affection we display in public. I don't like him kissing me in public, but if I want to kiss him in public it's okay with him.

I demand that he treat me like a lady. And of course, he can be friendly with other girls, but he knows it stops there. It's very satisfying to me when other girls are interested in him, because I know it's me he wants. I hate saying it this way, but he's *mine*.

Judy smiles when she says, "He's mine," because she realizes that these are the very words she objects to her boyfriend's saying about her. On the one hand, she desires fairness and reciprocity in the relationship. On the other hand, she feels a need to compensate for past humiliations by learning what it is like to be in control. In choosing a younger, rather obliging man such as Allan, Judy may feel that she needs to experience dominance as well as submission as she grows to achieve self-respect and mutuality in love.

NANCY AND KEVIN: GO AHEAD, MAKE ME OVER

Nancy, a divorced parent of thirty-seven, had her face surgically made over at the request of her boyfriend, Kevin. When he had first made the suggestion several months earlier, she broke up with him, not out of outrage but because she despaired of ever making herself look beautiful enough to please him. "I just couldn't handle it anymore," she recalls. "I couldn't cope with how he wanted me to be." Returning to him after briefly dating several other men, she arranged for cosmetic surgery without his asking a second time.

> Kevin needs to have a girlfriend who is beautiful. All his girlfriends before have been very modellike: big busts, tiny figures, perfect hair, perfect faces. He keeps pictures of them in his wallet. I broke up with him because he made me feel so self-conscious and insecure about my appearance that I couldn't stand it. When I came back to him, he didn't tell me not to have the makeover done. He didn't say, "You don't have to bother with it." So I had the work done on my face.
>
> I'm not flashy. I'm a plain, conservative person, but I take care of myself. I wear light makeup when I feel it's appropriate, but I never felt I had to wear makeup every day. I have some grey in my hair, and I have it dyed periodically, but I don't do my hair fancy, and I don't wear much jewelry. Kevin has made me feel self-conscious about my makeup, my wardrobe, everything.
>
> He's looking for a makeover class so I can have a color analysis and all. And he's going to show me how to dress. A friend of his has a store with very contemporary clothes, some of them quite flashy, and he's going to bring me in so she can show me what to wear. He's going to pay for the makeover, but not for the clothes, which he says I need anyway, so I'll have to pay for them myself. He says I can change my wardrobe gradually, replacing things one at a time as I can afford them. Meanwhile, I've been

giving away a lot of my clothes to a friend, who's been getting quite a windfall!

Kevin also wants me to pose for a photo wearing one of those little outfits — it's like a corset with nylons with the old-fashioned garters. I said, "Well, I guess so. I've never really thought about it. My body isn't that bad, but that's just not me." He said, "No, you have a really nice body, but you don't know how to show it."

My mother says, "Why are you doing this to yourself? Why do you pick someone who'll probably never think you're beautiful?" Many men I've dated have thought I'm pretty. Some say I look stunning when I'm all dressed up. My twelve-year-old daughter is furious with me; she thinks what I'm doing is terrible. She says, "You're giving away your clothes for a man? I can't believe you're doing this, Ma." I tell her, "It's something I've decided is worth it."

What keeps me hanging in there is that Kevin tells me I'm the nicest person he's ever known. He just wishes he could put my personality in another woman's body!

Why is it worth it for Nancy to accommodate herself so thoroughly to Kevin's specifications? Why would this woman have herself made over to conform to an image in her lover's mind?

Nancy came from a strictly religious family in which there was no drinking, no smoking, no sweets, and, it seemed, not enough love.

My father is a very cold person, unable to express love. He has never hugged, kissed, or physically touched us children. My mother is a cold person, too, though she'll occasionally hug you or give you a peck on the cheek. She knows she's not a warm, hugging person, though she would tell us she loved us.

All of the children were motivated to excel academically and to undertake professional careers in the face of financial hardship. Yet Nancy felt that she never got the appreciation she deserved. "Here I was," she laments, "an all-A student all the time, overachieving because I wanted some recognition from my father, and he never said a word to me about my grades." Another kind of appreciation likewise eluded her.

My father has never said anything critical of my mother's appearance. He's always told her that she's the most beautiful woman in the world for him, even though she says she knows she isn't. But they never said anything like that to me. My mother would say, "Beauty isn't what matters. It's what's inside that counts." I never got what I wanted to hear, which was, "You're pretty."

The man she married also helped to undermine her body image:

> My ex-husband did the same thing. Sometimes he'd sing the song, "If you want to be happy for the rest of your life, never make a pretty woman your wife." He played up my plainness, saying I wouldn't cheat on him because I was a nice, homey, plain girl. That's what I've always been told. Maybe that's why I'm so willing to accept it from Kevin, too. Obviously, I'm not happy about it.

Nancy attributes her disastrous marriage to her rigid, sheltered upbringing, which left her gullible and ill-equipped to make sensible choices. "Until I was seventeen," she recalls, "I had to bring my brother on my dates—what few dates you have when you have to bring your brother along!" A few years later, teaching school in a rural area where most of her colleagues were married, she fully expected that she would become "an old maid living on my pension, with no children, no living relatives." Thus, when a man she had only known for weeks proposed marriage, she had considerable incentive to "fall in love."

> My mother wanted me to wait; she thought there was something funny about him. But I said, "Why wait? People wait a lot longer and still make the wrong choice. I'm in love, and he treats me nice. What more do I need?" Actually, he was a con artist with women. I didn't know that he had been married before, that he had children, and that he wasn't even divorced when he married me!

Nancy believes that she fell into this trap because she was brought up to follow the rules and was never told that the rest of the world did not always do the same. High school valedictorian and honor student in college, she was not exposed to drug abuse and violence. Neither her intelligence nor her education protected her from her fiancé's dishonesty. "I asked all the right questions before we got married," she says, "and got all the right lies for answers."

She soon discovered that her husband was an alcoholic and drug addict. "He had only an occasional drink when we were going together, but he got drunk on our wedding night and never stopped." Nancy began working double shifts to pay the bills and support her husband's addictions as well. A few months after their marriage he began to beat her. In shame she hid her wounds, which included serious back injuries that required surgery. Nancy explains how these occurred:

Most commonly he would grab me and slam me into the edge of a wall or a counter. I was very submissive. Like the woman in *The Burning Bed* I would go into the kitchen and cringe in the corner, covering my head, hoping he wouldn't hit my face.

Nancy says that she stayed in this marriage for ten years for religious reasons.

In my family you marry for life; there is no divorce. My parents even tried to convince me to leave, but I feared I would go to hell if I did; they had taught me all too well. The other reason I didn't leave was that my father had drilled it into us that you stay a virgin until you marry and then you marry for life, because no decent man will want you if you're not a good girl. Divorce and remarriage did not seem a possibility for me because once I was divorced, that was it—I'd be a spoiled woman. My husband also would remind me of my religion—that this was for life, and that no one else would want me now because I was no good to anyone, anyone but him.

My parents left the church over what happened to me. They felt they had done me a terrible injustice, raising me like that.

Nancy's moral precepts, combined with a drastically limited sense of her options, led her to believe she had made her bed and now must lie in it. She felt that she was not entitled to take what others would regard as lifesaving steps to escape her desperate situation. She gives one additional reason for not leaving her husband:

To me it was like raising a sick child. You don't desert a child that's born with brain damage. I still cared about my husband even when I wanted to leave. At times I hated him, but I still needed to take care of him. That was my responsibility.

Nancy finally did leave her husband after he held a gun to her head and threatened to kill her. By then her daughter was old enough to protest, and Nancy called the police.

Understandably, Nancy's perceptions of men after her separation were filled with mistrust. If a man wasn't just after sex, he was after the financial security she could offer him. Amid this discouraging field, Kevin somehow stood out for her as less self-serving than the others.

I did a lot of dating before Kevin and in the months when I wasn't seeing Kevin, and I didn't come up short on marriage proposals. In a matter of a few days they're in love and they want to marry me. Something's wrong there, and I know it's something I'm supplying that they're very very needy for. One man wanted me because I was young. I looked beautiful to him because I was fifteen years younger than he was. There's always something men want me for. Either they want me to support them, or they go for me because I have a nice home that I've worked hard to earn. Kevin doesn't need any of that. He has an excellent job and his own home. So he has no ulterior motives if he marries me. He's the only man I've dated who didn't need me for something other than myself and my love. I'm secure with him that way. Unfortunately, I'm not pretty enough for him, which makes me insecure because he might leave me if he meets that perfect woman who's got my personality in the body he's looking for.

"I'm easy to please," says Nancy. "The only thing I require of men is that they love me, even if they're lying. If they say it, I'm going to believe it, at least for a while—I'm a little smarter than I used to be. If they love me and they're kind to me, those are the two things I need." Is that really so? The complexity of her situation and her motives defies her succinct and insightful summary. For instance, one man did give her that kind of consideration, and she rejected him.

After I broke up with Kevin, one guy I was dating was head over heels for me. It was wonderful, except that I didn't feel that way about him. I kept trying to feel that way, but I couldn't. He would have made an excellent husband for me, the kind my mother wanted me to have, who would be gentle and treat me nice and appreciate me more. But I couldn't do it. I kept thinking about Kevin, and since I obviously was in love with him, I decided that it was worth going back to him to experience that love. After all, he does think I'm a wonderful person. So I thought, "Well, small sacrifice, right? To have to work on my face, hair, body, and clothes." I just told him it bothered me and asked him to try to criticize me only a little at a time so I could try to fix those things.

The man Nancy loves, while financially secure, has insecurities of his own. "He's very self-conscious about being short," she notes. "Before he met me, he only went out with women who were taller than he is." Previously, Kevin seems to have taken considerable effort to woo tall, attractive women to compensate for his own unimpressive appearance. With Nancy he apparently changed his strategy. Nancy relates some things he has told her which suggest what he may be getting from their relationship.

I'm very attracted to him, although I know that most people think he's rather homely and too short. He's told me that this is the easiest relationship he's ever had, and that's why he's taken advantage of me at times. He didn't have to work at it at all; it was all just there for him. With all the other women he really had to work at it. He had to spend a lot of money on them, because beautiful women demand that. He told me, "You don't demand or expect anything." I guess I'm not beautiful enough to do that.

When Nancy broke up with Kevin, he became very upset and tried to tell her that she did not need to go through with the facelift after all. "I know he's a little insecure now because I *have* left once," she reports, "and he said he's worried about whether I'll ever walk away from him again." Perhaps he has become dependent on this woman with whom he can play the dominant role that other women have usurped in the past.

For her part, Nancy has concluded that "I've had far worse—I'm used to being beaten physically—so this hassle about my appearance is minimal in exchange for someone who is loving and kind." Now, as when she was married (although in a less extreme way), Nancy is a case of what we have referred to as low freedom of movement. That is, she feels a strong need for love, but has little expectation of being able to satisfy it outside of her present relationship. Rightly or not, she still fears that she has nowhere else to go.

Meanwhile, the makeover goes on:

I asked Kevin when we got back together whether he wanted me to have breast implants. Thank goodness—I hope he doesn't change his mind!—he said no, but not for the reason I had hoped. I thought he would say that big breasts aren't that important, but instead he said he heard the implants don't feel real. Wrong answer, Kevin, but I'm still relieved.

The facelift was painful, and it'll be a week before the stitches are off. I saw Kevin afterward, and he said he thought it was kind of a waste.

"A waste? You're kidding! What are you talking about?"

"I don't want you to feel you have to go doing these things for me. Why can't you do them for yourself?"

I wanted him to say that he realized it wasn't necessary, that he loves me just the way I am. But somehow it never comes out that way. It always comes out sounding like "Well, really, it doesn't do much good. You're still not going to look like my ex."

SHELLEY AND TED: A COSTLY BLUFF

Shelley is a very attractive, bright student who has difficulty finding constructive outlets for her wit and energy. With an older sister who seemed to monopolize the paths to her mother's approval, Shelley expressed herself by rebelling, thereby gaining her father's sympathy, since he was a secret ally. She was very attuned to men, but, without emotional support from her mother, lacked confidence in her ability to attract and hold them. Instead of projecting the strengths she had, she was quick to anger and tried to force people into meeting her needs.

In her junior year of college Shelley became concerned about finding a permanent mate. Her boyfriend, Ted, was in no hurry. He was just as easy-going as Shelley was intense. He majored in sociology to keep open a wide range of options for himself, and was not particularly concerned that he might graduate without clear goals in either his personal or professional life. His favorite pastimes were the evenings he spent carousing and the weekends he went camping with his male friends. To Shelley's outrage, these outings sometimes extended into time he had planned to spend with her.

In a typical scene, Shelley waited all Saturday evening for Ted to call as he had promised. At eleven o'clock he called and, in a lighthearted tone, asked if he could come over. Shelley exploded. A heated exchange followed, until Shelley finally blurted out, "I don't want to see you anymore." Over the next two weeks she became depressed as she waited for the phone to ring. Finally, she called a friend, and the two women went out to a night spot and flirted with men. When Ted saw her there, he became jealous. The next day he called her. As had happened numerous times before, the couple got together again, and Ted showed more consideration for a few weeks until the next incident.

It was a volatile relationship, with Shelley locked into a pattern of domination and control, and Ted into one of inconsistent compliance and resistance. When he felt the heat of her wrath, he was all the more likely to take refuge in friends and activities. She punished him actively; he punished her passively by withdrawing his attention from her.

Ted realized that Shelley would not follow through on her threats to break off the relationship. The same insecurity that led her to try to reduce Ted to docility also rendered her incapable of striking out on her own. Had she been able to be more sensitive to his needs, Shelley would have been a good catch for Ted. However, her punitive, irritable manner made the prospect of marrying her less attractive to him. Her tactics of control were counterproductive, since they perpetuated rather than resolved her problems with Ted. Short of finding a more suitable partner, her best hope lay in respecting Ted's need for independence and showing him that he could satisfy her needs in a way that would not compromise his own.

TACTICS OF ATTACHMENT: INGRATIATION

In between domination and compliance lie all the varieties of pleading, demanding, cajoling, and bribing that make up the repertoire of anxious romantic attachment. In the absence of mutual positive regard and secure attachment, people seek to meet their needs by striking tacit deals and obtaining promises of future reciprocation. These tactics come under the heading of *ingratiation*. As a tactic of insecure romantic love, ingratiation means giving services, goods, or other tokens or expressions of love in the hope of creating in the partner a sense of indebtedness and obligation. Its purpose is to elicit reciprocal signs of the partner's affection and loyalty.

Ingratiation grows out of traditional modes of courtship in which various gifts, attentions, considerations, and gestures (from preparing a dinner to taking someone out on the town) are used to win someone's favor.

However, if the gifts are inappropriately large, if they cannot be assimilated into the couple's shared emotional experience, and if they cannot be repaid in equal measure, then ingratiation is being used as a tactic. It works as long as the recipient values what is given and feels comfortable about repaying it with love and affection. The danger is that the recipient may not be comfortable with gifts given on those terms, but rather may see them as representing a burden, an obligation. Feeling guilty and angry to be receiving this accumulation of benefits that he or she is unwilling or unable to repay, the partner may end the relationship.

At first sight, ingratiation may seem to resemble compliance rather than domination. However, the sense of obligation it imposes makes it a manipulative strategy, and some variations have the character of extortion or blackmail. Ingratiation, when it gets out of hand, brings about a breakdown in the equality of the relationship. Usually, it is the person who receives less who feels aggrieved over a breakdown in equality. In the case of ingratiation, resentment is felt instead by the one who receives more.

Ingratiation represents an effort to buy security, like making deposits into a bank. Most relationships, however, reach a point in their development when the partners no longer keep mental ledgers in which they compare immediate gains and losses. Ingratiation as a tactic backfires when it retards the evolution of a relationship to that level of trust and intimacy. A person who is always trying to keep up an equal (or more than equal) exchange with his or her partner may keep the partner's focus on the superficial tally of the exchange rather than on feelings of love. You may genuinely like someone, but if that person keeps giving you things, you may start to think that you are involved with that person for the sake of the gifts rather than as an emotional attachment.

CHARLIE AND ELEANOR: YOUR LOYAL SERVANT

Charlie is a thirty-year-old graduate student who is anxiously attached to his girlfriend, Eleanor. Eleanor, who works six days a week as a nurse practitioner, resents the fact that Charlie has some free time during the week. Her disapproval of his "prolonged adolescence" as an "academic bum" contributes to his feeling insecure about the possibility of losing this woman, to whom he feels very attracted and whom he wants to marry. Charlie's response is to redouble his efforts to win Eleanor's approval.

> I quite frequently spend those free hours willingly, and with a zeal unknown to other activities I carry out for myself, doing things for Eleanor. (I realize, of course, that in a way I'm doing these things for myself as well.) For instance, I'd madly clean her bathroom for two hours so that she could have more time for herself—anything, *anything* to make her feel loved. I'd get up at 6:00 A.M. to get her child off to the sitter with her and get wound up in all the anxiety of her leaving in the morning. So after all this, after my cleaning her bathroom down to the last tile, what happens? She explodes in a fit of anger, saying that she has to pay back in guilt the things I've done for her. Just because I mention that I'm going to bed early because I'm exhausted from cleaning the bathroom, she gets upset and says I can't possibly be tired after staying home and doing something like that—not when she's been out working for eight hours.

Although Eleanor sounds ungrateful, she does have reason to say that Charlie is trying to make her feel guilty. His actions seem to say, "How can you not love me after all I do for you?" Eleanor, on the other hand, knows that if she cannot freely give Charlie her love, she surely cannot make it available for such a price.

Charlie also seeks tangible reassurance of his partner's love through frequent sexual contact.

> I am an extremely sexual person, what you would call a satyr. When I find a woman extremely attractive—and only then—I can't get enough of her. I would gladly make love with Eleanor daily—twice, three times daily. Unfortunately, she's not nearly as sexual. This causes discomfort for both of us: for her, because she feels guilty for not accommodating me; for me,

because I feel the anguish of unfulfilled attraction to someone who is
distant. Part of the distance, I think, comes from the work issue. She
seems to feel, "If you haven't worked all day, you haven't earned the right
to make love with me."

Of course, it is not unusual for a man and a woman to have different levels of
sexual desire. For Charlie, though, this is an especially sensitive issue.
Susceptible as he is to feelings of anxiety in the absence of recent confirmation
of his partner's love, he feels driven to have sex with great frequency so that he
can feel continually in contact with her. He has experienced this disparity in
sex drives with other women as well. He recognizes, for example, that a
woman with whom he was once involved might not have desired sex as often as
he did because of her preoccupation with her children. With his current
partner, however, he is unable to be so empathic. Instead of taking into
account that Eleanor may be tired after working all day, he acts as if he is
entitled to sex because of all that he has done for her. When she angrily resists
his demands and his attempts to make her feel obligated to him, he interprets
her refusal as a punitive denial of something he has earned.

According to Charlie, his insecurity stems from his lack of a strong male
role model with whom to identify. His father suffered from schizophrenia,
which clouded Charlie's early years with cosmic uncertainty.

> The first occurrence I recall was when I was four years old. I remember
> hearing some man making interesting and horrifying statements to my
> mother. I yelled out for my father, only to realize suddenly that the man
> *was* my father.
>
> I look at my father as a great provider and a good person who gave me as
> much as he could, but not as a strong, autonomous male. I think that my
> weakness as a person, as a man, lies in not having had that suave, bon
> vivant, confident, chum-type father relationship that would give me a
> sense of power, of manhood.

One might wonder whether anyone ever has the idealized father-son relationship that Charlie envisions. Nonetheless, Charlie's interpretation of his incompleteness, or incomplete sense of himself as a man fits his life history.
Working for a doctorate in his twenties, he dropped out for a time and then
switched fields, which delayed his emergence into adulthood for several more
years. He has continued to accept financial support from his parents, a fact
which contributes to Eleanor's as well as his own uneasiness about his
maturity and self-sufficiency. As he sums up his situation:

Driving me now is the sense that I have not achieved the earmarks of full maturation—a full-time job out in the world, marriage and having a child, and so forth. These things have escaped me for a variety of reasons, one being that I spent years being more interested in chasing women than in accomplishing those things.

Charlie spent his adolescence and young adulthood seeking immediate gratifications from women in place of education and self-development that would result in future rewards. As a result of this imbalance in his experience, he now relies even more on women—and on demonstrating his manhood frequently through sex—for basic reassurance of his worth. The foundation of his identity remains unstable, and he is vulnerable to disorientation when a woman he loves asserts her independence and freedom of movement.

When I'm involved with someone I'm very attracted to, I can't stay focused on myself. I lose myself, really. Other activities become trivial to me: I don't take the time to do them, and I don't care that I'm not doing them. I also have an extraordinarily difficult time coping when the woman I'm involved with seeks just that kind of space that I give up for myself. I view that as a threatening kind of separation. I get anxious for days thinking about the prospect of her going away for a day. For a day!

Charlie's anxieties are extreme, but his ability to articulate them sheds light on the little maneuvers many people go through to shore up the bulwarks of their emotional security. When Charlie pleads or bargains for love, he is seeking to build a favorable self-image that he fears might disappear at any moment if he is not hypervigilant. Most people do not live quite so close to the edge of existential uncertainty. Many people do, however, derive part of their sense of well-being and belonging in the world from their love relationships. This, then, is what is at stake in the tradeoffs, favors, demands, and manipulations by which all but the most fortunate establish who they are and where they stand in their closest ties with others.

TACTICS OF DETACHMENT: KEEPING A SAFE DISTANCE

When one or both partners in a relationship tend toward detachment rather than anxious romantic attachment, the tactics in which they engage are somewhat different. Whereas the anxiously attached individual's goal is to draw the partner into as close a relationship as possible, the detached individual and his or her partner enter into a more delicate kind of maneuvering. The detached person may try to establish a distance at which he or she can feel comfortable being intimately involved with another person. Not wanting to be dependent on love that can be withdrawn by the partner, a person who has suffered painful losses in the past may decline favors and intimacies in an effort to keep the ledger of love balanced, so that she or he can close out the account at any time. The partner, on the other hand, may use various tactics to bring the detached person into close enough contact for a relationship to exist at all. Such tactics may involve upsetting comfortable relationships and temporarily creating even greater distance, so as to shock the detached partner into acknowledging a need for real contact.

Previous chapters tell the tales of individuals who oscillate between detachment and anxious romantic attachment. After being drawn into an uncomfortably intense involvement, one may retreat to a place of safe isolation before venturing out again. For example, Alex (in Chapter 4), the engineer who opted for a peaceful existence after his wife left him, set limits on intimacy by seeing two women simultaneously. Couples also set limits on intimacy—and then adjust and revise them. The two partners may try out different degrees of closeness until they reach a stable working arrangement. Or they may simply bounce back and forth, merging and separating, closing ranks and retreating, in perpetual motion, reacting to the range of feelings they have toward each other.

JUNE AND TONY: CLOSENESS THROUGH DISTANCE

In the case of Marty and Fran in Chapter 2, a complacent husband who valued sports and friends over his marriage was made to realize how attached he felt to his wife when she suddenly left him. The story of June and Tony is a more subtle example of how such adjustments take place in the normal give-and-take between couples.

June and Tony were like many couples in which the wife feels unfulfilled emotionally in the face of the husband's preoccupation with work or recreation. They rarely went out together, and Tony spent much of his time out on business or at his workbench in the basement. June's response was to threaten divorce repeatedly. She would give monthly deadlines and announce that she would be moving out as soon as possible. She did not carry out these threats, however—nor was she about to do so, since she felt very attached to Tony and wanted to be closer to him.

Paradoxically, the turmoil seemed to bring the couple closer together in between the times when June shouted her threats of separation. When they were not at war with each other they went out together and talked intimately, mainly as a result of Tony's heightened interest in the relationship. To Tony, June's behavior was maddeningly inconsistent. She would let him get close only to push him away again. He complained:

> It's frightening. When we're out together and it feels so close, I know the next morning she's going to be a real bitch. How much longer is this going to go on? When can we get back to normal?

June, however, recognized that "normal" for Tony meant distant and detached. Now he was feeling the kinds of emotions she wanted him to experience, and he found them stressful. He would have liked nothing better than to go back to his old routines, which (like Marty) he would have done very quickly had he been able once again to feel securely in possession of his wife. To keep open the flow of feeling between them, June felt that she had to keep stirring up the waters with her dire expressions of discontent.

"She's always keeping me at arm's length," Tony protested. But arm's length was much closer than he had previously cared to be. By keeping Tony at arm's length, June kept him there *and no further.* By erecting a barrier between them, she drew him in to press up against the barrier, whereas before he had been drifting out of reach. Thus, what might have appeared to be a destabilization of their relationship was instead a process of adjustment and accommodation. Husband and wife exchanged signals to locate an appropriate meeting ground in the space between anxious attachment and detachment.

MARY LOU AND PAUL: THE DANCE OF DETACHMENT

Before their marriage, Mary Lou and Paul both had shied away from romantic involvements. Quite likely they were drawn to each other by the reserve they had in common, which made each less threatening to the other than a more demonstrative partner would have been. Even so, their mutual venture into intimacy required constant monitoring and fine-tuning, so that they could satisfy the need for closeness while preserving the distance that they also needed to maintain.

It was good for each of them to see that someone else shared the hesitations they felt about intimacy. Mary Lou had never known a man who was as open about his feelings as Paul. Hearing him talk, she recognized fears she had thought of as hers alone. It was as if he held up a mirror for her, in which she could observe and examine her inner experience with unaccustomed objectivity.

Still, there were tensions. Both of them wanted, yet feared, greater closeness. Paul's way of maintaining equilibrium was to give Mary Lou just enough emotional responsiveness to keep her involved, but not so much as to raise her feelings to an uncomfortably high pitch. When things got too hot, he would disengage from her.

At one point early in their relationship, before she recognized this pattern, Paul confided, "I feel I'm pulling away from you emotionally." Mary Lou reacted in a way that was typical for her. "He's going to leave me," she lamented. "I should never have gotten into this in the first place." Yet at that stage of their relationship, such a disclosure on his part might equally well have been an attempt to make contact with her and deepen the relationship. He could just as easily have stopped seeing her; instead, he expressed dissatisfaction with their relationship and sought to engage her in improving it.

Like billiard balls bouncing off each other and then ricocheting off the walls back toward each other again, Paul and Mary Lou seem to be reacting first to their fear of rejection and loneliness, then to their fear of losing their individual identities by merging with each other. Although they may moderate this pattern, this couple may have difficulty forming a stable, secure relationship. They have achieved a kind of equilibrium, but it is precarious at best and in danger of imbalance at any moment.

The stories in this chapter illustrate some of the tactics insecure romantic lovers use to meet their needs in intimate relationships. These tactics, which may be conscious or unconscious, are designed to elicit reassuring declarations of love from the partner. When such tactics are insufficient to provide the desired reassurance, the anxiously attached lover's preoccupations take a darker turn. Insecurity is then expressed in *jealousy,* the subject of the following chapter.

7

WHEN JEALOUSY

TAKES OVER

The office Christmas party was an awkward occasion for Linda, since she and Nick, who worked at the same firm, had recently decided to "cool it for a while" after dating for three years. Linda had not wanted the separation. In fact, she sometimes drove past his house to see whether an unfamiliar car was parked outside. Once or twice she stopped in to say hello, hoping that an impromptu visit might spark a reconciliation.

Linda brought a date to the office party; Nick did not. She noticed, however, that he was spending a good part of the evening with a young woman who had come with a female co-worker. "She's interested in him," Linda concluded.

Linda spent the night with her date, whom she had been seeing casually during the recent, troubled months of her relationship with Nick. As soon as he left in the morning, Linda was out the door, headed for Nick's place. When she got there she recognized the co-worker's car and, in her words, "flipped out." She goes on to tell the story:

> I banged on the door like a madwoman. When Nick came to the door, I screamed, "What the hell are you doing?"
> "What do you mean?" he said.
> "Who did you sleep with last night?"

"I slept alone."

"Like hell you did! Trudy's car is here, and Carole must be here, too."

"For your information, Trudy slept in the extra bedroom, and Carole slept on the sofabed in the living room."

I didn't believe him, of course. Meanwhile, the two women were in there hearing all this. I was acting like a lunatic. It was the worst thing I ever did in my life. I couldn't believe I did that. I was so mad at him.

"Which one did you sleep with?" I taunted him.

He threw it back in my face. "Weren't you with a date last night? I guess he took you home and then went home."

"No, he didn't."

"Then who are you, the pot calling the kettle black?"

"That's different."

"No, it isn't."

"Yes, it is."

When Nick started dating Carole, it was, according to Linda, "definitely the beginning of the end of our relationship." She describes the aftermath:

It was weird because I'd get snide when I'd see him. I'd ask him, "Are you still seeing Carole?"

"Yeah."

"Kind of petite, isn't she? I thought you liked full-bodied women."

"Yeah, but she's fun to be with."

"Yeah, but she's too thin. Besides, she's young—too young for you."

I think he kept seeing her just to spite me. I hope he didn't marry her for that reason.

As Linda's story illustrates, a feeling of entitlement to sexual exclusiveness is an important component of jealousy. Linda resented the fact that Nick was sleeping with someone else even though she was doing the same. The difference was that she did not want to be seeing anyone else; she did it only because Nick had made himself unavailable to her. Linda had trouble reconciling herself to Nick's "infidelity" because they had been going together so long. Apparently, the expectations of loyalty that a person develops in a long-standing relationship can persist even when anyone else would say that the relationship is over.

Doris married George ten years after she had ended an amicable first marriage for the sake of greater personal independence. Now fifty, she had known George for most of the decade since her divorce and had developed a comfortable, though not very passionate, relationship with him. Shortly after they were married, they went to the country club where George was a well-established figure. Doris was uncomfortable with the expansive greetings, accompanied by hugs and kisses, that the members exchanged. As they got ready to leave, a woman walked up to George and said, "We love you, bye-bye." George replied, "Love you, too." Doris describes her reaction:

> You might as well have thrown hot water in my face. I went right back to my office, hoping he would just let me be. He followed me in his car, and when we got there he asked me what was the matter.
>
> I said, "You can't go around telling people you love them. Not if you say you love me." I actually took my fist and pounded on his knee. "You can't do that! You can't say that! I don't toss 'We love you' around like that, and I don't think others should, either."
>
> "Look," he said, "I didn't say I was in love. I'm in love with you, but I can still love other people."
>
> "No, you love me, you love the children, but you really can't love anybody else."
>
> "My God, I can't cope with this! I have lots of friends. When I tell them, 'I love you,' I don't mean like I love *you*. You'll have to understand that, or we're going to have to call it quits here and now."
>
> That's what he needed to say at that point. All of a sudden I felt, "Oh, my Lord, he really will go." I knew that in a flash. And I said to him, "Promise me, then, that you won't say it in front of me. You can say it all you want, as long as I'm not around to hear it."
>
> That's the first and last time I displayed that kind of rage toward him. I was surprised to find myself pounding on his knee, like some child having a tantrum. I was embarrassed to face him for a while after that, because neither he nor I had seen that side of me. I've never in my life hit anyone; it hurt me to spank the children.

Although Doris never again confronted George with her jealousy, she still felt it regularly.

> Sometimes when he's talking to me I'm not listening to what he's saying; I'm listening to what he's not saying. I'm calculating when he left work, and when he arrived home. "Now what were you doing during that time?" I think. But I don't say it.
>
> I can't even meet him for a cocktail after work anymore, because I can't control my anger if I see a woman sitting at his table. It's just a bunch of friends talking after work; nobody means anything by it. But if I see someone sitting with him, I won't even go in. I'll get so angry I'll turn

around and walk out the door. It doesn't matter how old or young she is; it's somebody taking up his time instead of me.

Suppressing any direct expression of her anger, Doris began to suffer from severe headaches and high blood pressure. "I don't know who I'm mad at," she says. "I guess mostly I'm mad at myself."

> It's not George; it's me. He's very honest and up front about everything. He works so hard, he'd have very little time to do anything wrong if he wanted to, which he doesn't. But he's a gregarious person, and I'm a loner. He's always had platonic friendships, lady friends, who I think could become something more. But that's my wicked mind, my suspicious mind. The way I'm acting, I wouldn't want to live with me for ten minutes. A person can only take so much before he'll throw up his hands and leave.

Fearful of driving her husband away, Doris has begun to spend more time away from him to avoid friction. She has found that her jealousy abates when she is not in his presence, and she is not so concerned about where he is or what he is doing. "It's terrible to have to stay away from someone you love in order to feel good," she laments. She continues to try to understand why she has come to feel so insecure in middle age.

> My first husband came and went as he pleased, and it never crossed my mind to be jealous. And I don't think I love George so much more than I loved him. Maybe I'm getting scared now that I'm getting older and realize what I'd face if I lost George. I get panic attacks being around people, so maybe the prospect of finding another husband panics me as well. Yet here I am about to wipe out my marriage with my fear of losing it.

As Doris grows older, she has become less secure and confident of her husband's love. In reality, her claim of entitlement to sexual fidelity is respected by her husband. In Doris's mind, however, there is some question about whether he really is, or will remain, faithful. She realizes that her suspicions are irrational, yet she cannot dismiss them or mitigate the painful emotional reactions they cause her.

If Doris feels anxious when she is too close to her husband, Charlie feels anxious when he is too far away from his lover—indeed, when he is not in direct physical contact with her. In Chapter 6, Charlie spoke of his intense desire to merge, sexually and emotionally, with Eleanor, whose approval he sought with his slavish attention to household chores. "I get anxious for days thinking about the prospect of her going away for a day," he said. Not surprisingly, jealousy is a major component of Charlie's insecurity and possessiveness.

> I am extraordinarily jealous. The most trivial things make me feel, and at that moment believe, things that are so alien to the person I'm accusing that she finds me difficult to be with. It would be easier to deal with my jealousy if it were just a matter of "I feel threatened; I'm going to lose you; it frightens me." Unfortunately, my jealousy is accompanied by anger—a sarcastic, biting, childish, accusatory tone that makes the person at the receiving end of it want to run and hide, particularly if she does not agree that my perception of reality is correct. And I'd say ninety-eight percent of the time it's incorrect.
>
> If I'm ever going to live with a woman again, I need to tone down that jealousy. Given that it's been with me as long as I've been involved with women, you'd think I would have worked it through. I haven't been able to, I think, because it happens so damn quickly. It brews into a storm instantaneously, without my having the recourse of reflection. I don't have time to phrase things in a way that won't offend Eleanor. I don't have time to say, "I feel threatened. Will you help do a little reality testing with me, to tell me whether there's anything objectively to worry about?" At that moment I'm swept up in the things I'm saying. I believe them; I really do. Then five minutes, two minutes later I realize how absurd I'm being.

A recent instance of Charlie's jealousy occurred when Eleanor joined an exercise club. "I envisioned all these lithe male athletes in their gyrations," Charlie explains, "and Eleanor being attracted to one of them and leaving me for him, especially since things are so bad between us now." In reality, it is not Eleanor, but Charlie, who is so attuned to visual stimulation. He concedes that "she might look twice if she saw the most attractive man in the world, but I don't think she'd be tempted to leave."

But if Eleanor is not about to be tempted by a handsome face or a sexy body, what, then, might tempt her? In Charlie's view, there must be a rival somewhere. Charlie's jealousy arises not from anything Eleanor has done, but from his persistent expectations of disloyalty and betrayal on the part of women and his lack of confidence in himself to hold a woman's affection. If anything, Charlie is made more insecure by Eleanor's indifference to physical attractiveness, since he cannot anticipate from what angle a threat might come. Therefore, he feels driven to search for clues, images of men with whom she has been intimate in the past. As he explains:

> When I had a key to Eleanor's apartment, I got into the habit, the maddeningly joyful habit, of going over there and looking through her things—her pictures, letters, and so forth. It was a breach of her space, of her privacy, that she has found extraordinarily difficult to deal with. For me it was like a self-inflicted wound. I was driven to feel the pain, the jealousy, to be hurt by the jealousy, to say, "Aha, there, I was right!" rather than accept that these things were simply part of her past. I was on this demonic hunt to hurt myself, which I don't expect her to comprehend. When I first confessed that I went through her belongings, it put a lot of added stress on the relationship. I think it's also part of the reason we're taking this break from each other now.

Like Linda and Doris, Charlie tortures himself and alienates the object of his affection by his very obsession with her.

> This inordinate interest in Eleanor's every thought and feeling from her past is another dimension of my lovesickness. Others, presumably, would not be the least interested in going through somebody else's personal letters or would refrain from doing so for ethical reasons. My only explanation is that I was fascinated. I loved and hated every second of going through her photo albums and seeing other men. Most of all I wanted to find things written by the father of her child. I recently came across a letter from him, and it was quite painful for me to read it.

Although Charlie really does feel jealous and insecure, his accusations of disloyalty have a tactical quality, in that he uses them to demand reassurance of Eleanor's love. In this respect he differs from Doris, who hesitates to confront George with the particular provocations that (in spite of herself) set off her feelings of jealousy. Charlie, on the other hand, feels no compunction about confronting Eleanor. He goes digging for evidence with which to challenge her, hoping thereby to wring from her the definitive assurance of loyalty that always eludes him.

Both Doris and Charlie recognize the baselessness of their accusations, the irrationality of their jealous reactions, and even the morally compromising nature of their behavior. In Linda's case there really is infidelity on Nick's part, but it can hardly be called that when Nick has openly stated and openly acted on his intention to form a new relationship. Linda's irrationality lies not in suspecting disloyalty, but in feeling entitled to loyalty at this late date. Linda does, however, have one thing in common with Doris and Charlie: all three feel powerless to restrain themselves.

Jealousy is defined as the feelings, thoughts, and actions that arise when one believes that a significant relationship is threatened by a rival. Jealousy is one of three major indicators of an "attachment complex" that has its roots in childhood. The first of these indicators, anxious romantic attachment, typically occurs during the formation of a relationship, before the attachment is solidified. The last, depression, occurs after the relationship ends. Jealousy occurs somewhere between these two points—namely, when an existing relationship is threatened. Thus, measuring the intensity of a person's jealousy is one of three ways of "taking the temperature" of a person's attachment system. On such a thermometer, Linda, Doris, and Charlie would all register high fevers.

To be jealous (as opposed to envious), one must have an expectation of and feel entitled to sexual loyalty from one's partner. One may have this expectation without being fully aware of it; or one may have it but not have the self-confidence to invoke it, for fear of losing the relationship. The partner, meanwhile, may or may not agree about the extent of one's entitlement to sexual loyalty. In any case, when the partner is suspected of showing interest in a rival, there is an implicit judgment of disloyalty, injustice, inequality, or duplicity, and feelings of jealousy erupt.

In his book *Journey into Sexuality,* sociologist Ira L. Reiss presents evidence from many cultures showing that sexual jealousy exists in some form in all human societies. For example, even among the Lepcha, a sexually permissive Himalayan culture that has no specific word for jealousy, men and women become upset when their spouses have extramarital sexual relationships. Polygamous societies draw precise distinctions between permissible and taboo sexual involvements with multiple partners. The Eskimos, who have elaborate arrangements for sharing and swapping spouses, nonetheless are very suspicious of extramarital sexuality outside these prescribed and carefully regulated customs.

Sexual jealousy was found in all ninety-two cultures observed in a study by psychologist Ralph Hupka, and its strength in a given culture was proportional to the importance the culture attached to marriage. Sexuality symbolizes the marital bond and is closely linked with the expression of love, duty, pleasure, and kinship in a relationship of the greatest intimacy and importance. Jealousy arises out of a feeling that the partner is violating, abandoning, or devaluing a fundamental commitment by engaging in this form of intimacy with another person.

Jealousy may be felt when there is a real threat to the relationship (as in the case of Linda) or when the partner's disloyalty is merely a tormenting specter (as in the case of Charlie). Lovers often have good reason to be jealous. However, unfounded jealousy such as Charlie's can be extremely disruptive to a relationship. Where does it come from, if not from the partner's behavior? Some people learn in childhood to expect that they will be treated unjustly or that people cannot be trusted to be loyal. As adults, these individuals are likely to believe that they are being treated unjustly even when they are not. They carry their expectations of betrayal into ambiguous situations and react with jealousy in the absence of supporting evidence. Mildly flirtatious behavior by the partner can evoke sharp anger and a torrent of probing accusations.

Christine is an example of someone who can trace her jealous reactions to experiences she had when she was growing up. She relates this anecdote from a perspective of self-awareness:

> My father was unpredictable, and I feel the same thing in the man I'm seeing now. I'm very sensitive to his double messages. One day he mentioned this other woman he's seeing (we've been open about that) and started talking about some problems she was having. I let it go by for the moment. Three hours later we were having dinner, and I just blew up. I told him, "Don't you ever bring up her name to me anymore. I never want to hear her name again!"
>
> "I'm sorry, I'm sorry," he said.
>
> I mean, I just wanted to walk away. If I'd had my car, I would have got up and left him there. It was as if I couldn't figure out why he'd have anything to do with me after being with her. That came from my mother. She was selfish like that, wanting to be at the center of things. That's how I am, too. I couldn't stand the thought of his being with that woman and then coming over and being with me. "This will not do!" I thought. And I came on a little strong. Here we are in this restaurant, and he's like covering his face and saying, "Okay, okay." Poor guy.
>
> I dated one guy who would look at other women when we went out. He ended up with bruise marks on his shins that I'd give him under the table. That's terrible, I know.

Jealousy in some individuals has its roots in their lack of self-esteem. They may notice with envy the strikingly attractive features of a potential rival, and their own feeling of envy may lead them to assume that their partner is attracted to the object of that envy. This sense of comparative inadequacy and the suspicion of disloyalty that it arouses can motivate bitter remarks such as "I saw you looking at her. I bet you'd like to get her in bed, wouldn't you?"

Or, in some cases, people project their own desire to cheat on their partner and accuse the partner of cheating instead. Feeling sexually attracted to someone else, they assume the partner has similar feelings about others. These individuals become suspicious and vigilant even when the partner is entirely innocent.

People who experience jealousy sometimes use it tactically to eliminate perceived threats and gain reassurance of the partner's love. One may do this from a one-down position as Charlie does with Eleanor, sharing one's worry and anguish in an appeal to the partner's sympathy. Or one may do it from a one-up position, bludgeoning the partner with aggressive accusations of infidelity and threats of punitive retaliation. Recall Frank, Judy's insecure, domineering boyfriend in Chapter 6, whose jealous rages resulted in Judy's dancing with her eyes facing the floor so that she would not see any other man.

Extremely jealous lovers, whether acting out of self-doubt and fears of abandonment and betrayal or out of a need to dominate and to keep the partner responsive to their needs, can make the partner feel trapped, smothered, or always under siege. Constantly on guard and living on a tight leash of self-restraint, a person in Eleanor's or Judy's position may feel that she is losing not only her independence, but her personal integrity as well. Persistent accusations of disloyalty, whether made in a whining or badgering tone, can become a self-fulfilling prophecy, as the partner's love turns to hate and the jealous person "creates" a rejecting partner.

Whether jealousy rebounds on itself in this way depends on the relative power and resources of the two partners. A partner who is self-sufficient and has other options will not tolerate this treatment for long and will reject the jealous person, perhaps after a period of appeasement. Charlie, for example, runs the risk of rejection because Eleanor is an attractive professional woman who clearly has other options. Judy, as attracted as she was to Frank, did come to feel denigrated and abused and eventually left him. Although she was awed by Frank when she was seventeen, she separated from him as she grew more confident in her own right. Still, she needed to draw upon the support of her family to end the involvement.

WHEN DO WE BECOME JEALOUS?

What makes people jealous? What types of situations regularly provoke jealous reactions? To answer this question, Minor Chamblin, Carl Hindy, and Shelley Mackaman asked more than 150 people at the University of North Florida to write a paragraph describing each of the four most intense experiences of jealousy they had had in romantic relationships. This gave the researchers hundreds of stories from which to identify frequently recurring jealousy-provoking situations. The researchers then grouped the stories to see how often each type of situation occurred.

Seven types of situations that provoked jealousy were identified. They are listed here (with examples of each), starting with the one judged to be least threatening to the stability of a relationship and building up to the most threatening:

1. A former or desired partner with whom no present relationship exists shows interest in a third party or is known or believed to have a relationship with a third party. (This type of situation appeared in eleven percent of the accounts.)
    Examples:
    "I saw my ex-girlfriend out with a new guy."
    "The guy I was interested in asked my friend out instead of me."
    "I wanted to go out with her, but my friend asked her out first."

2. One feels neglected by one's current partner. There is no evidence that the partner has outside amorous interests. (This type of situation appeared in fourteen percent of the accounts.)
    Examples:
    "He worked late and was too tired to go out."
    "She went out with her girlfriends and didn't include me."

3. A third party shows interest in, or flirts with, the partner, who shows no reciprocal interest. (This type of situation appeared in eleven percent of the accounts.)
    Examples:
    "He tried to move in on my girlfriend."
    "She kept staring and making eyes at him [the partner]."

4. The partner is known or suspected to have behaved in a way, or to have been in a compromising situation, that suggests the *possibility* of infidelity. (This type of situation appeared in eighteen percent of the accounts.)

Examples:

"I saw my husband having lunch with a co-worker who is very attractive."

"My girlfriend was talking to her ex-boyfriend on the phone."

5. The partner is known or suspected to have flirted with or demonstrated casual interest in a third party. (This type of situation appeared in twenty-seven percent of the accounts.)

   Examples:

   "He [the partner] was staring at her and talking with her the whole time we were at the party and ignoring me."

   "He talked about his old girlfriend and how pretty and smart she was."

6. The partner expresses a desire to form other relationships or shows doubt about wanting an exclusive relationship. (This type of situation appeared in two percent of the accounts.)

   Example:

   "My girlfriend told me she wanted to date other people but keep me on as well."

7. The partner is known to have been unfaithful. (This type of situation appeared in sixteen percent of the accounts.)

   Example:

   "We went to a party, and he left with another girl."

   "I saw them in bed together."

Men and women experienced the different categories of situations in about the same proportions. As the figures given for each item show, feelings of intense jealousy were rarely reported when someone who was a former or desired (but not actual) partner showed interest in a third party (Item 1) or when a third party showed unreciprocated interest in the partner (Item 3). Intense jealousy was especially rare when the partner openly expressed interest in dating other people (Item 6). Predictably, feelings of intense jealousy were most commonly reported when there was direct evidence of mutual interest between the partner and a third party (Items 4, 5, and 7).

These findings support our idea that a sense of injustice is an important part of jealousy. In the case where a former or desired partner becomes involved with a third party, there is no betrayal on the partner's part, and there is also little threat to the relationship. The same is true when a third party shows unreciprocated interest in the partner. It is not surprising, then, that few people reported feeling jealous in these situations. (Whether jealousy occurs when a person is spurned by a desired partner depends on whether one is in a position to have competed for that person's affections and lost. Many men were envious, but not jealous, when Joe DiMaggio married Marilyn Monroe. But a man may be jealous when a woman rejects his advances in favor of his co-worker or roommate.) On the other hand, an open declaration by the partner of an intention to date other people would seem very threatening, yet even fewer people (by a wide margin) reported feelings of jealousy in this situation.

When the partner first asks for release from the commitment before becoming involved with others, one is more likely to feel rejection and depression than jealousy or anger. That depends, however, on the nature of the commitment. With a commitment of marriage, and especially one of some duration, feelings of entitlement are not readily relinquished just because one day the partner says, "I want out." Thus, one may still feel jealous after a divorce or even (as in the case of Linda, at the beginning of this chapter) after the ending of a long-standing relationship. This was not, however, an experience commonly reported by the young adults who participated in the study.

JEALOUSY AND ANXIOUS ROMANTIC ATTACHMENT

How is jealousy related to anxious romantic attachment? Is it essentially the same thing? Are the same people susceptible to both? To find out, we gave participants in our anxious-attachment study six questions developed by Gregory White for measuring jealousy in real-life situations. Two examples of these questions are:

"How intense were your feelings of jealousy in your relationship with this person?"

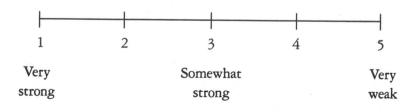

| 1 | 2 | 3 | 4 | 5 |

Very
strong

Somewhat
strong

Very
weak

"Compared to your other romantic relationships, were you more or less jealous in your relationship with this partner?"

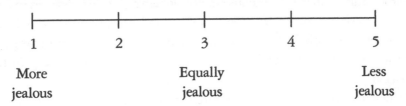

Participants were asked to answer these questions for each of their four most important past relationships—the same ones for which they answered the anxious-attachment questionnaire in Chapter 2 and the questions about their partners in Chapter 5.

Now, think of the four relationships you had in mind when you answered the questions in Chapters 2 and 5. How jealous were you in each? Did you experience the most jealousy in the relationships on which you scored highest on the anxious-romantic-attachment scale?

We found that the same people who tended to be anxiously attached to their partners also were likely to have relatively intense experiences of jealousy. Nonetheless, jealousy and anxious romantic attachment are not the same thing, although they are related.

We believe that a person who is susceptible to anxious romantic attachment is likely to experience jealousy, but that a person can experience jealousy without necessarily being anxiously attached. Why this is so begins to be clear when we look at the relationship between jealousy and the two main dimensions of anxious romantic attachment, which we have called romantic anxiety and romantic obsession. Jealousy was found to be more strongly associated with romantic obsession than with romantic anxiety, especially for women. In other words, jealousy tends to be felt more intensely by those who feel strongly attached to a highly valued partner than by those who feel anxious about their partner.

The strong link between jealousy and romantic obsession is consistent with what we understand jealousy to be: a response to a threat to a relationship's commitments. The relationship does not matter very much in the absence of a highly valued partner. It may seem surprising, however, that there is not a stronger association between jealousy and romantic anxiety, since we would expect people experiencing a jealous reaction to feel anxious. Under what conditions they do indeed feel anxious will become clear in the following sections, which explore the different ways people are jealous and the different reasons they give. These differences occur in the emotions people experience when they are jealous, as well as in the needs people are trying to satisfy in relationships where jealousy may arise.

THE EMOTIONAL EXPERIENCE OF JEALOUSY

There has been much speculation about what a person *feels* when in the throes of jealousy. Descartes thought of jealousy as a kind of fear. In *The Primal Scream*, Arthur Janov characterized it as an expression of anger. Freud emphasized the role of grief and resentment in the emotional makeup of jealousy. The many theoretical perspectives on this question suggest that jealousy consists not of a single emotional reaction, but of an array of emotions that may vary according to the individual and the circumstances. Different people experience different arrays of emotions when jealous. Our research sheds light on the emotions that occur in people who are jealous in their relationships.

Both men and women in our study experienced strong *distress* (indicated by their reporting that they were "downhearted," "sad," "miserable," or "discouraged") in relationships where they also experienced strong jealousy. This correlation was considerably higher for men, for whom distress was by far the emotion most strongly associated with jealousy. Distress was also the emotion most strongly associated with anxious romantic attachment—for *both* men and women. This common element of distress is consistent with the idea that anxious romantic attachment and jealousy are closely related emotional experiences with shared roots in a person's intimate attachments in childhood.

Otherwise, jealousy seems to have different emotional facets for women and men. These gender differences are more obvious with jealousy than with anxious romantic attachment (Chapter 2). Men—but not women—who were jealous, in addition to experiencing marked distress, also had strong feelings of *anger, contempt,* and *disgust. Shame* was felt more strongly in association with jealousy by men than by women, while *fear* was felt more strongly by women. We suggest that anger is the predominant emotion when a person's attention is focused on the partner's unfairness, and that fear is predominant when the person focuses instead on a threat to the continuity of the relationship. It may be harder for women to focus on the injustice done by a philandering partner. While a man may typically think, "How dare she cheat on me!" and become angry, a woman may think, "Hey, this means I may lose this guy," and get frightened.

To summarize these findings, men appear to experience jealousy outwardly, through emotions such as anger that motivate vigorous approach and attack. Women are more likely to experience it inwardly, through emotions such as fear that motivate avoidance or defense. This difference in emotional concomitants is more noticeable with regard to jealousy than with anxious romantic attachment. When a man feels that his relationship with a woman is threatened, he translates his anxiety into anger and attempts to reassert control.

When you recall that romantic anxiety in men also was accompanied by feelings of anger, contempt, and disgust, you can see how romantic anxiety can be strongly associated with jealousy in men, even though men typically did not report a feeling labeled "anxiety" in connection with jealousy. Both at the stage of anxious attachment and at that of jealousy, men have a way of experiencing anxiety *as* anger. They identify and express what they are feeling as anger, but their anger is fueled by anxiety, or a sense of being under siege.

Women who experienced jealousy more intensely when a relationship was threatened were often the very same women who experienced greater *sexual arousal* and *sexual guilt* at some point in the relationship. This was not true for men. Despite the trend toward greater equality in the ways women and men think, feel, and act concerning sexuality, women who invested themselves sexually in a relationship were more likely than men to have a jealous reaction when the relationship was threatened. If they were prone to feel guilty about sexuality, they were even more likely to feel jealous. Alternately, both the guilt and the jealousy were more likely to appear when a woman had invested herself sexually in a relationship and then perceived her partner to be disloyal.

JEALOUSY AND NEEDS

Why does one person feel mainly fear, while another feels mainly anger, in relationships in which they experience jealousy? One way of understanding these different emotional reactions is to look at the needs each individual is trying to satisfy. If someone is threatening to break up your relationship, what exactly is being threatened? What do you stand to lose? What kinds of satisfactions hang in the balance?

You have already answered these questions if you filled out the Ideal Partner Questionnaire at the end of Chapter 5. If you did not fill out the questionnaire when you read Chapter 5, you may wish to do so now. If you did, look back at how you scored on the six basic needs that people seek to meet in love relationships:

Need for Love and Affection

Need for Independence

Need for Dominance

Need for Physical Comfort

Need for Protection and Dependency

Need for Recognition and Status

The relative importance these needs have for you can explain a great deal about how you approach love relationships, including how you experience jealousy.

Next, here is an exercise you can use to identify the emotions you feel most strongly when you are jealous. Imagine how you would feel if each of the following five imaginary situations were to occur with your current partner. Listed above the five situations are thirteen different feelings that you might have. For each situation, circle a number between 1 and 7 on the scale beside each feeling to indicate how strongly you think you would experience that feeling in that situation. The higher the number, the stronger the feeling.

Feeling

anger   not at all ├─┼─┼─┼─┼─┼─┤ very strongly
                               1 2 3 4 5 6 7

guilt   not at all ├─┼─┼─┼─┼─┼─┤ very strongly
                               1 2 3 4 5 6 7

contempt   not at all ├─┼─┼─┼─┼─┼─┤ very strongly
                               1 2 3 4 5 6 7

fear   not at all ├─┼─┼─┼─┼─┼─┤ very strongly
                               1 2 3 4 5 6 7

shame   not at all ├─┼─┼─┼─┼─┼─┤ very strongly
                               1 2 3 4 5 6 7

distress ("feeling upset") not at all ├─┼─┼─┼─┼─┼─┤ very strongly
                               1 2 3 4 5 6 7

disgust   not at all ├─┼─┼─┼─┼─┼─┤ very strongly
                               1 2 3 4 5 6 7

surprise   not at all |—+—+—+—+—+—| very strongly
                              1 2 3 4 5 6 7

sadness   not at all |—+—+—+—+—+—| very strongly
                              1 2 3 4 5 6 7

aggression   not at all |—+—+—+—+—+—| very strongly
                              1 2 3 4 5 6 7

fatigue   not at all |—+—+—+—+—+—| very strongly
                              1 2 3 4 5 6 7

concentration   not at all |—+—+—+—+—+—| very strongly
                              1 2 3 4 5 6 7

anxiety   not at all |—+—+—+—+—+—| very strongly
                              1 2 3 4 5 6 7

Situation 1:
Your partner (spouse or lover) has been playing tennis every Saturday for the past two months with the same tennis partner. This Saturday you decide to meet your partner and his/her tennis partner for a drink, at which time you discover that the tennis partner is an unmarried and extremely attractive member of *your* sex.

Situation 2:
While at a dinner party with neighbors and friends, your partner spends most of the evening speaking with someone of *your* sex. Your partner seems to be flirting and the two of them seem to be having a very good time.

Situation 3:
Your partner comes home one night and raves about her/his new co-worker, who is of *your* sex. When you call your partner at work the next day, you find that s/he is out to lunch at a fancy restaurant with the new co-worker.

Situation 4:
You attend a high school class reunion with your partner and s/he is approached by a former lover. The former lover insists on reminiscing about their prior relationship, "that ended because [your partner] had felt we were too young to marry at the time."

Situation 5:
You return home early from a week-long visit with relatives and find your

partner having dinner with someone of *your* sex whom you have never met. Your partner tells you that s/he is an old friend who is in town unexpectedly and dropped in for a visit. They seem anxious and unsure what to say to you.

If you found yourself becoming more jealous as you went from Situation 1 to Situation 5, then you responded as most people have. Now look at your ratings of the thirteen emotions for each situation. Which emotions did you feel most intensely in those situations that made you feel especially jealous? Can you see a pattern in the emotions you experience in situations that evoke strong feelings of jealousy?

In a study similar to the exercise you just completed, Yola Harrison, Minor Chamblin, and Carl Hindy compared people's needs with their emotions in jealousy-arousing situations. Participants wrote page-long descriptions of their two worst experiences of jealousy. This exercise was designed to re-awaken the emotions associated with the two experiences while participants wrote their essays. At the same time, they filled out the Ideal Partner Questionnaire. The researchers then looked at which feelings clustered with which needs in the participants' experiences.

These observations suggest ways of making sense of the experience of jealousy. First, for people who scored high on all six needs, the emotions that predominated were fear, anxiety, and concentration. In Chapter 5 we spoke about people who try to meet all their needs within one relationship. This tendency to put all one's eggs in one basket leaves a person in a vulnerable position: first, because it is difficult to find one relationship in which all needs can be satisfied; second, because the person has so much to lose if the relationship is threatened.

It is to be expected, then, that people who score high on all six needs in love relationships also score high on fear and anxiety in situations that threaten the loss of a relationship. We believe that these individuals are anxiously attached and also highly susceptible to jealousy. They are people for whom an intimate attachment serves as a lifeline carrying a range of emotional nutrients. Naturally, they will have a strong reaction if this lifeline is cut off. Although they may have different ways of expressing this reaction—some through anger and aggression; others through sadness, guilt, or distress—fear and anxiety seem to underlie all of these expressed emotions.

Turning from this global tendency to be needy and vulnerable to the way specific needs cluster with specific emotions in situations evoking jealousy, this research suggests the following relationships:

IF ONE'S GREATEST NEED IS FOR:	THEN ONE IS LIKELY TO EXPERIENCE:
Love and Affection	Distress, Sadness
Independence.	Surprise, Anger, Disgust
Dominance	Anger, Shame, Aggression
Physical Comfort.	Fatigue, Concentration
Protection and Dependency.	Anxiety, Fear
Recognition and Status	Anger, Contempt, Disgust, Aggression

These associations between needs and emotions make intuitive sense. They support the general observation that the emotions a person experiences when a relationship is threatened depend on the needs the person is attempting to satisfy in the relationship. Do the emotions on which you scored high in reacting to the imaginary jealousy situations above match the needs on which you scored high on the Ideal Partner Questionnaire, according to the list given here?

To simplify the picture further, we can reduce the six needs to two large clusters of needs, with their corresponding emotions. Three of the needs (Love and Affection, Physical Comfort, Protection and Dependency) might be called inwardly directed. The other three (Independence, Dominance, Recognition and Status) might be called outwardly directed. As we see, inwardly directed needs are associated with inwardly directed emotions, and the women in our study experienced these more than men in relationships where they were jealous. Outwardly directed needs are associated with outwardly directed emotions; men experienced these emotions more than women.

We might conclude, then, that there are two general types of jealous reactions: the inwardly directed jealous reaction more common among women, and the outwardly directed more common among men. However, this distinction by gender is only a matter of degree, and we expect that it will erode as society moves toward greater equality in sex roles.

We believe that most of the people who experience jealousy as inwardly directed, men and women alike, are anxiously attached in proportion to the intensity of their jealousy. For them, the threat of losing their intimate partner means a loss of nurturance, of emotional support and security, of a human connection.

Those who experience jealousy as outwardly directed probably present more of a mixed picture. For some, feelings such as anger, aggression, contempt, and disgust are experienced in combination with—and at times may serve as a defense against—other feelings, such as fear, anxiety, or sadness, that could evoke shame. If these people tend toward intense jealousy, they likewise tend toward anxious attachment. The loss they feel when a relationship is threatened is the loss of the esteem that the partner's love conferred upon them. Charlie, at the beginning of this chapter, is such a person. He expresses his jealousy in the form of harsh, biting anger, but his emotional vulnerability is apparent. He may vent his rage at Eleanor, his girlfriend, only to be reduced to tears by some cutting remark she makes in response. Charlie is very anxiously attached to Eleanor, to whom he clings desperately, trying to control the source of sustenance to his self-esteem. As long as he is intoxicated with her, he is spared the need to attend to other areas of his life, where he feels even more threatened with incompleteness, failure, and self-reproach.

There are, on the other hand, people for whom feelings of anger and aggression so thoroughly mask other emotions that they no longer can recognize and express those other emotions. This occurs, for example, when *not* feeling angry becomes the only measure of contentment a person has. As a child (according to psychologists Donald Mosher and Sylvan Tomkins), the "macho" individual is shamed and tormented into feeling angry whenever he displays fear, anxiety, or sadness. As a result, he loses touch with these "unmanly" feelings and automatically feels anger in their place. With further exploration, as in therapy, he may be able to retrieve these feelings. In the absence of such a breakthrough, however, these detached individuals tend to experience the threatened loss of a spouse or lover not as a loss of nurturance and support (which they cannot admit they need), but as a loss of face, a loss of control, a loss of a status symbol or object of possession. Their anger is aroused by threats to their self-image, their prestige, their control over others.

An example is Rick, the man in Chapter 4 who fought with his wife in and out of therapy sessions, but was unable to articulate his feelings toward her. Growing up as a street kid, Rick learned that survival depended on one's act, one's game, one's toughness. Unfortunately, what had been an appropriate adaptation to the environment of his early years proved not so well suited to contemporary married life. Imprisoned in his machismo, Rick would react to someone trying to steal his wife the way he would to someone trying to steal his car. He might swagger and boast about his car and threaten people who came near it, and as a result of this vigilance he would have little fear that his car would actually be stolen. Rick would score high on jealousy, but low on anxious romantic attachment. Such jealous individuals, possessive but not outwardly anxious, appear to account for our finding that people who were prone to jealousy more regularly scored high on romantic obsession than on romantic anxiety. They would not admit to being anxious as readily as they would to being obsessed.

IN WHAT KINDS OF
RELATIONSHIPS DOES JEALOUSY OCCUR?

Certain elements of a relationship can be used to predict the likelihood that a person will experience jealousy, just as certain elements foreshadow anxious romantic attachment. In fact, the best predictor of jealousy in our study is the same one that best predicted the obsession component of anxious romantic attachment: the intensity of the person's love for the partner. According to our findings, the more one loves a particular partner, the more likely one is to feel jealous in that relationship. For example, a woman explained why she could easily accept her boyfriend's seeing someone else by saying, "I don't want a permanent relationship with him. He has nothing I'd want permanently." She did not value this man enough to want to possess him exclusively. On the other hand, the perceived strength of the *partner's* love was not strongly associated with the level of jealousy. Consequently, the disparity between the strength of one's own love and that of the partner's love, which had a large effect on romantic anxiety, does not prove so significant with respect to jealousy.

Chapter 5 told the story of Lynne and Scott, a passionately involved couple who went through a painful breakup. Lynne was intensely attracted to Scott, but was unable to win a permanent commitment from this chronically inconsistent lover. Even after she moved to New York to live with him, she was tormented by his secretive contacts with his ex-girlfriend and with other women as well. She expressed her frustration in jealous rages.

> In New York I became extremely erratic in my behavior toward Scott. I'd fly off the handle at the slightest indication that something was going awry. I threw wine glasses. I threw a picture of him and me against the wall. Any physical abuse between us I initiated. I would hit him—not that I could hurt him; I just pounded on him to listen to me. One night I completely lost control, and he threw me out in the hallway and locked me out of our apartment.

These violent outbursts were out of character for Lynne, a professional woman who characterizes her previous relationships as normal.

My mother reminded me that I had never acted that way before. She said, "You're not yourself, Lynne." My friends told me the same thing. I never had such exaggerated feelings of jealousy before. I think I'm attractive, and I feel good about myself intellectually. I've never been more secure about where I am in life. In previous relationships, if the man acted at all like Scott did, I got out. As soon as I felt the man didn't want what I wanted, I broke it off. But with Scott, if he even looked at another woman, I'd blow it all out of proportion. That's not normal. Men look—I know that, and I've never felt insecure about it, never!

Lynne could not react in a cool, controlled way to Scott's provocations because she valued him too much to let him go. She had been able to take an independent stance with other men, but Scott's behavior was a threat to a relationship in which she felt invested, and which she was determined to keep. "I did love him, and I didn't want to give him up," she says. "I was afraid to go back home and admit failure, but I was more afraid of the pain of giving him up."

Unlike the emotions associated with jealousy, the characteristics of a relationship that affect the occurrence of jealousy were similar for men and women. On the whole, they are the same characteristics that make it more or less likely that a person will be romantically obsessed. For example, jealousy was more commonly felt in relationships of longer duration, an association that was especially strong for women. This may have occurred because a longer-lasting relationship indicates a more highly valued partner, or because a person becomes more emotionally and sexually invested in a longer relationship, or because the passage of time gives a person a greater sense of possession of the partner. All of these issues are implicit in a comment such as "At first it didn't bother me that he was still seeing his previous girlfriend, but after I started caring for him it did." On the other hand, the number of hours a week the partners spent together did not have as large an effect on jealousy as it did on romantic obsession. Therefore, it is not the intensity of the relationship at any particular moment, but rather the involvement or identification with the partner that evolves over time, that motivates a person to be jealous.

The idea that jealousy arises when a person's sense of entitlement is violated is supported by our finding that less jealousy occurred in relationships where both partners were seeing other people concurrently. Although there may seem to be more occasion for jealousy in such nonexclusive relationships, those involved actually feel less jealous because of the way the relationship is defined: there is not an expectation that one partner has exclusive right of access to the other. Of course, there is *greater* jealousy when one is not seeing other people, but the partner is. These findings are parallel to those for anxious romantic attachment (and particularly romantic anxiety), which was lower when the nonexclusiveness of the relationship was reciprocal, but higher when it was one-sided.

In this passage, for example, a woman involved simultaneously in two nonexclusive relationships tells how she feels about sharing a man's affections:

> Michael, the man I'm half-seeing now, is seeing another woman. If I'm jealous at all now, it's of the time he's spending away from me, the loss of his company. I'm at peace that he has someone else. And Matt, the man I'm in love with, is still married, but I'm not jealous of his wife; I wouldn't trade my life for hers for a minute. She tells me he screws other women, but Matt says he's in love with me. I think he doesn't tell her anything, but she finds out what she can and imagines the rest. I'm sure there are other women, and I don't care. I've told him he should have other women; it would take the heat off me.

In her role as "the other woman," this woman is contented with the equilibrium (a balance of attachment and detachment) that she and her two lovers have reached. Compare her account with that of a woman who was involved in an exclusive relationship until her partner began to date someone else as well. For her, the same issue of having to share a man's time and attention was accompanied by a different set of feelings.

> Toward the end of our relationship he was dating me and someone else. It was like I was the "other woman" again. It was like going back to when we started, only now I was the one who was seeing him only once every week or two. I tried not to give him the third degree, because I knew it was getting to him. But I always thought about where he was and who he was with when we weren't together. I kept all this pretty much to myself, but the people closest to me knew how upset I was.

When people wrote stories about their four most intense experiences of jealousy, the intensity of the jealousy they expressed had more to do with whether the relationship was considered to be exclusive than with the seriousness of the provocation. The jealousy often was less intense when the partner in a nonexclusive relationship had sexual intercourse with someone else than when the partner in an exclusive relationship merely talked with a person of the opposite sex.

Finally, the more sexually active a relationship is (in comparison to other relationships one has had), the stronger one's feelings of jealousy in that relationship are likely to be. Again, we found this to be somewhat more commonly the case for women, in keeping with the observation that, as a rule, sexual feelings appear to be more closely tied to emotional attachments for women than for men.

THE PARTNER'S ROLE IN IGNITING JEALOUSY

Among the ten characteristics of the partner discussed in Chapter 5, the partner's *attractiveness* plays the most significant part in jealousy for men. The more attractive his partner, the more prone a man is to episodes of strong jealousy. A similar association holds true for women, but to a lesser extent. This is the same pattern as the effect of the partner's attractiveness on romantic obsession, but there the effects for both men and women were larger than they were with jealousy.

The partner's *consistency* also has some effect on jealousy, especially for men. The more consistent the partner, the less reason one has to be jealous. Lynne, for example, attributes part of the intensity of her jealous behavior toward Scott to the web of deceit and concealment that made it impossible for her to trust him or feel secure with him. "I never knew the whole story," she says. "I was going crazy not knowing what was going on."

It is surprising, however, that the impact of the partner's consistency is as weak as it turned out to be, given the much stronger association between the partner's consistency and romantic anxiety. One reason for this may be that we asked only about the consistency of the partner's expressed feelings of love and affection. We did not ask about specific forms of inconsistent, disloyal behavior (such as flirting or meeting secretly with another person) that would elicit a jealous response. Perhaps the partners were more consistent in their words than in their deeds.

Aside from these two modest effects, what the partner is like seems hardly to matter when it comes to jealousy. It is as if the partner could be chosen at random, and the likelihood of a person's experiencing strong jealousy would remain the same. Instead, jealousy appears to have more to do with the characteristics of the person who experiences it, as well as with how the two partners structure their relationship. In particular, whether they have a pact of exclusive loyalty to each other and whether they violate that pact are crucial to the emergence of jealousy.

JEALOUSY AND SELF-ESTEEM

Sue and Art, a couple in their twenties, were at a pool party when a voluptuous woman in a revealing bathing suit came up to Art and began speaking to him in what seemed a familiar manner. Watching from the other side of the pool, Sue inferred from the woman's body language that Art might be having an affair with her. She ran into the bathroom and punched a mirror, cutting her hand. She and Art left the party in embarrassment and argued heatedly all the way home.

Although this scene sounds like a typical violent outburst of jealousy, Sue and Art did not fit into any stereotype that it might suggest. Art was not actually unfaithful, and Sue was not excessively dependent on him. Nor was she a generally insecure person. She was bright, socially at ease, and successful as a coordinator in a day-care center. People found her attractive and responded positively to her outgoing personality and accommodating manner.

The tensions in this marriage usually were less overt than in the scene at the pool. Art had worked for several years to qualify himself to be a traveling management consultant. Now that he had attained this position, Sue felt neglected. She thought that Art was insensitive to her feelings about being home alone so many evenings while he was out of town. It made matters worse that Art, who was handsome and mildly flirtatious, sometimes "forgot" to inform her about where he went on his business trips. Actually, it was less forgetting than a reluctance to mention anything that might touch off a jealous reaction, such as if he were staying at a beachfront hotel. But when goaded beyond his limits, he would divulge his whereabouts in a taunting, suggestive way, upsetting Sue all the more.

During those evenings at home alone, Sue was driven to distraction by images of the kind of women Art might meet at beaches and pools. "Those blonde, tanned women in bikinis—bronze-skinned women in skirts split up the middle," she ruminated. "Of course, he'll be tempted. Why should he stick with me, when I'm so pale and plain-looking?" On the contrary, many of the people they knew would have said that Art was fortunate to be married to Sue, with her unpretentious competence and a certain appealing vulnerability that she projected. Art would have said so himself. Yet Sue could not look at herself in this positive light; instead, she blocked out evidence that people valued her or found her attractive. She did not believe that men ever flirted with her, even though her co-workers observed single fathers at the day-care center doing just that.

Sue's jealousy was tied to low self-esteem; she felt that she did not measure up to potential rivals in attractiveness. What was remarkable was that her self-doubt, while quite severe, was exclusively focused on her physical appearance. Sue was neither depressed nor generally lacking in self-confidence. Yet she was so convinced of her homeliness that she closed herself off to any feedback that might have told her otherwise. As her blind spot expanded, so did her jealousy. And since she felt herself to be so unattractive that men never flirted with her, she understandably felt insecure about her husband's fidelity.

Sue's image of herself as physically inferior to other women was so rigidly maintained and so out of keeping with the rest of her personality that it stood out as a tragic anomaly. What could account for this capable woman's blindness to her own attractiveness? The missing piece in the puzzle lay in the traumas Sue had suffered in her adolescence. The only daughter in a family with three sons, she grew up in a male-dominated environment where she was not appreciated—and did not learn to appreciate herself—for her femininity. Worse, she was abused because of it. When she discovered her brothers peeking through the keyhole to watch her undress, she told her mother, who said, "That's what boys do." After that she felt she could not go to her mother even when her brothers began to abuse her sexually. Outnumbered and overpowered by the men in her family, she accepted this treatment for several years, beginning in her early teens.

Here was a girl of twelve or thirteen, an age when a girl might look in the mirror and see her body beginning to mature. When Sue looked in the mirror, she saw her brothers peeking in at her, violating her. Abuse and degradation defiled her sense of her developing womanhood. Consequently, sexual approaches became threatening to her, and she blocked them out of her consciousness. When asked, "How would you feel if a man you knew made sexual overtures to you?" she answered, "I'd feel bad, because he'd be questioning my values, the kind of woman I am."

The guilt Sue experienced as a victim of sexual abuse meant that she felt attacked, not flattered, if she became the object of sexual desire. Unconsciously she chose to spare herself the pain, but there was a cost to her distortion. Deprived of feelings of pleasure and pride in her sexuality, she considered herself unqualified to compete with other women for her husband's affection. Assuming, as she did, that her husband would be attracted to other women, she naturally worried that he would act on those feelings. Her family experience had led her to believe that men, including her husband, did not restrain their sexual impulses or adhere to social mores. "That's the way men are," her mother had said, which in effect sanctioned her brothers' behavior.

A *Psychology Today* survey related jealousy to self-esteem in specific areas corresponding to what people thought was important to the opposite sex. People were more likely to be jealous if they believed that they lacked the specific attributes that were most valued by the opposite sex. They were less likely to be jealous if they believed that they possessed those attributes in high degree. Women in general believed, just as Sue did, that men most valued physical attractiveness and popularity in a woman. Men, on the other hand, believed that women attached greatest importance to a man's wealth and fame. Self-perceived deficiencies in these respective areas would leave women and men most susceptible to jealous reactions.

As Sue's case illustrates, self-esteem is not necessarily based on objective attributes, but rather on the person's subjective sense of her or his strengths and weaknesses. A woman whom others find attractive, or a man who is seen as a success story, can still feel insecure about having what it takes to win and hold a desired partner.

THE DOUBLE STANDARD: WHO GETS THE BLAME?

When Sue was riding home with Art after the incident at the pool, she said to him, "It's not *you* I'm really angry at—it's *her!*" In general, Sue was more tolerant of her husband's flirting with other women than of their flirting with him. It was when she thought she saw a woman coming on to Art that she was most upset.

Like Sue, a jealous woman typically blames the other woman. A jealous man, on the other hand, more often blames his wife or girlfriend. There seems to be a double standard for jealousy, based on an assumption that women are responsible for resisting temptation while men are not. Indeed, in many cultures women are expected to avoid tempting men. In Arab countries the woman is required to hide her face. Such a practice is based on the implicit view that women must avoid being a temptation to men. The responsibility lies with the woman who presents the temptation that men supposedly cannot resist. Therefore, the woman, not the man, is punished for unseemly behavior that leads a man astray.

We found that men who were jealous had some tendency to rate their partners as untrustworthy, while women did not. The fact that women blame other women for situations involving jealousy runs through our interviews as well. For example, this is how one woman experienced jealousy in her relationship with a male co-worker:

> I always imagined that other women were after him. I've got a great imagination, and I can build things up in my mind to the point where I practically make myself sick. One time, though, it was with good reason. There was one woman who regularly did business with our office. I kept saying, "I think she's after you." He said, "No, no." Then once he had to travel to her company to do business, and she invited him to spend the night with her. After that it was even worse. Even though he said he wasn't interested in her, I imagined that he was, and I worried about it on the nights when I wasn't with him. So every time she came to the office, I wanted to go for her throat. It was like "How dare you tread on my territory! You know he's mine."

In the following account, a woman who was involved with a married man describes how his wife's jealous resentment was directed at her:

> His wife is insanely jealous. She makes a life's work of chasing him around. I'd hire her as a detective if I could; she's brilliant. She has tapes of everything he's done, even before me, but I was the only serious threat. She taped him and me sitting in the car, talking. She taped him making love with her—where she placed the microphone, I don't know, but she got every detail—and sent it to me. Bizarre. Even today, she blames me totally for wrecking her life, which I think was wrecked long before me. She has threatened my life on the phone, and she and I once had an extended confrontation in which she would sit in my neighborhood, case the house, and follow me around. She was so threatening that he put in a burglar-alarm system in my house. It's exciting, if nothing else.

Thus the dynamics of jealousy turn women against each other, even though infidelity is obviously a two-way street.

ATTRIBUTING ONE'S OWN IMPULSES TO THE PARTNER

A young man felt so insecure about his girlfriend's loyalty that he practically held her prisoner. He discouraged her from seeing her friends and grilled her with so many questions whenever she had been away from him that she began to think it was not worth the trouble to do anything on her own. In an incident that shows the extent of his irrationality, he saw a man drive by in a fancy car and whistle at his girlfriend. For the rest of the day he pursued her with questions like "What did he look like? Was he attractive?" Pointing randomly to a man in a supermarket line, he blurted out, "Is that him?" Yet when asked, "What do you think might happen to end this relationship?" he replied, "It would end if I had an affair." This man, for whom jealousy was a consuming preoccupation, nonetheless understood that he, not his girlfriend, was the one who was likely to be unfaithful.

People who have had affairs or who feel tempted to do so while in committed relationships often imagine that their partners have had similar impulses. Men and women alike can imagine that their partners share their own inconsistent or indecisive feelings. "It's not me that's fickle; it's him," one may think. More often, it is men who do this, in keeping with their tendency to blame the woman in situations that provoke jealousy. The need to blame arises not from anything the woman has done, but from the man's own fear or guilt.

One may be aware of one's own urges even while attributing them to the partner. For example, a man who feels attracted to others besides his wife or girlfriend may assume that because he has such feelings, she must have them, too. Like a shady businessman who assumes that everyone else is trying to cheat him because he knows that he is trying to cheat everyone else, this man is fully aware of his own illicit desires; he may simply be mistaken in attributing them to the woman as well. He may also be expressing indirectly his guilt and fear of retribution for his infidelities in past relationships.

Charlie, who agonized over the thought of Eleanor's falling for a good-looking man at her exercise club, was conscious not only of his own susceptibility to such attractions, but also of the groundlessness of his suspicions about Eleanor. With considerable self-awareness he describes how he would transfer ownership of his feelings to her:

> Perhaps my jealousy stems from the fact that I'm so visual, so I think everyone else is visual, too. Physical attractiveness, pulchritude, stirs me. It doesn't stir Eleanor. What you do when you're jealous is to think that your perception of reality is the other person's. You project it onto her and accuse her of things that perhaps you're frightened of doing yourself, like responding to an extraordinarily attractive woman in a way that would jeopardize the relationship.

Most men, although aware of their wayward impulses, may not be aware of the connection between those impulses and their attribution of similar impulses to their partners. Less common is the man who is unaware of his own wayward impulses, but nonetheless attributes them to his partner and reacts as though they were really there. A man may, without realizing it, use such false suspicions to restrain his own behavior. By believing that he must be vigilant to keep his wife or girlfriend from misbehaving, he redirects his energy from the sexual desires he finds threatening to the safer outlets of anger and a sense of injustice.

When a man feels a strong impulse toward polygamy, consciously or not, he may not easily be reassured that his wife or lover is immune to similar feelings. And anyone, man or woman, who is keeping a delicate balance between loyalty and temptation may suspect that his or her partner is not above such frailty.

COPING WITH JEALOUSY: HOW PEOPLE RESPOND

In the study in Florida in which people wrote brief accounts of their four most intense experiences of jealousy, they were asked to include a description of how they responded to each provocation. From these accounts the researchers identified six ways in which people reacted to these threatening situations, listed here (with examples) in order from the least to the most drastic response.

1. One responds passively, doing nothing to the partner and displaying no emotional reaction. There is no hint to the partner that the situation provoked feelings of jealousy. (This type of response appeared in thirty-two percent of the accounts.)
   Examples:
   "I didn't do or say anything."
   "I just pouted or sulked privately."

2. One responds passively, but does something to reveal emotional distress or discontent without confronting the partner about what provoked this reaction. (This type of response appeared in sixteen percent of the accounts.)
   Examples:
   "I just asked a couple of questions about her."
   "I made a sarcastic remark."
   "I left."

3. One directly communicates one's concern to the partner, but there is no emotional outburst or angry confrontation. (This type of response appeared in ten percent of the accounts.)

Examples:
"I took him aside, and we talked about it."
"I asked him what this was all about."

4. One directly confronts the partner about the situation in an emotionally charged manner. (This type of response appeared in twenty-five percent of the accounts.)
   Examples:
   "I gave him a nasty look."
   "We argued about it."

5. One punishes, threatens to punish, or retaliates (perhaps physically) against the partner. (This type of response appeared in eleven percent of the accounts.)
   Examples:
   "I threatened to leave him."
   "I threw something of his away."
   "I became abusive."

6. One terminates the relationship. (This type of response appeared in seven percent of the accounts.)
   Example:
   "I left him."

The most common response was the most passive one, in which the jealous person neither confronted the partner nor revealed his or her emotional distress. On the whole, the more intense the jealousy, the more drastic the response. This makes intuitive sense, and was true for both men and women.

Nonetheless, a recent study by psychologist Karen Derecho Earnest has confirmed that men are more preoccupied than women with sexual threats to the relationship and more likely to respond with expressions of anger and attempts to reassert control. These may take the form of verbal or physical aggression toward the woman or the male rival. Women are more preoccupied with threats to the emotional and social bonds represented by the relationship; in response, they are more likely to seek support from others and to make an effort to repair the relationship. Earnest, who recorded the reactions men and women had after they imagined particular scenes of disloyalty and betrayal on the part of their current partners, also found that women who were attracted to macho men tended to react in much the same way those men did—that is, with anger and aggression.

The fact that women express less anger when they are jealous does not mean that they necessarily *feel* less anger. Women share a great deal of anger with their therapists or female confidantes that they do not reveal to their male partners. It appears that women are socialized to value continuity in relationships and to play the active role in preserving relationships, rather than to insist on defending their rights as men commonly do. A woman may feel the same sense of injustice and inequity that a man does, but she learns to inhibit the expression of these feelings in the interest of holding things together.

Doris, the middle-aged woman (in the story at the beginning of this chapter) who suffered unexplainable fits of jealousy, felt intensely angry. Yet she suppressed her anger for fear of losing her husband. "That's the first and last time I displayed that kind of rage toward him," she reported. Instead, she bottled up her anger and felt it in the form of headaches and high blood pressure. She directed her anger inwardly, saying, "I guess I'm mostly mad at myself." Her case illustrates what researchers have found—namely, that women who are jealous blame themselves more often than do men, who are more likely to direct their anger toward others. Unfortunately, both men and women are conditioned to act in ways that perpetuate the power of men over women. As our society becomes more egalitarian, these patterns may be changing, so that women and men will be less likely to act according to stereotype. As Ira Reiss concludes:

> It takes power to be able to respond to a wound by attacking. Thus, in a more gender-equal society, not only would female premarital sexuality be higher but . . . so would the expression of sexual jealousy by wives.

COPING WITH JEALOUSY: RECOMMENDATIONS

We have seen how people typically act when they are jealous. How might they respond more constructively when they believe there is reason to be jealous? How, as individuals and couples, can we minimize the destructive effects of jealousy on relationships?

The approach we recommend can be broken down into six stages. These are not rigid categories. Rather, they describe the essential components of a fluid, interactive process. Still, we can identify at least an approximate sequence of steps by which the clarification and resolution of issues occurs. These steps are:

1. Identify and articulate feelings precisely.
2. Discover the roots of both partners' reactions in their past.

3. Engage the partners' capacity to empathize.
4. Negotiate agreements.
5. Explore the function served by persistent disagreements.
6. Last resorts: separate, accommodate, or seek professional help.

1. Identify and articulate feelings precisely. In working therapeutically with couples, we ask the person who is feeling anger and resentment to clarify, as precisely as possible, what they feel. Why do they feel they are being abused? What rights do they feel are being violated? Putting the grievance into words may not, however, be a simple matter. Indeed, this first step may be the most difficult as well as the most crucial in the whole process. The two partners may not know themselves well enough to articulate their needs accurately, or one of them may fear the other's criticism or ridicule, which inhibits him or her from revealing important needs or fears.

Too often, the jealous partner issues a barrage of vague threats and grievances, seasoned with negative emotions such as anger, fear, and distress. These expressions of discontent tend to be strung together illogically, as in this sequence: "You goddamn bastard, how can you do this to me? You don't care at all about me, all you care about is yourself and those little tramps you're always giving the eye to—I mean, you care more about that trashy woman next door than you do about me—what business do you have going into her house to lend her the vacuum cleaner? Look at you, carrying on this way, coming home late from work all the time—why, you should thank me for all the things I've put up with for you, and here I am, not knowing if you're going to throw me out next week and move in with her—I have half a mind to throw you out first and go home to my mother."

Such overly generalized emotional reactions, heartfelt though they may be, present an obstacle to identifying and resolving the problem. For one thing, the couple cannot negotiate a solution until they know what they are negotiating about. Second, the hostile, accusing tone of such a tirade may hurt the partner, who may then dismiss the potentially threatening complaint, on the basis of its overwrought, confused presentation, as "the same old crazy stuff." Instead of responding with empathy, the partner becomes, or stays, distant.

The first step, therefore, is to disentangle the various resentments the jealous partner may express and to ask, "What are you angry about? What are you afraid of? What, specifically, makes you feel so betrayed?" The answers, though, may not be quick in coming. Even when one specific grievance is articulated, it may serve merely as an excuse for discharging the emotions aroused by a deeper issue that feels too painful to admit and confront.

If the jealous person's upset is disproportionate to the stated complaint, that is a clue that a deeper problem lies elsewhere. For example, Sue and Art initially identified their marital problems as caused by the many nights a week Art spent away from home, how little he told Sue about his whereabouts, and how enthusiastic he looked when he spoke with other women at social gatherings. These issues by themselves easily could have been negotiated. However, they took on their meaning not in isolation, but as they expressed a deep-seated insecurity Sue felt due to her history of sexual abuse.

2. *Discover the roots of both partners' reactions in their pasts.* When a person's jealousy seems irrational or unexplainable, one needs to look deeper into the person to find what the reasons really are. A disproportionate reaction to what would seem to be manageable problems suggests that the person is reacting to something that is not visible, something in her or his past experience. At the same time, don't overlook anything in the other partner's past that may be exacerbating the situation. It may be less threatening to the jealous person to explore the partner's background first.

Imagine a black box with a tiny p (for provocation) on one side and a huge JR (for jealous reaction) on the other. Inside the box is a string of personal associations that connects the p with the JR, each link enlarging the provocation until it looms as a major threat. It is like a multistage amplifier whose components (the pre-amp, the power amp, etc.) act in series to produce the sound that finally blasts out of the speakers. For Sue, the sight of Art speaking animatedly with a woman at the swimming pool connects inside the black box with a set of childhood experiences that includes her brothers abusing her and her mother telling her that men are sexually irresponsible and can't be changed. As a result, an innocuous scene touches off a major personal crisis for Sue, and Art turns away in bewilderment and annoyance. Every person's black box is wired differently, and the path of the wiring must be traced to discover the unique personal associations that touch off those "unexplainable" jealous reactions.

The same is true for the other partner. It can be useful to look into Art's black box, too. When Sue asks, "Will you call me Tuesday and tell me where you're staying?" why does he see it as so much more than a minor courtesy she is requesting of him? Why does he view it as an imposition, a sign of distrust? Perhaps his hypersensitivity to issues of control, his resistance to "crazy demands," has its roots in his relationships with his mother and father. Art's mother was schizophrenic, and Art identifies with his father's struggle not to be overwhelmed by the effects of her illness. This is the childhood origin of his unyielding determination not to be "run" by Sue's "crazy" behavior.

3. *Engage the partners' capacity to empathize.* Neither partner will negotiate seriously until they feel that they can be responsive to the other partner's needs and can trust the partner to be responsive to theirs. The two steps outlined above—untangling key concerns and exploring their significance in the light of the jealous partner's life history—are crucial in creating an empathic relationship around issues that have provoked jealousy. To these steps we add another: articulating the grievance in a credible, considerate way, so as not to attack and alienate the partner, but to bring about empathy and understanding.

The jealous partner's feelings need to be stated in such a way that they can be heard. The fears and insecurities need to come across as real, deeply felt, and sincerely expressed—which is not how they appear when they are blurted out amid a string of vulgar epithets in a fight. The other partner needs to open up and listen, and the therapist can help by asking this partner to recall times and circumstances when he or she may have had similar feelings. Respect is to be offered even as it is sought, as when the jealous partner says, "I don't want you to change your behavior just to placate me. I want you to change because you understand how I feel."

The value of deciphering the black box of personal history lies in demonstrating to both partners that the jealous reaction cannot be dismissed as irrational; rather, it is understandable in terms of its own deeper logic. This revelation frees the jealous partner from having to be defensive about his or her feelings and attacking as a result. It frees the other partner, too, from attacking or withdrawing from the jealous partner.

As Sue commented after she saw the connection between her jealousy and the abuse she suffered as an adolescent, "For once I feel like someone understands me, like I'm not crazy." Out of this greater self-acceptance she no longer felt the same need to attack Art. Art, who previously had reacted to Sue's "craziness" with irritation, passive indifference, and even a degree of provocation, became more sympathetic once he appreciated the underlying conflicts that fueled her demands. When he saw that she had reasons for acting as she did, he no longer felt that he was caught in a power struggle, and he became more willing to change his behavior. Similarly, Art gained self-awareness, and Sue gained sympathy for him, from understanding that his rigidity in the face of her demands stemmed from having watched his father cope with his mother's mental illness. As Art sat massaging Sue's neck and shoulders in their therapist's office after she revealed her childhood traumas, it seemed clear that the couple would be approaching their problems thereafter with greater mutual sensitivity and concern.

These first three steps in coping with jealousy in a relationship are also illustrated by the case of a young couple named Marge and Don. Marge complained that Don came home fifteen to thirty minutes late from work every day, and thereby delayed dinner for her and their two children. Committed to building his career with a Long Island management consulting firm, he was chronically unable to arrive home on time. Somehow, this small discrepancy in his schedule made Marge feel isolated and neglected. She brooded as well about *why* he was late. Why couldn't he finish his work on time? Was he dallying with a secretary?

To their marriage counselor, Don's lateness in itself hardly qualified as a serious marital problem. It was not out of the ordinary for a serious young professional person to come home at 6:15 or 6:30 P.M., and the couple (if they wanted to) could just set their expectations—and their dinner hour— accordingly. It was ironic that a specialist in time management was always late, but that was not a problem that required psychological counseling.

Nonetheless, Marge's disappointed expectations and jealous fantasies required a second look. Something was bothering her, but what? The counselor searched for answers in numerous places suggested by his discussions with the couple. Was Marge unusually perfectionistic? Did she resent that Don was being more considerate of his employer than of her? The counselor dug wherever he was given a lead, but came up short of a convincing explanation.

As the weeks went on, Marge mentioned several times that she felt close to her family in Illinois and wished she were living back there. The couple had relocated several times to take advantage of job opportunities for Don, and Marge was feeling rootless and disconnected. The counselor saw a possible link between these feelings and Marge's complaint that Don was not paying enough attention to her.

"Have you thought any more about moving back to Illinois?" asked the counselor.

"I can't get Don to look for jobs there."

"You mean you *do want* to move back there."

"It's not so bad here. If only he would come home on time, it wouldn't be so bad."

Finally it became clear why Marge attached such importance to a seemingly insignificant conflict. Without realizing it, she had focused her discontent on the immediate irritation of having to wait for Don to come home at night so that she could avoid raising a question with weightier implications for their life together. The counselor pressed the issue, and Marge finally burst into tears and said, "Yes, I want to move to Illinois."

Then the counselor sought a similar clarification from Don, who was talking about particular advantages and disadvantages of his present job. He and Marge thought they could reason with each other, sort out the details, before they acknowledged fully the momentous issue that stood between them. When Don said flatly, "I don't want to move," it was out in the open. Now Marge revealed that she actually had contemplated taking the children to live with her parents in Illinois and leaving it up to Don whether he wanted to come with them. Her father had been diagnosed with a terminal illness, and Marge wanted the children to get to know him while there was still time. She and Don sat, red-faced and glaring, agreeing that they had gotten down to a primary source of their difficulties.

Marge had framed a complaint of neglect, with overtones of sexual jealousy, to express her sense of loss at having been uprooted from a supportive family environment. Her feelings were understandable, since she depended, more on her husband's attention in the absence of other emotional ties. Still, the underlying conflict had to be brought out in order to be resolved. It had taken a few months of counseling to identify the problem, but it was an important breakthrough. Now Marge and Don could begin to negotiate a compromise or a tradeoff (for example, by setting a time limit for moving or by agreeing that they would move when certain conditions were met). But until they felt secure enough to state the problem out loud, they were negotiating on different fronts.

4. Negotiate agreements. Once the underlying conflict has been stated, we inquire whether the jealous individual has asked his or her partner to change specific behaviors. In other words, does the couple have a clear understanding about what each partner expects of the other, and has each agreed to meet the other's expectations? If not, trouble lies ahead. We emphasize the importance of forging such agreement; this is a cornerstone of a contented relationship.

Let's say that a woman believes that it is not appropriate for her husband to go out to lunch with a woman whom she does not know. Has she asked him in advance not to do this, or is she reacting after the fact with feelings of resentment that he might not have anticipated? Once she tells him that she feels he is being unfair to her, he may agree or disagree. If he agrees not to do what threatens and offends her, then this irritant will be removed, and she will no longer feel jealous on that account. What if he does not agree? He may believe that he has the right to have lunch with other women as long as these contacts remain platonic. In that case, the couple needs to explore whether they can resolve the disagreement.

The husband may really need his wife's help in understanding the pain that his activities with other women cause her. He, on the other hand, must be able to convey to her in earnest that the satisfaction he gets from these activities really poses no threat to the relationship. Seeing how she feels, he should try to find a way to reduce this threat she experiences. The goal is to find a reasonable modification of his behavior that will enable her to experience the safety and trust that she needs. In other words, the couple should try to identify the minimum sacrifices they need to make to live together peaceably. We emphasize the value of cooperating to meet each other's needs and of sharing equally the sacrifices that are required to continue any relationship.

Perhaps they can agree to disagree. That is, the husband may refuse to give up having lunch with other women, despite his wife's feelings. The wife may reconcile herself to the situation because of other values the marriage has for her. By explicitly recognizing this choice she is less likely to feel jealous. If she finds, however, that she cannot be contented on these terms, she may choose to leave her husband and find a man who will accept the conditions she considers essential for a satisfactory relationship.

This approach helps couples clarify what is permissible and what is not in a relationship. It turns implicit agreements or disagreements into explicit ones. Sometimes a man and woman may be working from two different implicit contracts governing their commitments to each other. By acknowledging the differences, they can work to resolve them—or at least satisfy themselves that they have tried.

5. *Explore the function served by persistent disagreements.* It would be wonderful if every couple could resolve their differences after a few hours of therapy. Occasionally that does happen, but the process of clarification and resolution often is longer, more complex, and less certain. Misunderstandings and broken agreements testify to the difficulties couples have in achieving mutual understanding.

If a couple cannot come to terms by negotiating in good faith, or do not keep their agreements, or if the agreements leave them still feeling dissatisfied, it may be necessary to repeat the first three steps. Perhaps the underlying problem was not identified accurately and articulated clearly. Perhaps they needed to explore more how one partner's discontent is rooted in past experience. Perhaps there was an attempt to negotiate differences before achieving the necessary foundation of empathy and trust. Sometimes it takes a failed negotiation for a couple to see that they were digging in the wrong place even when they thought they had discovered the real problem.

If a fresh look does not lead in any new directions, one needs to ask, "What function might this persistent disagreement be serving in the relationship?" One or both partners might have reasons to want to maintain the conflict rather than resolve it. For example, it might give the jealous partner a sense of control she or he would not otherwise have. It might contribute to an imbalance of power, an edge that one partner is reluctant to give up. Art, say, might derive a sense of superiority from thinking of Sue as "a little crazy." Marge might find it hard to stop punishing Don for making work his main priority.

6. *Last resorts: separate, accommodate, or seek professional help.* Unresolvable conflicts may come about as a result of a lack of good faith in negotiations. For example, one partner, despite all promises to the contrary, may continue having extramarital affairs. Alternatively, intense emotional reactions based on past experience may overpower the outcomes of present negotiation. The partners may not be conscious of the reasons why they have such strong emotional reactions, or they may be conscious of them but feel powerless to change them. They may, in fact, be deeply incompatible, yet unprepared to bear the losses involved in separating.

When behavior antithetical to a healthy relationship is deeply ingrained, one might need to consider ending the relationship. Judy had to leave Frank because he was not about to change; he came from a background where the extremes of jealous domination he exercised were considered normal. Judy did not share that background, and she could not forever accept his unfounded accusations without damaging herself severely. Lynne had to leave Scott because her jealous reactions were all too well founded; his fickle, indecisive behavior had become a way of life.

When jealousy seems irrational even to the jealous partner, one solution (odd as it may sound) is for the jealous person to acknowledge the irrationality and nonetheless to ask the partner to accommodate the jealous reaction so that they can live in peace. Then the partner should look for the smallest effective accommodation. This accommodation will not only remove a perceived threat, but also provide reassurance of the partner's concern for the jealous person's feelings. If the partner can make this adjustment without feeling violated or chronically discontented, the couple may be able to live with potentially disruptive feelings and expectations that otherwise would take a long course of therapy to address.

When a person reaches the point of admitting, "I know this is hurting both of us, but I just can't help myself," then the focus of the problem shifts from couple therapy to individual therapy. The partner whose impulsive behavior provokes the jealousy may be the one to benefit from in-depth therapy. Or it may be the jealous partner, still experiencing excessive emotional reactions after receiving ample assurance of the partner's good faith.

In difficult cases, the couple and the individual can work on the problem simultaneously. Charlie and Sue both want to moderate the jealousy they feel toward their partners, but they cannot do so all at once. Charlie and his partner, Eleanor, could benefit from articulating the assumptions behind their day-to-day irritations. What does Charlie expect from Eleanor in return for the chores he does for her? What does she feel she owes him in return? Does she feel burdened by the implicit obligations he imposes on her? Can they agree about how often and under what conditions they will make love? Such negotiations would not, however, take away Charlie's deep-seated, intensely felt insecurity, which fuels the agonizing jealousy that he knows has no basis in present reality. To address this larger issue, individual therapy probably would be needed.

Sue and Art could also make adjustments in their daily interactions so as to put helpful boundaries around Sue's jealous reactions. For example, Art would do well to be completely open with Sue about his travel plans and his casual interactions with women, even at the risk of precipitating a jealous scene. Were he to do so, this kind of information would not come out later in a more damaging light, and Sue would understand more clearly that she is responsible for her jealousy. She still, however, would need to come to terms (through therapy, group support, and self-awareness) with the major traumas in her adolescence that led her to feel inadequate as a woman, and thereby made her so susceptible to jealousy. In the end, whether a solution is found through negotiations, couple counseling, individual therapy, or all of these together, the goal is not only to remove the symptom of jealousy, but for the couple to reach a deeper understanding and appreciation of each other and greater satisfaction in their relationship.

8

DEPRESSION:

LOVE'S HANGOVER

Here is how some of the people we interviewed described their feelings at the end of a relationship:

> *Carol:* "There's a great big knot in my stomach, and my chest is tight most of the time. I can't even contain myself from crying when I'm on the phone talking about business."

> *Ray:* "I started going crazy. And then I just fell apart. I felt all this emotion in my body. I thought, 'I'm going to walk in the ocean and drown myself.' I couldn't sleep at night. I was sick. Sick sick sick. I cried and cried and cried for days and days and days. I've gone through an emotional trauma that is beyond any pain I've ever experienced."

> *Gail:* "That hurting, aching feeling was there—when I'd go to bed at night, when I'd wake up in the morning, and during the day, too. I went through such gut-wrenching feelings of misery."

For the person whose intimate attachments are fraught with insecurity, the third and last stage of prime vulnerability comes when the relationship ends. As we have seen, anxious attachment most commonly occurs early in a relationship, although for some people it may persist throughout the relationship. Jealousy occurs when the relationship appears to be threatened by a sexual rival. *Depression,* the third type of emotional reaction commonly associated with insecure love, occurs in response to the perceived loss of love from a partner.

We have followed the story of Lynne and Scott through the stages of anxious attachment (in Chapter 5) and jealousy (in Chapter 7). It is a classic case of a person becoming emotionally involved with a partner who is very attractive, but highly inconsistent. After Scott finally made up his mind first to take a job in New York, and later to invite Lynne to live with him there, he continued to have secret phone calls with his ex-girlfriend as well as clandestine meetings. In her frustration and anxiety, Lynne became uncharacteristically violent, throwing things against the wall and hitting Scott to try to get him to listen to her. Scott used her disruptive outbursts as a reason, or pretext, to call it quits. Lynne returned home to Ohio to reestablish the connections she had severed and pick up where she had left off.

Lynne had hoped to marry Scott. That dream left her with a draining emotional hangover as she returned to the day-to-day business of life, including the need to find employment. She describes the depression she experienced:

> I've never before felt the insecurity that I felt with Scott. I've never felt the crazy jealousy that I felt with him—never. And I've never had this bad a depression after a breakup. I've been busy with my friends and all, but still, the mornings and the evenings. . . . Waking up every single morning thinking of him. I really have to fight to get out of bed sometimes—it's that heavy. I feel the sadness when I hear certain songs on the radio.
>
> When it gets really bad, my mother or a friend comes and talks sense to me. But that has to come from within, and it's not sinking in. I can't get over this, and I don't understand it. Miss him? Miss what? I mean, there were so few really good times. We had good chemistry; we had fun together. But when it came down to the real fundamentals of a relationship, we didn't have it. So what do I miss? This is what bothers me.

Many who have gone through a painful breakup, especially one they did not initiate, will recognize Lynne's bewilderment, the gap that separates her intellectual understanding from her emotional reactions. She can *say* exactly why Scott is not worthy of her loyalty, and why he and she are not compatible, but she still *feels* a gnawing sense of loss, of bereavement, of emptiness. She carries on from day to day with an absence of energy or enthusiasm, and the daily routines of life become a chore and a struggle. When Lynne is in this frame of mind, every other relationship, experience, or feeling loses meaning and value for her. She fears, therefore, that against her better judgment, she might be unable to resist any renewed overtures from Scott.

> It's not completely out of my system. I still harbor the thought of calling him. I find myself coming home looking for letters or phone calls or even the obscure possibility that he would fly back here and beg me to marry him. Subconsciously and even consciously I sometimes wish that would happen, even though my head tells me that would be the biggest mistake of my life, because I don't think he's capable of giving what I want and need. I do want to be loved; I do want to be the only one in his life. I definitely want to feel that I'm Number One, and I'll make the other person feel the same way. But I'm not sure Scott is capable of it.
>
> Sometimes I say, "He's just incapable of giving." Then I ask, "Is it just because he's not ready to be committed? Maybe the timing was bad because he was on the rebound. Maybe he just needs another year." My friends tell me, "No, absolutely not, he is selfish, he's a liar, and he will never give you a hundred percent. He will never give you what *you* need, Lynne. Maybe someone else could handle it, but not you."
>
> Intellectually I can say that, but I miss everything else about him. So I let myself say, "Maybe if I had been a little more independent . . . ," or "Maybe it was the situation." I go back and forth. There are moments when I get beyond it, but not days. My friends tell me I have to move on, but I can't. Or maybe I don't want to.

Part of the hook that keeps Lynne obsessed with Scott is the guilt that he played upon when he broke up with her. As *he* represented the breakup, it occurred not because he was disloyal, but because she was too insecure, or too impatient, or too dependent. Even afterward he hinted that he really wanted to be married, and that it was too bad Lynne had messed things up. Lynne took the bait.

> I look back and say, "Was he all that bad? Maybe it was just a reaction to me and my jealousy. Maybe if I had handled it differently, he would have felt closer to me." Because that's what he tells me. I know it takes time, but I wish I could make the guilt go away. I wish I could say, "Dammit, I wasn't wrong." I wish I could believe that, because that would help me move on.

To the already severe loss of the man she loved, Lynne added the pain of self-reproach, the haunting thought that maybe it had all been her own fault. If only she had acted differently, if only she could have one more chance to do it right. . . .

Lynne's depressed reaction to the breakup with Scott illustrates what psychologists such as Robert Weiss have called the "attachment-distress syndrome." People who lose a relationship of primary importance (that is, a family member or loved one) continue to focus their attention on the relationship for some time after it has ended. They experience emotions ranging from anger toward the lost person to guilt because they believe they may be responsible for the loss. They feel an urge to make contact with the lost person and are alert to the least sign (real or imagined) that the person may return. They suffer from great restlessness, sleeplessness, feelings of fear and panic, and loss of appetite.

It is not only insecure lovers who experience the attachment-distress syndrome. Anyone who suffers the rupture of a highly significant bond may have similar feelings and show similar symptoms. This includes, for instance, children who are separated from their parents as well as people mourning the death of a loved one. Weiss quotes a woman who had a strong feeling of panic, "out of proportion to what was actually happening," when her husband left her. She recalled that this was the same feeling of abandonment she had had as a child in the hospital when her mother went home each night. Depression after a great loss is a universal experience, regardless of age or circumstance, and for many people it follows a pattern set early in life. It may occur following the breakup of a secure relationship of long duration. For example, a woman whose husband dies after forty years of mutual contentment may react to her bereavement in some of the same ways Lynne did.

Nonetheless, Lynne's experience with Scott bears little resemblance to a long, happy marriage. Lynne and Scott had a stormy relationship that lasted about a year and a half. Scott was a highly attractive, but fickle lover, and Lynne never felt secure with him. Besides, although she valued him highly in some ways, she did not value him unequivocally. As she says, "there were so few really good times," and "when it came down to the real fundamentals of a relationship, we didn't have it." Lynne recognized that Scott was not right for her. One would hardly say that she loved Scott as our recently bereaved widow would have loved her husband after forty years together. Yet Lynne felt intensely, albeit anxiously, attached to him. She was like the people in divorce groups who say, "Here I am feeling so depressed, yet I *hate* the man. Why?" People form strong attachments regardless of how they feel, or say they feel, about their partners. When these attachments (brief, troubled, or obviously doomed as they may be) are broken, those who have felt bound to them go through a grief reaction similar to that experienced by a securely attached person.

Does this mean that depression is unrelated to anxious romantic attachment? No, it simply means that depression is not *necessarily* a sign of anxious romantic attachment. We cannot say that a person who feels depressed when a relationship ends was anxiously attached in that relationship. Many people feel depressed when they lose a valued partner. However, a person who is anxiously attached to a particular partner is likely to be depressed when the relationship ends. It is not coincidental that someone like Lynne, who was anxiously attached to her lover and went through fits of jealousy, became severely depressed when he left her. A person who tends toward anxious romantic attachment also is prone to jealousy when a relationship is threatened and to depression when the relationship ends. All three are aspects and characteristics of insecure romantic love.

People can have many reasons for being depressed. We are concerned with just one of those reasons—depression in the aftermath of anxious romantic attachment. Here is a case of a person who was anxiously attached in a relationship and became depressed when the relationship ended.

GAIL AND BRIAN: THE YOUNG HAVE SUCH LOSSES

Gail and Brian started dating when they were seniors in high school in a town in western Massachusetts near Amherst. They had known each other throughout their school years, but Gail had never expected Brian to take an interest in her. A star on the school's football team, Brian had his pick of the prettiest girls at school, and he was more self-assured and experienced in dating than Gail. For her, Brian was quite a catch. A muscular, well-proportioned athlete, he was overwhelmingly attractive to her, as he was to others. A great part of his attraction lay in the unaccustomed status he conferred on her.

> I'd seen the way other girls were so attracted to him; he was the type of
> person you'd notice. I liked being with him just because I knew a lot of
> other people liked him. Maybe that's how it started.

What drew Brian to Gail, she speculates, was that "I didn't go running to him, even though he was so popular. I was different from a lot of the girls he had dated." As the relationship progressed, she says, "I got to know him on a more personal level than the others had. I didn't see him just as macho, but also as sensitive."

A few months after they started going together, Gail told Brian that she loved him. "You can't love me," he said. "It's too soon." This was unfamiliar terrain for him, and for her as well. "He was my first love," she remarks. When they graduated, Gail went off to college in the Midwest, while Brian stayed in the area where they had grown up so that he could attend the University of Massachusetts at Amherst. It was then, in a tearful farewell, that Brian reciprocated Gail's declaration of love. For Gail, it meant that "I felt important; I felt needed. He singled me out as being special, different from the other girls."

If anything, the relationship intensified during the year they spent apart. Gail recalls how she felt at the time:

> I was much more emotional, more attached to him than he was to me, but I felt comfortable knowing that he cared for me when I was hundreds of miles away. He could have started dating somebody else, but he didn't. I was surprised. I kept waiting for him to do it, because I really was insecure.

After a series of visits that seemed to increase their attachment, Gail transferred to Amherst for her second year to be near Brian. The relationship picked up where it had left off. Gail moved back in with her parents in the town nearby and visited Brian on campus on the weekends. As the year went on, however, Brian became elusive and noncommunicative.

> He didn't come home or call me as often as he had. I sensed that he was getting itchy. I didn't try to smother him. I knew he was in a demanding course of study and had to study a lot, and I respected him by letting him do his thing. Maybe he was also getting pressure from his friends to date other girls. His friends never saw me because he never wanted to hang out with me at school. At first I thought that was strange. Then I started attributing it to myself, like "What's wrong with me? Why doesn't he want to be with me?"

Never fully secure in the relationship, Gail now began to show more evident signs of anxious attachment.

> He was all I thought about. I tried to predict his every move, and why he did what he did. When we were apart, I'd wonder what he was doing, why he wasn't calling me, and whether he was thinking about me as much as I was thinking about him, which was constantly. Most of the time he'd give me subtle reassurances. My friends would say, "Oh, when you're not around, all he talks about is you." Every so often I'd get a card from him. He was not predictable, that's for sure. Maybe I found that exciting.

At times I was on top of the mountain, even when I wasn't with him, just knowing that he was out there, thinking about me. More often than not, though, a bad feeling would follow a good one. I'd fall asleep at night still hoping he would call. Sometimes he'd call late at night, and I'd be ecstatic. Otherwise I'd have him on my mind all night and wake up the next morning thinking, "Wow, he didn't call. Maybe he was out with some girl." It was such a letdown.

At that point in their lives, Gail and especially Brian were not very articulate about their feelings. As a result, their relationship broke up in what for Gail was a mystifying and frustrating way.

By now we saw each other only for occasional weekends. He said, "We have to be more casual." I said, "Okay, okay, just don't cut me out completely." I wasn't dependent on him to do things for me. I didn't need to see him every day, and he didn't want us getting too mushy in public, like people who have to live, sleep, eat, and breathe together. In that respect we were mature for our age. But I was dependent on him for his devotion, his affection, for all that we had shared, and for the things he had said that made me feel unique and special. And to lose that for no valid reason, like all he could say was, "You know, Gail, I need to finish my education, and I have to concentrate on my work." I didn't understand that. I needed to hear something from him, even if it was "I don't love you anymore," or "I just want to see other girls." I pleaded for an explanation, like "Harpo, speak!" But he said nothing; he couldn't deal with me directly.

So I had to come up with his excuses myself, terrible things to cut myself down to size and make me feel I wasn't good enough for him. "Oh, I guess I'm not attractive enough," I'd think, and do everything in my power to look better. Then he'd tell me I was getting too skinny! So nothing was good enough. I'd imagine horrible things, like that he was seeing someone else. But I kept it to myself, because I couldn't talk to him.

Brian engineered the breakup in passive, indirect ways. In Gail's words, "He did things to get me to break up with him, like making insensitive remarks. He was hoping I would be vindictive toward him, but I wasn't." Like Lynne, Gail turned her disapproval upon herself, seeing herself as deficient. Given the ambiguous message of Brian's silence, she interpreted it in a way that reflected her feelings of insecurity and guilt. "I didn't deal with it very well," she says in retrospect. "I'd get so upset and cry, and he couldn't handle it."

The slow unraveling of the relationship concluded when Brian did not invite Gail to spend Spring Weekend with him on campus. The meaning of this omission was unmistakable, and Gail accepted the inevitable.

Finally I said, "Forget it. Good-bye. That's it." I was heartbroken, because he'd always said he could never just leave and not say good-bye, but that's what he did. We were so young — we never sat down and talked about how we felt.

That summer, living a few minutes away from Brian as she had back in high school, she saw constant reminders of him — for instance, at parties where she ran into his friends. She lived in fear and hope of seeing him, but never did. She continued to be obsessed with him.

I saw him in my mind every day and expected to run into him around every corner. I dreaded seeing him going out with somebody else. My friends would say, "Oh, forget about the jerk. He's going out with one of his old girlfriends." I'd say, "Yeah, yeah, you're right," but I was dying inside. It was bad enough that he dumped me like he did, but to go out with an old girlfriend that he'd said he didn't care about anymore! I started doubting everything he'd ever told me. No, I thought, he had never loved me, never cared about me. I went through a bitter time that summer, a bitter, angry period when I just hated him.

Now that she had lost him, Gail could at least direct some of her anger outward, at Brian, rather than blame herself completely for her supposed inadequacies. Like many jilted lovers, she alternated between cursing the man who had left her and longing for his return, between railing at his unfairness and blaming herself for failing to hold his interest. Although she found sympathetic listeners in her sister and her friends, she still suffered inwardly in this, the most intense period of her depression.

I felt so out of control. Things had gone so far out of proportion; I didn't know what to do. That hurting, aching feeling was there — when I'd go to bed at night, when I'd wake up in the morning, and during the day, too.

Gail lost the desire to eat — a problem she had never had before. In an echo of her desperate effort to lose weight so she would be appealing to Brian, she turned on her body with a vengeance. For several hours a day she worked out at her health club, and all the while she was hardly eating. As she lost weight, the people around her became concerned.

Here I was trying to make myself look better, and I was wasting away to nothing. My friends would see me, and I'd get these looks. But nobody said anything to me until my Dad stepped in. He said, "I don't like the way you're looking. You'd better cut it out and start eating." I'd break down and cry, saying, "Oh, no one understands me. No one understands how I feel." I felt so alone. I was reaching out for something, but I didn't know what it was. I was such a mess; I didn't care about myself or anything.

Gail's eating habits slowly returned to normal after her father threatened to take her out of the health club and hospitalize her. But she faced a new challenge when she returned to school in September and began to have occasional, uncomfortable run-ins with Brian.

Throughout my junior year I tried to block Brian out of my mind, but I knew he was there, and I thought about him constantly. I went through such gut-wrenching feelings of misery. I started dating casually, going out a lot, just letting myself go and not caring about my schoolwork. It even affected my grades. That didn't last long, because it wasn't me at all. It made me feel even worse about myself.

The following year, Gail began to feel more comfortable around Brian, even when she saw him with another woman. "A year and a half had gone by, and a lot of the hurt had subsided," she explains. That year she and Brian had their first serious talk since their breakup, and both of them acknowledged feelings they had been unable to put into words at the time. With further growth and reflection, Gail could put her experience with Brian in perspective.

When I see him now, I feel so strong. I can stand there and be proud of myself, and not feel insecure, as if I'm a little nobody compared to him. Sometimes he seems nervous to me now; it's a strange thing. Looking back, I can understand why he couldn't deal with all this when he was nineteen—lots of guys can't. At the time it was misery for us both, but we grew.

I still melt when I see him. It's such a bundle of weird, conflicting feelings. But what I called love then was different from what I would call love now. Now I would never enter into a relationship for the reasons I did then, to impress people and bolster my ego. And if I felt it was the same type of relationship, where somebody kept me feeling unequal and in the dark about everything, I would get out. I learned a lot from it, but it's not what I would want now.

Although she has dated a number of men and says that she now knows what she wants from a prospective partner, Gail had not (at the time of this interview) been involved with anyone seriously since Brian.

Gail's severe depression was in part a consequence of youth and inexperience. She and Brian, who were not very articulate with each other about their relationship, provide a good illustration of the kind of protracted disengagement sociologist Diane Vaughan describes in *Uncoupling,* where one partner breaks up with another through drift and indecision. Gail saw signs of trouble, but Brian reassured her in an elusive and misleading way. Not wanting to hurt Gail (and perhaps not wanting to lose her until he had found a suitable replacement), Brian could not bring himself to confirm her fears and forebodings. Without clear warning signals, Gail could neither work out the problems in the relationship nor prepare herself realistically for its end. Moreover, she had little past experience to bolster her against such a loss. With no other relationships behind her, she had placed all of her emotional eggs in this one basket.

In a sense, what we call anxious romantic attachment describes the emotional turmoil typical of adolescence. For some people, though, it continues into adulthood, and these individuals remain perennial adolescents in respect to love. To understand why this happens, we can turn back to our discussion of needs at the end of Chapter 5. A person whose needs are all being met in one relationship will not readily give up that relationship. Even if the partner is not meeting those needs very well, one who has little hope of finding a better way to satisfy them will still feel dependent on that partner. This is true whether one regards oneself as too old to attract another suitable partner or too young to have tested one's attractiveness.

As social psychologist Stanton Peele and writer Archie Brodsky emphasize in *Love and Addiction,* when one is dependent on a single emotional tie as a primary source of well-being, that connection comes to be so highly valued as to seem essential to one's existence. If it is broken, then one may feel oneself to be without moorings. Charlie, the anguished, plaintive lover in Chapters 6 and 7, gives an apt description of addictive love:

> Sometimes I feel like I want to crawl in Eleanor's back pocket and never emerge. This loss of self seems to be so key to all my significant relationships—this constant, all-pervasive urge to be with the woman at all costs, despite the fact that I don't even enjoy her company all the time.

Charlie is dependent on his girlfriend in proportion to his lack of other meaningful involvements in life. In the words of *Love and Addiction,* "When a person goes to another with the aim of filling a void in himself, the relationship quickly becomes the center of his or her life." The extent of this dependency is revealed when the relationship breaks up. "Since the relationship has been the person's one essential contact point with life, its removal necessarily leaves him in a disoriented agony."

FROM ANXIETY TO DEPRESSION

A forty-year-old man married to a twenty-five-year-old woman refused to accept that their marriage was over after six years. His wife had moved out to live with a younger man, but occasionally she would visit him and rekindle his hope that she would change her mind, although she only dropped by when she wanted to borrow money from him. From the start it had been a tragic mismatch. A reserved, highly intellectual man fell in love with a beautiful woman in her late teens who gave him the attention and respect he had never received from attractive women in his own peer group. He was a warm, sensitive person, and she drew him out of his isolation when she needed a moment of respite from her own world of parties, drugs, and motorcycles. But she could not be the homemaker and spiritual companion of his fantasies, any more than he could fit into her youthful social scene.

As she matured into a more self-confident woman, she sought new worlds to conquer. But despite the evidence that she had little further interest in her husband, now entering middle age, he continued to think obsessively of her and to grasp at any hint that she might come back to him. Having dated relatively little before their marriage, he refused to date other women until their divorce was final. In the meantime, he kept saying to himself, "She *has* to change. She *has* to come back. I've put so much into this, like I never did before—I *have* to make it work!"

Clinging to hope in a situation grown increasingly hopeless, this man was like a person gambling at a slot machine, putting in quarters again and again and pulling the lever even though the losses mount. What keeps a person gambling? Apparently, the occasional jackpot leads one to anticipate winning another eventually. Even if the rewards are few and far between, one refuses to believe that the losses will outweigh the gains.

Perhaps one tides oneself over during dry spells by fantasizing about the pot of gold—a picture of which is often placed prominently on the slot machine for just that purpose. Then, too, the occasional wins *feel* all the more rewarding by contrast to the repeated frustrations, like crumbs of food to a starving person. The slot machine withholds, withholds, and rewards; withholds, withholds, withholds, and rewards. These rewards mean more than the same amount of money would in less tense circumstances. They also mean more to one who finds life outside the gambling casino not very rewarding, and who therefore places great hope in the possibility of a magical transformation of one's circumstances.

The more one invests, the harder it is to walk away from the slot machine. To walk away is to admit the reality of the losses which until then have seemed just temporary setbacks. One may feel humiliated; one may have acted in a way that is "not like myself." But none of that will matter if one can make that one big score.

The slot machine is an example of what learning theorists call "inconsistent reward" or "partial reinforcement." Instead of winning on every play, one learns that if one keeps playing one will win some of the time, and that expectation keeps one in the game. Psychologists have found that inconsistent rewards can be *more* effective than consistent rewards in motivating a person to continue behaving in a certain way. That is because one never knows whether the rewards have really stopped, or whether one simply has hit a dry spell. If you reward a person consistently—say, every third time—for doing something (such as pulling the lever on a slot machine) and then stop the reward, the person quickly will discontinue the behavior. He or she has no basis for expecting the reward to be resumed once it has been interrupted. If, however, you reward the person *in*consistently and then stop, the person will continue the behavior much longer, since he or she has learned to expect a resumption of the reward.

John Paul Scott cites an early experiment by A. E. Fisher that gave a striking demonstration of the power of inconsistent reward. The experimenter took three groups of fox terrier puppies (who were fed automatically by machine) and gave them three distinct forms of treatment. He treated one group with consistent affection, the second with consistent coldness and rejection. Toward the third group he acted inconsistently, sometimes treating them kindly and sometimes coldly. It was this third group of puppies that kept chasing after the experimenter, seeking his approval and affection. They were more attached to him and dependent on him than the puppies that were consistently rewarded or consistently punished.

We see a similar pattern, tragically, in children whose parents neglect and abuse them, but then "make it up" to them with exaggerated kindness. A child treated in this manner often feels a powerful bond with the parent and may spend considerable energy trying to figure out what will make the parent act like the good parent, rather than the bad parent, all the time. Unable to face what it means to have a bad parent, the child has no alternative, psychologically, but to make the parent into a good one.

The anxiously attached individual also experiences inconsistent rewards. Anxious romantic attachment is marked by a strongly felt, yet insecure emotional bond with another person. One experiences the bond as insecure either because the partner is inconsistent or because one is predisposed to experience relationships as tenuous and uncertain due to past experience with inconsistent lovers or parents. Indeed, both may be the case, in that the partner's behavior may reinforce one's prior insecurity.

For the anxiously attached lover, positive feedback (the partner's interest, affection, or reciprocated love) alternates with negative feedback (the partner's inattention, neglect, disapproval, rejection, or greater interest in others). Although the negative experiences might lead some people to give up the relationship, one who finds the positive experiences intensely rewarding will wait out the negative ones in the expectation that an ecstatic sensation of romantic fulfillment will come up again.

This is the pattern of reward and punishment that binds a person into an anxious romantic attachment. Lynne felt frustrated and even compromised by Scott's behavior, yet she found something about her involvement with him so rewarding that she could not turn away from him. Brian's behavior was somewhat aloof and mysterious, but also somewhat reassuring. He would pull away from Gail, but then come back, acting as if nothing had changed between them. It was a combination that kept Gail guessing, but kept her involved.

Understanding anxious romantic attachment as (in part) a product of inconsistent reward helps explain how people experience its two components, romantic anxiety and romantic obsession. It is evident that being rewarded inconsistently can make a person feel anxious, and we have seen that romantic anxiety is associated with the partner's inconsistency. Romantic obsession, on the other hand, can serve as a mirage to carry a person through the drought between rewards. Like the person dreaming about the big jackpot while the slot machine takes his quarters, the anxiously attached lover may obsess about a partner who at the moment is aloof or rejecting. By gaining temporary satisfaction through fantasy, one acclimates oneself to the inconsistency of the real gratifications bestowed by the partner. Thus, in similarly uncertain situations, some people mainly feel anxious; others use obsession to take their minds off the anxiety; while still others experience a mixture of anxiety and obsession.

Since inconsistent rewards can lead a person to maintain an attachment with greater tenacity, a marriage or love affair may well have a long, drawn-out conclusion for the anxiously attached person. A person who is accustomed to filling the empty spaces in a relationship with obsessive fantasies can keep up that diversion for a considerable time as the reality of the end slowly sinks in. At the same time, a person who harbors even the slightest hope of a reprieve will make active efforts to win the partner back. People can play out a losing game with amazing determination when, in the past, those efforts have sometimes paid off—especially if they think it is the only game in town. (This is true even when the losing game is a stalemate between two partners—say, a spouse and a lover—neither of whom is a satisfactory choice, yet the person cannot break out of the dilemma and look elsewhere.)

This protracted process of disengagement is described in Diane Vaughan's book, *Uncoupling*. The partner who ultimately initiates the breakup, while showing signs of discontent, creates such a smokescreen that the other partner can disregard the faintly perceived signs of the impending severance. The initiator may do this out of a reluctance to hurt the partner, as well as out of a desire to hold on to the partner as long as possible—at least until the initiator has a new relationship in place and has resolved any ambivalence about the breakup.

In this way, the two partners tacitly conspire to disguise the initiator's intentions for the "benefit" of the partner who, about to be jilted, is only too happy to avoid facing the inevitable. One partner is trying to let the other down gently, while the other still thinks it possible to preserve a valued relationship. When the breakup comes, even after a long, gradual loosening of ties, it still may come as a shock. Vaughan's analysis (exemplified by Brian's slow, indecisive withdrawal from Gail) shows how the inconsistent rewards experienced by the anxiously attached lover can continue right through to the end of the relationship, keeping hope alive and anxiety boiling.

As the truth starts to sink in, the partner who is about to be left enters into an intensified phase of anxious romantic attachment, the symptoms of which become more extreme in a crisis. Here the person may resort to desperate tactics to rekindle fading passion and force tokens of love from a partner who is frustratingly distant. In response, the initiator may feel increasingly guilty and delay the final blow while seeking to help the partner understand and accept what is happening. This compassionate reaction can leave the initiator open to further emotional manipulation. For example, the anxiously attached partner may give free rein to her or his distress in the hope of evoking sympathy. Many relationships have been prolonged by implicit or explicit threats of suicide—or, less drastically, by appeals such as "But what will I do? Where will I go? How will I get along?"

As long as there is hope, as long as there is an attempt to save the relationship, these intimations of desperation are still expressions of anxiety rather than depression. A newly jilted lover who is still playing the game, nagging the ex-partner ("Come on, you know you still love me—just a little, maybe?"), feels a great deal of anxiety, frustration, and sadness, but also intermittent hope. However, as the hopelessness of the situation becomes apparent, these feelings come to be intermingled with, and dominated by, depression.

A person may alternate for some time between anxiety (uncertain hope) and depression (hopelessness). Waves of depression are followed by indications of renewed hope (often in the form of fantasies). The shift from anxiety to depression does not happen all at once. Rather, there are days when one is anxious and days when one is depressed. There are even moments of anxiety and moments of depression within the same day, the same hour. Hope is like fumes to an engine running out of gas on the road to despair—it sputters, catches fire and runs for a while, peters out, then catches fire again.

ED AND HOLLY: PLAY "MISTY" FOR ME

That was how it was for Ed, a popular thirty-eight-year-old disc jockey who played golden oldies on a radio station in the Midwest. Not long after a tense therapy session in which Ed despaired of being able to put his life back together now that his girlfriend had left him, his therapist turned on the car radio to hear Ed playing Bobby Darin's "Dream Lover." The song was part of a "dream sequence" Ed had put together that day: the Everly Brothers' "All I Have to Do Is Dream," Jimmy Clanton's "Just a Dream," Johnny Burnette's "Dreamin'," Roy Orbison's "Sweet Dream Baby." Yes, the therapist mused, the relationship had been something of a dream, a fantasy. Holly, an attractive, childlike woman of twenty, had fallen in love with a voice on the radio, a name known to all her friends, a virtual fountain of tickets to an endless season of rock concerts. When she introduced herself to him at an event where he was the emcee, Ed was flattered and intrigued. He had his fantasy, too—one of youthful romance and simple devotion—which he tried to realize through Holly in the wake of a painful, humiliating divorce.

Ed and Holly lived together for a few years. Each felt a great need for the other, but their needs were incompatible. Holly needed Ed to take responsibility for her, while he needed to escape from responsibility through her. Their fantasies were incongruent with the divergent realities of their lives. In particular, Holly, age twenty-four, could not accept Ed as the father of two teenage children. The children regarded her as more a peer and a rival than a parent. Unable to deal with these complicated emotional currents, Holly moved out.

His fantasy ended, Ed came to therapy distraught and needy. Obsessed with Holly, he saw her name wherever he looked, in newspapers and street signs. She fed his obsession by calling to seek advice and give consolation, as well as to justify herself and blame him for not having done more for her. The tantalizing possibility that she might come back to him was out there, unspoken, although both of them knew that the cycle of mutual discontent would only repeat itself. Meanwhile, Ed comforted, or tortured, himself by saying things like, "I've never felt so alive as when I was with Holly and felt her admiration."

Actually, their relationship had been stormy, uncommunicative, and not always mutually fulfilling. Ed, however, isolated the best parts of it to enshrine after the fact. During the relationship, too, such thoughts had carried him through difficult moments. The idealized image of Holly that he cherished had stretched the partial reinforcement he got from her erratic, self-preoccupied behavior into something that he experienced as nearly complete satisfaction. Even after her departure, he continued to live on memories of his peak experiences with Holly.

His therapist, who now made a point of listening to Ed on the radio, heard him play strings of songs about lost love, longing, and despair. There were songs about the futility of loving a younger woman: "But you lived on the morning side of the mountain, and I lived on the twilight side of the hill." The therapist wondered whether Ed was trying to woo Holly back with these songs, as Holly always used to read a message for herself—or for other women who called the station (of whom she was jealous)—into every song he played. Ed denied that there was any significance to his selection of songs. "They're all like that," he said. "Popular songs are always about breakups and incompatibility, about falling out of love."

Ed went on to say that he was feeling better and that he realized it was all over. Holly would never get along with his children, and he would only destroy himself trying to change her. That day he went back to the radio station and played a set of songs having nothing to do with broken romances or unrequited love. The set ended with "I Can See Clearly Now." Contrary to his own contention that every song had the same message, he seemed intent on showing that he could let go.

That same day, however, he lost control of himself and had to leave the studio early. Crying and shaking, he called his therapist and asked for medication. He revealed that he had phoned Holly from the station and begged her to come back, and that she had refused. That was right after he had announced his acceptance of the finality of the breakup. In retrospect, it seemed clear that as long as Ed hoped to reach Holly by playing certain songs, he could cushion himself from the depression he would otherwise face. Challenged by the therapist to relinquish that fantasy, he felt himself losing hope. Whether in a desperate attempt to regain that hope or to test the reality that he was beginning to acknowledge, he confronted Holly directly. He got the answer that he probably knew he would get, but was not ready to accept. Ed was at the transition point between anxiety and depression, and it was likely that he would flip back and forth more than once before he reached a stable resolution.

In our initial study of anxious romantic attachment in men, those who scored high not only were more depressed when a relationship ended, but also stayed depressed longer, than those who scored lower. But we cannot say very precisely what they meant by depressed. How can we ever specify the day when a relationship ends, when hope is forever lost? The men in our study may have been thinking of the entire final act before the curtain fell on the relationship, including its anxious as well as depressed scenes. That is, they might have given similar answers to questions such as "How long and drawn out was the ending of the relationship?" and "How distressing was the ending of the relationship?" What we learned from their responses was that those who have experienced the inconsistent rewards of anxious romantic attachment have greater difficulty letting go.

It may be that inconsistent reward creates a stronger as well as a longer-lasting attachment, increasing the likelihood of severe depression when hope is finally lost. In a chemical analogy, the strength of a molecular bond is measured by the energy released when it is broken. A person who has to be dragged away from a slot machine will have a strong sense of disorientation. Similarly, the power of inconsistent reward to bind a person to a relationship is remarkable, judging from the painful ruptures it often takes to break such attachments. As hope dwindles to nothing, the jilted lover may experience insistent fantasies. As one man put it, "Now I've got the worst of both worlds. I'm still 'in' the relationship, even though I don't really have it anymore." At the other extreme, the reinforcement may go on for so long, infrequent as it has become, that only by some dramatic act of rejection can the tie finally be severed.

Ironically, it is often the jilted, formerly anxiously attached partner, desperate to relieve the tension and pain that by now far overshadow any positive gratifications from the relationship, who acts decisively to end the obsession. In an adolescent example, a boy in high school continued to visit his ex-girlfriend after school in her parents' candy store. He felt drawn to make these visits even while he found them frustratingly inconclusive, for he felt that the girl was keeping him on a longer and longer string. One day he came into the store, bought a cream pie, and, in full view of her parents, pushed it into the girl's face. He exited quickly, bowing out with feelings of relief and ecstasy, knowing that he could never show his face there again.

In a more serious, adult situation, Lynne did essentially the same thing when she threw fits of temper that led Scott to lock her out of their apartment. These tantrums, she says, were "my way of leaving. I think in my heart I knew it had to end, but I didn't have the strength to end it, so I let him throw me out." Worn out waiting for inconsistent rewards that had become increasingly sparse, but still somehow compelling, she finally let go and accepted the prospect of depression, followed by whatever unknown alternatives the future would bring.

DAVID AND JOAN: TO LOVE AGAIN

At the end of Chapter 6 we saw how some couples adjust the level of intimacy in their relationship so that both partners can be comfortable with it. Sometimes this fine-tuning occurs throughout the duration of the relationship and becomes part of the couple's normal pattern of interaction. Sometimes it takes the form of an acute crisis, in which one partner uses the threat of separation or divorce to make the other partner more responsive. In the case of David and Joan, actual divorce proceedings figured in the readjustment of the marital relationship. The couple appeared to have an evolving relationship during and after the divorce process, and it was difficult to tell whether or not they really were disengaging from each other. Joan was the initiator of this prolonged, ambiguous separation, and her mixed motives wove a web of inconsistent reinforcement around her husband, David.

David, a forty-year-old market research specialist, had never been emotionally demonstrative toward his wife, who was several years younger. However, his reserved, self-sufficient air masked his dependency on her in many areas of daily life with which he did not engage actively. Keeping his mind on his work, he allowed Joan to structure their personal life. She felt that by assuming this role, she was held back in her own development. Joan wanted to complete her education, but somehow never did so because David always left her with "something to take care of."

After Joan moved out and filed for divorce, David seemed transformed. Having taken his emotional life for granted up to that point, he began to blossom into poetic self-expression, articulating his feelings in journals as well as in soul-searching talks with Joan ("now that it's too late," he would add). He felt intensely lonely and admitted that

> I miss Joan as I never thought I could or would. I was never an affectionate person, and yet now I crave the affection and physical contact I denied her. Now I'm in her shoes, and I see how she felt.

David was another of those men, like Marty in Chapter 2, who appear detached and self-satisfied in relationships until their bluff is called. Men often are more acutely distressed than women when a relationship ends, having been less conscious all along of the underlying problems in the relationship. Men also bounce back more readily if they can reestablish themselves in the same or another relationship.

David expressed his distress dramatically. He had few friends and had lived alone only briefly in the past. He felt adrift in the absence of the one emotional relationship (limited as it was) that he had taken the trouble to form. He did not, however, fall into an extended, immobilizing depression; nor did he bounce back and reconstitute his comfortable life in some other relationship. Neither resolution was possible because he and Joan remained involved even though she refused to take him back. He was caught in the bind of inconsistent reward and, with it, undying hope. "If only I knew what she really wants, I could resolve this," he would say.

Unfortunately for both of them, it was not clear whether *she* knew what she wanted. She may have been letting him down gently, cushioning the blow for fear he might become self-destructive if cut loose too abruptly. At times, though, it seemed she herself was having difficulty letting go. She may even have resorted to divorce as the only way left to bring about lasting changes in their relationship. She may have feared that, if she relented, she would be overwhelmed by his entreaties and promises, but nothing really would change.

Whatever her intentions, she colluded with David to place him in a classic situation of partial reinforcement. She would invite him for dinner, and he would come with flowers and a poem of his own creation. Seizing the opportunity, he would come over again the next day and the next. Then she would complain that she felt pressured, and he would try his best to back off. If he declined an invitation because "I don't want to crowd her—I want her to have some space," David would expect to see Joan three times the following week. "My emotions are churning around," he declared. His hopes would soar when he received a promising invitation, only to collapse in misery when he saw that she had taken off her wedding ring.

Through it all, the couple spoke more intimately than they ever had when they were together. Expressing a sense of puzzlement, Joan reported:

> He's telling me things now that he never did in all those years: what I mean to him, how he feels about me, how I've had an impact on him in ways I never knew. I believe he means it, but it makes me feel guilty.

More grist was added to the mill when, after the separation, David was diagnosed with non-insulin-dependent diabetes. He made sure to remind Joan that this disease made him less salable on the marriage market. "I really feel my mortality now," he told her. "I might live another twenty or twenty-five years, but unless they find a cure I'm not going to live to a very old age."

David played on Joan's guilt and compassion as a tactic to put off any definite reckoning and keep his hopes alive indefinitely. When Joan said that she might need at least a year to make up her mind for certain, he said, "Take your time. Don't feel pressured. You don't have to decide by any particular date."

However, David was not always sure that he wanted to stay in perpetual uncertainty. Even as Joan saw other men, she and David were sexually intimate during a few weekend outings they took together over a six-month period. Although he felt powerless to resist this closeness, David was unnerved by it; it felt *too* close. He suffered another rough landing when Joan called off the divorce one day, only to change her mind the next. "I can't let go of her," he said. "I can't stand the limbo. I need a decision."

Did he really want a decision? With insight and frankness he explained, "I want her to search out her emotions and come to some conclusions. But if she comes to the wrong conclusions, I'll really be shaken up." At one point Joan announced, "I've decided I want to be on my own." Taking that as his final notice, David cried all the way home. In that mood he concluded, "I feel all alone. I feel like I'm just functioning in a vacuum. I feel empty." This is the depression that signifies lost hope.

Yet for David, though devastated at the moment, it was not the end of the line. When the divorce became final he was sad, disappointed, and angry, for it put a seeming end to any future plans the couple had made. "I'm just going along, taking care of myself from day to day," he sighed. Even then, however, Joan did not allow his hope to be extinguished. "This doesn't mean," she said, "that a year or two from now we might not find each other again."

The first time he went out with another woman after the divorce, David saw the movie *Fatal Attraction*. He understood how someone might want to kill the person they love, just to end the pain. If the loved one were dead, she wouldn't be there to bestow acceptance or rejection, to be the object of unrequited desire, to be ultimately unattainable. David was not a violent person, but he wished for something drastic to happen to bring him deliverance. He had fought tooth and nail to keep from sinking into depression, but there was a point where even that would be preferable to the anguish of keeping up the fight.

WHAT THE DATA SHOW

Participants in our study of anxious romantic attachment were asked to complete the Beck Depression Inventory (short form) to measure how depressed they felt "when my relationship with was over." The Inventory included multiple-choice statements such as the following:

3) I get too tired to do anything.
2) I get tired from doing anything.
1) I get tired more easily than I used to.
0) I don't get any more tired than usual.*

Similar multiple-choice statements explored the following symptoms or aspects of depression:

- feelings of sadness
- loss of appetite
- feelings of disappointment or disgust with oneself
- feelings of personal failure
- inability to work
- difficulty making decisions
- feelings of guilt or unworthiness
- feelings of being unattractive
- feelings of hopelessness about the future
- loss of interest in other people
- feelings of dissatisfaction
- thoughts of suicide.

Participants responded to these thirteen items concerning each of their four most important past relationships—the same ones about which they answered the anxious-attachment questionnaire (Chapter 2) and the questions about jealousy (Chapter 7). Their responses enabled us to relate the experience of depression when a relationship ends to those of anxious romantic attachment and jealousy when the relationship is still in full swing.

People who were anxiously attached to their partners often were more prone to marked depression when those relationships ended. As with jealousy, and by an even wider margin, people who scored high on romantic obsession were especially likely to become seriously depressed. (The association between depression and romantic anxiety was weaker, especially for women.) Romantic obsession reflects the strength of the attachment a person feels to a particular partner. We noted in the previous chapter that jealousy is felt in response to the threat of losing a partner to whom one feels emotionally bound. Now we see that the loss of such a partner—and such a bond—is central to the experience of depression in the aftermath of a relationship. The stronger the bond, the more depressed one is likely to be when the partner leaves. Along the same lines, among the characteristics of relationships we measured, the one that best predicted depression was the intensity of the person's love for the partner. The more you love someone, the more depressed you are likely to be if you lose that person.

The emotions men and women experienced in relationships that were followed by depression were similar to those they experienced in relationships where they became jealous—but with some interesting differences. Since participants indicated *distress* by reporting that they were "downhearted," "sad," "miserable," or "discouraged" (words that correspond closely to depression), it is not surprising that distress was the emotion most strongly associated with subsequent depression for both men and women. What is surprising is that, for men, distress was less strongly associated with subsequent depression than with jealousy.

Although people may experience similar feelings of distress at any stage of a relationship, an individual actually experiences such distress when that individual feels most vulnerable. For example, a person who has no inkling that anything is wrong until the partner leaves may be all the more prone to depression after such a sudden turnabout, even though that person has had no reason to feel distressed during the relationship. Likewise, men may be more susceptible to feelings of distress in situations involving jealousy than after a breakup because a man's image of himself tends to be tied in with his beliefs about his partner's loyalty. If his partner is disloyal, his sense of his own adequacy is threatened. In keeping with the double standard that still influences our attitudes and emotional reactions, women typically do not feel so diminished by a partner's disloyalty.

Anger and *fear* were other emotions experienced during the relationship by men who subsequently became depressed. In jealousy-provoking relationships, women experienced more fear than men, while men experienced more *shame* than women. In relationships that ended with significant depression, the reverse was the case: men experienced more fear, while women experienced more shame.

Other emotions women tended to feel strongly in relationships whose termination later caused depression were *joy, sexual arousal,* and *guilt* specifically associated with sexual arousal. Of course, one does not experience joy and depression simultaneously. Rather, one apparently is more depressed upon losing a relationship that once had reached higher peaks of joy. Women who reported great joy during a relationship plummeted to great depths of despair when it ended. Women were also more likely than men to experience joy in the same relationships in which they felt a high degree of sexual arousal. For these women the joyfulness of the relationship might have been related to their sexual involvement—the very element that exacerbated their depression when the relationship ended. The fact that depression in women was associated with emotions related to sexuality suggests once again that sexual investment in a relationship leaves some women especially vulnerable to a depressive aftermath if the relationship comes to an unwelcome end.

The duration of the relationship, which had a great deal to do with jealousy (for women especially), had little to do with depression, again for women especially. On the other hand, the number of hours per week the partners spent together, which had little effect on jealousy, was one of the best indicators of depression for men. In other words, jealousy grows out of a sense of entitlement and having one's rights violated, and that sense of entitlement becomes greater the longer the relationship lasts. Depression, on the other hand, grows out of a sense of irreversible loss, and its magnitude is related to how large a place a relationship has in a person's life at any given time. Men become significantly more depressed, though only slightly more jealous, when they have been spending more time with a partner. The amount of time one spends with someone is an index of how large a part of one's life that person is, and how large a gap is left to fill when they are gone. Depression, then, has less to do with entitlement or possession than with the day-to-day experience of the relationship and with the value a partner has as a companion, a constant presence around whom one builds one's life.

People who become so absorbed in a romantic relationship that they cut themselves off from other friends and family may be setting themselves up for depression. Adolescents especially run this risk, since they often are overly influenced by our culture's romantic ideal. For an adolescent, a romantic involvement may serve as a way of separating from one's family and establishing one's individual identity. One may feel most independent of parental tethers while soaring on the clouds of romance, only to find oneself floating aimlessly once the love is gone. One teenage boy spent so much time with his girlfriend that he practically grew up with her family. Without a close family of his own, he allowed himself to be "adopted" by them. When his girlfriend broke up with him, it was as if his whole family had died. Cut off abruptly from his primary source of sustenance, he suffered a severe depression.

TWO TYPES OF DEPRESSION

Thoughts often are the key to feelings. In a study conducted by psychologists Cynthia Wickless and Irving Kirsch, people kept diaries in which they noted when they experienced certain emotions and recorded the thoughts that immediately preceded those emotions. Anxiety usually was preceded by thoughts about the possibility of some bad occurrence or outcome. Anger usually was preceded by thoughts about being treated unfairly or abused. Depression usually was preceded by thoughts about hopelessness or inevitable loss. Wickless and Kirsch's research is a glimpse into the process of how anxious romantic attachment, jealousy, and depression come about. There is a particularly close connection between the cognitive state of hopelessness and the emotional state of depression. If you *think* things are hopeless, then you probably will *feel* depressed.

We can think of depression as taking two main forms, *grieving depression* and *self-punishing depression.* Each is associated with thoughts about hopelessness, but these thoughts have a somewhat different character in each case.

Grieving depression results from a loss of nurturance and support on which one has relied. It grows out of a feeling that one can neither win back the person who provided this nurturance and support nor find anyone else who can fill the same needs adequately. Together, these beliefs add up to a vast sense of loss and hopelessness, one which is more severe if one has placed all of one's eggs in one basket—that is, has depended on one partner to satisfy a range of basic needs.

How susceptible one is to this kind of depression depends in part on the available options, which are related to one's self-image and beliefs about access to potential partners. It also is related to one's ability to mobilize social skills and act confidently to achieve a goal. Cultural roles play a part as well, such as in the case of women who were taught not to ask men out, which results in reinforcing feelings of powerlessness and hopelessness. Social norms for men, on the other hand, may prevent them from seeking emotional support when they feel depressed.

Gail had reason to be depressed on all three grounds. Having had no significant relationships before she met Brian, she was neither aware of options that might be available to her nor confident of her ability to make those options a reality. She may also have assumed that she had to wait for a man to approach her rather than choose and pursue a partner if she so chose.

Gail found herself in a state known as *learned helplessness.* In experiments by psychologist Martin Seligman, dogs were subjected to a series of electric shocks. Their first reaction was one of intense anxiety. However, some dogs had an opportunity to avoid the shocks by running over to another compartment of their cage at the signal of a buzzer or light, and they quickly learned to do so. Another group of dogs was restrained from escaping the shock. After struggling against their restraints for a while in a distressed manner, these dogs gave up and passively endured the shock. Even after they were given the same opportunity to escape that the other dogs had, they learned the new behavior only slowly and with difficulty. This is what is meant by learned helplessness, and in these dogs it was accompanied by symptoms of depression such as loss of appetite and loss of weight.

As these experiments demonstrate, anxiety can lead either to active attempts to cope with the source of the anxiety or to feelings of helplessness and depression, depending on whether one believes that effective remedies are at hand. In human experience, learned helplessness occurs when people live in an environment that teaches them that nothing they do affects their destiny. This belief leads to intense grieving or fatalism rather than active, resourceful behavior.

Freud thought of grieving depression as (in part) a reaction to past losses. When a person has a depressed reaction that is disproportionate to present circumstances, an explanation may be found in the person's past experiences. For example, a woman who suffered a breakdown at the time of her divorce had been abandoned by her father at an early age. For years she bought birthday and Christmas gifts for him and saved them along with letters she wrote, but could not send, to him. In a delayed reaction to the unmourned loss of her father, she experienced suicidal despair after she discarded these items. "I'd be better off if he had simply died," she lamented. Later, she relived this overwhelming loss when she and her husband separated.

A person who has not adequately dealt with earlier deprivations of love (such as those resulting from the death of a parent or parental divorce) may be hit hard when a later source of love is withdrawn. Ed, the disc jockey (earlier in this chapter), had not mourned either the breakup of his marriage or the loss of its early promise in years of bickering and humiliation. Instead, he had immediately fallen in love with Holly, a hero-worshiping young woman, with whom he entered into a relationship laced with overtones of escapist fantasy. In a sea of past losses, Holly buoyed him up, enabling him to postpone coming to terms with his life. When she left him, he was thrown back into the abyss, and he experienced her loss as if it were the aggregate of all the losses he had not previously mourned, against which her presence had insulated him.

Sometimes the hopelessness that leads to depression at the end of a relationship occurs not because no other potential partners are available, but rather because no one quite good enough is on the horizon. In such cases, depression results from setting unrealistically high standards for a partner (what we call high minimal goal levels in Chapter 5) and being unwilling to compromise those standards. The higher one's standards, the less optimistic one can be about finding a satisfactory replacement for the partner one has lost. In Gail's case, her only boyfriend was one whose social status was higher than her own, lending her prestige in the eyes of her peers. She felt that she didn't deserve him and would not be able to find another like him. These assumptions led her to feel depressed until she adjusted her standards and ceased to value the appearances that Brian represented.

This pattern can be observed in professional women who apply to the choice of a mate the same high standards that have brought them success in other realms. Since there are not enough men available who meet those standards, some of these women delay making a commitment almost until the end of their childbearing years, perhaps settling for an affair with a married man along the way. If a woman in her late thirties loses what has been a workable relationship, or perhaps is finally disappointed by a married man who has been promising to leave his wife, she may find herself devastated—not because there are no men available, but because she despairs of finding a man who meets her standards in time for her to raise a family.

Self-punishing depression involves feelings of self-criticism, guilt, and failure. It comes about when a person's self-esteem is unstable and easily influenced by events and circumstances. The same uncertainty about one's own worth that predisposes a person to anxious romantic attachment and to jealousy also contributes to depression. In all three cases, one interprets ambiguous information negatively, in a way that undermines one's sense of self-worth. If one is uncertain about one's attractiveness and desirability, one may become anxious and fear possible rejection with little or no evidence. One may then go on to suspect disloyalty and abuse, which may lead to anger and jealousy. People whose self-esteem is uncertain and variable are especially vulnerable to depression. Suppose the partner shows signs of discontent—for example, by saying, "Let's not be so serious about this" or "I think we need more time apart." Given this warning, a more secure person may become anxious, even jealous. A less secure person may leap to the conclusion that all is lost.

While a person may become anxious or jealous for no good reason, people rarely become depressed without some evidence that something is wrong. Feelings of hopelessness do not arise in solid relationships, only in shaky ones.

People do, however, magnify a threat to a relationship into a premature conviction that the relationship is over. Uncertainty about one's self-worth turns a possible loss into what feels like a certain loss—at least some of the time, since feelings of anxiety commonly alternate with depression. One day things seem hopeless, the next day merely uncertain.

In adolescence and early adulthood, relationships that are threatened are, in fact, likely to end. People in that age group typically feel uncertain about their self-worth, which they have not had enough experience to confirm. In other words, they have not developed what is called a "coping expectancy"—a realistic sense of how well they can play the game, based on the experience of having played it repeatedly before. The longer one's history, the more stable one's expectations, for good or for ill. For instance, a person who has had several divorces may have negative expectations about future relationships.

For these reasons (and others as well, including the high value they attach to their first taste of sexual fulfillment), young people facing the breakup of a romantic involvement are especially prone to dramatic experiences of hopelessness and depression. Think of what it must be like to have had only one serious relationship, and to have that relationship end. How can one feel confident about one's future without the memory of having bounced back from periods of deprivation to form new relationships? How can one put a formerly all-encompassing relationship in perspective without having learned from experience that other relationships will offer different satisfactions?

Gail, for example, showed this vulnerability during and after her relationship with Brian. Separated from him by the conditions of student life, she rarely was able to be with Brian enough to feel secure about him. Moreover, she had no prior romantic experiences to give her a stable feeling of self-confidence in her dealings with men. Lacking reassuring feedback either from her present boyfriend or from her past experience, she became anxious before she had much reason to be, and began to be depressed before she was finally rejected.

Whether or not one is likely to become depressed following a breakup depends on how one interprets the cause of the event. First, does one blame oneself or blame other people or events? Second, does one believe that the breakup was caused by something stable (that is, fixed or relatively unchangeable) or unstable (that is, situational or circumstantial)? As shown on the following grid (developed by social psychologist Bernard Weiner), these two questions give us four possible ways of interpreting causation:

WAYS OF INTERPRETING THE CAUSE(S) OF A BREAKUP

	STABLE	UNSTABLE
INTERNAL	"I'm just not good enough for her." "I'm a loser." "I guess I'm too much of a wimp." "With my metabolism, I'll always be too fat." "I'm not smart enough or interesting enough for the kind of man I want." (*self-punishing depression*)	"I wasn't at my best with him. Too many things were going on for me." "Job stress prevented me from giving the relationship the attention it deserved." "I met her on the rebound, and I was still preoccupied with my previous relationship." "I was too impatient. If I'd just given him more time . . ."
EXTERNAL	"He just got tired of me. There's nothing I can do about it." "I can't blame him for not wanting to take on three kids." "She's too self-centered—she'll never settle down with anybody." "She decided I didn't fit in with her family and friends." "He's too tied to his mother." (*grieving depression*)	"She met this guy, and he swept her off her feet." "At this stage in his career he's too involved to commit himself to a relationship." "His old girlfriend came back. We'd still be together if she hadn't shown up for their class reunion." "Our relationship fell victim to the stress of her dissertation."

The more one believes that the breakup was caused by something that cannot be changed, the more one will see the situation as hopeless and become depressed. Those who see the cause as lying within themselves are more susceptible to self-punishing depression; those who see the cause as lying elsewhere are more susceptible to grieving depression. For example, the man who married a beautiful young woman, only to have her leave him and take advantage of his generosity when she became bored with domestic life, had little reason to experience self-punishing depression. He might well have attributed the breakup to a stable external cause, such as "She's just no good" or "She was too immature to know what she wanted when she married me." However, he still had reason to grieve, since his belief that he lacked other options made his wife's departure a great loss for him.

Most people do not, however, fit neatly into one of the four boxes. For one thing, these causal attributions themselves are not stable. One day Gail may think that Brian left her because of some permanent defect on her part, and she will be depressed. The next day she may decide that he left her because he is a jerk, and she will feel angry. The day after that she may conclude that she and Brian broke up because they never had a chance to spend much time together, and she will feel sad and anxious, but not hopeless.

The link between depression and the assumptions people make about why things happen provides a very useful basis for therapy. People can change their explanations for a breakup, and therapists can help people adjust their thinking in constructive directions and emphasize the kinds of thoughts that do not maintain depression. Using the cognitive-behavioral approach to depression developed by Aaron Beck and his colleagues, a person can learn to identify and avoid self-defeating thoughts—in particular, the tendency to see deficiencies in oneself. Instead of blaming oneself, one can learn to acknowledge causes that lie outside one's control, to look for causes that can be changed, and to understand that most things in life have multiple and uncertain causes.

Ideally, one neither disowns one's share of responsibility nor blames oneself completely. Short of that high level of consciousness, recent research has indicated that well-adjusted persons err in the direction of taking credit for their successes (internal attribution) and defending themselves against responsibility for their failures (external attribution). Depression-prone persons, on the other hand, tend to be overly critical of their shortcomings. To avoid this extreme, instead of jumping to the conclusion that "I wasn't good enough for her," one may be able to moderate the severity of postrelationship depression with thoughts like these: "I wasn't at my best in that relationship. She was too footloose, and I guess we had some bad breaks, too. I don't see why I shouldn't be able to find someone who's more compatible."

Therapy for depression is not necessarily a simple matter. Attributions of causality cannot be treated in isolation when they reflect a deeper self-doubt, a more pervasive sense of personal deficiency. One woman dieted whenever she was not involved with a man, but when she did get involved she gained weight again. It seemed that she wanted to create an external reason for being rejected, so that she would not have to blame herself for the rejection that would then occur. Lamenting bitterly that men were only interested in women's bodies, she then made sure that her body would not be one that attracted men's interest. Another woman did not have intimate relationships because, she said, it would be unfair to subject anyone to her depression. Her depression was self-fulfilling, an excuse for avoiding interpersonal involvement.

Cognitive-behavioral therapy may not be adequate when a deep sense of deficiency, of disqualification, motivates one's search for negative attributions about oneself. In some cases, such attributions represent an escape route from potential relationships. One woman had an unshakable belief that she was ugly, despite the fact that friends insisted she was attractive. For this reason she felt that she never would have a fulfilling social life. Shy and lacking in self-confidence, she gave the impression of being dour and fearful rather than outgoing and vivacious. This self-presentation, which reflected her feelings about herself, probably had more to do with her lack of social success than did her appearance. The same attitudes that fueled her depression may well have contributed to the outcomes about which she was depressed. To change her fixed belief in her unattractiveness, she would need to address the feelings and experiences that reinforced her negative view of herself.

In other cases, simply reorienting a person's understanding of the causes of a breakup can have remarkable success in lifting postrelationship depression. A man blamed himself for the failure of his second marriage, believing that he had been self-indulgent, and unresponsive to his wife. This reasoning had a ring of plausibility, since his first wife had left him because she felt he was neglecting her in favor of recreational activities with his friends. But it was too simple and too punitive an explanation for the more recent breakup. His second wife, twenty years younger than he, had not been a realistic choice. Her interests and his had diverged in ways that made the marriage problematic even with the best intentions on his part. Once he realized this was so, he recovered quickly from his depression. He was able to shift from seeing only internal causes of the separation to recognizing external causes as well. This move from self-recrimination to a broader, more complex appreciation of the breakdown of a relationship is a major element in the recovery from depression.

9

INSECURE LOVE IN

THE MAKING: DAUGHTERS

Paula: "I never felt like my parents loved me. They didn't outwardly belittle me; it was something I sensed. I was always doing things to try to please them, but they'd find something wrong before they'd praise me."

Celeste: "I was everything my parents wanted, a beautiful little girl with long red hair. Everything I wore was red and white. I was taught always to perform a certain way in front of adults: 'Shine, Celeste, Shine!'"

Joyce: "My parents hated each other; they only said bad things about each other. I remember seeing a nasty fight between them when I was five years old. My brother was pulling my Dad off, and my sister was pulling my Mom off. They were just screaming. I don't know how they got them to stop. The last time I saw my parents together, my mother had a skillet in her hand."

Deborah: "My mother was chronically depressed, and to grow up with someone who's that way, especially with an absentee, alcoholic father, is the pits. It was the same with both of them—not knowing whether they're going to be thrilled to have you come home and throw their arms around you and ask how your day was, or whether you're going to walk through the door and get yelled at."

Nancy: "My father never drank, never smoked—he's a very strict, stoic man. He was determined to raise his daughters real strict. I had to bring my brother on dates until I was seventeen—what few dates you get when you have to bring your brother with you."

Linda: "We always had plenty of food and clothes, but there was never any real love. They were always drinking. My father would pull up in the driveway, and my mother would be the perfect housewife, at the refrigerator getting him a beer and a shot of vodka. They never laid a hand on us; the abuse was never physical—it was mental. For me it was 'Why can't you be like your older brother?' For my younger sister it was 'Why can't you be like Linda?'"

The most fascinating findings of our study have to do with family backgrounds and childhood experiences. If you believe you are anxiously attached to a spouse or lover, what clues can you find in your early years to explain how you came to be that way? Can you understand the experience of anxious romantic attachment, or of jealousy, or of depression when a relationship ends, in light of your upbringing and early family relationships? What is there about the way you were raised by your parents, about the relationships you had with them, and about their marriage that may have left you vulnerable to insecurity in love relationships? We have found answers to these questions, both for women (in this chapter) and for men (in Chapter 11).

By answers we do not mean definitive explanations that apply to everyone. Rather, the value of our research lies in stimulating people to think about their own family experiences. There is no reason to expect that any reader's childhood should have been exactly like the most common patterns found in our research. But those patterns do show what kinds of childhood experiences typically make a person susceptible to anxious romantic attachment. By comparing them with your experiences, even if those turn out to have been quite different, you can get a clearer idea of the influences that were important in your own development.

THE MAKING OF THE ANXIOUSLY ATTACHED WOMAN

Typically, for the woman who becomes anxiously attached to men, the parental home was not a secure, stable, nurturing place. She experienced her father as hostile—either in a critical, controlling way, which undermined her confidence in her ability to hold a man's affection; or in a neglecting, rejecting way, which left her yearning for emotional involvement with others, especially men. Disharmony and dissatisfaction in her parents' marriage led her to have pessimistic expectations about intimate relationships, and she may have suffered emotional consequences of her parents' conflicts. Her mother probably was lax in exercising parental control, allowing her a great deal of freedom to do as she wished. In addition, her mother may have been passive and weak-willed, and therefore powerless to protect her from—or substitute for—her father. Or else her mother tried to compensate in a fussing, indulgent, and emotionally involved way that reinforced the separation between daughter and father. The distinction was blurred between a child's role and a maternal role, and the daughter became involved in an overly close, dependent relationship with her mother that may have been a prototype of her future relationships with men.

With parents who were disengaged from each other, and with too much discipline from one parent and perhaps too little from the other, the young woman lacks the sense of security that would have come from a firm, but nurturant family structure. Driven by unfulfilled needs to seek that security elsewhere, she invests herself, anxiously and obsessively, in romantic involvements.

This summary of our findings breaks down into two somewhat different family types, one for the woman who is high in romantic anxiety, the other for the woman who is high in romantic obsession. A detailed picture of each will be presented after the following story, which combines important elements of both. Here is a young woman whose case might serve as a typical illustration of anxious romantic attachment, as well as of the family relationships that lead up to it.

JOANNE: THE PERSISTENCE OF INSECURE ATTACHMENT

At twenty-one, Joanne had been involved in only one serious love affair. She had dated others before Keith, but he had been "the first person who thought I was great, the first one who really liked me a lot." He also was an attractive young man with a charismatic personality: outgoing, socially adept, well-liked, but somewhat self-indulgent and heedless of future consequences.

Joanne started seeing Keith during her senior year of high school in a suburb of Los Angeles. She became aware of her growing commitment to him when she found herself regretting her earlier decision to go to Ohio State University. More and more, she was thinking about how she would miss Keith. She did go to Ohio State, however, and throughout the year she and

Keith exchanged frequent letters, spoke on the telephone twice a week, and visited on holidays. Only later did Joanne learn that Keith had picked up a woman the very night he dropped her off at the airport.

Joanne left Ohio State at the end of her first year. She said that she wanted to take some time off because she did not know what she wanted to study, but in retrospect she realized that she had come home to be near Keith. The couple found an apartment and lived together for the next year while both were out of school and working full time.

In these close quarters, conflicts began to occur. Joanne, who was not as gregarious as Keith, objected to his having guests over every night. She also resented the time he spent with his family, since her family did not lavish the same attention on her. In matters such as these Keith seemed impervious to her demands. He spoke in a conciliatory way, but did not change his behavior. Frustrated that her needs were not being met, Joanne became more insistent. "I suppose I acted as though I was asking him to put me first," she said later, "ahead of his family and everyone else, but if he had treated me a little better I probably would not have felt that I needed that." In other words, she got into a vicious cycle in which her complaints and demands provoked, and were provoked by, Keith's inconsistency and inconsiderateness.

Joanne recognized that she had formed an obsessive attachment to Keith, and she was uncomfortable with it.

> I think I resented him because he had become such a major force in my life. I came home from Ohio because of him, and now he was affecting my whole life: whether I went to college, where I went, and so forth. I was scared that he was having that much effect on me.
>
> I think my self-esteem was worse when I was living with him than it ever was in my life. After a while I didn't want to go out much, because I was afraid people wouldn't think I was very attractive. I gained a lot of weight when I lived in that apartment, and I smoked and drank a lot. I wasn't in school; I didn't have hobbies or interests like Keith did; and I didn't know what to do with myself. I was uncomfortable being with people because I didn't feel good about myself.

Joanne sensed that Keith was not as fully committed to her as she was to him. He no longer was so attentive to her; he no longer went out of his way to show her how much he cared for her. He was her whole life, but she was not his. She began to ask him whether he still found her attractive, whether he still enjoyed being with her. As she said later, "Now I think my asking questions like that scared him and made him want to back off from me a bit." As she expressed her anxiety about his love for her, he became more inconsistent, which gave her more reason to be uncertain and anxious.

The following year Joanne enrolled in a small college in the Los Angeles area. Feeling increasingly desperate about her relationship with Keith, she resolved to up the ante by proposing that they live apart and spend less time together. But Keith adapted so comfortably to that situation that Joanne was left feeling "even more desperate and vulnerable, so I'd try even harder." Now that they had agreed that they both would be free to date other people, Joanne was forced to confront the disparity between her commitment and his.

> I still felt like he was my boyfriend, while I don't think he felt that I was his girlfriend. Instead, he felt I was somebody he was dating. He had more of a feeling of independence than I did.

Joanne interpreted her greater devotion to Keith as a sign of personal inadequacy. She might have felt better if she could have thought of herself as deeply in love with him and as feeling hurt that he didn't fully reciprocate her love. Instead, she saw herself as "needing him and unable to survive without him. And I was mad at myself for that."

While Joanne merely went through the motions of dating other men, Keith exercised his new freedom with relish. Joanne was jealous when he dated other women.

> I didn't understand why he wanted to date anyone else, what was wrong with me that I didn't fully satisfy him. I'd feel all this self-doubt about whether I was attractive enough for him.

Worse yet, Keith was not honest about his other involvements. When Joanne learned about his dates from friends, he would deny all the stories. Joanne was understandably pained. "I was more hurt by his inability to trust me anymore, even as a friend, than by what he had done."

In the spring of that year an incident occurred that crystallized Joanne's dilemma. She and Keith had been spending more time together again. They were having a good time, and Joanne's hopes were on the rise. Then she found out—through the grapevine, as usual—that he had disregarded her feelings about something very important to her.

> He knew that if there was anything he could do that would really hurt me, it would be to sleep with this one particular woman. He did it anyway, but

when I asked him if he had, he said he hadn't. Then I found out about it from someone else a few months later. I was very hurt that it happened at all, and I was furious at him for lying to me and ruining the good things that were happening between us now.

He lied to me so much that I could never figure out when he was lying. But I forgave him anyway, and that's when I realized how much I loved him. I didn't want to forgive him for his affair with that woman; it hurt me way too much. But I put up with it even though I knew he was going to do it again. I knew that he wouldn't change and that I was too much in love with him to do anything about it.

Joanne now saw clearly that she was unconditionally attached to an inconsistent and unfaithful partner. Wanting to get as far away from Keith as possible to put things in perspective, she spent the summer working on a forestry project in Maine. There, in an atmosphere that encouraged physical exertion and healthy living, she began jogging and working out daily.

I got obsessed with making my body look good so that Keith would want to be with me. My goal was that he and others as well would think I was attractive. If he saw others approve of me, he would know what he was giving up.

On her return to Los Angeles, however, she sensed a certain reserve in Keith that convinced her once again that things were hopeless. She became physically inactive again—smoking, drinking, gaining weight, and feeling depressed. Keith still gave her mixed messages. One night he would be sexually intimate with her; the next night he would not even talk to her when she saw him in a bar. Here, in stark relief, is the inconsistent partner who precipitates romantic anxiety. Joanne was devastated.

I couldn't understand how he could be so close to me one night and then not even acknowledge me the next. It hurt so much because it made me feel that he was ashamed of me. I was still drawn to him sexually and aroused by him, but making love with him made me feel vulnerable, because I knew how much it meant to me and how I would end up getting hurt because it didn't mean as much to him. I wanted to be stronger than he was. I wanted to reject him because I knew it was happening anyway, and I wanted to do the hurting rather than get hurt. And I was mad at myself because I couldn't say no, even though I knew I would be treated badly.

Under the stress of this assault on her self-esteem, Joanne developed symptoms of anorexia and bulimia. She would run several miles a day for a few weeks, become exhausted, and then stop running for a few weeks out of guilt and self-disgust at her "failure." She would starve herself to lose weight, eat in binges when starved beyond endurance, and then, in her guilt, make herself throw up the fattening food.

Not knowing how else to get Keith out of her system, Joanne took a semester off and went to Spain. There she regulated her diet and exercise, and she restored a positive body image. At that distance, too, she could have positive thoughts about Keith and care about him as a friend. Although she thought about him every day, she resisted writing to him.

Returning home with renewed self-respect and inner peace, Joanne hit one final low point before overcoming the worst effects of her romantic obsession. Contrary to her intentions, she saw Keith almost immediately and accepted the affection he offered. The next night, after they both had drunk too much, he confessed his love for another woman and revealed that he had disclosed intimate information about Joanne to this woman. Joanne felt betrayed, violated, and discarded. It made her feel "like nothing mattered at all." She went home and took an overdose of tranquilizers, and late that night she received emergency treatment.

Why did she do it? "Because I wanted people to see how I felt, and because I just didn't care anymore."

Later, she summarized her years with Keith in these words:

> I was so obsessed with Keith for so long. Even in Spain I thought about him every day, and for a long time before that. I still think about him every day, but it's getting to be different. I'm feeling better each day, gaining more self-respect so I don't feel like there's something wrong with me because things didn't work out.

Joanne's story could be called a prototype of anxious romantic attachment. Her experiences illustrate with great clarity the feelings, thoughts, and actions that are part and parcel of the syndrome. Her family background also exemplifies the patterns we found to be most common for women who experience anxious romantic attachment.

Joanne's father, an air traffic controller, was a workaholic with a strong belief in traditional moral and religious values. He emphasized the importance of hard work and discipline and the need to earn whatever one was to have in life. Visitors to the house, such as the children's friends, found him unfriendly, irritable, and intimidating. Joanne describes him as distant and seemingly indifferent to his children. He never spoke with her about emotional matters, only about "things like paying my bills at school or checking the oil in the car."

When Joanne was in high school, her father let her know that he did not approve of a daughter who stayed out late partying instead of doing her homework. Every report card she brought home was an occasion for a lecture.

> He'd tell me I had the ability to get much better grades. It was my decision, he'd say, and I'd have to suffer the consequences of getting bad grades. It would affect my future by limiting my options for going to college. It would affect how much money I'd have to pay to go to school and how long I'd have to work to pay off the loans.

When Joanne was in the hospital recovering from her overdose, her father brought in her homework on his first visit. "I told him to take it home," she reports, "but he left it anyway." Perhaps this was his substitute for the emotional communication with which he was uncomfortable. But it left Joanne feeling hurt and rejected.

This father was a demanding person who valued achievement. He always gave Joanne the impression that he expected more from her, that she wasn't good enough the way she was. He enforced his demands by instilling anxiety. As she put it, "He never gives me any feedback unless it's critical. So I always wonder whether I'm doing the right thing, whether he's pleased with what I've accomplished." Guilt was another means of control he employed, as seen in Joanne's description of the arguments she had with him:

> We'd start out talking reasonably, rationally. But then every time I said anything to him about the way I felt, he'd never express any understanding, or any attempt to understand. I'd get frustrated and angry and end up yelling at him again. He'd get flustered and hurt, and I'd feel guilty.
>
> We've never resolved one of those conversations. I'd just storm out and then apologize later. After I'd apologize, that would be the end of it. But he'd never come to me. He'd wait forever for me to come to him.

All told, Joanne's father was an aloof, forbidding, somewhat hostile figure. He combined the *controlling* tendencies which (as we shall see) would predispose a daughter to romantic anxiety with the *rejecting* tendencies that would predispose a daughter to romantic obsession. Joanne experienced rejection not only from his lack of warmth or emotional communication, but also, ironically, from the inconsistency of his discipline. Although he appeared to be a strict father, his enforcement of rules depended on his mood. "Sometimes if I asked him something he'd say okay; another time he'd say no," Joanne related. "I never understood his logic." There seemed to be something expedient about his style of discipline: either he didn't care enough to keep track of his own rules, or else he was serving some unstated purpose. Perhaps he wanted to reward and punish her for other things by his selective enforcement of rules.

He was also inconsistent in his love, a characteristic of some fathers that leaves their daughters more likely to experience both romantic anxiety and romantic obsession. Joanne was fearful of crossing her father, and she never quite knew where she stood with him. Evidently she did not derive from her relationship with her father the emotional security that might have bolstered her confidence in relationships with other men.

Regarding her mother, Joanne said, "She wants to avoid making trouble with my father. She hates it whenever anyone fights or disagrees. If my father gives the final word, she doesn't go against it." Clearly, Joanne's father exerted control over his wife as well as his children, while her mother accepted a submissive, self-effacing role. From Joanne's standpoint, their marriage left much to be desired.

> As far as I can see, they just talk about everyday things, family stuff and finances. If there's more to it, I don't see it. I think both of them would say they have a happy marriage, but they don't seem very happy. If they value security, permanent companionship, loyalty, then they're happy, because that's what they have—a stable relationship.

Joanne opens a window into the dynamics of this family when she states, "My mom once told me that she didn't have anyone she could talk to very much besides me because she couldn't talk to my dad about anything emotional." A woman is more likely to experience romantic anxiety if her father disapproved of her mother's style of communicating. This seems to have been the case in Joanne's family, where her mother learned to suppress communications that her husband, Joanne's father, did not want to hear. Instead, her mother directed these emotional communications at Joanne, which suggests the possibility of an alliance, or *coalition,* between mother and daughter.

This coalition does not seem to have been very strong when Joanne was a child. Joanne did not feel that she could be any more open about her lifestyle with her mother than her father, for her mother could no more understand her staying out all night while she was in high school than could her father. Moreover, her mother counseled her to accommodate, not defy, her father. As Joanne explains, "She didn't want me to disagree with my father; she told me to be more understanding." When her mother asked Joanne whether she might want to take a year off from school before starting college, nothing ever came of the idea, since neither Joanne nor her mother would risk the unpleasantness of bringing it up to her father.

Thus, Joanne's mother was not a very potent ally against an overbearing father. Yet the fact that her mother thought to suggest the year off from school shows a degree of sympathy and insight that her father lacked. Joanne acknowledges as much when she says, "I was messed up, and Mother wanted to help me, but I didn't want to bother about it." This potential closeness between mother and daughter ripened into an active alliance only after Joanne left home and began living on her own. She began to confide in her mother, as well as to support her (though ineffectually) against her father's autocratic rule.

> My mother works full time, and I feel that it's unfair that she also has to clean and always have dinner ready on time. I feel she deserves time to relax. I help her because no one else will lift a finger, and she accepts it. My dad won't even put away his dishes. Sometimes I tell my father that he ought to do more, but it's stupid for me to say anything. He just answers that he does a lot of things at home, like taking care of the cars. He says that Mom made the choice to work, and that he doesn't care if she has a career as long as she makes dinner and does all the things he's used to.

Mother and daughter turn to each other for support and consolation in the face of a father who withholds affection and approval from both of them. Joanne's story describes the most common family pattern leading to anxious romantic attachment in the daughter.

THE MAKING OF ROMANTIC ANXIETY

The following list summarizes the characteristics of the type of family that most commonly instills a *high* level of romantic anxiety in a daughter:

FAMILY TYPE: HIGH ROMANTIC ANXIETY

Parents' personality and child-rearing traits:
father hostile and controlling
mother lax in disciplining daughter

Parents' marital relationship:
marital conflict and dissatisfaction (mother especially dissatisfied)
father dissatisfied with mother's communication style

Daughter's relationships with parents:
daughter not emotionally attached to father
daughter in coalition with mother

The pieces of this family picture fit together in ways that make intuitive sense. The parents do not get along well with each other, and they may be discontented with their marriage. The daughter, experiencing her father as hostile, does not form an emotional bond with him. In contrast, she finds her mother more indulgent and may form an alliance with her against the father.

The type of family that most commonly instills a *low* level of romantic anxiety has essentially the opposite characteristics:

FAMILY TYPE: LOW ROMANTIC ANXIETY

Parents' personality and child-rearing traits:
father warm and well-adjusted
mother strict in disciplining daughter

Parents' marital relationship:
marital satisfaction (mother especially satisfied)
father satisfied with mother's communication style

Daughter's relationships with parents:
daughter emotionally attached to father
daughter not in coalition with mother

Here and in the section below on romantic obsession, our findings about family relationships and upbringing are based on the recollections of the research participants as well as other family members. Ratings of each parent's personality are based on reports by both parents. Ratings of child-rearing behavior are based on the accounts of four people: the participant, the mother, the father, and a brother or sister. In rating the parents' marital relationship we have each parent's unique perspective, as well as those of the participant and her brother or sister. For the participant's relationship with the parents, we have the participant's and her brother's or sister's report.

Thus, we see the parents and the participant through their own as well as others' eyes, and the biases of any one family member are to some degree offset by those of another. For example, you, your sister or brother, and your mother and father might have very different points of view about your father's warmth toward you. But by having your view and your sister's or brother's, as well as your mother's and father's, we get a more objective picture of your father's relationship with you as you were growing up.

In presenting what we learned, we include some samples of the questions asked, both to make our portrayals of childhood experience more concrete and vivid and to enable you to answer some of these questions yourself. By asking yourself these questions, you can see how closely your experiences (or, in the case of a man, your partner's) resemble those that most commonly lead to anxious romantic attachment in women.

THE FATHER'S ROLE

For women, the father's personality is pivotal in the family dynamics that lead to romantic anxiety. This is not to label the father as the villain, since the personality and child-rearing behavior he shows are influenced by his child-hood experiences as well as by his relationship with his wife. In some cases the father may simply be reflecting the stress that exists in the family. Nonethe-less, the child-rearing behavior of the father which involved the daughter is the factor most clearly associated with her subsequent experience of romantic anxiety.

A woman who is *high* in romantic anxiety is likely to have had a *hostile, controlling* father. This father is a strict disciplinarian who, quoting the questionnaire, "believes in having a lot of rules and sticking to them" and who "insists that I must do exactly as I'm told" (Schaefer). He places a high value on achievement and attempts to instill this value in his daughter. To enforce his demands he uses psychologically coercive methods. One of these is withdrawal of affection ("[He] will avoid looking at me when I've disap-pointed him"; "[He] is less friendly with me if I don't see things his way"). Likewise, he instills feelings of anxiety ("If I break a promise, [he] doesn't trust me again for a long time"; "[He] says someday I'll be punished for my bad behavior") and guilt ("[He] tells me of all the things he has done for me"; "[He] feels hurt when I don't follow advice").

Always keeping his daughter anxious, this controlling, hostile father appears inconsistent in his love for her, as shown by statements such as the following:

> "My father could be warm and affectionate, but sometimes he said cold, cutting things to me."
> "I couldn't tell from day to day how my father would respond to certain things."
> "The things that didn't seem to bother my father one day would make him angry the next."
> "You were all right if you stayed on my father's good side, but it was best not to cross him."
> "There were times when, no matter what I did, I could not avoid making my father angry and upset." (Schwarz and Zuroff)

By contrast, the father whose daughter scores *low* on romantic anxiety tends to be *warm* and *well-adjusted*. This father is egalitarian and accepts his daughter as an individual ("[He] likes me to choose my own way of doing things" [Schaefer]). He is nurturant: that is, responsible, easygoing, and forgiving toward others. He is self-confident and has a positive attitude toward life, as well as being gregarious, socially skilled, and oriented to the opposite sex. Overall, then, he is warm and supportive, relates to others in positive ways, and is comfortable with himself and the world. Understandably, his daughter feels emotionally attached to him.

PARENTS' MARITAL RELATIONSHIP

According to a number of indicators, the romantically anxious woman comes from a maritally troubled home. Her parents had low scores on a scale rating their marital happiness from "very unhappy" to "perfectly happy." They tended to experience frequent marital conflict over issues ranging from automobile maintenance to in-laws to children's sexual behavior. They showed relatively low marital adjustment, measured by how much they agreed or disagreed on important issues, as well as by questions such as:

> "Do you ever wish you had not married?"
> "If you had your life to live over, do you think you would marry the same person?" (Locke and Wallace)

The status of their marriage was relatively uncertain, as revealed by their endorsing statements such as:

> "Thoughts of divorce occur to me very frequently, as often as once a week or more."
> "I have considered a divorce or separation a few times other than during or shortly after a fight, although only in vague terms." (Weiss and Cerreto)

Typically, both parents were dissatisfied with their marriage, the mother more so. The father tended to be dissatisfied specifically with his wife's style of communication and with the level of communication in their marriage, as shown by his answers to questions such as the following (which were asked of both parents):

> "Does your spouse have a tendency to say things which would be better left unsaid?"
> "Do you find your spouse's tone of voice irritating?"
> "Are you and your spouse able to disagree without losing your tempers?"
> "Does your spouse accuse you of not listening to what s/he says?"
> "Does your spouse insult you when s/he gets angry with you?"
> "Do you fail to express disagreement with her (him) because you're afraid s/he'll get angry?"
> "Do you feel that s/he says one thing but really means another?"
> (Bienvenu)

Viewed from the other direction, the better the parents' marital adjustment, the less anxious the daughter is in her own romantic relationships.

We found that the daughter is more likely to perceive her partners as inconsistent in their love if her mother lacked warmth, and was rejecting and inconsistent in her love. Our findings suggest that the daughter's relationships may replicate a vicious cycle of bad communication and disengagement in her parents' marriage. Her father, finding her mother irritable, insistent, or irrational in attempting to make contact with him emotionally, reacted by withdrawing further from her. The daughter, anxious about whether men will accept her, may anticipate—and perhaps find—the same frustrating indifference in her spouse or lover. She then overreacts when she feels him withdrawing, thereby re-creating the pattern she saw at home. Her partner, stung, pulls back to a safe distance to reconsider, and she becomes all the more anxious in the face of his mixed messages and wavering commitment.

A woman who has witnessed such an impasse between her parents may either accept or reject that example. If she identifies strongly with her mother and lacks other role models, she may react to her frustrations with men in the same ways that displeased her father and thereby risk the same disapproval. On the other hand, she may make a conscious effort to avoid repeating the self-defeating pattern she observed. She may monitor her behavior carefully, thereby breaking the pattern and winning greater loyalty from men. She runs the risk, though, of reining in her desires so tightly that she does not assert herself sufficiently to meet her needs.

PARENT-CHILD RELATIONSHIPS

A daughter is likely to experience romantic anxiety when she has not felt a close *emotional attachment* with her father. For example, she would agree with the following statements on the questionnaire, which indicate a low level of emotional attachment:

> "My father and I get along all right on the surface, but down deep I wonder if we even know each other."
> "Very often I have envied other people who have had so much more fun with their father than I."

This lack of emotional attachment to her father would be indicated by her *denying* the following statements, which indicate a high level of emotional attachment:

> "I am very happy with my present relationship with my father."
> "My father and I have a great deal of mutual respect, faith, and confidence in one another."

She would also indicate her relative lack of attachment to her father by her answers to questions such as these:

> "How close do you feel to your father?"
> "How much do you depend on your father for advice and guidance?"
> "How often do you and your father talk about your personal problems?"
> "In terms of your basic temperament and emotional reactions, how similar are you to your father?"
> "How much do you want to be like your father when you are an adult?"

In the absence of a close relationship with her father, the daughter is likely to form a coalition with her mother against her father, as revealed by her endorsing statements such as these on the questionnaire:

> "I get along much better with my mother than I do with my father."
> "In most of the disagreements between my mother and father, I find myself supporting my mother."
> "I can count on my mother to side with me (take my part) if my father is unreasonable."
> "My mother sometimes sides with me against my father even when I know my father is right."
> "I sometimes feel that I understand my mother much better than my father understands her." (Schwarz, 1989b)

Note that the alliance may involve the daughter's supporting the mother against the father and/or the mother's supporting the daughter against the father. Moreover, a coalition is not necessarily an emotional attachment; it may be merely an expedient alliance. The child may perceive the coalition as justified (". . . if my father is unreasonable") or unjustified (". . . even when I know my father is right"). As mother and daughter side with each other, they create a barrier that father cannot cross. But the daughter ends up feeling anxious later on in her romantic involvements with men.

The parents' dissatisfaction with their marriage appears to be one of the factors that trigger this pattern of child-parent relationships. Note that we do not see the father forming a compensatory attachment with his daughter if he is unhappy with his wife; if anything, the daughter is somewhat more likely to be attached to the father if he is happy in the marriage. Nor do we see the daughter competing with her mother by getting close to her father when the mother feels estranged from him. Instead, the daughter usually lines up with her mother, allying with her in accepting or rejecting the father. It may be that the mother's acceptance of the father makes it safe for the daughter to align herself emotionally with him. Or it may be that the father who enjoys his wife's high regard is simply a nicer, warmer person, one to whom his daughter can feel close as well. Whatever its origins, if there is a sense of closeness and emotional security within the family, the daughter is insulated against excessive anxiety in her love life.

THE MOTHER'S ROLE

More often than not, a woman who is high in romantic anxiety experienced *lax discipline* by her mother. That is, she would describe her mother with statements such as the following:

"[She] does not insist I obey if I complain or protest."
"[She] gives me as much freedom as I want."
"[She] doesn't tell me what time to be home when I go out."
"[She] doesn't check up to see whether I have done what she told me."
"[She] seldom insists that I do anything." (Schaefer)

In direct contrast with the dictatorial, punitive father, the mother who fits this profile does not exert much control over her daughter's behavior. She does not enforce rules strictly; instead, she allows her daughter a great deal of autonomy.

Other characteristics of the mother that affect the daughter's susceptibility to romantic anxiety do so indirectly. The mother's traits influence her relationship with her husband, as well as her husband's disposition toward their daughter, and the formation of alliances or schisms within the family. We can see the effects of the mother's characteristics most clearly by looking at them in combination with the father's.

For example, a woman whose mother was *rejecting* and *self-abasing* is likely to be very *high* in romantic anxiety if her father was hostile and controlling. (A self-abasing person might be described as submissive, fearful, preoccupied by feelings of inferiority and guilt, thin-skinned, and sensitive to criticism.) But if her father was warm and well-adjusted, a woman with a rejecting, self-abasing mother is likely to show a very *low* level of romantic anxiety.

Finally, regardless of whether her father was hostile and controlling or warm and well-adjusted, a woman whose mother was *dominant* is likely to rank near the *middle* on romantic anxiety. The term "dominance" here is meant to describe an outgoing, imposing, attention-getting person, one who has a large impact on others. She is forceful, assertive, spontaneous, enthusiastic, and impatient. "Dominant" and "self-abasing" are close to being opposites, and the same person rarely shows both traits.

The most secure situation for a daughter is to have a warm father and a nonthreatening mother, since she can then form a strong attachment with both parents. If, in contrast, the father is hostile, the daughter needs a powerful, self-confident mother for protection and to provide a substitute attachment and alliance. If the father is warm, however, a dominant mother may actually be a *source* of anxiety.

For the daughter whose father is hostile, a self-abasing mother is of little help. This mother, out of her sensitivity to her husband's criticism, may turn the rejecting side of her nature against her daughter, leaving her without support from either parent. Interestingly, though, we find that among women with hostile fathers, those who score highest on romantic anxiety are those whose mothers are neither especially dominant nor especially self-abasing. While all families with hostile fathers are likely to show high marital conflict, it is in this middle group of mothers that the parents' marital adjustment is poorest. It is in this group, too, that the daughter tends to be in coalition not only with her mother, but with her father as well (as described below).

We might speculate that in these families the mother does not have a clearly defined role that complements the father's. She neither submits to him nor competes with him. If she either accepted his control or challenged it, she would be engaging with him in a way that would make her a lightning rod for his controlling tendencies. By not doing so, she may be leaving the daughter to bear the brunt of the father's domination. The daughter may then respond to this pressure by entering into shifting, expedient alliances with her mother and father for the sake of emotional survival.

THE ROOTS OF ROMANTIC ANXIETY: A TROUBLED FAMILY PORTRAIT

Here is a family whose tone is set by a strict, demanding father. He and his wife are not happy with each other, and she especially is dissatisfied. Their daughter tends to side with her mother against her father, with whom she does not have a good relationship. He acts in a critical, hostile, and controlling manner toward her. She and her mother, both unhappy with the father, gravitate toward each other. The two women may or may not have a close emotional attachment to each other. Their coalition may reflect such an emotional bond, or it may be little more than a self-protective alliance against a formidable adversary, the father. It may be mutual or one-sided. The daughter may seek to be protected by her mother, or she may protect her mother, extending her sympathy and support in the face of the father's attacks. The mother may protect herself by forming a possessive coalition, interfering with the daughter's relationship with the father so that she herself will not be isolated and outnumbered. Therefore, the daughter may end up without a strong emotional attachment to either parent, because the mother has preempted any attachment to the father by drawing the daughter into a coalition, not an emotional attachment. Or the daughter may react in anger because her bid for a coalition is rebuffed by a mother who is too weak, passive, and fearful to oppose her husband.

Given that the daughter typically sees less of her father than of her mother, it is remarkable that her father seems to have such a large influence on her development. Her relationship with her father may be a prototype for later heterosexual relationships and the basis of her initial expectations about whether she will experience warm acceptance or rejection and inconsistency from men.

Unfortunately, these expectations have been conditioned by a man who set high standards and punished her when she failed to meet them. Uncertainty, coupled with painful consequences, makes for great anxiety. The daughter of such a critical, disapproving father carries into her adolescent and adult relationships a feeling of insecurity about whether she will ever be able to please a man. She enters into each relationship not knowing in what proportions to expect love and rejection, having received mixed and inconsistent messages from her father. Although her father has been relatively disdainful as parents go, that does not mean he was never loving. Parents generally are loving to some degree, but a relatively cold or rejecting parent is more inconsistent than most in expressing that love. Remember that love-inconsistency was part of this father's profile. He kept his daughter guessing, kept her anxious about his love for her. That uncertainty about her acceptability, transported to a relationship with a lover or husband, becomes romantic anxiety.

PEGGY: REPLAYING THE STRUGGLE

Peggy, a forty-six-year-old Minneapolis beautician, comes from the kind of family background that leaves a woman susceptible to romantic anxiety. Peggy has not slept in her own bed in the year since she and her husband separated. She sleeps on the sofa with the TV always on, "so that I won't be alone." The main event in her complicated love life is an on-and-off affair with a married man, of whom she says, "I love everything about him except that he lies. He's hurt me so much. But when I'm with him, I know he cares. Then I feel like a whole person." She wants to fill her emptiness, even if she must suffer the inevitable pain at the hands of an inconsistent partner.

Peggy dates other men as well, but finds that they cannot distract her from her obsessive thoughts of the married man she loves, whose shadowy presence in her life enables her to disqualify anyone else from serious consideration. His possessiveness is an additional barrier: he checks up on her when he is not around. He has a key to her apartment and might walk in at any time. Perhaps she sees other men as a hedge against rejection or in the hope of being discovered and provoking his jealousy. Her relationship with him—half-

imaginary, half-real—is just absorbing enough to shut out other possibilities. As we have seen in previous cases, anxious romantic attachment
sometimes goes with its opposite, detachment. On the one hand is the wish
for an all-encompassing romantic union; on the other is a fear of involvement
and reluctance to give oneself fully.

How did Peggy come to be this way? Why does the experience of wholeness
in her relationships elude her? Peggy's father was an alcoholic, and as a child
she would hang around outside the bar he frequented and try to persuade him
to come home. Peggy was a parental child—one who assumes adult responsibility in the family to compensate for her parents' weaknesses or failures. She
dated little in her teens because her mother needed her help in taking care of
her brothers and sisters. "I missed out on my childhood because of my father's
drinking," she says.

Peggy's account of her childhood touches upon some of the main themes of
our research findings:

> My earliest memory was when I was four or five—my father coming in
> drunk late at night and my mother cooking him supper at 1:00 A.M. My
> mother and father fought all the time; their marriage was always stormy. I
> never saw them kiss, never saw any tenderness between them. He thought
> he did her a favor by marrying her, and she felt grateful to him for giving
> her a home and children. He always drank, but he always worked. She
> tried so hard to please him—she'd do anything for him—but he was so
> nasty. I can remember my mother getting angry and not talking to him for
> days. When they fought it would hurt me inside; I'd go to my room or
> leave the house. I can't stand fighting, and even now I'm afraid to do
> anything that might get people angry at me.
>
> Once my mother and I went to the bar and found my father with
> another woman. My mother didn't say much, but I saw how hurt she was.
> She was always throwing him out of the house. My worst fear was that
> they'd divorce, and that I'd be torn between them. She had plenty of cause
> to leave him, but she never did—she always loved him.
>
> My mother was always arguing with my father about me. When I was a
> baby, she kept him away from me; she wouldn't let him hold me. I don't
> know why, since he only hit me once for being bad. It was as if she wanted
> to keep me for herself. I really had no relationship with my father. He'd
> make me feel bad for wanting the kinds of clothes other girls had, but then
> sometimes he'd buy them for me. My mother spoiled me, though; she gave
> me as much as she could. She worked every day in a tailor shop and saved
> up the money to buy me things. I'd throw a tantrum if I didn't get what I
> wanted, and I wasn't well liked by other children.

Here are the three key elements: lack of attachment to father, coalition with mother, and marital discord between the parents. We do not know whether Peggy's mother formed a coalition with her infant daughter in response to her husband's drinking and absences, or whether her father reacted with frustration to his wife's possessive attitude toward the baby. Probably it was a vicious cycle.

Some of the characterizations in Peggy's story are difficult to reconcile. Her mother always loved her father and was grateful to him, but they never showed affection for each other. Her mother did everything she could to please her father, but withheld the infant Peggy from him. Whether or not her mother was able to resolve these conflicting emotions, they are present in Peggy's experience of her parents' marriage, and they carry over to her own relationships with men. Thus, she simultaneously shows signs of anxious romantic attachment and fearful detachment.

Asked what she learned from her mother about men, Peggy says, "I wasn't going to let any man make me helpless." Peggy repeatedly expresses anger at her mother for not being more assertive and for accepting an incomplete relationship with a man. Yet Peggy herself is reliving her mother's struggle to win acceptance, respect, and security from a man. As a child, Peggy wanted her father to show attention to her mother more than anything else. Now she looks for a man who will love her more than anyone else. She ends up, however, with men who withhold from her the full measure of devotion that she seeks. As a result, she again experiences the anxiety she once experienced through her mother.

KAREN: DAUGHTER OF A DOMINANT MOTHER

In general, women who have dominant mothers rank near average in romantic anxiety, regardless of whether their fathers are warm or hostile. However, some women with dominant mothers and warm fathers experience a high degree of romantic anxiety. Karen illustrates this less common family pattern.

Karen is a tall, attractive, outgoing woman in her late thirties. She is a divorced mother of a teenage daughter. Intelligent and energetic, she has been very successful as a Wall Street stockbroker. Despite the air of independence and self-confidence that she projects, she holds back in relationships with men because of intense fear of rejection and unwillingness to risk herself.

Karen's father was pleasant, well-mannered, and cooperative, but as time

went on he receded into the background of family life. When he and his wife
fought, she always seemed to come out on top, so after a while he just gave up
and accepted defeat. From Karen's earliest years, her mother isolated her from
her father. Even now, Karen says ruefully, "I'd like to get to know my father
more, but I can't while my mother is around." In this respect Karen
anticipates an important family theme associated with romantic obsession—
that of isolation from the father. As Karen tells it, her mother was the
unapproachable bulwark of the family.

> My mother is very strong. I admire the way she raised four children and
> worked at the same time. She was always herself; she did a lot on her own.
> She gave the impression of being flawless, perfect, independent. Either
> that or she pretended to be, since she didn't let anyone inside to see who she
> really was.

Karen's story diverges from the more typical case of Peggy in that Karen's
mother's assumed the hostile, controlling role usually played by the father.
"With my mother," says Karen, "either you are subservient or you tell her off.
There's nothing in between." Karen's mother had great difficulty with emotional communication.

> She can't say, "I love you," and she can't look me in the eye and speak to
> me. She just sent me a Christmas card addressed to "Mrs. _____,"
> using my ex-husband's name, even though I've been divorced for years.
> Recently she told my daughter in front of me that she's proud of me, but
> she can't praise me directly. She makes me feel like I'm not important
> enough to talk to or listen to.

While Karen was growing up, her mother was so critical of her she began to
doubt her own worth, particularly in relationships with men. After Karen
introduced a man she was dating to her parents, her mother told her, "He's too
good for you." Karen, remembering the incident with regret, concludes,
"Actually, he was just right for me." Later, when Karen's husband-to-be gave
her an engagement ring, her mother warned, "Don't let it go to your head."
These devastating remarks recall some of the more extreme fathers we have
seen. Karen's mother, anticipating rejection on her behalf, stood in for the
rejecting man. Even when a man responded positively to Karen by proposing
marriage, her mother felt a need to negate his message.

As a result, Karen has carried with her the mental image of her critical
mother as a kind of punitive conscience.

When I was getting divorced, it was a long time before I could bring myself to tell my mother, because I knew that in her eyes it would mean that I had failed. She had always told me I was going to be a failure. Not long ago a relative came to visit, and my house was a mess. I caught myself saying to her, "Don't tell my mother." And here I am, thirty-seven years old.

Karen emerged from this background driven to succeed, determined to outdo any standards set for her, yet strangely unmoved by her successes and unsure of their meaning. Like her mother, she presents a strong, independent front, but feels weak and vulnerable. With men she anticipates rejection without good reason, and since she associates rejection with intense pain she usually ends up rejecting a man before he can reject her. Detachment is her way of dealing with her insecurity.

She shows her ambivalence toward men by gravitating to weak men who will not satisfy her. "When I date, I usually end up getting bored," she says. "Give me a room with fifty men, and I'll pick the two weakest, the ones who want to be controlled. But I don't like them, as soon as I see what they are." More controlling men are alienated by her manner. "A lot of men tell me I'm too assertive; they're intimidated," she reports. "I can't play stupid with men; that's why I don't have many men. I'm not going to massage a man's ego. With women I can relax more and be myself. But if I play tennis with a man, I play to kill." Fearful of men, Karen needs to master, vanquish, or avoid them.

Karen's insecurity has carried over to her relationship with her teenage daughter, with whom a disagreement turned into a severe rebuff. After an argument with Karen, her daughter went off to stay with her father, Karen's ex-husband, perhaps only temporarily. Karen, however, reacted as if someone she loved had died.

That's it—I don't have a child anymore. She's gone. She's growing away from me, and I'll never again share my life with her. I'm very hurt. It's a big slap in the face. It's going to affect the whole rest of my life. I put everything into that kid. Now it's like losing my arm. I have to put her out of my mind. I can't be like a yo-yo, my hopes going up and down. I won't get rejected twice, not by the same person. After so much rejection you just close your door. No, I'll just have to bury her. I'll disown her. I'll turn her room into a study.

Weeks later, she admits, "It's still with me every day."

Karen's feelings toward her daughter, as she describes them, are akin to anxious attachment. Feeling rejected by her mother, Karen is overly sensitive to any signs of rejection by her daughter. She responds by reciprocating the rejection she feels. She spurns her child, not out of indifference or neglect, but because she cannot bear the emotional turmoil brought on by her child's inconsistent feelings toward her. Aware of her tragic dilemma, she says, "I'm acting a lot like my mother, and I don't want to be that way." She means that her own outspokenness as a child likewise may have been too painful for her mother to bear. Karen risks perpetuating her mother's defensive rejection of her—that is, her mother's inability to express emotional needs in a positive, loving way. If Karen and her daughter act out this conflict repeatedly, her daughter may come to experience (if she has not already) the same feelings of rejection that haunt Karen.

On the other hand, the estrangement between them may not last very long. Karen presents herself verbally as more extreme than she actually is. She carries with her deep scars from her childhood and adolescence, but she also brings great resources: her intelligence, her social and professional skills, her worldly success, and the concern for people that is evident beneath her controlled exterior. Probably she is less withdrawn from people than she says she is; to some who know her, she is not that way at all. She is learning to acknowledge her needs and seek support from others. Perhaps most important, she is beginning to recognize how attractive she is and to see herself as worthy of love.

THE MAKING OF ROMANTIC OBSESSION

The following list summarizes the characteristics of the type of family that most commonly instills a *high* level of romantic obsession in a daughter:

FAMILY TYPE: HIGH ROMANTIC OBSESSION

Parents' personality and child-rearing traits:
  father hostile and rejecting
  mother lax in disciplining daughter

Parents' marital relationship:
  low marital adjustment

Daughter's relationships with parents:
  daughter not emotionally attached to father
  daughter in coalition with mother

This family picture is similar to the one we saw for romantic anxiety—which we would expect, since a person often experiences romantic anxiety and romantic obsession simultaneously. However, you will see some subtle differences if you compare this list of family characteristics with the one for High Romantic Anxiety. In particular, the father's rejection is much more important in romantic obsession, and his controlling tendencies are less important. Also, the parents' marital conflict has less influence on the development of romantic obsession.

The following characteristics describe the type of family that most commonly instills a *low* level of romantic obsession:

FAMILY TYPE: LOW ROMANTIC OBSESSION

Parents' personality and child-rearing traits:
  father warm and accepting
  mother strict in disciplining daughter

Parents' marital relationship:
  high marital adjustment

Daughter's relationships with parents:
  daughter emotionally attached to father
  daughter not in coalition with mother

THE FATHER'S ROLE

A woman who is *high* on romantic obsession is likely to have had a *hostile, rejecting* father. This father has some of the same qualities as the typical father of a woman high in romantic anxiety; in particular, his daughter experiences him as inconsistent in his love for her. However, his hostility takes a somewhat different form. Although he may have some controlling tendencies, he is not so much coercive as rejecting. Thus, according to his daughter, he "doesn't talk with me very much" and "wishes I were a different kind of person" (Schaefer). In contrast to the strictness of the hostile, controlling father, he can be inconsistent in his discipline ("[He] soon forgets a rule he has made"; "[It] depends upon his mood whether a rule is enforced or not"). In his lack of involvement with his daughter, he is erratic in discipline as well as in love.

By contrast, when the daughter scores *low* on romantic obsession, the father tends to be *warm* and *accepting*. This father has some of the same characteristics as the fathers of women who are low in romantic anxiety; specifically, he is egalitarian, warm, and accepts his daughter as an individual. However, he places more emphasis on acceptance and positive involvement with his daughter. These qualities come through in characterizations such as these:

> "[He] smiles at me very often."
> "[He] seems proud of the things I do."
> "[He] often praises me."
> "[He] is very interested in what I am learning at school." (Schaefer)

Almost invariably, his daughter reciprocates this emotional attachment, just as the daughter of a hostile, rejecting father reciprocates his lack of attachment. In fact, the father's warm, accepting nature is the characteristic that best predicts whether the daughter feels emotionally attached to him.

Women whose fathers were hostile are likely to experience *both* romantic anxiety and romantic obsession. Those whose fathers were warm are likely to experience neither to any significant degree. The differences between the two are, however, revealing. High romantic anxiety is associated with a demanding, controlling, punitive father, while high romantic obsession is associated with a detached, indifferent, rejecting father. Low romantic anxiety is correlated with having an easy-going, well-adjusted, nurturant father, whereas low romantic obsession usually means that one has had an involved, accepting, encouraging father.

These are only differences of degree, since many of the hostile, controlling fathers were also rejecting, and the warm, well-adjusted fathers often turn out to be accepting fathers. Nonetheless, the distinctions clearly make sense. A strict, demanding, emotionally coercive father is likely to make you feel anxious; a father who withdraws from you in anger or disapproval will leave you searching for a close emotional attachment elsewhere. Similarly, a father who projects self-confidence and is socially at ease will make you feel comfortable; a father who accepts you and interacts with you in positive ways will leave you feeling secure in your emotional attachment to him, secure in your valuing of yourself, and therefore not desperate in attaching yourself to others.

MARITAL AND PARENT-CHILD RELATIONSHIPS

Marital disharmony is part of the family picture leading to romantic obsession in the daughter. If the parents have shown good marital adjustment, the daughter tends to be somewhat less obsessive in her own relationships. However, romantic obsession is not as strongly affected by the father's dissatisfaction with the mother as is romantic anxiety. On the other hand, the daughter's lack of an emotional attachment to her father and her formation of a coalition with her mother are even more crucial to the development of romantic obsession than of romantic anxiety. The daughter's vulnerability partially stems from her need to compensate for her father's uninvolved, rejecting attitude toward her and for the emotional distance that separates her from him. And, as discussed below, the tendency toward romantic obsession is further reinforced by a possessive, child-centered (and child*like*) mother, who is intent on forming a mother-daughter alliance.

"I never knew my father" is a common refrain among romantically obsessed women. Often it is accompanied by anger at the mother for keeping the father at a distance. Stephanie put it this way:

> You know, I never really knew my father. It seemed my mother was always interrupting. Whenever my father spoke, my mother would finish the sentence. She'd say, "You know what he means."
> So I never got much love from my mother, and I *couldn't* get it from my father. Maybe he would have been more affectionate toward me if my mother had let him—who knows?

Stephanie felt she needed to move to a different state to put a long, painful episode of unrequited love behind her. Her sister Lisa had a more extreme experience of romantic obsession. First, Lisa suffered an emotional breakdown when the man she loved ran off and married another woman. Later, when this same man was left comatose after an automobile accident, she visited him regularly for two years until he died, even though she was married at the time. She kept these visits secret from her husband. Lisa said that she knew the man loved her despite the fact that he could not respond visibly to her.

What was Lisa so unwilling to give up? It was not so much the loss of a partner that made her depressed. Rather, it was the loss of an experience of acceptance. She clung to a memory of the fulfillment of her wish to be loved, to have the acceptance she never got from her father. This intangible sense of acceptance and acceptability may be more important than any particular relationship, in that it motivates what one seeks from relationships through-out one's life. When a girl feels cut off from her father, she may wonder, "What's wrong with me? Why isn't my father interested in me?" As an adult, then, she seeks reassurance by clinging to a man who confirms that she is, indeed, lovable. As long as she feels he loves her, she feels good about herself. To lose him would mean again feeling bad about herself, so she will not accept losing him. She will not let go, for she would be losing a part of herself that makes her feel good.

In the first story in this chapter, Joanne was obsessed for years with a boyfriend whom she described as "the first person who thought I was great, the first one who really liked me a lot." When he dated other women, she questioned her attractiveness, wondering "what was wrong with me that I didn't fully satisfy him." When he failed to acknowledge her publicly while he was out socializing with others, she felt very hurt "because it made me feel that he was ashamed of me." These insecure, self-doubting reactions reflected Joanne's early experiences of rejection by a father who was lost in his work and who seemed indifferent to his children.

Joanne's father kept himself remote from his children by his own choice. The coalition between mother and daughter was understated, becoming more evident as Joanne grew up. In the case of Elaine, the ballet dancer whose story began this book, the separation between father and daughter was enforced by a domineering mother. Elaine's marriage was threatened by her intense, adolescentlike infatuations with male mentors, which led to embarrassing declarations of love and sometimes to unsatisfying one-night stands. When asked what she most regretted in her life, Elaine said, "I regret that I never really got to know my father. My father never shared himself with me." Considering that her father was physically present throughout her childhood, it is remarkable how little Elaine knew about him. She saw him as sad, as not taking pleasure in life, and as the object of verbal assaults from her mother, who said cutting things to and about him. Elaine wanted to rescue him ("I thought I could have been a better wife to him"), but her mother allowed her little time alone with him. For his part, her father acquiesced to this treatment.

In later years Elaine expressed much anger at her mother, who not only had stood between her and her father, but also had stopped her from dating a boy she liked at school. Without direct experience in obtaining affection from men, Elaine resorted to extravagant fantasies when faced with a reserved, emotionally undemonstrative husband. Idealizing her mentor as a romantic object, she was perhaps imagining the loving father she had wished for. At the same time, when she provoked her husband, she was repudiating the withholding father she actually had.

THE MOTHER'S ROLE

Lax discipline characterizes the mothers of romantically obsessed women as well as romantically anxious women. Otherwise, the mother's personality and child-rearing behavior influence the daughter's susceptibility to romantic obsession indirectly—that is, in combination with the father's characteristics and in the context of family relationships as a whole.

We found that, when the father was hostile and rejecting and the mother *possessive* and *child-centered,* the daughter is high on romantic obsession. As seen by her daughter, a possessive mother "worries that I can't take care of myself unless she is around" and "wishes I would stay at home where she could take care of me" (Schaefer). A child-centered mother "gives me a lot of care and attention" and "makes her whole life center about her children." These characteristics portray a mother who is overly involved (or, as family therapists would say, enmeshed) with her daughter. She smothers her with attention and concern, acting as if she lacks confidence in her daughter's ability to get along on her own.

A mother who has these traits sometimes has childlike qualities as well. That is, she is anxious, fearful, dependent, sensitive, high-strung, and dreamy. Lacking self-confidence and emotional reserves for coping with the stresses of reality, she takes refuge in daydreams and fantasies. She may, therefore, involve herself in her daughter's life in an attempt to satisfy unfulfilled needs of her own, perhaps living out her fantasies through her child. Troubled by feelings of inadequacy, she may fear for her daughter's well-being and intervene protectively—which can cause the daughter to become dependent and insecure, a mirror-image of the mother.

If the mother is possessive and overinvolved in her child's life, there is a potential for a coalition between mother and daughter. If the mother, in addition to being insecure, also is lax in exercising control, the coalition may be one between peers; that is, the mother may act as a pal rather than a parent to her daughter. A hostile, rejecting father can activate that latent coalition by polarizing the family, pushing the daughter into an alliance with her mother. According to this interpretation, conflict between parents promotes an alliance between generations.

Alternately, the latent female coalition may become a source of conflict, provoking the father to a hostile response. In other words, the mother overinvolves herself with the daughter to the point where the father feels that his authority and control over the daughter have been undermined by his wife's indulgence. He reacts with hostility or rejection, intensifying the mother-daughter coalition. According to this interpretation, an alliance between generations will make a war between parents more likely. Either way, a daughter who has become accustomed to an overly close, mutually dependent relationship with her mother may cope with her anxiety about heterosexual relationships by attaching herself to men in the same obsessive way.

On the other hand, the daughter is less romantically obsessed when the father is hostile and rejecting and the mother is *assertive* and *forceful,* and displays self-confidence and initiative as well as ambition, aggression, dominance, and a need for power. These mothers are not possessive or child-centered, as are the mothers of romantically obsessed daughters.

The assertive mothers described here might be regarded as cousins of the dominant mothers who seem to moderate the effects of the father's characteristics on the daughter's level of romantic anxiety. Assertive mothers do the same with respect to romantic obsession, at least when the father is hostile and rejecting. In particular, the mother's assertiveness appears to protect the daughter against the worst effects of the father's hostility and rejection. In contrast, women with hostile, rejecting fathers and assertive mothers may tend to show defensive detachment, as discussed in Chapter 4. These women, in fact, score moderately high on romantic anxiety even though they are moderately low on romantic obsession. (An example is Joyce, the hard-boiled but vulnerable woman in Chapter 4 who will appear again in this chapter.)

Finally, the women who were *lowest* in romantic obsession were those with warm, accepting fathers and mothers who were neither especially possessive and child-centered nor especially assertive and forceful. It appears that a daughter is insulated from obsessive romantic attachments when her mother does not interfere with her relationship with a warm father, either by being too warmly enveloping or by being demanding and coercive.

THE ROOTS OF ROMANTIC OBSESSION: A TROUBLED FAMILY PORTRAIT

Whereas the key factor in romantic anxiety is a personal one—namely, the father's threatening, punitive nature—with romantic obsession the issue seems to be more of a structural one—namely, the daughter's sense of being cut off from her father and overly involved with her mother.

The daughter is vulnerable to romantic obsessions with men in proportion to the absence of a close emotional attachment to her father. If she does not have a good relationship with her father, she tends to place greater value on her male partners. At one extreme, a woman who feels cut off from her father tends to approach relationships with men in the desperate, vulnerable way that reflects intense romantic obsession. She brings to these relationships an insecurity that originates in the dislocations of her childhood home.

At the other extreme, a daughter who feels too attached to her father may not feel free to break away from the family and form emotional attachments with other men. There is an unhealthy overinvestment in the father that inhibits normal development, as with the daughter who spends her life taking care of her father or measures all men against him and finds them wanting.

LYNNE: SEARCHING FOR A FATHER

In several chapters we have followed the story of Lynne, the young professional woman who found it agonizing to break up with Scott, her attractive but inconsistent lover. Lynne illustrates especially well the family characteristics associated with the development of romantic obsession in women. From her earliest years she was used to seeing her parents fight. Her father was hot-tempered and volatile: "he could blow up over the slightest thing, and this caused me a great deal of pain as a child." In addition, he was unfaithful to his wife and beat her frequently. Well-organized in his professional and personal habits, he provided materially for the family, but that was about all Lynne could say for him. As she put it:

> My dad is just not capable of giving warmth and love; he doesn't know how
> to express it. He provided a roof over our heads, food on the table, a model
> of good work habits, and strict discipline in terms of dating. Mom made
> up for all the other stuff, the love.

Lynne's father combined the characteristics of the hostile, controlling father with those of the hostile, rejecting father. Her response was to try to win his affection by way of his approval—that is, by emulating and appealing to his achievement values. "I remember following him around a lot, being his little helper," she says. She excelled in school (later putting herself through college when her father refused to pay) and became the family prodigy and show-piece. "At parties," she recalls, "my father would set up a stage and a microphone for me, and I would sing and play for everybody. He was proud of me."

Lynne had to content herself with this kind of conditional admiration from her father. Meanwhile, she was drawn into the darker side of her family's life. "My father was always beating up my mother, and we always had to see it. My sister and I tried to retreat to our room, but she would come in and cry to us." Desperate for support, her mother made a bid for a coalition with her daughters. Lynne, who accepted some of her father's values, met her mother halfway.

> I kind of felt sorry for her because he was so big and mean. But then I was disgusted with her because of her drinking. She drank to numb the feelings, I guess, but I couldn't sympathize with her. It was two-sided: I hated him for what he was doing to her, but I disrespected her for taking all that garbage from him.
>
> While I was growing up, I couldn't stand her sloppiness. There was a kid I was friendly with, and his mother was a neat housekeeper and a teetotaler. I wanted her to be my mother. She spoiled my friend rotten, and when I was with him she spoiled me, too. I wanted to be the center of attention the way he was. As it was, while my mother was good to me, she favored my sister, so I was left to fend for myself.

Lynne both identified with her father's disapproval (in a futile bid for his love) and allied with her emotionally distant mother against his brutality.

As Lynne grew to adulthood, the mother-daughter coalition was strengthened and came to be accompanied by a warm emotional attachment. Throughout the ordeal of her up-and-down relationship and prolonged breakup with Scott, Lynne turned to her mother first and last for support. When she was depressed, when she was unsure about what she was feeling or what she should do, she called her mother. When her friends didn't want to hear any more about Scott, her mother remained her most loyal confidante. "She's been a patient saint," Lynne says, "because every time I talk to her it's 'Scott, Scott, Scott.'"

This is how Lynne describes her relationship with her mother currently:

> I call my mother daily. I lean on her completely. She is my best, best friend in the world, and I love her dearly. She's not perfect, and I wish she were different in some ways. But I rely on her for a lot of moral support, and that makes her happy, too.

She has reached a degree of mutual understanding with her father as well, but her description of her relationship with him makes clear with which parent she feels really intimate:

I don't know why he did what he did to my mother, but I forgive him. He's made mistakes, and he never helped me financially, but he's done things for me lately that he never did before. I do need my father. I do need a man to call up once in a while. I rarely call him, though it's nice to know that I can. But he still isn't "Daddy" the way my mother is "Mommy."

It is heartening—and it bodes well for her future relationships with men— that Lynne can be at peace with her parents after the wounds she suffered and those she witnessed when she was a child. Still, however, there are vestiges of the childhood relationships that may have set Lynne on the path to romantic obsession: mother as ally; father as remote, withholding, impervious.

CHILDREN OF DIVORCE

Families of divorce frequently show patterns similar to those which led to anxious romantic attachment in the daughters of the intact families in our research. Couples who are headed for divorce generally have poor marital adjustment and much dissatisfaction and conflict. After the divorce, the parents struggle for the daughter's allegiance. Thus, a woman whose parents divorced while she was growing up may well have had a version of the childhood experiences that leave a woman vulnerable to insecurity in love relationships. Often she has had a quite severe version of those experiences.

In particular, it is romantic obsession that is a common by-product of divorce. When the parents are estranged from each other, the custodial parent is in a position to undermine the absent parent. Since the mother usually has custody, especially in the case of a daughter, it is the father who is absent, and that alone may constitute rejection in the eyes of a child. In addition, if the mother feels hostile and bitter toward the father, she may paint the father's absence in a negative light. In this way, divorce can predispose the daughter to feel alienated from her father; but at the same time, she may harbor fantasies about him and long for the confirmation of her worth that he is not there to give.

The circumstances of divorce and its aftermath can lead to a progressive rupturing of a girl's relationship with her father. Whatever steps the father takes to rebuild his life after the divorce—finding employment out of state, meeting another woman, remarrying, buying a house, fathering a child— may be experienced by the child as additional signs of abandonment. No sooner does she adapt to one upheaval than her father upsets the applecart again. Each new change feels to her like another blow, a recapitulation of the loss. As she grows up, she may direct this obsessive longing toward other men; she may feel the same repeated blows when she sees signs that another man is rejecting her, and the same sense of loss at the conclusion of a romantic involvement that she felt after her parents' divorce (accompanied by the loss of her father).

The following stories are of an adult woman and a teenage girl whose families were shattered by divorce. They serve to dramatize the effects of separation from the father, whether through actual abandonment or extreme parental conflict.

JOYCE

In Chapter 4 we told the story of Joyce, who presented herself as strong and in control—the image of the hard-boiled woman—yet just below this surface she felt very vulnerable. She suffered an emotional collapse when she felt betrayed by a man who "was like a dad, or my perception of what a dad should be." She explained, "My real dad and I never really had a relationship. I don't think I ever really knew him." As a result, she reflected, "I have never felt special to any one person. No, I have never felt real."

Joyce's parents "hated each other." The children were compelled to witness and intervene in violent fights between them, and an ugly divorce ensued when Joyce was five years old. Her father then kidnapped her from their Tennessee home and took her to live with him in Detroit. There he married a woman who verbally abused her, while he himself was not much more empathic. As Joyce recalls:

> My dad had a very large ego; he was macho and easily became insecure. And he would just lose it, totally lose it, if you did one little thing wrong. Some little kids can joke with their daddies and mommies, tease them and they'll tease back. You could not do that with my father. I called him a sourpuss one time, and I caught hell. Even now I have a hard time kidding with people.

This was an unsympathetic father, hostile and controlling. Joyce experienced him as erratic in his behavior and inconsistent in his love. "He was so unpredictable," she explains. "One minute he'd be so gentle, the next minute he'd be raving mad." Joyce sought a closer bond with him, only to be rebuffed, as in this poignant incident:

Once when I was still very little he got some mail, and his wife threw it away. "She's throwing away my daddy's mail!" I thought. So I took it out of the trash can and hid it in my room. When I got him alone and showed it to him, instead of thanking me like I expected, he got real bent out of shape. "If she said to throw it away, you should have thrown it away!" he yelled. I was crushed. I thought I was protecting him.

Joyce had tried to bring her father into an alliance with her, but instead he allied himself with her "wicked stepmother." As a result, she says, "the distance between us kept growing wider."

Joyce keenly felt the lack of an emotional attachment to her father. "I didn't have the usual Daddy-little girl relationship, like 'You're precious,' 'You're wonderful,' and all that. So when I got into my teens I started looking for it outside the home"—that is, from a succession of boyfriends.

First, though, Joyce turned to her mother. Forbidden by her father to communicate with her mother for several years, she began making furtive long-distance calls to Tennessee in her early teens. Finally, not knowing how he would react, she told her father that she wanted to see her mother. He consented. "I was in shock," she recalls.

It seemed too good to be true that her father was putting her on a plane to Tennessee. What she found there was also too good to be true.

Mother expects this little bitty thing to get off the plane, and here she gets this adolescent. She didn't know what to do. Everything was wonderful while we were getting to know each other. It was hunky-dory; she was spoiling me rotten because she missed me so. I said I would stay three weeks, and I stayed three months.

At this stage, Joyce formed an alliance with an indulgent mother against a strict father.

When she returned to her father in Detroit, Joyce found that she missed "having my mother around—the family unit, parents and kids." She told her father that she wanted to live with her mother. "You can go on with your life," she said to him, "but it's really tough on me." Again her father let her go, this time for good.

So Joyce moved back to Tennessee. When she arrived at her mother's home, however, she was in for another surprise. The coalition her mother had formed with her during her visit lasted only as long as her mother was competing with her father for her presence and her loyalty:

It was like, "You're here for good now, and I'm the boss. You're going to be in by ten o'clock, and you're going to do this and this and this, and before you go out on Saturday, all your chores are going to be done." I was free labor for her until I moved out.

Joyce describes her mother as a domineering, but secure woman who made growing up an arduous experience. Contributing to the emotional aridity of Joyce's teen years was the fact that, now that she was living with her mother, she was not allowed to speak to her father. Her parents, who had raged violently at each other before their divorce, hardened their hearts against each other afterward.

If you lived with one, you couldn't talk to the other—that's how it was. I never heard any warm stories about Mom from Dad, or warm stories about Dad from Mom. They only gave me awful stories about each other. I could not talk to them about each other, it was only after my father died that my mother told me how they met. I think that's where a lot of my problems with relationships come from.

When Joyce was about to be married (a marriage that lasted only a few years), she asked her father to give her away at the wedding. He declined, on the grounds that her mother was going to be there. "You don't love me enough to be in the same room with my mother?" Joyce asked.

"I guess not," he said. Then he added dryly (he was a medical pathologist), "I hope I'll be around when she dies, so I can do the autopsy."

At that Joyce lost her temper. "That's it. You two have used me as a pawn for twenty years. That's it. I'm through." She did not speak to her father again for several years.

Some years later, her mother said she was too busy to travel five hundred miles to visit Joyce in the hospital, where she was recuperating from an overdose of tranquilizers brought on by a feeling of abandonment at the hands of a man she secretly loved. Evidently, Joyce's parents were so uncomfortable with their past connection to each other that they did not know how to deal with the daughter they had in common. Although they may have wanted to love her, they reacted to her out of their deep alienation from each other. Joyce did call her father near the end of his life and learned that he had kept informed about her through her brother. Ambivalent toward her father as he was toward her, she was pleased to have reestablished even that much of a relationship with him.

Looking back on her life to date, Joyce describes the sources of her insecurity in romantic love relationships in a way that comes very close to our research findings:

> If you grow up with very insecure, jealous parents, which I did, you'll carry on that pattern. It's going to take a lot of work to change it, and you have to be aware of it first. You need to have that feeling of being special to someone. If that need is met in your formative years, then you can stay with one person and feel special. But if you've never had that, then you're going to go through life looking for that one special feeling—and you're not going to find it with a mate. It's got to happen early, or you're going to have to work through it. The insecurities in a one-to-one relationship with a man are real hard unless you have that daddy or someone else you can go to.

BECKY

When a teenager who is just beginning to date shows all the signs of anxious romantic attachment, we know that her insecurity has not come from bad experiences in dating. Rather, it has deeper roots in the assumptions and expectations about intimate relationships that she learned from her parents. Some anxiously attached young people will continue to be anxiously attached in adult life, as Joyce was. Others will have positive experiences that will give them greater emotional security and make them less susceptible to romantic anxiety and obsession.

Seventeen-year-old Becky came to therapy with the complaint that she was "boy-crazy. I fall in love very quickly. I have to have someone to love and to love me back. I always need to have a boyfriend to tell me how cute I am, or I go into a deep depression and feel that no one wants me. How come?"

Becky was bright, verbal, level-headed, and otherwise successful, but she had difficulty setting boundaries for her relationships with boys. She was drawn into talk of love and marriage by a boyfriend she had barely known for a week, only to find that he talked that way with other girls as well. Their relationship lasted only a few months and was volatile from the start, but Becky did not end it because she wanted so badly to prove that she was a sensitive person who could make contact with a difficult male. In the end, the boy broke up with her in anger, and Becky was crushed.

A day later she had a new boyfriend, a drug and alcohol abuser. "He's irresistible—a sweet-talker," she said. When her therapist asked her what she would do if she found her mother living with a man like him, she said, "I'd insist that he leave." But she was determined to stick it out with this boy so that she could "help" him.

Becky's emotional vulnerability can be traced to problems in her family. Recently she had shown up on the doorstep of the father she had never known. Her parents, who divorced when she was an infant, lived a continent apart. Her father did not try very hard to stay in contact with her, and her mother thwarted his half-hearted efforts. As a young child, Becky cried when her mother would not let her talk to her father when he telephoned. Now, after her mother remarried, she left home and made her way from San Francisco to New York, where her father lived with his second wife.

From the outset, Becky's life was set up as a coalition with her mother, with no possibility of an attachment to her father. Becky lived with her mother and a succession of single "stepfathers." One of these men stayed on longer than the rest. The couple was always fighting, and Becky naturally blamed all the fights on him, since her mother incessantly complained to her about him. Becky assumed an alliance in which she defended her mother against this man, whom she saw as an intruder. Indeed, her mother was happy to seek comfort in Becky when she had problems with her lover. Suddenly, without warning, she eloped with him. Becky felt shocked, hurt, and betrayed.

Becky saw her mother as self-centered and not really interested in her. Her mother is an intelligent but depressed-looking woman with an immobile facial expression and a critical, undermining tone. Her personality is a combination of the qualities of rejection and self-abasement (which may lead to romantic anxiety) and immaturity and possessiveness (which may lead to romantic obsession). Drifting into an unsettled second marriage in her late thirties, she seemed forever at loose ends. Employed as a palm-reader at a beach resort, she upset Becky by predicting a future for her full of bizarre incidents and broken relationships.

Becky was placed in the role of the parental child, who must create the order that is missing in the household. Suppressing her anger at her mother for fear of hurting her, she showed an emotional sensitivity beyond her years. But when her mother remarried, Becky felt that a special tie had been broken. She began to drink, smoke marijuana, and skip school. Her grades plummeted. It was then that she ran away and asked her father to take her in.

Becky was delighted to find that her father had matured since he had walked out on her mother, and that he and his wife were reasonable people who cared about her. "I grew up thinking my father was a jerk," she said, "but now I see his side of things." In her new home Becky excelled in her schoolwork and tried in every way to please her new family. Insecure about being accepted, she worked hard to show what a worthy person she was—to her father and stepmother, to the peers she befriended, and to the boyfriends whose tokens of love and approval meant so much to her.

Bending over backward to be sensitive and solicitous to others, Becky now found herself unable to ignore an appeal from her mother to return to California to live. "Mom needs me," she explained. Her father and stepmother wanted her to make her own decision, and she agonized over conflicting obligations. She was beset by guilt for deserting her mother, but did not want to disappoint her father. Finally she did go back to her mother, and to a future which, while uncertain in the short term, was promising in the long term. Despite the way her mother had drifted away from her, Becky still clung to the hope that they could form a close alliance—a hope that was bound to be crushed again. Nonetheless, she had grown immeasurably by establishing a relationship with her father, who would now be a major source of emotional support for her.

JULIE: A FRAGILE BOND

Our research has identified the most common family patterns associated with intense insecurity in romantic love relationships. There are, no doubt, other, less common family patterns that also lead to this experience. One such variation in family background is illustrated by Julie, whose relationship with her husband was described in Chapter 2.

Julie is strongly obsessed; she stays home all day, revolving the household around her husband, waiting for him to call and reward her by suggesting they go out on the town. She is anxious as well; she is susceptible to sudden, explosive bursts of temper when she feels he is neglecting her. Julie expresses both romantic obsession and romantic anxiety when she says that "there is no one else I want to please" except her husband, yet she finds her love for him "scary."

Julie is an extreme case of a woman who feels cut off from any paternal relationship. Born out of wedlock, she never met her father. This alone would lead her to be romantically obsessed with men. In addition, her mother seems never to have accepted her completely. Her mother had intended to give her up for adoption until the hospital staff persuaded her to take the baby home. Julie ended up being raised by her grandparents for several years until her mother married. Even then, her mother, clearly favoring her "legitimate" children, kept a distance from her. It was as if her mother found Julie an embarrassing reminder of her past and wanted her out of sight. Julie was not given the same educational advantages as her sister and brothers; instead, she was told to go out and work. She believes that she married her first husband, the only man she had ever dated, because her mother made her feel that she had no alternative, either for marriage or for a career.

Julie's first husband was an abusive alcoholic who was unfaithful and did not earn a steady living. Her second husband is not only a good provider, but also a reasonably accepting and supportive, if somewhat complacent, partner. Yet as noted in Chapter 2, Julie has acted toward both men in similar ways — with exaggerated devotion punctuated by unpredictable outbursts of anger. Clearly, she is responding not to her husband as he is, but to prior circumstances in her life that conditioned her uneasy reactions to men in intimate relationships. Julie has had a recurrent dream in which a faceless man comes up to her and gives her flowers and cupcakes. The dream expresses the link between the romantic love she craves in the present (flowers) and the nurturance she feels she was denied in childhood (cupcakes).

For Julie, this lack of nurturance resulted in part from not having a father, and in part from having a rejecting mother. Julie may be a good example of the effects of the maternal-infant bond on adult romantic relationships. Psychoanalyst John Bowlby and psychologist Mary Ainsworth described three types or qualities of emotional attachment of infant to mother. Each corresponds to a pattern of caretaking behavior on the mother's part. There is one type of attachment in which the infant is contented and secure, the mother reliably attentive; a second in which the infant is aloof and avoidant, the mother abusive or overstimulating; and a third in which the infant is temperamental — sometimes demanding, sometimes turning away, sometimes angry, often anxious — as if mimicking a mother who responds insensitively and inconsistently.

This third group of infants is called "anxious-ambivalent." These infants may demand contact with the mother, but reject such contact when it is offered. They tend to approach the mother until they come within what they regard as a safe distance, at which point they stop. They may react noisily when the mother leaves, but then turn aside cautiously when she returns. Perhaps we can find an echo of this anxious-ambivalent style of infant behavior in Julie's inconsistent feelings toward Mike, her husband — elaborately submissive most of the time, but with disproportionate eruptions of anger and pain. Preoccupied constantly with Mike, thinking of him as her whole world, she sometimes finds this consuming emotional attachment unbearably intense. It is then that she begs Mike to release her from her misery if he does not love her with the total consistency and devotion she demands.

There may well be a continuity between the kinds of attachment infants form with their mothers (secure, avoidant, anxious-ambivalent) and the kinds of romantic attachment formed by adults (secure, detached, anxiously attached). As we learn more about anxious romantic attachment, further research may establish a link with parent-child relationships not only in childhood and adolescence, but in infancy as well.

JEALOUSY IN THE MAKING

The family pattern that leads to jealousy in women resembles that of romantic obsession. This is to be expected, since people who are romantically obsessed typically experience strong feelings of jealousy (as discussed in Chapter 7).

As with romantic obsession, the father's child-rearing behavior and his relationship with his daughter are key factors in jealousy. If the father is hostile and rejecting, the daughter is likely to be jealous when her relationship with a man is threatened by a rival. But if the father is warm and accepting, the daughter is not likely to show strong feelings of jealousy. Likewise, the more emotionally attached to her father a woman feels, the less she is likely to feel jealous in her romantic involvements with men.

In some other respects, however, the family pattern associated with jealousy diverges from that associated with romantic obsession. In particular, the better the parents' marital adjustment and the more satisfied they are with their marriage, the less likely the daughter is to be jealous, which is not the case with obsession. On the other hand, the mother's lax discipline and the coalition between her and her daughter do not play the same important roles with respect to jealousy that they do with romantic obsession.

DEPRESSION IN THE MAKING

Severe or prolonged depression at the end of a relationship, which also is closely linked with romantic obsession (as shown in Chapter 8), has similar antecedents in the father's child-rearing behavior and in the father-daughter relationship. The more hostile and rejecting the father, the more depressed the daughter is likely to be when a romantic relationship ends. The more warm, accepting, and well-adjusted the father, the less depressed the daughter is likely to be, particularly if she has a strong attachment to him.

The mother's child-rearing and personality characteristics and the mother-daughter coalition do not appear to bear any relationship to the daughter's susceptibility to depression at the end of a relationship. Nor does the parents' marital relationship have any effect. In the case of depression, the woman's personality is more important than family relationships. Personality is the focus of the following chapter.

10

THE QUESTION OF PERSONALITY:

WHO ARE YOU IN REAL LIFE?

"I just wasn't myself yesterday," you may have heard yourself say. Or "I just couldn't be myself with Chris." Of course, you were yourself. Who else could you have been? But people are so complex and many-sided, so capable of variation, that the consistent core that makes you the same person yesterday, today, and tomorrow is easily obscured. You may present different sides of yourself to your friends, your co-workers, and your family, and they may each describe you in ways that sound very different from one another. Yet something about you is constant; something carries over from one situation to the next, one relationship to the next, one year to the next.

That something is personality. Following a general description of the personality of the anxiously attached person, this chapter will report what our research has revealed about personality characteristics of anxiously attached women. Men's personality traits will be covered in Chapter 11 in conjunction with their family backgrounds.

We have seen that feelings of insecurity in romantic relationships are triggered by circumstances outside of yourself. Romantic anxiety is affected by the inconsistent behavior of your partner, romantic obsession by the partner's attractiveness. Your partner's disloyalty may touch off feelings of jealousy, while your partner's departure may be a prelude to depression. Even so, there is something in you that determines how you respond to these

events. That is what the relationship between family background and insecure love implies. For since we can predict with some reliability how you will
react to "Chris" on the basis of experiences you had with your parents twenty
years ago, those experiences must have shaped you in some way. That shaping
is preserved over time and affects other parts of your life and your relationships with people, including romantic love relationships.

THE INNER EXPERIENCE OF
ANXIOUS ROMANTIC ATTACHMENT

Psychologists Keith Cohen and James Clark found that people who as
children had been especially attached to blankets, teddy bears, and other
stuffed animals (what psychologists call transitional objects) tended to be
more tense, excitable, restless, and impatient as adults. They were more easily
angered and upset and expressed more emotion generally. Is there a parallel
between the child who clings to an object to get a feeling of comfort and
consistency and the adult who clings to a love relationship?

Our sense of why people become anxiously attached to others comes from a
number of sources, including our detailed observations of anxious romantic
attachment, our findings about family backgrounds and childhood experiences, and considerable psychological theory and research. According to John
Bowlby and Mary Ainsworth, the consistent availability of the mother to the
infant can begin a lifelong confidence in the availability of other sources of
love and affection. But if the mother is unreliable or unpredictable, then the
child, lacking this early working model of emotional availability and support, grows up feeling insecure about having her or his needs satisfied. Our
own research, while it focuses on the father as well as the mother and on later
stages of childhood and adolescence rather than infancy, likewise shows that
parental inconsistency and rejection in childhood are at the root of insecure
love in adulthood. There is good reason to believe that the pattern of anxious,
obsessive attachment to a love object begins early in life. We see this clearly
for women, who are most susceptible to anxious romantic attachment when
they have grown up feeling cut off from their fathers. The picture is more
complex for men, but the themes of rejection and inconsistency on the part of
both parents, along with hostile control and domination, are prominent in the
backgrounds of many men who are anxiously attached to their wives or lovers.

A person with a background of parental inconsistency and rejection enters
adulthood without having a stable expectation of love and affection. Those

who are anxiously attached are more likely to be those who have had positive as well as negative experiences of parental attachment, and who therefore approach adult romantic involvements with intense hope as well as intense fear. They have had a taste of the acceptance and affection they desire, but cannot feel secure in its possession.

The child grows up with a self-esteem that is variable and easily influenced by the reactions of others. As an adult, he or she continues to be engaged in a day-by-day, moment-by-moment search for confirmation of his or her worth. The anxiously attached lover, having once looked intently for signs of a parent's love or indifference, approval or disapproval, now looks to others who offer, or at least symbolize, the elusive promise of secure, reliable love. If you do not carry within yourself a stable sense of personal worth, you become dependent on positive feedback from others to maintain good feelings about yourself. You will also be sensitive to negative feedback and, more interestingly, to a lack of feedback, which throws you into a quandary and leads to a distorted, judgmental, and negative view of yourself. You are subject to widely fluctuating moods, ranging from elation to despair. These are the mood swings that characterize romantic anxiety.

Think of a time when you have been desperately, wonderfully in love with someone, or when someone has been in love with you. Anxiety and uncertainty are not all there is to love, but they provide evidence of the strength of one's love and add to the power of the feelings of love. Moreover, when you find you have goose bumps, sweaty palms, and a pounding heart, there are strong cues all around you (just think of all the songs on the radio) to label those as symptoms of being in love rather than anxious or insecure. Is it love, or is it insecurity? Or is the insecurity really love? The riddle is posed by the captions from a Jules Feiffer cartoon:

> *Patient:* Last time you told me that I should try to get in touch with my emotions. So, on Monday I felt competitiveness, on Tuesday I felt elation, on Wednesday I felt frustration, on Thursday I felt hostility, and on Friday I felt depression. When will I feel LOVE?
> *Therapist:* That IS love!

It is this mixture of intense and sometimes incongruous feelings that our culture defines as falling in love. It includes the hope, the tantalizing possibility, of having your feelings of worth and desirability confirmed by a positive response from a highly valued person. It includes mounting excitement at the signs that someone to whom you are physically attracted may feel the same about you. These would be exhilarating sensations for almost anyone. But they are especially intense for a person whose self-esteem is especially shaky. As a way of repairing or coping with the damage done to self-esteem in childhood, a person may cling to the reality, belief, hope, or even fantasy of being loved by a desirable person. This feeling of acceptance, of reflected glory, can be so rewarding that people take great risks (including the risk of rejection) to experience such fulfillment, even temporarily. It is a heady gamble, one that transforms painful uncertainty into a high-rolling adventure, where the positive stakes are as large as the negative ones.

Why do people put so much energy into stressful and often unsuccessful romantic pursuits? They may do so to reduce uncertainty, to render the unpredictable predictable, to return to the scene of past losses and triumph over them, to gain mastery over experiences that have been painful or frustrating, or, simply put, to obtain what they see others as having and yearn so much to have for themselves. Uncertainty is a challenge, and sexual attraction often is heightened when the reward is less than a sure thing. When this positive excitement exists together with a more threatening uncertainty about oneself, anxious romantic attachment is at its zenith.

THE ANXIOUSLY ATTACHED WOMAN

What kind of person is formed by the childhood experiences described in Chapter 9, experiences that we know lead to patterns of anxious romantic attachment? What other facets of personality are found together with romantic anxiety, romantic obsession, jealousy, or depression? Here is what we found out from the women in our study and from others who knew them well.

ROMANTIC ANXIETY

When a girl grows up in a family in which her parents fight a great deal and her father is rejecting and coercive toward her as well as toward her mother (who may be overinvolved with her), she may come to believe that she is not very lovable. She may assume that other men, like her father, will not accept her. This belief may have no basis in reality; on the contrary, this young woman may be very desirable—only she has no way of knowing it. Growing up in a hostile atmosphere, she learns to expect that men in general will be critical of her.

This negative self-image and uncertain expectations may cause her feelings and moods to fluctuate greatly, depending on the signs of approval or disapproval she gets from others. Given her experience of paternal rejection, she is anxious to be accepted and, to protect herself, all too ready to interpret ambiguous signals as bad news. If a man really does like her, she delights in the possibility that what she has always believed about herself is wrong. "Hey, I'm okay," she thinks. She is euphoric in proportion to the depth of her prior despair. And so she gets hooked on a feeling, one long in coming, that she does not want to lose.

She may have developed a positive self-image in other areas (such as professional accomplishment) where enough evidence of success has accumulated since her earliest school years, and enough current reminders and feedback are available, to outweigh her father's denigration and other discouraging experiences. In romantic relationships, however, her self-esteem remains fragile, and her relevant experience has been more limited. In the face of possible rejection, her old doubts lie just beneath the surface. They are always pressing forward threateningly, and she needs reassurance of her lovableness to keep them at bay. If the man she has just begun dating does not call for a couple of days, she begins to wonder whether she will ever see him again. If he does not call by the weekend, she may sink from elation to depression. Although recent experience has told her that she *is* lovable, in the absence of reinforcement of that message she falls back on her childhood notion of herself as unworthy of love. This is one version of the romantically anxious woman—unsure of herself, easily led to believe more or less of herself on the basis of how she thinks others are reacting to her, and thus subject to mood swings. In this state she feels disempowered; she believes that she is living too much at the whim of others, particularly her partner.

In another version, a woman may have reacted to parental conflict and rejection during her youth by becoming aggressive, nonconforming, and adventure-seeking. Taking her mother's side in the marital struggle (and maybe gaining at least her mother's support in return), she reacts to the feeling of being put down by her father by fighting fire with fire. This stand-tough attitude that she slowly acquired during her formative years carries over to relationships with other men, where she guards against possible rejection by struggling to stay one step ahead. Beginning in childhood, she has met threats to her self-esteem with a strong-willed assertion of her adequacy. In some cases, her hurt and anger find comfort in heavy drinking. She may, by getting into scrapes with authority, rebel against her father's values or reproduce the conflict of a divided family.

In the family in which this woman grew up, she had to be ready to defend herself against imminent danger. In such an emotional jungle (where the rule was: "Be alert or be eaten"), she developed sensitive "tiger detectors" that would fire off an aggressive response when she felt threatened. Now, in her adult relationships, her tiger detectors fire needlessly, causing distress for herself as well as for others. When men withdraw in response to her aggressive defenses, her anxiety only heightens.

Whatever anxieties she may have at the outset, a woman who appears confident and assertive runs the additional risk of being rejected by men who are threatened by her self-assurance. Such experiences may instill uncertainty about her attractiveness and desirability to men. As a result, she may become anxious about entering into new romantic involvements.

To understand the woman who is high in romantic anxiety, it helps to look at the woman who is *low* in romantic anxiety. Her most prominent qualities are two that she shares with her parents: warmth and self-discipline. In general, nurturance and firm guidance are the parental qualities most important in raising a child who is emotionally secure. The daughter absorbs these qualities, both from observation and from direct teaching, and carries them on in her own life and relationships.

The woman who displays little anxiety in her love relationships comes across as a warm person. She likes being with people and is not afraid to be open. She is gregarious, socially at ease, and responsible and supportive toward others. Cooperative relationships, involving give-and-take with a number of people, bring out the best in her. She is known both to family and friends as a nurturing person. At the extreme, such a woman risks being caught up in roles that involve giving a great deal to others without getting much in return. As a result, she may come to feel drained and even "used." But by and large, she is likely to be secure enough to get out of an unrewarding or inequitable relationship.

Although the romantically anxious woman may potentially have these qualities, often they are hidden from herself, if not from others, behind her feelings of fear and inadequacy. With a father who was cold toward her and a mother who may have been too distracted by marital conflict to be a model of warmth, she may have difficulty becoming a warm, nurturing person herself.

An important dimension of personal warmth is the ability to trust an intimate partner. A woman who feels she can rely on her husband or lover to be honest and trustworthy tends to be relatively low in romantic anxiety. This trust is expressed by questionnaire statements such as the following:

"You can rely on men to be truthful about their feelings."
"You can rely on a man calling you if he says he will."
"It's rare that men will hurt you to get what they want."

In contrast, statements such as the following show a lack of trust:

"It's better not to trust a man until you have proof of his sincerity."
"Most men will use any trick or line to get a woman into bed."
"If a woman doesn't watch out, she'll be used." (Gurtman)

Psychologist Michael Gurtman, who developed the measure of "heterosexual trust" used in our study, showed that a woman is better able to trust her male partner when her father was consistent in his love. For a woman, secure love appears to be rooted in the experience of trustworthiness on the part of men (beginning with her father) and in the belief that she can tell when a man can or cannot be trusted. If, on the other hand, she saw her father as untrustworthy—sending mixed messages, saying one thing and doing another—she may not easily place her trust in a man's love.

When we speak of the woman who experiences relatively little romantic anxiety as self-disciplined, we refer to a number of characteristics having to do with her personal and social adjustment, self-control, and self-satisfaction. This woman tends to conform to conventional norms and customs; that is, she is conscientious and dependable in her work, respectful and proper in her dealings with people, restrained in her expression of emotions, and regulated in her behavior. Adept at organization and planning, she can carry through a task from beginning to end and can delay gratification for the sake of achieving long-range goals. Known for her toughness and strength in the face of adversity, she can be counted on in a crisis. Some individuals may accomplish all this at the cost of being a bit rigid and inhibited. Even so, women who are low in romantic anxiety tend to know themselves well, to be comfortable with themselves and their lives, and to feel that they are living up to their image of what they should be. They have a secure sense of value and responsibility.

How and why does the romantically anxious woman differ from this picture? In some cases, she may have trouble making herself do the things she knows she needs to do. She may procrastinate. The aches and pains, the daily inconveniences, the unexpected things that all too easily seize her attention may divert her from working to achieve her goals. Instead of sacrificing for the future, she puts off unpleasant tasks for the sake of enjoying the present with a great deal of vitality and pleasure. Some women who are high in romantic anxiety are very spontaneous and open to change. These same women, however, may feel at a disadvantage in competitive environments, and at times they may feel uneasy that they are not doing enough to build for the future. Although speaking one's mind directly in a social or work situation can help clear the air, it can also make people angry. Nonconformity has its advantages, but a person can also be punished for challenging authority.

To see how this free-spirited woman expresses herself in romantic involvements, recall the story of Amy in Chapter 5. Although she says she wants a stable relationship, she passes up men who might offer the security of a long-term involvement. Men with whom she experiences warmth, companionship, trust, and communication she relegates to the status of buddies. Instead, she pursues the dream—and occasionally, for a time, the reality—of a captivating, intensely gratifying lover. "Maybe it's just the conquest I want," she reflects. "It's as if I'm saying, 'I can have him; I don't want him. I'll find somebody else I can't have.'" Amy may not know what she wants most, or she may feel she wants different things at different times. But she regularly chooses brief, highly romantic unions that flatter and gratify her somewhat shaky self-image in preference to relationships that might bring her stability and lasting satisfaction, but without that intensely gratifying boost to her ego.

The difference between women who are low in romantic anxiety and those who are high seems largely one of upbringing. When the parents are firm, consistent, and nurturing in their discipline, the daughter is likely to adopt their values. But when the parents are in conflict, one parent may be warmer, more firm, or more punitive than the other. Typically, if the daughter sides with the mother in family conflicts, the father may become more strict and rejecting while the mother becomes more permissive. Such disagreements undermine the daughter's development, since a child, when faced with two different standards, most often takes the path of least resistance.

But this is not the whole story, since highly responsible, self-disciplined, productive women can and do experience intense romantic anxiety. Some women who rate themselves (and are rated by others) as low on discipline may have considerably more self-discipline than those ratings would indicate. We infer this from the fact that the romantically anxious woman tends to underestimate herself. She freely expresses self-doubt as well as other feelings. More often than not, she is disappointed in herself. She feels that she is not living up to her potential, to her own image of what she should be. In fact, she may be more responsible and better organized than she realizes. But the excessively harsh image of herself that she formed in childhood leads her to doubt herself in these areas just as it leads her to doubt her attractiveness to men.

A person who expresses this sense of inadequacy (however unwarranted) may unwittingly convince others that she is indeed inadequate. A person who lacks confidence in herself is unlikely to inspire confidence in others. In particular, a woman who readily expresses feelings such as those associated with romantic anxiety may seem hardly the person to call upon in a time of crisis, even though she may be very capable of rising to the occasion. By the way she represents herself, she may convince those around her to see her in the role she has been assigned in her family—that of an incompetent, dependent person. And some of those people may not need much convincing, since they are the family members who assigned her that role in the first place!

ROMANTIC OBSESSION

The picture is much the same for romantic obsession, but not as strongly so, with fewer personality characteristics associated with either high or low romantic obsession. In particular, the whole set of traits associated with warmth (such as gregariousness, nurturance, and trust) are unrelated to romantic obsession. The fact that a woman is a warm person does not make her any less likely to be obsessed with her partner. Similarly, aggressive, nonconforming behavior is not so strongly associated with romantic obsession either, although a romantically obsessive woman is more likely to have engaged in teenage delinquency and to be a heavier alcohol user as a young adult than one who is nonobsessive.

Otherwise, the major personality characteristics associated with romantic obsession are the same as those associated with romantic anxiety. The romantically obsessed woman tends to be subject to the cycles of anxiety and depression, of elation and self-doubt, described above. She is likely to be less disciplined and less well adjusted than average, at least in her own opinion.

The romantically obsessed woman's vulnerability to mood swings comes from the great value she places on the relationship and on the man who thinks so well of her. With her self-esteem so much in question, the idea that she is loved gives her a feeling of euphoria. She thinks about her lover, fantasizes about their interactions—she is in love with love. Thus, when someone values her, she is riding high, feeling on top of the world; but the flip side, despair, comes ever so quickly when the positive feedback ceases. So intense are the feelings at each extreme of the cycle that she experiences both the ups and downs as highly dramatic events.

JEALOUSY

Jealousy, too, is found in conjunction with feelings of inadequacy, changeable moods, and periods of discouragement about the prospect of being loved. Again, uncertain self-esteem links a woman's good feelings about herself to acceptance by a man. In contrast, personal qualities that reflect warmth and discipline are associated with the relative absence of jealousy, as they are with the relative absence of romantic anxiety.

Physical characteristics also play a part in jealousy. The more attractive a woman is, and the thinner she is, the *more* jealous she is likely to be. The fact that thin, attractive women are more jealous is consistent with the idea that jealousy arises from a sense of entitlement. The more physically desirable a woman considers herself to be, the more deserving she feels of her partner's loyalty, and the more indignant she is when that presumption is violated.

More attractive women generally are just as secure or insecure as less attractive women, and entitlement and insecurity are not necessarily intertwined. Typically, it is the other way around: those who feel more secure are in a better position to insist on their rights. How, then, can jealousy be associated with both entitlement and insecurity? Probably there are at least two main groups of jealous women. First, there are those who feel entitled to speak up when their partner violates their rights. Second, there are those who perceive disloyalty because they feel insecure, even when no actual infraction has occurred. Whether a woman becomes jealous depends on a combination of factors: what agreements she has with her partner, whether her partner keeps those agreements, and how she reacts to real or imagined violations. With all of these elements, it is not surprising that there is not a consistent set of personality traits associated with jealousy.

A sense of entitlement can be expressed by an outspoken, critical style of dealing with people. Jealous women have a tendency to be aggressive, but this is not so much rebellion as domination and demandingness. This is a woman who is outspoken about what she wants, what she expects, and when she is upset or displeased. She may register her grievances loudly and forcefully to compel her partner to respect her rights.

In dramatizing her jealousy, she is expressing her strong need for companionship and support. Somewhat dependent on others, she attracts people to herself to satisfy her needs. She soaks up human contact, which she sometimes seems to pursue impulsively and excitedly, as if in a headlong rush. With her self-doubt and expectation of rejection and the need she feels to have people in her life, she may appear thin-skinned and quick to presume betrayal. Like an actress who must always have center stage, she has little tolerance for rivals. On the lookout for slights, she may (in her more aggressive variation) take the offensive, as if to squeeze loyalty from her partner. Her dilemma is that her behavior may drive her partner away and thus make her feel more insecure.

When asked about the frequency of a variety of sexual fantasies, women prone to jealousy reported a slightly higher frequency of homosexual fantasies than women low in jealousy. Such fantasies may express a wish for intimacy and reassurance without the stresses and threats that relationships with men often entail. If the fantasies indicate a degree of bisexuality, a heterosexual woman who feels some sexual attraction to other women may more easily imagine her male partner also being attracted to other women. This could make her feel intensely jealous, and especially so if she is unsure of her own femininity.

According to one interpretation of jealousy presented in Chapter 7, people who have the impulse to be unfaithful more readily imagine that their partners have similar impulses and may even be acting on them. Our composite portrait of the jealous woman as impulsive and excitable, as self-dramatizing even while she is dependent, suggests that she may feel drawn to have affairs outside of her committed relationship. Her suspicion of her partner may arise from her own vulnerability to outside stimulation.

DEPRESSION

While women who retaliate actively against the father's rejection and hostility are more likely to be jealous when a relationship is threatened, they are not so likely to be depressed when a relationship ends. A vigorous, hang-tough stance serves a woman well when a relationship ends, since it leads her either to attack the partner or rival or to cope actively with her loss rather than blame herself.

In contrast, women who *are* prone to depression at the end of a relationship tend to be those who have more difficulty throwing off their fathers' negative images of them. Although these women may be somewhat nonconforming, they usually are not aggressive. On the other hand, and not surprisingly, they are prone to anxiety, mood swings, and severe depressions, whether or not in response to the breakup of an intimate relationship.

This type of reaction could go back to a woman's childhood, when her mother comforted her and sympathized with her distress over her father's hostility (as opposed to encouraging her to resist actively her father's derogation). It corresponds to what we referred to in Chapter 8 as self-punishing depression—the kind of depression that involves feelings of self-criticism, guilt, and failure. Under the stress of rejection by an intimate partner, the woman is jolted back to her childhood, when a critical father pointed the finger of blame at her. Self-punishing depression is tied in with the uncertain and fluctuating self-esteem that is at the root of anxious romantic attachment.

The other main type of depression, grieving depression, is a reaction to the loss of nurturance and support on which one has depended. It is associated with a different set of personal characteristics: social isolation, a lack of personal energy, and a lack of experience and confidence in attracting and getting along with others. Grieving depression is expressed by feelings of helplessness and hopelessness, based on the perception (which may be realistic) that the lost relationship will not easily be replaced. It is equivalent to learned helplessness—namely, the feeling that nothing you do will accomplish anything, that you cannot cope with your problems and losses.

How these characteristics contribute to depression at the end of a relationship becomes clearer when we look at the ones that seem to protect a woman against depression. One such trait is extroversion, being oriented to and involved with people. People who are introverted, especially to the point of being socially withdrawn, are more hopeless when they lose a relationship because they realize they will have trouble initiating another one. The extroverted person can have more hopeful expectations, with a confidence based on past successes in forming new relationships. Indeed, an extroverted woman may have not only a larger network of friends to buoy her up, but also other, secondary relationships with men, any of which could help fill the void in her life.

The same is true for a person who is warm, nurturant, and comfortable with others. These are social skills that contribute to positive expectations about finding new relationships. People who reach out to help and support others find themselves highly valued and able to make friends readily. They have less reason to be depressed because their personal qualities are so well appreciated.

Personal discipline, like personal warmth, reflects a kind of upbringing that instills a stable, favorable self-image. A woman whose parents approved of her and taught her to feel good about herself is bolstered against self-doubt and self-recrimination when she loses a man's love. When one is disciplined, organized, and assertive, one is more likely to take effective action to cope with whatever might cause those feelings and less likely to succumb to self-pity, to feel hopeless and helpless.

A woman who is independent and self-reliant, who is forceful and takes initiative, who copes well with pressure, and who has leadership ability—even to the point of being domineering—is less likely to be depressed at the end of a relationship. In contrast, one who panics in a crisis or who expresses dependency on others with a disgruntled, underdog outlook is more prone to postrelationship depression.

Finally, a woman is more likely to be depressed after a relationship ends if she believes in a moral code that makes her feel guilty for having sex. If she believes that she has betrayed her moral values, then the end of a relationship brings self-doubt, even a sense of unworthiness, that she may experience along with feelings of depression.

CELESTE: TAKING CONTROL

Joanne, the student in Chapter 9 who suffered repeated bouts of anguish over her boyfriend's cavalier behavior, illustrated anxious romantic attachment in the context of a shy and not very assertive personality. She reacted inwardly to frustrations and disappointments instead of fighting back. Celeste, a thirty-eight-year-old Southwestern businesswoman, has a more extroverted personality; she is outgoing, forceful, and feisty. She, too, is subject to the mood shifts typical of anxious romantic attachment, but her mood swings are counteracted by her high energy and blunt manner. Although threats to her self-esteem may cause her to be depressed for a time, she soon rallies to confront her problems.

Intelligent, forceful, and adventurous, Celeste would not strike business associates or casual acquaintances as a romantically insecure woman. A tall, voluptuous redhead, she attracts attention at social and professional gatherings. Yet this is a woman who responded to our advertisement seeking the life stories of people who had a pattern of insecurity in love relationships. Celeste's story, told mainly in her own beguiling words, dramatizes some of the complex interrelationships between anxious romantic attachment and many other facets of personality.

Celeste's parents "drank and fought all the time." Her father was a construction supervisor, "a real macho type—gung-ho, intimidating, a man who looked like he could kill." Her mother was "a strong woman, the one who really raised me since my father was away so much." As if to belie the chaos in their home, her parents taught Celeste to look good and perform well for others; she was expected to "shine" in her long hair and pretty clothes. "Even now," she says, "I can turn on that pattern when it's necessary for me to cope. Other women do this, too—you go out of where you're really at to sparkle and shine."

Beneath this proper public display, there was a dark side to the family life Celeste experienced as a child.

> My father would come home after a long day and make me get down in front of him and take his boots off—his stinking, lousy boots. "Daddy worked hard," he'd say. "Pretty Celeste, come over and take these boots off." I'd look at my mother, and she'd say, "Help your father." I can't tell you how much I hated that.

Between the ages of seven and ten Celeste was sexually abused by her father. The abuse stopped when she threatened to tell her teacher. Unable to call on her mother for support, Celeste did, at crucial moments, summon the strength to resist her father, but only at great emotional cost. She could not entirely avoid learning the lesson that life would be less threatening if she submitted and obeyed. Looking back on the pain of her childhood, Celeste reflects, "I couldn't come to terms with my feelings toward my father. I wanted to love him, but I hated him." She adds, "The abuse wasn't just sexual; it was also psychological. I could never be good enough for them— even now, when they call me a slut to my children's faces because I sometimes see more than one man at the same time."

Celeste's parents did not let her go out socially until she was seventeen, when her father began selecting her dates. When she went away to college, she says, she was "the Virgin Queen of the West." Even so, her beauty and vitality soon made her a prominent figure during football weekends on the campus of a Southwest Conference powerhouse. As homecoming queen she began a sexual relationship with a star athlete. "I initiated," she explains. "I thought, 'I'm twenty-one—the hell with this.'" With this man she showed the high-strung reactions and bravado that would mark her later relationships.

> I would break out in sudden jealous rages. One time he was sitting in a bar
> talking to a girl, and I walked up and hit him in the mouth. He was six
> foot six and 250 pounds. He picked me up and said, "You hurt me." I said,
> "Wonderful," and busted his lip open.

After college Celeste parlayed her personal magnetism, together with her
network of contacts, into a job as a legislative aide to a local congressman.
Single life in Washington was raw, fast-paced, and anarchic; in Celeste's
words, "half the government was stoned." Although she relished attention
from men, Celeste was suspicious of the kind of attention she got. "I couldn't
stand the way men looked at me outwardly, never inwardly," she says.
"Nobody noticed my IQ."

In singles bars Celeste developed a self-protective routine, responding to
men in a contemptuous, bellicose way that discouraged most of those who
approached her. But she could melt before the occasional man who had the wit
or the will to break through her defenses. One such man was Elliot, who
owned his own advertising agency. Impressed by his self-possession and
touched by a "romantic, poetic" remark he made, Celeste went home with
Elliot the night she met him—something she rarely had done. Eight months
later she married him "because anything had to be better than that raucous
scene—anything besides going back to my parents." In addition, she says,
"Back then I didn't feel right openly maintaining a sexual relationship outside
of marriage. I couldn't have lived with a man at that time." Bold as she was,
Celeste could not completely shake off the constraints and inhibitions with
which she had been brought up.

Celeste, who had been "active, a go-getter" in college, tried to maintain a
comparable level of activity after her marriage, but the demands of keeping
house for an aspiring businessman kept her home much of the time.

> I hardly went out during the first several years of my marriage. I felt totally
> isolated. I'd read a lot, take courses. I'd stay in the house and knit; my
> hands were going fifty miles an hour. I went through periods of depres-
> sion, which I pulled myself out of by being a workaholic, which I still am.
> Activity was a way of occupying myself.

Her outgoing energy blocked, Celeste agonized about what Elliot was doing
while she was cooped up at home.

> Even during the first few years he drank a lot, and sometimes he was out
> very late. He was never really unfaithful, but jealous thoughts were

constantly on my mind. If he looked at a singer in a night club I'd be jealous, which was absurd. I'd say, "Why aren't you paying attention to *me?*" or "What does she have that I don't have?" Once when we were drinking at a New Year's party, a woman came over and kissed him, and I knocked his party hat off.

Elliot was, according to Celeste, "a handsome, strong, beautiful man. To look at him you wouldn't know I was a stronger person than he was. I didn't know it at first, either. He was already drinking too much, and I was drinking more than I should have, too." As his alcoholism progressed, Elliot withdrew sexually from Celeste. Claiming that she was overweight and unattractive, he put pressure on her to get in shape physically. Celeste tried to please him.

> Elliot told me to jog, so I'd run faster and better than anybody else. Exercising did keep me in shape and pretty attractive, but I hated it. He had me working out at a health club—all those sweat hogs, men, I got to lift weights with the best of them. They'd come over to help me, and they'd sweat on me, and I'd say, "That's one." Then they'd spit in this bucket in the corner, and I'd say, "That's two. I'm outa here." There were limits to what I'd take.

Celeste got her chance to get out in the world when a model who was to appear in one of Elliot's advertisements suddenly became ill on the day of the shooting. Elliot persuaded Celeste, fresh from her exercise and weight-loss routines, to pose in a bikini beside a new automobile. After that Celeste began to spend time in Elliot's office, where she recaptured the focused energy and effectiveness she had shown as a congressional aide. She began writing copy and soon found she was gifted at it. Not surprisingly, she was a whiz at client relations as well. "Why didn't I think of putting you to work before?" exclaimed Elliot.

At first, having his wife as a partner inspired Elliot to greater successes. But before long he was drinking more and working less, and Celeste was devising projects and expanding the business on her own.

> To the world I had it made: handsome husband, beautiful children, good career, new car, furs—everything looked good. And I was miserable.

As Elliot grew weaker he lost his hold on Celeste. When he became incontinent, she finally said "I'm outa here" to their marriage.

With the smell in the bedroom from his drinking and wetting the bed, I said, "This is the limit." I stayed married much longer than I should have, but I still feel guilty about leaving. I feel I should be there taking care of him.

This was Celeste's dual nature—submissive when she felt overpowered, yet intimidating to keep from being overpowered. As she puts it, "My parents, my husband—they all abused me, but they were all afraid of me. Everybody walks on eggs around me. It's strange because I've always been obedient, always tried to do what's right."

Having freed herself from what had become a degrading marriage, Celeste set out to make up for years of unfulfillment.

I did more in one year than I had in a decade. I ate at every restaurant between here and San Francisco. When I dated, they sent the limos for me. I don't know how, but that's the type of man I attracted because I didn't give a damn about attracting anybody—I didn't care.

One night I went to a party, and the men were boasting about their careers: "*I* do this," and "*I* do that." After the second vodka and tonic I had taken all I was going to. I was being introduced to this big, handsome man, and I was supposed to be the pretty, quiet lady. I said, "Wait a minute. I don't care what you do. I want to tell you what *I* do." He called me the next morning and asked me to go to Paris with him. I said, "Sure," and the limo pulled up. I did a lot of that that year. I made up for a decade of knitting.

Back in the dating bars, Celeste again put on her protective shell, weeding out all but the most resolute men with her disdainful sarcasm. One who persisted was Doug, an unhappily married man who was to play a significant role in Celeste's life.

I went out to singles bars with my girlfriends. Mostly I'd dump on the men there; if one made a pass at me I'd say, "No, thanks. I don't need you." This guy Doug sent a drink over to our table. I ignored him for a while, but then we struck up a conversation. He wanted very badly to get to know me. When we got up to go, he said, "I'll take you anywhere." All I would tell him was my first name and what business I was in. I didn't give him my phone number. I wasn't interested in anybody following me home.

He gave me his card, so I could have called any time, but it was not something I did. Besides, I knew he'd find me. He'd made clear how he felt about me, and he was the kind of man who didn't take no for an answer.

But with all that, I still felt down in the dumps when I didn't hear from him after a few days. By the weekend I was really depressed. "What did I do! Why did I make it so hard for him?" I thought. "Could I have so totally misread him?"

When he did call a week later, I was in heaven. "What took you so long?" I said. He told me he'd gone crazy researching me—he'd had people at all these companies trying to find out who the hell I was. Finally, he dreamed the name of my company; I must have told him without realizing it.

There began a "wildly crazy romantic relationship," in which "exciting Celeste, woman of the world," introduced Doug to an intensity of passion he had never experienced. "It was magic, absolute magic," she says. At the same time, the strength of her obsession with him left her vulnerable to depression as she realized that Doug, unable or unwilling to extricate himself from his marriage, was beyond her reach as anything more than an illicit lover.

As I look at it now, I would have done anything to have Doug. I loved him more than anything in my life. I felt that for the rest of my life I would leave anything, anyone, to go to Doug. If I married someone else, and Doug came back, I'd go.

But there were down moments, too. There were moments, like when Doug didn't call me on my birthday, when if it weren't for my responsibility for the children I wouldn't have cared if I lived or died. I had no desire to live. There were times when I went through hell. Yet I never would make him come to me. I never would go to his wife and say, "He loves me." I tried to help him clarify things, but it had to be his decision; otherwise it would never have worked.

Again, Celeste deferred to a powerful man and accepted his terms. This time, though, she got something important in return. Doug nurtured her self-esteem, which first her parents and then her husband had undermined.

My husband used to tell me, "This is as good as it's going to get. You can't dance, you can't screw, and you ain't going to amount to anything." But Doug said, "You can do anything you want to do." He was my mentor and still is. He brought out in me the strength I needed to do what I had to do.

In their personal relationship and in joint business ventures, Doug showed Celeste that she was better than she thought, or had been told, she was. Celeste already had gotten encouraging feedback from her accomplishments in her husband's business. Now, with Doug's support, she was ready to start a public-relations firm of her own.

In the wide-open economy of the Sun Belt, Celeste seems headed for success. Perhaps more important, she believes that she is striking a better balance between meeting others' needs and her own. "All my life I've been trying to get things together while everyone around me is going wild," she remarks. Indeed, even her love affairs have had the character of helping relationships.

> People sometimes look at me funny for seeing a married man, or for dating more than one man at a time. But I don't think I'm doing wrong. I know these guys are a lot better off since they met me. They've lost weight; they've got a new job; they're paying their taxes; they've got a better relationship with their kids—whatever. That's why they stay with me.
>
> People tell me their secrets. I do make a change in their lives. Maybe it's intuitive, maybe it's because I've been there. Somehow I know how to go into people to find out what they need. I can define another person's need, and if I choose to I can go in and make a positive change in his life. I was never able to do that for myself.

Now she has found a vocation in which she can do it for others and for herself as well.

> It's tough, putting myself on the line for the first time by starting this company. But it's amazing what I've done in a few months—from a concept to a corporation. If you know me, though, it's not so amazing. What's different is that I'm focusing my energies on making this company work for me, instead of going in and saving everybody else's life. I could never do something for money; I had to do it for people. But now I'm creating something that combines the two. It will make money by helping people. I don't want to do it unless it feels good. I want to keep the integrity in it. And I want to be a star, too.

Living at a pace that most people would get dizzy just watching, Celeste continues to juggle her relationships with men. To balance her passionate involvement with Doug, she likes to have a man who is more available, more of a known quantity, one who can be her "stability factor." One of these men she calls her "best friend—some sexual, but very little. He loves me, but it isn't exciting enough with him. Maybe if I ever get really healthy, he'll be the man I'll end up with."

Now that she has launched her new enterprise, Celeste finds herself less emotionally dependent on Doug, or on the stimulation of romance generally.

I always used to think, "Bring on something new." Now I want to settle down where I am. I'm not so ready to follow Doug wherever he goes. The things he could have offered me—the excitement of money and travel and planes—I may be able to get on my own.

People were afraid that one day I'd run off with Doug into the sunset, and that would be the end of the business. But I have responsibility now; somewhere I've made a commitment to the business. And that seems to have made me more attractive to Doug. He says that only now that I'm making it on my own is there a chance for us to get together, because when I was the insecure little girl who only wanted to play house with him, I would have been just like his wife. The question is, do I need Doug, and do I need him for the same things? Now that I'm becoming the superstar, I may need someone to be in the background and provide stability for me.

Currently, the excitement in Celeste's life has shifted from romance to business. There her energy, drive, and variable moods are very evident.

I have bouts of depression, but right now I'm so high it's unbelievable. For five days I work at an incredible energy level, motivating my people, and then exhaustion sets in. Friday afternoon I'm comatose. Then the doubts arise: "What if I fail?" I worry, "Am I substituting work for love?"

Perhaps she is, but Celeste's recent development also represents a real growing up, a more satisfying integration of the different parts of herself than she had previously achieved.

INSECURE LOVE IN

THE MAKING: SONS

The questions are the same for men as for women, but the answers are different. In the first place, when it comes to insecure love, sons are not affected as much as daughters by the push-pull of parents' marital conflict. Whether there is an atmosphere of strife or of harmony in the home seems less important to sons than to daughters. Instead, fathers and mothers have certain qualities that similarly influence how strongly the son will experience anxious romantic attachment. Both the father's and the mother's characteristics are important; the two parents act in ways that either reinforce or counteract each other's influence on their son. The same father might have different effects in combination with different mothers, and vice versa. As a result, there is more than one path to romantic insecurity for men, more than one family type associated with a given level of romantic anxiety or romantic obsession in a son.

THE MAKING OF THE ANXIOUSLY ATTACHED MAN

Some men who are anxiously attached to women have had cold, domineering parents, the kind of parents who demand great things of their son, but are unresponsive to his need for warmth and affection. These parents set high standards for achievement and keep their son perpetually anxious about meeting those standards. With their rejecting attitude toward him, they do not support him in developing the self-confidence he needs to tackle the demands placed on him.

Other anxiously attached men have had warm, loving, easygoing parents who let their son do almost anything he pleases. Such blanket acceptance is not so different from rejection, since it denies the child an opportunity to gain approval by meeting his parents' expectations. If he has no way of knowing when he is doing well and when he is not, then he does not get the satisfaction of feeling good when he does measure up.

Thus, the all-rejecting parents, with their impossibly high standards, and the all-accepting parents, with no standards at all, are as much alike as they are different, at least in their impact on their son's self-esteem. In the one case, the son goes out into the world intent on finding the emotional security he did not have at home, but doubting his ability to find it, since his past efforts have met with disapproval and rejection. In the other case, the son has had all the emotional security and approval he could want, but has not earned it. Therefore, if he does try to recapture this sense of connection and acceptance in romantic relationships, he is likely to be anxious because he does not know how one goes about obtaining it. So anxious, in fact, that he may prefer just to stay home and dream about it.

As we saw in Chapter 4, romantic insecurity can take the form of avoidance, or detachment, instead of anxious attachment. A man who has felt rejected by his father and ignored by his mother (because she lavished all her warmth and approval on her husband, not her son) is likely to sidestep romantic involvements rather than endure the anxiety of bidding for an acceptance he has never known. Another variation is the man whose parents acted in a harsh, dominating way, articulating high standards, but did not care enough to check up on his behavior. His mother may have been overtly rejecting, but his parents mainly showed their indifference by letting him evade their supervision. This man tends to be detached in a different way. Sexually active but emotionally uncommitted, he approaches relationships as an opportunity for conquest rather than intimate sharing.

All of these family backgrounds, in one way or another, set a man on a path to insecurity in his romantic relationships with women. What they all lack is that combination of love and firmness, of support and challenge, that seems to offer a young man his best chance at emotional security. The parents of men who are not anxiously attached (or detached) are not weak or afraid to assert themselves. Rather, they exercise appropriate discipline in a way that conveys a caring involvement with their son. He then learns that he can live up to their standards and model himself after their success.

NEIL: THE PAIN OF INVOLVEMENT

Neil is a man of forty who is trying to summon the courage to phone the women referred to him by a dating service. He plots out the conversations in advance, thinking, "If she says that, then I'll say this. But what if she says so-and-so? I suppose I could say such and such, but she might take it the wrong way." Still, his fear of saying the wrong thing or "sounding like a turkey" prevents him from picking up the phone.

Recalling his first serious love in college, Neil says, "I ruined that relationship. I fell in love with Bonnie, but I couldn't express my feelings to her. I just wasn't sure enough of myself. It was so frustrating." He goes on to describe how his insecurity dampened the spirit of the relationship:

> Everything was so forced. I put pressure on myself to buy her things, to bring her small gifts, tokens of my affection. It wasn't enough just to go out together, but I had to take her to a special club or downtown restaurant. When anything went wrong, like getting lost, I made it into a major tragedy, rather than something we could laugh and joke about. It would detract from our time together. Instead of talking about lighter things, I'd concentrate on getting lost, running out of gas, and whatever else might happen to us.

Neil never did more than kiss Bonnie, but her other friendships made him very jealous. As she became increasingly aloof and unavailable, he called her more and more frequently. Finally, his pursuit of her ended when he went up to her room during a dormitory dance and found her with another man. Although a number of her friends were in the room, the man was lying on her bed "in a way that made me feel they had been intimate." Neil was mortified. The people in the room may barely have noticed him; no matter, he felt like a fool. How could he ever again show his face among her friends? Besides, he thought, she didn't want him around anyway. He felt devastated.

> I thought of myself as a failure. I worked it out that she had found someone who was more outgoing, more easy-going, more fun to be with, more sure, more confident of himself.

Somewhere Neil had learned to blame himself, to count himself a failure, to compare himself unfavorably with others. Actually, Neil was an attractive man who did not know his true worth. But his feeling of unworthiness made him act in such a way that he became less attractive, even to women who took an initial interest in him.

Neil felt very depressed afterward. He drank heavily for several months. He showed his obsessive preoccupation with Bonnie by asking around about her, as well as by "putting myself in places where I thought I might run into her by accident." She was attractive and popular, and he envied the men who went out with her.

The pain Neil suffered is evident from the fact that he did not have another serious romantic involvement until he was in his late twenties. The trauma of the breakup and the self-reproach with which it left him brought on a decade-long period of detachment, of avoidance of emotional risks.

Then he met Pam, twelve years his junior. An attractive, unmarried man in his prime, Neil appeared knowledgeable and confident to a girl of her age. His reserved manner may even have impressed her at first, and it was she who actively courted him. They began going out together, but did not become sexually involved until Pam was eighteen, because Neil thought it would be wrong to take advantage of her youth. But when they did become sexually involved, it was Pam who initiated. By then, Neil was utterly in love.

> She was unlike anyone I had ever met. She was beautiful, absolutely stunning. There was music in her voice. She was innocent, delightful, lascivious—she could be anything and everything to anyone. To me she could do no wrong. I could never say no to her, even when she asked for something that I thought wasn't right. I loved her so much, I only wanted to please her. I couldn't stand the thought of losing her.

For a shy, conscientious, sensitive man, this was an experience beyond anything he could have envisioned. Recognizing how different he and Pam were in age, cultural background, and temperament, "part of me, the rational part" resisted becoming seriously involved with her. "But I couldn't get her out of my head," Neil recollects. He was swept away by the currents of her passion combined with his. They married—only to be divorced ten years and three children later, when Pam, as Neil put it, "just grew tired of stable married life." Neil wistfully sums up the denouement:

I don't feel I ever did anything to cause this breakup, except by being who I was. When I think about how much I put into that relationship, how much I wanted her to try to work out our problems with me—but she had no desire to do so. Maybe I wasn't the exciting person she made me out to be when she was sixteen.

Again, Neil was left with obsessive thoughts of his lost love:

The other day I was in a shopping mall, and a woman came down the aisle who for an instant I thought was Pam. I felt myself freeze on the spot. I felt as if I'd had a heart attack. I became very, very anxious. I did not think I could react that way to anything. It means that I still have very strong feelings for her. I'd hesitate to call it love. It's a lot of things—anger, hurt, sorrow.

Neil is a prototype of anxious romantic attachment. He is so apprehensive and wary around women that he goes for long periods without making an approach, even though it means denying himself the satisfaction of intimacy. But when he is approached, he says, "it just happens—it just comes over me." When he is romantically involved with a woman, he has obsessive thoughts and feelings about her, not only during the relationship but long after it ends. His family background, too, is typical of anxiously attached men.

Neil's father, a career military officer, exercised his habits of command at home as well as on duty. While working long hours at the base, he made sure that his family life went by the book, with each child performing his or her assigned chores. On Sundays he took the family to church and tested the children on their catechism. He was equally concerned with their performance in school. A well-educated man with several advanced degrees, he was, according to Neil, "particular about my getting good grades and being able to do all the multiplication tables without error." Neil remembers his father as strict in matters of courtesy and deportment; no one dared use "bad language" in his presence. "One time," says Neil, "he was so angry and upset with us that he walked out and drove around the neighborhood for a while. I spent that time worrying about the spanking I might get when he came back."

Neil's mother, an "Old World–type lady," devoted herself to home and family. "She stayed home and didn't even learn to drive until all the kids were in school," Neil relates. "She cooked the meals, did the laundry, and took us to Scout meetings." Deferring to her husband intellectually, she supported his strict disciplining of the children and his emphasis on learning and good grades. Her own energy, however, went more into having the children fit in socially. She dressed them in proper clothes, saw that they joined the right clubs, and supervised them on group outings. When Neil was in his early teens she made a point of signing him up for a ballroom dancing class, so that he would learn to be poised and comfortable in social situations.

However different their personalities and interests, Neil's parents worked together smoothly in their complementary marital roles. "I'm not aware of any discussion in which they'd be pitted against each other," Neil remarks. "They very much presented a united front." He goes on to describe their relationship:

> Maybe they don't fit today's standard of equality, but their relationship certainly has been a model for me. They're loving toward each other. They both know how to give and take, and they compensate for each other's weaknesses. They've been faithful to each other for more than forty years.

Neil, who respects his parents deeply, feels that he has failed to live up to their standards.

> I think I've fallen way short, both in my career and in the family life I would like to have had. I've had high standards for myself, for my wife, for my kids. I wish I could have done more. I wish I had a lot of money. I wish I could have had a military career like my father. I feel that way even though what I do, I do well.

Ironically, Neil believes that his parents might be more forgiving of him than he is of himself. He says, "If they were asked whether I've disappointed them, they'd probably say, 'Oh, he's had a rough time of it lately, but he's hardworking and he's honest.'" But Neil, who has adopted their standards as his own, remains disappointed in himself.

Although they were loving parents, devoted to their family, Neil's father and mother had certain characteristics that typically lead to a son's being anxiously attached in romantic relationships. They were strict parents who maintained a disciplined household. In their different spheres of activity they were controlling and domineering, the father pushing his son toward intellectual achievement, the mother making sure he would be socially acceptable and proper. Neil's mother took her cues from her husband and reinforced the lessons he gave the children; it was not like her to break ranks. These parents taught Neil their high standards, but they were not so successful in imbuing him with the self-confidence that he could meet those standards. Instead,

Neil grew up believing that he was unequal to his father's imposing image. He felt disapproved of and destined to fail, and he carried over those expectations to his relationships with women.

THE MAKING OF ROMANTIC ANXIETY

We have found one family type primarily associated with a high level of romantic anxiety in men, another associated with an intermediate level, and two others associated with a low level. In each case, we can see how a boy growing up in a particular type of family is likely to have certain kinds of experiences that influence how anxious he feels when he becomes romantically involved with women.

HIGH ROMANTIC ANXIETY

The following box lists characteristics of each parent which, together, contribute to a *high* level of romantic anxiety in a son. The more of those characteristics the parents have, the more likely the son is to be high in romantic anxiety.

HIGH ROMANTIC ANXIETY

FATHER

Achievement-controlling, nonnurturant, and/or hostile, rejecting **COMBINED WITH** Dominant, nonpermissive

MOTHER

Intellectually stimulating, nonnurturant, and/or rejecting, critical **COMBINED WITH** Autonomous, assertive, nonpermissive

---

In this type of family, the parents are demanding and controlling. They place great emphasis on achievement, particularly intellectual achievement. It is not simply that they expose their children to opportunities to learn, giving them books and puzzles and taking them to plays, concerts, and art exhibits. More than that, they pressure their children to excel, to be better than others, and they do so in a coercive way.

The father might be described by his son as a bossy man who "expects me to be successful in everything I try" and "says he would like me to be an important or famous person someday" (Worell and Worell). Valuing academic performance over extracurricular pursuits, he "is unhappy that I'm not better in school than I am" and "says that my teachers often expect too little of me." Himself orderly and fastidious, the father emphasizes the importance of neatness, organization, and planning. While he is rational, conservative, moralistic, and self-controlled, he comes across to his son as critical, demanding, mistrustful, and easily angered. He keeps his son anxious much of the time.

The mother reinforces these attitudes and values. She, too, encourages—indeed, pressures—her son to develop independent thinking. Exalting rationality and objectivity, she lets her son know that she expects original ideas and achievements from him.

These parental qualities might produce an exemplary citizen, a model of successful accomplishment, if they were accompanied by warmth and empathy—that is, if the parents gave the child emotional support in meeting the high standards they set. But the parents portrayed here typically do not provide such nurturance. Instead, the father of the romantically anxious son, determined to maintain order, enforces his standards in a punitive way, while the mother projects ambition for her son more than warmth, affection, or nurturance.

Having one parent who is controlling, achievement-oriented, and nonnurturant makes a man more likely to experience romantic anxiety. Having two parents like that inclines him even more strongly in that direction. These parents present a united front to a child, as if to say, "Getting B's on your report card isn't good enough. You're not going to get anywhere unless you get A's. If you want to be anybody, you have to go to one of the best colleges."

Other parental characteristics also contribute to romantic anxiety in the son. A man is even more likely to score high on romantic anxiety if his father is not only *achievement-controlling,* but also *dominant,* and if his mother is not only *intellectually stimulating,* but also *autonomous* and *assertive.* In addition, parents such as these are more likely to be strict and not at all *permissive.*

The word "dominant" sounds like "controlling," but we use it here to describe a different style of fathering, a different combination of personality traits. Some of these traits overlap with those included as part of achievement control, while others do not. For example, the dominant father exercises control over his son by instilling guilt and anxiety. He exerts an intrusive form of control; for example, the son reports that the father "keeps a careful check on me to make sure I have the right kind of friends" and "asks other people what I do away from home" (Schaefer). In these respects dominance is closely related to achievement control.

On the other hand, the dominant father does not apply the same discipline to himself that he does to his son. Rather, people see him as spontaneous, flamboyant, and headstrong, as well as aggressive, manipulative, and self-indulgent—the kind of person who sweeps people up in his enthusiasm and clears away all obstacles from his path.

An intense preoccupation with achievement often is found together with a tendency to dominate others. We can picture a man whose life is well ordered, a man who appears rational and controlled as long as things are going his way. However, when his control is threatened and he cannot impose a structure of his own choosing—for example, when his son challenges his authority—he may vent his frustration and seek to reestablish control through aggressive outbursts that make him appear disorganized and even irrational. This behavior may serve as a model for his son when the son's control is threatened in romantic relationships. We then see the panic and rage of an anxiously attached man when the woman to whom he has looked to satisfy his needs withdraws from him.

This, then, is the typical father of the romantically anxious man—a father who dominates the people with whom he associates, who always has to have the last word, and who expects too much from his son, from whom he will not take any back-talk. His counterpart is the mother who regularly asserts herself and seizes the initiative. She may appear as an ambitious, self-confident, forceful woman who pushes her son to excel in school and in a career. Like the dominant father, she takes an independent, nonconforming stance and is somewhat indifferent to and mistrustful of others. These two parents share an impulsive, self-centered disposition and a prepossessing air. Themselves not very amenable to control, they nonetheless assume considerable control over their son and do not allow him much latitude to make decisions for himself.

Finally, sons who are highest in romantic anxiety come from families in which the parents also have acted toward them in a rejecting manner. The father is *hostile* and *rejecting* as well as dominant. He not only is a strict disciplinarian, demanding and critical; he also is hostilely detached from his son. His son feels that he "is always getting after me" and "makes me feel I'm not loved" (Schaefer). For her part, in addition to being autonomous and self-assertive, the mother is *rejecting* and highly *critical* of her son, as well as inconsistent in her love for him. She tends to be an irritable, opinionated woman who rubs people the wrong way, and her son is one of those who most feel the brunt of her anger.

In our personality tests, men from families like these were rated low on masculinity, high on femininity. Lacking a close emotional attachment with either parent, they nonetheless tend to form a coalition with the mother, presumably for protection against a threatening father. They avoid social situations and have had relatively little romantic involvement.

Such a man, we might infer, feels inhibited from expressing himself. He may be easily cowed, as if unable to risk challenging his parents. He carries into his later relationships the memory of the father who treated him as a rival and slapped him down when he appeared to challenge the father's dominance. Comfortable with the low-profile position he was taught to take in the family, he becomes anxious when placed in a situation that calls for self-assertion—for example, when he wants to present himself to a woman as a successful, self-assured man. He may struggle with this inhibition, overcoming it only during sporadic outbursts when he feels frustrated and angry.

The romantically anxious man's parents are critical of people in general and implicitly convey to him that their approval is contingent on his distinguishing himself from the herd. They may put him on a pedestal, but the pedestal is always teetering. "There but for the grace of God go I," or "I'll be on the chopping block next," he may think as he hears his parents cut down someone else.

This ever-present anxiety often is worsened by the fact that the parents cannot be dismissed as obviously hypocritical, unreasonable, or uncaring. They might say, "I just want the best for my son"—a statement that may arouse anger in the son, but at the same time makes the parents an elusive target. Since the son would pay a high price (outwardly and inwardly) for rejecting his parents, he may feel compelled unconsciously to accept their standards as his own and to judge himself by them. He swallows his anger, but remains vigilant in later life to the hidden meanings in what people say, the wounding knife-edge sheathed in apparently innocuous remarks. Wary of having relationships ruined by these unspoken conflicts, he does not accept the feelings of others at face value. Eventually, he may come to resemble his father, perfectionistic yet emotionally vulnerable, controlled yet subject to petulant outbursts, and act toward his sons as his father did toward him.

The parents may indeed want the best for their son. They may believe they are supporting him, since they are giving him structure and discipline and pointing him toward success. However, they have placed their faith in punishment rather than reward, in the motivating power of the fear of failure and rejection rather than pride in one's skill and mastery. Thus, they can only greet their son's initial successes with admonitions such as "Now that you've done this, it's time to work on this and this and that." In other words, an accomplishment is not something to be savored, but merely serves as preparation for the next hurdle.

This negative motivation, this need to prove one's worth over and over again or risk punishment and humiliation, may become a recurrent theme in the son's life. Never quite sure whether his parents approved of him, he cannot approve of himself except by demonstrating perpetually his capacity for achievement. As a result, he may achieve success, but at the cost of continual insecurity about his worth and acceptance by others. Indeed, he may seem driven to succeed, but never secure or happy even when he does. As psychoanalyst Alice Miller puts it in *Prisoners of Childhood*:

> It is thus impossible for the grandiose person to cut the tragic link between admiration and love . . . he seeks insatiably for admiration, of which he never gets enough because admiration is not the same thing as love. It is only a substitute gratification of the primary needs for respect, understanding, and being taken seriously—needs that have remained unconscious.

A leading scientist, for example, recalls how as a boy he watched his father rebuilding an automobile in the garage. Wanting to emulate this activity, the boy took up building model cars. Whenever he completed one, his father would give it qualified praise, saying, "That's very good, but next time you should do this and this and this differently." Simultaneously encouraged and criticized, the son would walk away feeling unfulfilled. In his words, "It got to the point where I just wanted to break the damn thing and go do something else." Subsequently, he felt the same lack of pleasure in the accomplishments of a career that had brought him international distinction.

Parents who contribute to instilling such insecurity and futile striving are not likely to have foreseen such consequences and certainly did not intend them. They may be just as demanding and punitive toward themselves as toward their children. Moreover, they may be expressing insecurities and fears that go back to their relationships with their own parents. To be emotionally secure, one needs to be accepted by one's parents and loved for oneself. One who has not experienced this love and acceptance may seek to obtain them from one's child. Instead of being nurtured, the child is cast in the role of a nurturer, always attentive to the parent's need for attention and gratification.

At the extreme, for example, a father may treat his son as an extension of himself, perhaps even as the ideal self that his own mother or father might have loved and accepted. The child, then, is compelled to be perfect or suffer humiliation—not because his father consciously wishes to humiliate, but because he is exercising the same tactics of emotional survival that his parent practiced. The child is held responsible for shoring up the parent's fragile self-esteem. When he fails, he not only disappoints himself, but hurts his father, jeopardizing his father's self-esteem and with it his own. This pattern may continue through the generations, down to—and beyond—the man we observe to be romantically anxious.

Insecurity pervades the life of the romantically anxious man, especially his love life. He is anxious in romantic or sexual situations because he has learned to experience these as achievement situations. He worries about whether he will pass or fail the courting test, for rejection, to him, is a mark of failure. Perhaps his parents have told him, "You've got to marry the right kind of woman; your life will be miserable if you don't." If he achieves this goal, he may (as with other successes) quickly move on to new challenges without stopping to enjoy the one he has mastered. Nonetheless, the loss of a wife or lover is like a feared irretrievable loss of his acceptability, dignity, and sense of worth. It may have looked as if he did not value the woman when he had her, as he had never learned to be happy with success. But when he is faced with the prospect of losing her, his "love" becomes an urgent priority.

In addition, he may hunger for love out of a sense of incompleteness and deprivation. His anxiety about being accepted by women may come in part from a need to recoup the love denied him by one or both of his parents. Yearning for a complete emotional union while anticipating disappointment, he searches for the ideal woman who will gratify him as he has never before been gratified; yet his early experiences of helplessness in the face of parental rejection lead him to approach real women with suspicion, mistrust, and anger. This volatile mix of desperate hope and fatalism appears to underlie the intensely alternating emotions that are a prominent sign of romantic anxiety: elation when the lover's wish for perfect affection and approval seems about to be fulfilled, rage when he suspects betrayal, and despair when he loses hope of maintaining love.

MODERATE ROMANTIC ANXIETY

The characteristics of parents listed in the following box describe a type of family associated with a *moderate* level of romantic anxiety in a son.

MODERATE ROMANTIC ANXIETY

FATHER
1. Permissive
2. Meek, reflective, cautious
3. Nondominant

MOTHER
1. Permissive
2. Warm, deferent

In this type of family, the father is thoughtful and introspective, but also cautious, somewhat submissive, and overly self-controlled. In contrast to his own self-discipline, he allows his son a high degree of freedom and treats him as an equal. The mother is equally permissive and egalitarian. The son might make statements such as the following about either his father or his mother:

> "[He] lets me do anything I like to do."
> "[She] doesn't tell me what time to be home when I go out."
> "[He] can be talked into things easily." (Worell and Worell)

The mother accepts her son's individuality, encouraging him to choose his own way of doing things. At the same time, she is attentive to the standards and customs of the people around her. A truthful, hard-working, responsible person, she tries to inculcate similar values in her son, telling him that "good hard work will make life worthwhile." She teaches him conventional religious values and, as he describes her, "sees to it that I keep my clothes neat, clean, and in order" (Worell and Worell). This simultaneous emphasis on individualism and conformity reflects the different sides of her own nature. Warm, sensitive, and compassionate, she is generally nurturant toward her son and therefore supports him in being himself. Patient and nonassertive toward her son, she subordinates herself to others as well, and this deference goes with her willingness to conform to others' standards.

Together, these are low-key, supportive, self-effacing parents. They do not impose their will on others; rather, they blend into the social atmosphere, moderating their impulses for the sake of the general good. If both parents fit this description, it does not make much difference whether or not they are also achievement-controlling and intellectually stimulating. In either case, their son usually is in the middle range on romantic anxiety.

It makes sense that warm, undemanding parents would not directly instill much anxiety in their son. But what they do not provide is a clear sense of values to live up to, feedback about how well he measures up, and guidelines for recognizing his own worth. Their bland attitude and vague expectations reduce his motivation to win approval by leaving him in the dark about how to go about doing it.

Why don't men from such families score lower on romantic anxiety? Quite likely because they did not see in their fathers a good model of the kind of self-assertion they need when they approach women, and because they did not get from their mothers the kind of approval of their masculine qualities that would bolster their confidence. Such a man may well end up like his parents, passive and meek. We can imagine him before the high-school prom, screwing up his courage to ask a girl to be his date. His parents have not shown him—as parents who were more assertive as well as nurturant might have done—how to cope with anxiety actively by making known his desires in appropriate ways.

LOW ROMANTIC ANXIETY

Men who are *low* in romantic anxiety are found predominantly in two family types, and the men who come from these homes are very different from one another. The first type includes the following parental characteristics:

LOW ROMANTIC ANXIETY: NURTURED TYPE

FATHER

Nurturant and/or warm, accepting	COMBINED WITH	Dominant, nonpermissive

MOTHER

Nurturant and/or non-critical, nonrejecting	COMBINED WITH	Autonomous, assertive, nonpermissive

---

Parents of men who are low in romantic anxiety tend to be *nurturant*—that is, warm, compassionate, and supportive. In addition, both fathers and mothers of romantically nonanxious men tend to be good-humored, gregarious, full of vitality, and comfortable with their gender as well as their sexuality. Mothers in this group are especially accepting of people and concerned about making friends. They are personally well adjusted, having a positive attitude toward life and little need to ponder disturbing questions.

These, then, are parents who are warm, easygoing, sociable, and not especially worried about success or failure. When this easygoing nature is combined in the father with qualities of *dominance* and *nonpermissiveness,* and in the mother with qualities of *autonomy, assertiveness,* and *nonpermissiveness,* their son is very likely to be low in romantic anxiety. We might picture a fatherly football coach who maintains strict discipline, but who wins the loyalty of his players by showing that he cares about each of them as an individual. His standards are high, but he motivates more through approval than disapproval. When someone makes a mistake, instead of branding the person a failure and rejecting him, the coach encourages him to try again. He is empathic, telling his players, "I went through what you're going through myself."

In this family type we often find, combined with parental dominance and assertiveness, a tendency to be *accepting.* In fact, the mother is consistent in her love for her son and not overly critical of his actions. She is an unselfish woman, tolerant and cooperative in her relationships with others. Her mate is the sort of father about whom a son might say:

> "[He] is easy to talk to."
> "[He] cheers me up when I am sad."
> "[He] seems to see my good points more than my faults." (Worell and Worell)

This is an outgoing man who mixes well with people and values friendship along with social and sexual contacts. He involves himself fully with his son and is comfortable dealing with him on equal terms.

If both parents have the combinations of characteristics listed in the box, then we get a strong and consistent picture of firmness and control combined with warmth and nurturance. Men from this type of family have close emotional attachments with both parents and tend to be in coalition with their fathers. Somewhat nonconforming and sexually experienced, they rank above average on masculinity and low on femininity. In their relationships with women, some remain stably attached and show little jealousy, while others play the field, but the latter, too, appear self-assured and well adjusted.

Evidently, a man will show little anxiety in his relationships with women even when his parents are both imposing, even domineering people, provided that they also are strongly accepting and emotionally supportive of him. He can then identify with his parents' dominance rather than be overwhelmed by it. He is comfortable with his father and apparently benefits from having a mother who is outgoing and assertive as well as loving. To the extent that she praises and rewards him for asserting himself appropriately, her encouragement means all the more to him because she is a formidable person in her own right. In this way she helps build his sense of competence and manliness, which in turn makes him feel confident around women.

The second family type that is found for sons low in romantic anxiety consists of a father and mother who are both rejecting toward the son, but apparently close to each other, since the mother has an empathic, accommodating side to her nature. A man brought up by parents like these is likely to be very different from one who comes from the kind of family just described.

LOW ROMANTIC ANXIETY: REJECTED TYPE

FATHER
Hostile, rejecting
toward son   **MOTHER**

and/or   **COMBINED WITH**   Warm, deferent
                                                  toward husband

MOTHER
Rejecting, critical
toward son

A *warm, deferent* mother, combined with a *hostile, rejecting* father, usually leads to low romantic anxiety in the son. The hostile, rejecting father avoids emotional involvement with his son, does not treat him as an equal, and disciplines him by making him anxious. Similarly, the son is likely to be low in romantic anxiety if the warm, deferent mother is also *rejecting* and *critical,* as well as emotionally inconsistent.

In this type of family, the parents seem well matched for each other, but in a way that does not benefit the child. The mother defers to her husband; her warmth and nurturance are lavished on him, not on her son. While the parents may have a workable (if unequal) relationship, the son is left out in the cold. He usually does not feel a close emotional attachment with either parent, especially not with his father. Often he is found to be in coalition with his mother, but the lack of an accompanying emotional attachment to the mother indicates that the coalition is a reaction to the father's rejection.

Largely rejected by both parents, the son gets no support from either for learning the kinds of behavior that would lead to successful relationships with women. There is no one to reward him for living up to parental expectations and standards. He may wonder why his warm, loving mother doesn't care for him, and he may attribute her indifference to his own inadequacy.

As a result, he typically avoids social contact, has little sexual experience, and appears withdrawn and lacking in self-confidence. He fits the picture of detachment presented in Chapter 4. A man can avoid anxiety simply by not pursuing or seeking acceptance from the object of his love. He may safely engage in obsessive fantasies at a distance without arousing the fear of rejection.

Here we have two groups of men, both low in romantic anxiety, who are at opposite extremes in their personalities and their social and emotional relationships. One group is emotionally secure and involved; the other avoids anxiety by not entering the competitive arena, where rejection is possible. Such detachment is much more common among men than among women.

JIM: A FATHER'S LONG SHADOW

Jim, like Neil (earlier in this chapter), comes from a family whose tone was set by a dominant, demanding father, one who insisted on achievement but did not nurture his son in developing the skills needed to succeed. With this background, he experiences a high degree of romantic anxiety. Jim, described in Chapter 4, is a man in his early twenties who practically keeps his fiancée prisoner to ensure her loyalty. Jealous and insecure, he questions her closely when they have been apart even for a short time. He sometimes wishes he didn't care for his fiancée as much as he does, since his feelings of attachment to her are inseparable from the anxiety that causes him so much discomfort. He wonders whether it is worth it to have such an emotional investment in a relationship that he might easily lose.

Jim is a shy young man, ill at ease socially, who always felt at a disadvantage because he was short and thin. His father was an automobile dealer who lectured and corrected him with an egotistical manner fed by his own success. Jim recalls "the way my father laughed and put me down when I threw a ball over his head, and the way he got angry when I was helping him fix something and I made a mistake." Throughout Jim's adolescence his father taunted him with the epithet "loser"—telling him, for example, that he would be a loser if he could not afford to buy a new car by the time he got his driver's license. After that, Jim reacted with fury whenever he thought someone was calling him a loser.

Here we see Jim's father controlling him, pressuring him to achieve, and doing so in a hostile way. Jim's father showed the dominance, combined with insensitivity and lack of nurturance, found in parents of men high in romantic anxiety. Nor could Jim turn to his mother for support when faced with his father's rejecting behavior. An intense woman who usually gave an impression of frantic activity, Jim's mother would be overinvolved with him one day, then would seem neglectful the next day when some other duty claimed her attention. Her inconsistency toward Jim was not deliberate, but Jim had ample reason to regard her and his father jointly as unsympathetic, nonsupportive, and rejecting.

"I never had a real father," Jim says wistfully, "one who would play with me and encourage me to learn. The father I had wasn't the father I wanted." As an adolescent Jim would fume with frustration and bitterness, vowing to tell his father off or to gain some great triumph and "throw it up in his face." Jim's anger at his father surfaces whenever he feels that he has failed or has been rejected. In particular, it cast a shadow over his early dating experiences in his teens, when he found himself tongue-tied with girls. "I wouldn't know what to say—a million thoughts would race through my mind," he recalls. Many teenagers have such difficulties, but Jim's interpretation of them showed how he had learned to expect the worst, and how he associated any rejection with his father.

In one poignant instance, a girl Jim wanted to date showed many signs of reciprocating his interest; she would call him on the phone and initiate conversations with him when she saw him. At a dance to which they went together, he found her dancing with another boy when he expected her to dance with him. Losing his temper, he went on a tirade in the middle of the dance floor while the embarrassed girl tried to quiet him, and others held him back physically. In the midst of a stream of accusations directed against the girl, he blurted out, "I don't even have any friends!" This was something he would say to his father, whom he blamed for his unpopularity and poor social adjustment. The girl must have been puzzled by this utterance, which had nothing to do with her. But it made sense in Jim's inner world, where he saw all rejection as coming ultimately from his father.

Jim allowed one moment of misunderstanding to wipe out all the encouragement, all the positive signals this girl had given him. He was always tuned in to signals of rejection, real or imaginary. Not surprisingly, when he did form a relationship he guarded it anxiously and jealously.

VINCE: THE AMBIGUITY OF INDISCRIMINATE LOVE

If Neil and Jim wear their romantic anxiety on their sleeves, Vince covers his with a tough masculine exterior. His underlying insecurity is similar to theirs, but his way of coping with it is different. Vince is a leader of industry whose drive, energy, and dominating force just don't seem to work out when he applies them to intimate relationships. Although very choosy about women, he falls in love quickly and totally and *must* have complete commitment in return. He overpowers a woman with attentions that all too often seem forced. "Why don't these women respond?" he asks in a tone of frustration. "I pick all the right concerts. I buy only the best seats. We go to the best restaurants. Why, if I like somebody I'll spend a hundred on her just like that." Vince pours himself into planning a vacation trip with a woman — going to the travel agent, studying the maps, comparing prices, scheduling the time. But then he finds the trip itself a letdown. For Vince the pleasure lies in setting the stage, orchestrating the relationship. For the woman, all this planning has the feel of an impersonal service rather than a spontaneous, mutual experience. There is no room for her to participate. It is all done for her, rather than with her. Vince cannot leave room for mutuality; he needs his rigid routines to overcome his fear of a woman's independent will.

In the name of honesty and efficiency, Vince approaches women with the high-powered presentation that serves him so well in business. It is like a sales pitch, with the wining and dining of the customer and the showcasing of the product. We can picture him sitting imperiously with his feet up on the desk, saying, "What's there to talk about? By rights you *should* love me." He explains:

> When I'm interested in a woman, I don't want to play games; I don't want to manipulate and mislead. I just put it all on the line. If she wants me, fine. If not, the sooner we find out, the better. Either it's a relationship that's going to matter or it isn't. If it isn't, why waste her time and mine?

Unfortunately, this "straightforward" approach does not give the woman, let alone Vince, a chance to find out whether she wants him. For his part, he shows no interest in the woman as a person. Vince says that he is trying to communicate love and caring, but the woman hears him pressuring her to comply, demanding outward signs of affection before she has any inner basis for giving them. Wanting commitment right away, he is so intent on establishing the status of the relationship that he does not give it time to blossom. The harder he tries, the more he works at it, the worse it is. Then he gets angry at the woman because she does not feel loved by him and does not return his love.

Twice married and divorced, Vince is a highly intelligent, impressive-looking man whom many women would find desirable. Acknowledging his desirability, but in a way that reveals his defensive and problematic attitude, he says, "I know there are cattle cars full of women who'd love to have me, but they're not the ones I want." The ones he wants are the ones who are a challenge to master—successful women who are likely to resist, and even compete with, his dominance. He wants to have a woman give herself up to him, subordinate her existence to his, but he wants this woman to be one who also has a strong personality and an independent existence.

Vince can be ecstatic when he feels in charge—when he is planning, organizing, impressing people, working toward a goal. Yet he has to keep finding little ways to pump up this euphoria, for his inflated sense of himself is his defense against the depression he feels when he is not the object of attention, as well as the anger he feels when he is rejected. Who is he angry at? Why does this successful man need to prove himself over and over again? What is at the root of his insistent need for respect, for dominance?

Vince's father was a hard-driving, self-absorbed entrepreneur who did not find room to include his son in his personal image of success. Again we have the dominant, coercive father, bent on high achievement. No one was going to compete with him, not even his son. Neil or Jim might have been cowed by this treatment, but Vince defended himself by going on the offensive. Rebuffed in his efforts to gain approval by emulating his father, he started a business of his own rather than carry on his father's successful enterprise. This is what he means when he calls himself a self-made man. He is self-made with a vengeance, recreating himself in a desired image so as to banish feelings of inadequacy.

Meanwhile, Vince's mother compensated for his father's rejection by doting on him uncritically.

My mother promised me that I wouldn't have to experience the bad things in life. She made me believe I never had to be frustrated, because she'd take care of me. I was dependent on her for all my happiness—and then she died.

"Good Vinnie, good Vinnie," his mother was always saying. But the approval she lavished on Vince seems to have come with disabling strings attached. Perhaps her praise was so indiscriminate that he experienced it as meaningless, even demeaning. Perhaps it contained an implicit message that her approval, arbitrarily given, could be just as easily withdrawn. To the extent that he felt dependent on her praise, he felt anxious about the prospect of living without it. It did not make sense; he had one parent whose approval he could not win, and one whose approval he could not lose. How was he to know when he really was doing the right thing?

Whatever sense of incompleteness or deprivation led his mother to treat Vince in this way, he felt simultaneously overvalued and not valued at all. He desired powerfully the ideal, perfectly gratifying mother that she sometimes was to him, but all the while feared being engulfed by her—feared, too, that she might withdraw all her unearned praise of him if he refused to be engulfed. This was the dual image of womankind that he carried into adult life—the selfless nurturer to whom he felt accustomed and entitled, and the devouring predator whom he needed to master.

Vince's mother stood as a buffer between him and anything in the world that might threaten him, including his father. She rescued him, protected him, put him on a pedestal. She treated him as a child—special treatment that was contingent on her continued presence in his life. Vince wanted her to be proud of him as a man, but she somehow withheld that dimension of approval. Her death carried out her implicit threat that she could take away the acceptance she had given him. Vince was left with an unfulfilled wish to please his mother and make her proud of him, and with unresolved anger toward her for dying without giving him the benediction he sought.

With a father who was not satisfied with anything he did, and a mother who acted as though she was thrilled by everything he did, Vince had difficulty obtaining realistic feedback about the appropriateness and effectiveness of his actions. Even as an adult he was constantly testing limits, struggling to master and control an environment in which uncertainties and threats lurked everywhere. In his career he succeeded by virtue of his native ability and years of observing how his father operated. In his personal life, however, he was not able to get beyond his anger toward his mother and father, which darkened any intimate involvements he undertook.

Initially, he was drawn to unassertive women, but they did not satisfy him for long. Increasingly, he has campaigned instead to win more formidable women, so as to gain a more discriminating kind of approval—approval that he can have the satisfaction of winning after at first being denied it. Rejected by his father and overwhelmed by his mother, feeling that his life lacks an independent foundation, he needs to gain control over anyone who appears to have such a secure foundation. If he fails, he feels rejected and humiliated himself. Success, on the other hand, provides only ephemeral satisfaction, a thrill that must be renewed repeatedly. As he puts it, "Like a little kid who puts together a puzzle, I have to dump out the pieces and do it all over again. It's like fox hunting—releasing the foxes so I'll have to chase them down again."

THE MAKING OF ROMANTIC OBSESSION

We have identified two family types that are associated with high romantic obsession in men, as well as two groups associated with low romantic obsession. Moreover, the differences between the two groups of men who score low—those who are emotionally secure and those who are detached—are quite marked.

HIGH ROMANTIC OBSESSION

The characteristics of parents listed in the box below describe one of two types of families of men who are *high* in romantic obsession.

HIGH ROMANTIC OBSESSION: REJECTED TYPE

FATHER

Achievement-controlling, nonnurturant   COMBINED WITH   Firm, nonpermissive

MOTHER

Intellectually stimulating, nonnurturant, and/or rejecting, critical, strict   COMBINED WITH   Firm, nonpermissive

---

Some characteristics of this family structure are already familiar. The father is controlling and achievement-oriented; the mother is concerned with stimulating her son's intellectual development; and the parents are neither nurturant nor permissive. In this type of family the mother also tends to be *rejecting, critical,* and *strict.* This is how a son high in romantic obsession might characterize his mother's attitude toward him:

"[She] makes me feel I'm not loved."
"[She] thinks I am just someone to 'put up with.'"
"[She] doesn't seem to think of me very often." (Worell and Worell)

As seen by her son, she is a strict disciplinarian, just like his father.

"[She] wants to control whatever I do."
"[She] is always getting after me."
"[She] sees to it that I know exactly what I may or may not do." (Worell and Worell)

In our personality tests, these men show an unusual mixture of adaptive and maladaptive traits. They are about average in the strength of their attachment to, and coalition with, both parents. Strikingly, they impress others as very unmasculine in their mannerisms, yet they come out about average, compared to other men, on such sex-stereotyped personality traits as dominance, aggressiveness, caring for others, and communal involvement. Social situations seem to arouse anxiety in them, and they tend to shy away. As a result, they have relatively little dating or sexual experience. When they do get involved in relationships, they tend to stay attached to their partners, whom they rate high on consistency. Perhaps in proportion to the value they attach to their partners, they are especially prone to depression when a relationship ends.

These men seem to crave the love and affection they have not received from their parents. Moreover, since past experience has given them ample reason to fear disapproval and rejection, most of them are high on romantic anxiety as well as romantic obsession. Not having basked in the approval of their parents, they are all the more dependent on the approval of others. Uncertain about their worth and acceptability, they look to their female partners not only to compensate for their mothers' rejection and lack of nurturance, but also to give them the kind of positive feedback that will raise their self-esteem. For such a man, being loved by a woman is a measure of his value. That may account for the strength of his obsession.

Neil and Jim, whose stories illustrated the rejecting family type for high romantic anxiety, also rate high on romantic obsession, and their families fit the rejecting type for high romantic obsession. In this family type one or both parents tend to be coercive, achievement-oriented, nonnurturant, and rejecting, as well as firm in their discipline. Neil and Jim both had fathers who set higher standards for achievement than their sons could meet comfortably. While Jim's father was more rejecting than Neil's, neither father established the kind of rapport that would have motivated the son to strive for achievement. In both families the mother, instead of making an alliance with her son, reinforced the father's values by organizing the household around her husband.

We also found a second family type that leads to high romantic obsession in men. Surprisingly, the parents' characteristics here are the opposite of those in the previous box.

HIGH ROMANTIC OBSESSION: NURTURED TYPE		
	FATHER	
Nurturant	COMBINED WITH	Permissive
	MOTHER	
Nurturant and/or non-rejecting, noncritical	COMBINED WITH	Permissive

Yet men with parents like these also score high on romantic obsession—even though they do not score high on romantic anxiety, where they tend to fall in the middle range.

These men report that they have little dating or sexual experience and avoid social situations. Unlike other men high on romantic obsession, they feel strongly attached to their fathers as well as their mothers. They are extremely conforming and rank low on drug and alcohol use. At the same time, they show little communal involvement or caring for others. While normally masculine in their mannerisms, they are the least dominant and aggressive of men. Overall, they give the impression of being timid, withdrawn, and socially isolated.

In their most important romantic relationships, they do not remain attached for long, and they rate their partners low on consistency and very low on attractiveness. Normally, people are obsessed with partners whom they consider attractive. These men, however, are highly obsessed with partners who are not very attractive in a physical sense. It is possible that they defensively downgrade their partners after they have been rejected, or that they are so unassertive they become deeply attached when a relationship finally comes their way, even if the woman was not their first choice.

There is also another possibility—namely, that these men actually do choose partners who really are not very attractive. These are men who tend to avoid relationships altogether and thereby keep their romantic anxiety down to a moderate level. Lacking self-confidence, they may also shy away from the highly competitive, anxiety-provoking arena represented by attractive women, where they would face—or fear—probable rejection. Instead, as another way of moderating their anxiety, they may approach women whom others consider less desirable, women for whose affection there is less competition. Even with these women their relationships tend to be short, which may reflect their own undesirability as partners. These men do not exude the self-confidence that women might find attractive. Thus, their relationships may be characterized by considerable mutual dissatisfaction. Still, their need for love is so great that they obsess over the less attractive partners they have chosen.

Why is it that two parents who are permissive, nurturant, and not particularly demanding, controlling, or rejecting have a son who is romantically obsessed? The son of these parents seems to be smothered with love and support. In addition, neither father nor mother appears to provide him with a model of self-confident assertiveness. Perhaps he is so comfortable in his parents' home and so ill-prepared to venture outside of it that he fails to develop either the courage or the skill to seek out intimate relationships. With parents who gratify him whatever he does, he may never learn to discriminate what will provide him with gratification outside his family from what will not. If he is pushed to take the risks, he is probably anxious and acts like the anxiously attached—that is, clinging and campaigning for reassurances of the woman's commitment; or else he backs out prematurely at the first glimpse of possible rejection. Instead, he avoids the stress and expresses his desires through romantic fantasies.

We have seen two groups of men, from different types of families, who are highly susceptible to romantic obsession. Yet they differ strikingly in the ways in which romantic obsession fits into their personal histories and their social and emotional experiences.

LOW ROMANTIC OBSESSION

Men *low* in romantic obsession are raised in two very dissimilar types of families. One type includes the following parental characteristics:

LOW ROMANTIC OBSESSION: NURTURED TYPE

FATHER

Nurturant   COMBINED WITH   Firm, nonpermissive

MOTHER

Nurturant and/or non- COMBINED WITH   Firm, nonpermissive
rejecting, noncritical

When the parents are nurturant but not permissive (that is, when they exercise firm rather than lax control, but do so in a caring way), and when the mother is not rejecting, not too strict, and is consistent in her love for her son, he is likely to be low in romantic obsession. This is very similar to the pattern we saw for low romantic anxiety, the same combination of firmness and emotional support that allows a child to feel secure. A child can experience this kind of firmness as a form of parental involvement, as opposed to permissiveness that could be perceived by the child as parental indifference.

What is this group of men actually like? Very little about them is remarkable. They feel a close attachment to their mothers, and they are moderately masculine in their mannerisms; however, they are low in qualities such as dominance and aggression. Otherwise, they rank near the average on most of our personality tests. On the whole, they appear to be a well-adjusted group.

The second family type associated with low romantic obsession also resembles one of the patterns we found for low romantic anxiety—namely, the one that led to detachment. The following parental characteristics are found in this family type:

LOW ROMANTIC OBSESSION: REJECTED TYPE		
	FATHER	
Achievement-controlling, nonnurturant	COMBINED WITH	Permissive
	MOTHER	
Intellectually stimulating, nonnurturant, and/or rejecting, critical	COMBINED WITH	Permissive

It is as if the family type described above had been turned inside out. Instead of the parents being involved with the child in two ways (firm and nurturant), they appear doubly uninvolved (permissive and rejecting). Men from these families are predominantly macho types rather than shy and retiring. They feel attached to their fathers and have an extremely strong tendency to form a father-son coalition against their rejecting mothers, to whom they have a very weak attachment. This paternal identification seems to influence much of their personality. They can be characterized as dominant, aggressive, antisocial, and nonconforming, with high levels of drug and alcohol use. In keeping with the image of the detached man, they keep their feelings hidden safely behind a cool exterior. Likewise, they are not prone to depression when a relationship ends.

As to their level of involvement in social life, they seem to split into two groups: some actually avoid relationships, while others are Don Juans, outgoing but noncommittal. As a group they rank highest in sexual experience among the men studied. Given the way they feel about their mothers, it is possible that their expression of sexuality involves a degree of hostility toward women. They rank their female partners high on attractiveness, but low on consistency. This image of a glamorous but fickle woman may reflect the type of women they pursue, the way they perceive these women, and/or the impact of their macho detachment on their relationships. They may pursue attractive women, but then have difficulty retaining their affection. Their own social behavior—in particular, their exploitiveness, disloyalty, and antisocial behavior—might cause women to leave them. Since they are emotionally uncommitted, they are not likely to inspire commitment in their partners.

As a rule, this sort of man comes from a family where he was pressured to achieve, yet was left to his own devices. His parents may have neglected him in favor of their own interests and their relationship with each other. Particularly in light of his mother's overt rejection, the son would appear to have no basis of security and self-confidence from which to take the risks involved in intimate relationships. At the same time, he might react defensively to this maternal rejection by devaluing women and showing that he can live without them.

DAN: ALONE AND ADRIFT

In the story that follows, Dan, an exceptionally intelligent young man, comes from a family that has many (but not all) of the attributes of the rejecting family type for *low* romantic obsession. His parents share with that family type the qualities of being both achievement-oriented and highly permissive; however, rather than being actively rejecting, Dan's mother is distant and uninvolved like his father. And Dan is not the angry, exploitative, super-masculine type of detached man we typically see in the rejecting family type. Dan does, nonetheless, show evidence of detachment, but in a more subtle way. He is much like the classic narcissistic personality, a person who is basically self-absorbed, but who manifests attachment when the relationship aggrandizes the self.

A woman who had recently broken up with Dan described him this way:

> Dan was a sweet guy in so many ways, but he wasn't really comfortable with himself. He couldn't accept how great he was—or *who* he was, even. He couldn't tell who he was and who he wasn't. In the end, I think that's why I couldn't relate to him.
>
> We'd be going along great, and then Dan would pull these stupid little things. He had this antique mechanical adding machine that he bought at a flea market. One day I heard him telling a neighbor how it had been his father's and his grandfather's and his great-grandfather's—he even described the desks in the great-grandfather's office! It was an elaborate story, like he had rehearsed it and told it a number of times.
>
> Then there was the time we went to a record store, and this pimply-faced kid behind the counter started chatting with me, very friendly like. Dan stood around waiting, and then for the next few hours he was bitchy and demanding with me. I don't believe he was actually jealous; he

wouldn't think I could be interested in that kid. It was more that he had to be the center of attention; he couldn't stand to watch while somebody else showed off some trivial expertise. It was that fragility, that need he felt to out-phony all the other phonies, that set me off about him and ruined things between us.

Dan has been many things—teenage adventurer, spiritual seeker, working-class hero, sensitive poet. After a brief, court-ordered stay in a drug rehabilitation center, he got a job as assistant to the chief of a ward in a state training school for the mentally retarded. He describes himself as "an addictive personality, an all-or-nothing personality—either I'm completely indifferent to something or I throw myself into it."

Dan began making up stories about himself in childhood. "I've played a lot of my life as a character in a play," he says. Fearing that "underneath it all I'm an uninteresting person, with nothing real for anyone to get hold of," he fabricates his past, tailoring his story to the listener "to impress people that my life is more exciting than it is. It seems I'm hiding myself by lying all the time." With women he hides behind a romantic facade. He sings paeans to closeness, but if a woman gets close, she finds a costume, a routine, a role. Movingly simulating (even to himself) the emotions associated with romantic love, Dan remains safely removed from the action. His "stage" identity protects him from rejection, but also from acceptance, for he knows that he is being accepted only as an actor, or a con artist. He lies in order to be loved, but he must discount the love because he knows he is lying.

Dan describes the relationship he had with his parents as distant. "They did their duty, but they were not very affectionate," he says. "They were not harsh, but I didn't get a clear sense of values from them." Dan felt that he and his sister were shut out by their parents' closeness to each other.

> When I was growing up I got the idea that my parents' first allegiance was to each other, their second to us. While I never heard them say, "I love you," to each other, my mother made it very clear that my father was the primary person in her life, and vice versa. And so I got a real sense of security from knowing that they would stay together, but a corresponding insecurity from feeling that I was of secondary importance to them.

Actually, Dan's parents, who were almost forty when he was born, had wanted very much to have a child, but from his first years they were in awe of his intelligence. It was if they did not know what to do with him. Believing themselves incapable of disciplining him, they gave Dan few restrictions or limitations.

Dan describes his father as passive and hard to understand.

> I have a hard time thinking about who my father is. He never talks much. He jokes a lot, but never says much. It's hard to get an opinion of any kind out of him. He'll make jokes that suggest his opinion, but even if the question is "Where do you want to go for dinner?" he won't be decisive. He'll say, "You decide." He'll play dumb to get my mother to commit herself or to explain things more. He makes decisions that have already been made tacitly by everyone else.

Dan believes when he was a child he did not have much rapport with his father. "We'd play catch out in the back yard, but otherwise I felt estranged from him," he recalls. "If I had to spend a few hours with him and I felt that I didn't have anything to say, I'd go to another room and read a book."

Dan has found his mother to be noncommittal as well.

> I feel she hides her intelligence and tries to present herself as more emotional, less intellectual than she actually is. She thinks about things a lot, but has a hard time coming out with what she's thinking. She wants to make it seem as if she's just intuitive.

With each parent at pains to appear deferential to the other, it was as if no one was taking the lead. The family seemed to drift, and Dan felt its lack of direction acutely.

If Dan wanted to please his parents, he decided early on that it was hopeless.

> Reading my father's high school yearbook when I was seven or eight years old, seeing his picture a hundred times with this long description of how wonderful he was as a football player, a basketball player, a dancer, a swimmer. I remember thinking even at that age, "I'll never be able to be that good at those things."

Since sports were important to his father, who had been a star athlete, Dan tried out for the school teams, but his performance was only fair. Though unable to live up to his father's standards in sports, he might well have outdone him academically. In an intelligence test he took before he started school, Dan scored in the genius range. His parents held his score up to him,

saying, "You are a genius, so you should be able to excel at anything."
However, despite their stated concern with academic achievement, they did
not follow through and try to hold him to the standard they set.

> I wanted to be held more accountable, but I wasn't. If I brought home Bs
> and Cs and Ds in grade school, they were upset from Friday afternoon to
> Saturday evening. After that it wasn't mentioned again until the next
> report card came out.
>
> In high school I graduated near the bottom of the class while winning
> National Merit honors for high SAT scores. I would deliberately not read
> the books assigned for English class—books I often came back to later.
> Just by listening to class discussions and by being glib and verbal I could
> get Cs and Ds on the tests.
>
> I wanted to be told, "Knock this off," but I never was. My parents just
> ignored it. They'd say, "Maybe we should put you into a private school
> where you'd be challenged more."

Both as a child and in retrospect, Dan was struck by how permissive his
parents were:

> I was given almost complete freedom. My parents would let me do
> whatever I wanted to do. I feel like I've been completely alone and adrift in
> the choices I've made, within very broad limits, since I was nine or ten.
> And that was scary for me. When I was twelve I could stay up till eleven-
> thirty at night; it was no big deal. I didn't have to tell them where I was
> going or who I was going to be with. When I was fifteen I had a couple of
> girlfriends I could bring in after school and take upstairs to my room with
> the door shut and mess around. My parents would just call,
> "Dinnertime—come on down!" Then after dinner we'd go back up to my
> bedroom. I can remember riding in the car with my parents and necking
> with this girl in the back seat for an hour at a time, and my parents
> wouldn't say anything. I wanted them to say, "Knock it off." I wanted
> them to ask, "What are you doing?" "How long will you be gone?" "What
> courses are you taking next year, and how do they fit into your plans for the
> future?" But they didn't seem to care.

In retrospect, Dan does not believe that his parents were as uncaring and
unaware of him as they appeared to be. At the time, however, he felt keenly
their lack of support:

> My gut reaction is that they didn't care, but I don't think that's true.
> Somehow they were emotionally incapable of setting up any structure for

me. I believe they cared for me and thought they were doing the best thing for me by letting me make my own decisions and live with my own mistakes. But it was terrifying to be a twelve-year-old living with his own mistakes.

Dan reacted to his parents' permissiveness as if it were a form of rejection—which, in a sense, it was. Dan had no guidelines for pleasing his parents, who acted as if nothing fazed them. He begged and goaded his parents to set limits for him, but his appeals went unanswered. Without the experience of being rewarded for gratifying their wishes, he did not feel secure in his relationship with his parents—or in his later relationships. "I never learned what was okay and what wasn't," Dan concludes.

Dan's parents were not actively rejecting; if anything, they were more bewildered by Dan than hostile toward him. Dan himself did not turn out to be the macho character depicted in our discussion of the detached male, rejected by his mother, strongly identifying with his father, and seemingly hostile or unfeeling toward women. Rather, Dan was as uncertain of himself as his parents were of how to raise him.

His identity crisis was made worse by his family's precarious position in the neighborhood where he grew up. Dan's father was a skilled craftsman who, living in a university town, did not enjoy the status he might have elsewhere. Dan, who played and went to school with the children of professors, picked up his parents' feeling of unease with their position in the community. "There was this sense that we were moving down in the world," he recalls, "but I wouldn't have been comfortable saying anything to my parents about it." Instead, he made up stories about himself and his family to gain status among his peers. Ashamed of his origins, he was willing to distort reality to look better than he was. This habit of falsifying himself lingered on to curse his young adulthood.

Trapped inside layers of insecurity, Dan entered into romantic relationships primed to employ the manipulative skills he had used as a child to bolster his self-image. He invented a more glamorous, or at least more coherent, personal history, complete with a "family heirloom" adding machine purchased at a flea market. He reinvented himself, he says, "for sympathy, to make me seem more interesting, to inflate my importance, to heighten the passion."

It was no wonder that the identity he appropriated most frequently and lovingly was that of John Lennon, the original "working-class hero"—a man who inspired the world, but who remained a needy, petulant child. In

Lennon's dualism—one face turned toward peace and harmony, the other toward drugs and degradation—Dan found something that struck close to home. Physically Dan presented an incongruous image: his hair short in front like a priest, long in back like a juvenile delinquent of the 1950s. His John Lennon T-shirt was visible under his starched white shirt; a backpack was slung over his three-piece suit. He lived his life as a mixed metaphor.

If there was a turning point for Dan, it may have come in his therapeutic efforts with Catherine, a profoundly retarded young woman at the state training school. Dan could not impress Catherine with his stories; she would not understand. For that very reason, he was touched that someone would like him just because he was warm and caring. "It's nice to spend several hours a week with someone who just gives me good feelings," he remarks. About his work at the training school Dan says:

> I can't put anything over on these people. I can be amusing; I can be helpful; I can show them love and caring. But they're not going to be fooled into thinking I'm this great person.

It is too soon to tell whether this is just Dan idealizing and rhapsodizing, or whether it really is a turning point. He has begun seeing a woman who works with him at the treatment center, and his relationship with her has been characterized by a lack of pretense and an open sharing of feeling that are unusual for him. In a romantic relationship as well as in a helping relationship, Dan may be sensing the possibility of loving and being loved, and thereby of attaining the personal identity and inner security for which he has been searching.

JEALOUSY IN THE MAKING

The only parental characteristics that are clearly associated with jealousy in men are those of the father; the mother's characteristics appear not to affect how jealous the son tends to be.

Among the characteristics we typically see in the father of a jealous son are strict control and intrusiveness, combined with rejection, nonpermissiveness, and self-assertiveness. This is a punitive father who induces anxiety and guilt to make his son obey him and meet his high standards of achievement. One way he punishes his son is by emotional withdrawal, and at times he seems hostile and rejecting. At other times he intrudes into his son's life in a possessive, controlling way. The father's overbearing involvement with his son and strict enforcement of rules leave little room for autonomy. This father is a strong-willed, determined, aggressive individual. Egotistical and headstrong, he commands the attention and acquiescence of others.

Men whose fathers fit this profile seem to model their personal style and their interactions with women after the way they were treated by their fathers. Besides being prone to jealousy, the sons also tend to have attractive partners and to be high in romantic obsession. These are men who date attractive women, obsess over them, and become jealous about them. They take after their fathers in their assertiveness and competitiveness as well as in their coerciveness. Such a man may end up with an attractive partner by virtue of being assertive, and he may feel that she bolsters his self-esteem. His jealousy may stem either from insecurity and distorted perceptions arising from the fear of losing a self-enhancing relationship, or from the actual attention that rivals pay to his highly attractive partner.

Having a firm, self-assertive father is not in itself sufficient to yield high jealousy in the son. Fathers who are *not* controlling in a hostile, punitive, or intrusive way, even though self-assertive and rejecting, have sons who turn out not to be very jealous at all. A man with an assertive but noncoercive father dates less attractive women, does not obsess much about them, and does not express much jealousy. He may be less fanatical about the physical attributes of the women he pursues, or he may only attract less beautiful women because he is not so handsome and outgoing himself. Perhaps he does not seek to exert control over women because he did not learn the exercise of control from his father. His father did not dominate him, so he does not try to dominate his partners. Alternatively, if the father was an assertive man who did not encourage his son to be equally assertive, the son may not have been equipped to compete with his father. With this background, he may prefer to avoid competing with other men as well, and therefore will not insist on his partner's loyalty.

Men reared in a permissive, laissez-faire atmosphere tend to show a moderate level of jealousy. Their fathers are nonassertive, nonrejecting, and lax in discipline. These fathers are compliant, let others take the initiative, and defer to their judgment. They carry over this personal style to their parental role, for they are accepting of their sons and do not interfere with their lives. Sons of this type of father, although moderately secure, seem capable of feeling and expressing concern over threats to their relationship.

DEPRESSION IN THE MAKING

With regard to depression at the end of a relationship, the picture of relevant parental characteristics is simpler. The more the father exercises control in a hostile, punishing way (including strict enforcement of rules), the more the son is depressed when a romantic relationship ends. In addition, the more influential the father is relative to the mother in family decision-making, the more depression the son experiences. This finding suggests that when the father's hostile-controlling nature carries more weight in the family, it has a greater effect on the son. Finally, the son is more subject to depression when either or both parents are rejecting, less so when they are accepting.

Our findings regarding the parental characteristics associated with breakup depression are similar to those found for people who are depression-prone generally. Such individuals tend to be reared with strict control combined with a lack of warmth. This is consistent with the theory of learned helplessness discussed in Chapter 8. A child whose parents are rejecting is bound to be unhappy. If the parents are also strict, unsympathetic, and controlling, the child learns that there is nothing he can do to change that condition. He is helpless to create or restore the love that he misses. In adulthood, the loss of an intimate romantic relationship can re-create that feeling of helplessness and hopelessness, and the more important the loss, the more likely that depression will follow.

12

QUESTIONING, COPING,

EXPERIMENTING

The experiments for personal growth we recommend in this chapter proceed by trial and error, like scientific experiments. They provide insight even if they seem to fail, for science progresses as much by "failed" experiments as by "successful" ones. To interpret the results, you will find you must often go back to the preceding chapters.

You may want to try different exercises from someone else, or the same exercises in a different sequence, and you will come up with different answers. These experiments are tools for testing yourself, your partners, and your relationships. They are not a short-cut to change, but they can help you learn things to use to bring about change.

In exploring how both you and your partner can contribute to the insecurity you feel in a romantic relationship, the exercises will take you back to the discussions of these questions throughout the book. We believe the best possibility for change lies in applying the insights you gain from our research to your own relationships, so you can understand and then modify any negative expectations you learned in childhood as well as in previous romantic involvements.

It is difficult to change lifelong patterns of insecurity. Yet seemingly minor readjustments can have a powerful eye-opening effect. A person learns to change his or her behavior by practicing small, everyday skills, skills previously placed out of reach by anxiety. As you will see from our examples, small changes often can lead to positive cycles of growth between two people and within oneself. To start with, small changes can interrupt negative cycles that may have been going on for some time. This process gains momentum as layers of futile or destructive interaction are peeled away, allowing you greater hope and self-confidence as well as increased understanding and sympathetic involvement between you and your partner. Moreover, success in making these small changes can spark further progress just by confirming that you can change and that trying makes a real difference.

A therapist can do much to aid this process. The therapist assists in identifying the problems you want to work on, tailors the self-help exercises to those problems, and prepares you for the possible consequences (both positive and negative) of taking new risks. During the initial period of exploration, when any new step may feel as if it has more danger than promise attached to it, the therapist can encourage and reward you for taking that step. It can help a lot for a therapist simply to give you permission to do things that initially feel foolish, awkward, or out of character, but that free you from accustomed roles or habits that are of no benefit. Anticipating the pitfalls you may face, the therapist can interpret how you feel when you approach unfamiliar territory and help you cope with your fears. Later, the therapist calls attention to the rewards you may reap, thus enabling you to appreciate those rewards more than you otherwise might.

If you are highly motivated, you may benefit from doing the exercises in this chapter on your own. If, however, you need more support, you may find it helpful to work with a therapist, who can structure such exercises for you and supervise you in carrying them out. A therapist can also assist you with individualized insight and in-depth exploration tailor-made to your particular needs.

IDENTIFYING THE BASIS OF YOUR INSECURITY: YOUR PARTNER OR YOUR PAST?

The insecurity you feel in love relationships may come from the way your partner acts toward you, or it may come from the way you expect your partner to act toward you—that is, from expectations that you bring to each new relationship based on past experience. Usually, to varying degrees, it comes from a combination of the two. The following exercise can help you distinguish between past and present sources of your insecurity and clarify the relative importance of each.

Think of three or four important relationships you have had, not including your present relationship or the one in which you were most recently involved. (We'll get to that one later.) For each relationship, think about how much your partner's behavior contributed to the insecurity you felt, and how much was based on your own feelings and preconceptions. The chart below gives you nine lines on which to write the names of these partners. The lines are labeled with numbers ranging from 1 (if your insecurity was caused entirely by your partner) to 9 (if your insecurity was caused only by yourself). Write the name of each of the partners you are considering on the line that best fits what happened in your relationship with that partner. For example, if you feel that "the lion's share of it was Ken's doing, but I made things worse," you might write "Ken" on line 2 or line 3.

One more instruction: Please do not write more than one name on any line. Even if you have had several relationships in which you believe your insecurity was caused almost entirely by your partner, or several in which you believe it was caused almost entirely by yourself, see if you can distinguish among them so that you can put each one on a different line.

PARTNER   SOURCE OF INSECURITY

1. _____   PARTNER ("Let's face it, he was a jerk.")
2. _____
3. _____
4. _____
5. _____   SHARED ("We're both equally guilty.")
6. _____
7. _____
8. _____
9. _____   MYSELF ("I hate to admit it, but it was my own fault.")

Now think about the relationship you most want to work on as you read this chapter. Most likely this is your current relationship or your most recent breakup. Which of the past relationships listed above does this relationship most resemble with respect to the source of your insecurity? Or is it different from all of them? Write the name of this current or recent partner in the appropriate place, either beside another name or on a line of its own.

If you have not previously experienced the intense insecurity that you have felt in this relationship, then it is likely that something about your partner is making you insecure. But if you have had similar feelings in a number of relationships, then either the insecurity is coming from your past, or you may be choosing partners who make you feel insecure.

If you listed all of your partners on lines 1 through 4, you might consider why you are always choosing inconsistent partners. Here are some possible reasons:

1. *You may be setting your sights too high.* If you always choose partners who are the most physically attractive, socially skilled, and successful, then you may be taking on a lot of competition. People who rank high in status and power or are very physically attractive can be highly desirable partners, but the attention they get from potential rivals can lead them to be inconsistent toward you.

2. *You may be pursuing people who do not reciprocate your interest.* If you choose partners solely on the basis of how attractive they are to you, you may be ignoring the cues they give out about how interested they are in you. See if you can find a relationship that develops through mutual declarations of interest rather than one-sided pursuit.

3. *You may be trying to satisfy needs that few partners can meet.* As discussed in Chapter 5, you may be looking to your partners to satisfy too many of your needs, including needs that are not readily fulfilled in romantic relationships. Before you conclude that all of your partners have been inconsistent in satisfying your needs, ask yourself what it would take for them to be consistent and how easily your needs could be satisfied in conjunction with theirs. You may be giving so little that your partner is not motivated to give much in return, or you may be giving so much that you are bound to be disappointed by what you get back.

4. *You may be underestimating yourself.* If your partners really have been inconsistent, perhaps even abusive, you may be selling yourself short, choosing partners who are incapable of love because you don't feel confident enough to risk yourself with worthier individuals. Without realizing it, you may feel more comfortable with partners who you believe will not reject you. Yet this can be a costly choice, since these partners act in a rejecting, inconsistent way and will eventually make you regret your decision to get involved romantically.

5. *Your partners may actually be consistent, but you may not trust your own lovability.* Have your partners really been so inconsistent, or might you be reading inconsistency into their behavior? Perhaps some of them have tried to give you reassuring messages that you have not heard because you do not think yourself worthy of their love. In other words, this is an opportunity to

reconsider the way you rated your relationships on the exercise above. Maybe some of the names you wrote on lines 1 to 4 belong on lines 6 to 9.

If, for whatever reason, you regularly choose partners who disappoint you, you may want to examine what leads you to make these choices. Choosing the wrong partners can be another expression of insecurity that harkens back to childhood. This can be a bad habit extending back over a number of relationships, none of which met your needs.

To identify the factors in your background that may lie at the root of your insecurity in relationships, you can look back at the last three chapters. If you are a woman, did you find your father remote or hostile? Were you frustrated in your desire for a close relationship with him? Were your parents in conflict with each other? If so, what was your role? Were you and your mother allied against your father?

If you are a man, did you find your parents harsh and demanding? Did you feel pressure to achieve, combined with a lack of love and support from them? Was your father unsympathetic and tyrannical, while your mother had little left to give because she was so busy catering to your father? At the other extreme, were your parents so warm, loving, and protective that you never learned what it would be like to look for love outside the warmth of the family circle?

For a person of either gender, were your parents inconsistent and unpredictable in their affection? Were they so absorbed in their own needs that they were insensitive to yours and emotionally unavailable to you? Then there are the more extreme instances of divorced, absent, or abusive parents that are illustrated by some of our case histories.

Now that we have reviewed some possible causes of insecurity, both in your partner's behavior and in your family background, take another look at the numerical rating you assigned to your present (or most recent) relationship in the exercise above. You may wish to reconsider that rating and move this partner's name to a different line.

Based on that rating, if you believe your insecurity in your current or most recent relationship has been due mainly to your partner, you may find the next section, "Coping With Your Partner's Contribution to Your Insecurity," especially helpful. If you believe your insecurity is mainly something that you have brought to the relationship from your past experience, you will be especially interested in the section that follows it, "Overcoming Your Own Insecurity." And if you feel that "it's part me and part him" (as it so often is), you may wish to go through both sections.

COPING WITH YOUR PARTNER'S
CONTRIBUTION TO YOUR INSECURITY

There are four stages in a relationship when you might find your partner acting in a way that makes you feel insecure: (1) when you are just meeting a potential partner; (2) when you are going out with someone, but are not yet in a committed relationship; (3) when you are in a committed, stable relationship (married or unmarried); and (4) when a relationship may be about to end. We will look at how you might experience your partner's behavior at each stage and what you might do to reduce your insecurity.

BEGINNINGS

If you feel anxious on a first date—and especially when anticipating meeting the person—then your partner's actions would seem to have little to do with your insecurity. At this point, the partner is still an unknown quantity. When you still don't know very much about your prospective partner, do you worry that she or he will not find you attractive? Do you fear that he or she will think you are not bright enough, or won't find you interesting enough to want to see you again? If so, these feelings of insecurity probably are coming from within yourself, from your past history. To deal with feelings of insecurity at this stage, turn to "Beginnings" in the following section, "Overcoming Your Own Insecurity."

WHEN YOU ARE NOT YET COMMITTED

When you are dating someone prior to making a commitment to each other, the terms of the relationship are still being defined. Indeed, the two of you probably are testing whether you want to have a committed relationship. This is the time to ask for what you need to be comfortable with this person. It is the most critical time to deal with anything your partner may be doing that makes you feel insecure. If your partner is unresponsive to your needs now, even when approached in a gentle, considerate way, he or she is much less likely to accommodate you later when you are committed. At this stage of the relationship, people too often make the mistake of not asking the questions they need to ask. In fact, many partners are willing to tolerate just about anything—even actively repress their own needs to save the relationship—or think they might negotiate things after the relationship is committed.

Marianne, for example, who had just gone through a difficult divorce after years of abuse by her husband, was relieved to meet a "regular Joe" who seemed, by comparison, benign and good-natured. However, he expressed his uninhibited good spirits in ways that she found unsettling—for example, by making suggestive remarks to and about women they saw out on the street. Marianne always felt on edge about this, but dared not say anything for fear of losing this man. In fact, she said nothing at all to him about the future of their relationship, even though they both acted as if it were serious. In this way, Marianne boobytrapped herself for bigger problems later on. Not wanting to unsettle the relationship, she allowed it to have a shaky start. She did not take the initiative needed to give it an enduring foundation. Marianne can test out the future by asking for a change now. But if this man cannot avoid casting his eye toward other women when the relationship is new, the chances of his changing his ways later are not great.

Your needs—whether or not they seem weighty, essential, or sensible— deserve to be treated with respect by your partner. You, too, need to see your needs as legitimate and not let them remain underground, submerged by unspoken arrangements that fall into place between you and your partner. What is crucial, though, is how you go about trying to have your needs met by your partner. The way you approach your partner can either reduce your insecurity or make it worse.

Assuming that something your partner is doing is making you feel insecure, have you shared your distress about this behavior with your partner? It is an elementary question, but one too often overlooked. Many people make the mistake of saying nothing at all about their dissatisfactions, either because (like Marianne) they are fearful of sharing their insecurities, or because they feel that their partner *ought* to know without being told. The grievance then smolders until it bursts out in an angry explosion, to which the partner may reply in kind. Or it may continue to smolder, with subtly expressed anger feeding into a silent power struggle, an adversarial relation- ship rather than a cooperative one. This alternating silence and anger makes for a stalemate in which couples often find themselves, both before and after they are committed to each other.

Jane, for instance, was upset because her boyfriend forgot about her birthday. When her therapist asked whether she had let her boyfriend know how she felt, she answered, "Why should I have to? He should know. I haven't cooked dinner for him for a month. That should tell him something." Jane's reaction is justified, but her way of communicating, or not communicating, is ineffective. Her boyfriend cannot be expected to change if he is unaware of what is bothering her, and he cannot be expected to understand subtle, implicit, indirect communications. Even if he is conscious of the problem, the lack of constructive dialogue pushes the couple toward an adversarial relationship. However much we want our partners to know what we are feeling, we cannot expect them to be mind readers. It is a good precaution to check and make sure that you have told your partner what is hurting you.

The other extreme, angry rage, proves equally futile. Tina regularly became angry when her boyfriend showed up late for a date. Sometimes, when she really made a scene, he would walk off and leave her to stew. "It seems that your anger isn't very productive," remarked her therapist. "Why shouldn't I sound angry?" Tina snapped. "I *am* angry. You mean I'm supposed to just bottle it up?" Tina has every reason to be angry when her boyfriend has been indifferent to her feelings. However, by attacking him she puts him on the defensive, and that may interfere with persuading him to act differently. If he feels attacked, he is not likely to make an effort to meet Tina's needs. More likely, he will say, "I work all day long; why should I have to worry about being a few minutes late? It's not fair."

Sometimes it seems people think that the only way to break through a partner's indifference and get his or her attention is to raise the decibel level or the forcefulness of the utterance. But that only raises the level of the partner's defenses. The really powerful persuader that many people have not tried, even if they think they have, is to say what they want to say in a straightforward, nonangry way. Imagine Tina calmly telling her partner, "Maybe you've had a lot on your mind lately, and that's made it difficult for you to get here on time. But I want to remind you that it does make me very upset and uncomfortable when you're late. Would you please try to be on time for our next date?" She might then ask him to commit himself to being on time and express appreciation if he agrees.

This recommendation for Tina is an illustration of the Schwarz Three-Part Method for stating your needs to your partner:

1. Express sympathy for the needs of your partner—in particular, the needs that contribute to the behavior that is a problem for you.
2. In a way that can gain your partner's sympathy, share how your partner's behavior has been a problem for you. Avoid laying heavy guilt on your partner. Avoid being punitive. Concentrate on *your* feelings, not his or her lack of consideration.
3. Describe concretely how you want your partner to act in the future, and under what specific circumstances. Then ask for a commitment—

that is, a promise to try to act as you have requested. Show your
pleasure over receiving your partner's commitment to change.

The Three-Part Method is a way of asking for change that is less likely to upset
your partner and more likely to elicit the response you are looking for. How it
works is illustrated by the case of Shelley and Ted (from Chapter 6). Ted, who
liked to go out carousing with his friends, sometimes found it hard to break
off and get back for his Saturday night dates with Shelley. Instead of calling
when she expected, Ted would finally get to a phone booth late in the evening
and propose that he come and spend the night with her. Shelley, understandably enraged, would attack him bitterly, which only made Ted go off again
into his carefree lifestyle, leaving Shelley increasingly anxious when he did
not call her for several days. The two of them repeatedly fought because they
had not agreed to any contract defining their mutual commitments. Shelley
became jealous, insecure, and upset when Ted did not live up to her
conception of their relationship; Ted, meanwhile, distanced himself and
acted according to his own conception of it. Although Shelley was a very
attractive and bright woman, she seemed so controlling and possessive that
Ted found himself resisting her control more than trying to accommodate her
needs. It was a vicious cycle: Shelley's romantic anxiety was touched off by
Ted's frustrating elusiveness, which in turn was exacerbated by her abrasive
personal style.

In therapy Shelley learned the Three-Part Method: to show sympathy for
Ted's needs, to state her own needs and desires, and to request from him a
commitment to act in specified ways. Then she said to him [Step 1], "I can
understand that you enjoy being with your friends, and that when you've had
a lot to drink you want to keep doing that. [Step 2] But it's Saturday night.
I've worked hard this week, and I was looking forward to seeing you. I was
very disappointed when you didn't call earlier. [Step 3] I really would like you
to commit Saturday night to us. In the future, would you do that?" For the
first time, the couple really discussed their expectations of each other. Ted
thought carefully about when he would commit himself to meeting Shelley
and when he would not, and he kept his commitments. He had not taken her
seriously when she had been enraged and seemingly out of control. But with a
smoother, more sympathetic, more assertive style, she presented her needs in
such a way that he had warmer feelings toward her, and their relationship
became more cooperative and mutually rewarding. She also applied the

Three-Part Method elsewhere in her life (particularly in her job) and gained rewards for it there as well.

Not everyone finds it so easy to apply the Three-Part Method. It can be hard to get past the inhibited silences, the unproductive ruminations ("Damn him—he should know better—how come he doesn't care about me?"), the fruitless tirades. We recommend that you start by practicing your new, calm, straightforward approach in the mirror. Start with Step 2: rehearse telling your partner what bothers you. But don't expect it to come out right all at once. Just say it, even if saying it makes you feel choked up, frustrated, and angry. In fact, say it until it comes out sounding angry! Then keep saying it, all the while trying to be more and more relaxed. When you can say it to the mirror very calmly, without being angry, self-conscious, or blaming, add Step 1 (expressing sympathy for your partner's needs) and then Step 3 (asking for a commitment to change) to your rehearsal. When you have all three parts worked out and feel relaxed saying them to the mirror, that's the time to say them to your partner.

As you stand in front of the mirror, put yourself in your partner's place. Be mindful of what you want your partner to feel and what would be most *productive* for you to have him or her feel. These two things may not be the same. If you want your partner "to feel as hurt as I do," see if you can keep that wish in check. Too often we imagine, "The more I make him (or her) suffer, the more he (or she) will remember to act differently." But that is not what motivates change; on the contrary, it causes rigidity and resistance to change.

Try not to lose sight of your goal; speak to your partner in a way that stands a greater chance of success. Admittedly, this is not easy. If it were, you probably wouldn't need this exercise. It is easy to fall back into sarcasm, threats, or a flareup of temper. Keep in mind, though, that shaming, blaming, and angry threats, even when they do get results, often have serious *negative side effects.* They make partners defensive, angry, and retaliatory. They create an atmosphere of hostility unconducive to cooperation. And they tend to destroy your partner's love for you, lower your partner's self-esteem, and drive her or him away.

Do what you can to create a *cooperative atmosphere* rather than an angry, vindictive, adversarial one. If your partner defends his or her past behavior, it is best not to attack these rationalizations. Keep the focus on the future, and concentrate on what will please you *next* time. Use the Three-Part Method to open up a dialogue. Don't expect instant harmony; more often you will need to negotiate an understanding. Your partner may reveal important needs of which you were unaware, needs that are in conflict with your request. With this new information, you may decide to back off a little and work out a compromise. The essential thing is that there be a frank exchange, a full disclosure of the partners' respective needs. Only then can a compromise be reached that each partner considers fair and is willing to accept and live with.

What if the Three-Part Method initially does not work for you? There are some partners who will not respond to direct requests, since for them to change means admitting they were wrong in the first place. If your partner is like that, you might stop asking for large changes and start unobtrusively rewarding small changes. Be alert to any sign of positive movement. Pay careful attention to when your partner *is* on time, and let him or her know that you have noticed the change and are pleased by it. Try to avoid the pitfall of throwing in barbs that have the unintentional effect of punishing your partner for changing, like "Thanks for remembering my birthday, even though you missed the last three," or "Why did it take you ten years to finally shape up?"

What if you make your requests exactly as recommended, and your partner says, "Okay, I won't do it anymore," but then he keeps doing it? Again, calmly share your concern with your partner and try to obtain a renewed commitment for future change. Old habits are hard to break, and new habits form slowly. Even when a commitment is made, change does not always happen immediately. A person may need several reminders.

When a partner repeatedly makes a sincere commitment to change and is unable to keep it, it is reasonable to address that as a problem and ask him or her to do something about it. Alcohol and drug problems are especially difficult to resolve. Nonetheless, you should express your concern. If you see no change, you can ask the person to get professional help. If that fails to bring change, you can withdraw from the relationship. It is best not to gamble that you will have more success at a more committed stage of the relationship, since failure at a later stage will be more tragic for both of you.

Thus far we have assumed a degree of mutuality and good faith in the relationship that can be tapped—and should be nurtured—when you want to change a long-standing pattern of interaction. Not everyone, however, has a responsive partner. As reasonably as you may state your request, you may get an uncaring response such as, "Tough luck—that's just the way I am." If you find such indifference and intransigence distressing, you need to evaluate what this relationship means to you.

That is the strong advantage of raising such issues now, before you are committed to the relationship: you still have time to get out without emotional devastation. On the one hand, you must decide whether you are willing to put the relationship on the line to insist on the changes you want, and that involves consideration of the risks that breaking up entails. Months of loneliness before finding a new partner, and even years of searching to find the right partner, may be preferable to a life with the wrong partner. Still, walking away without putting the relationship on the line would be selling yourself short and giving up a struggle you might have won. On the other hand, if you find yourself willing to accept any provocation or abuse to keep the relationship, it may be advisable to consider the basis of your choice and perhaps examine this issue with a therapist.

Whatever the outcome of the dialogue with your partner, the act of asserting yourself by initiating a dialogue is itself an antidote to insecurity. At the outset, it may feel unnatural to speak to your partner in such an unfamiliar way; that is why rehearsal can be valuable. In the long run, though, calmly discussing your respective needs and expectations can only make you feel more self-confident and powerful. By taking on the role of a secure person, not only can you create a more positive self-image, but you can actually become the person you are play-acting.

COMMITTED RELATIONSHIPS

In committed relationships, negative patterns may be deeply ingrained. If one partner is financially or emotionally dependent on the other, the partner who is favored by this imbalance of power may have little incentive to change, especially since it may be difficult by now for the other partner to leave the relationship. Couples get frozen into rituals of interaction that, despite their stated intentions, serve to protect the status quo. It may seem you are trying and trying to change things, but they become more and more rigidly the same.

Chuck, for example, would stonewall his wife's needs until, in her frustration, she burst into an angry tirade. Then Chuck would remark disdainfully, "You have to learn to control yourself, Maureen," and walk off indignantly, refusing to work toward a resolution of the conflict. To break the cold, intolerable silence, Maureen apologized for each outburst and then struggled to hold in her feelings until her next abortive attempt to have Chuck consider her needs. Although she spoke of wanting to be more independent, she stifled her discontent over and over again out of fear of losing him. Irritated by Maureen's unpredictable outbursts, Chuck referred to them as "her anger problem," as if she had a disease. "You've got to see her," he would say. "She really goes off the wall when she's angry. Every time she does it, I feel as if she's destroying our foundation, and we have to start all over." Yet he did not understand why Maureen felt insecure about their marriage.

To break out of such a cycle, the Three-Part Method illustrated above can be used in the committed stage of a relationship just as in the earlier stages. The following table lists rules for resolving conflicts, Do's and Don't's that are worth keeping in mind as you address the chronic dissatisfactions that stand between you and your partner.

PRINCIPLES OF CONFLICT RESOLUTION

Do's

DO pick a relaxed, cheerful time to start a discussion of your conflict.

DO show sympathy for your partner's needs.

DO share your pain and hurt more than your anger.

DO explain your preferences in ways that gain your partner's sympathy.

DO ask for a *specific* change in the *future.*

DO ask for a *commitment* or at least a *promise* to try.

DO encourage your partner to share his or her feelings concerning this topic and your request.

DO, if criticized, acknowledge any part of the criticism that is true *before* justifying your actions.

DO keep the focus on the *future* and on *one* topic of change.

DO accept compromise as a solution, but only when the sacrifices are equally balanced.

DO acknowledge your partner's cooperation.

Don't's

DON'T attempt serious conflict resolution when either of you are in the heat of anger.

DON'T judge, blame, shame, threaten, or punish.

DON'T dwell on the past.

DON'T provoke strong guilt.

DON'T demand an apology.

DON'T put your partner down with negative labels—for example, "lazy," "alcoholic," "sexist pig."

DON'T attack your partner's justifications for past conduct.

DON'T cross-complain in response to criticism.

DON'T introduce or respond now to a second topic until the first has been resolved.

DON'T demand surrender on a new (second) topic of conflict as a precondition for resolution of the original (first) topic.

DON'T accept an unfair or unworkable agreement.

DON'T give up the effort to resolve the conflict; it won't go away.

Sue and Art (in Chapter 7) demonstrate how a persistent conflict can be resolved by a direct, sincere statement of underlying needs. Whenever Art went on a business trip, Sue demanded that he keep her informed of his whereabouts at all times. He resisted even though it would not have been much trouble to make the calls she requested. He felt controlled and demeaned by the demands stemming from her jealousy. His own unexpressed way of changing her behavior was to not reward it, not "even privilege it with a response." His method of teaching her obviously was not working, but instead was increasing anger on both sides, intensifying the adversarial atmosphere, and making it harder to switch to a different approach.

However, when he learned that as a child she had been sexually abused, he could really feel for her and come to a much deeper understanding of why she might be feeling insecure. No longer interpreting her requests as an attack on him, he stopped struggling against her jealousy and started giving her the reassurance she wanted and needed. Once he did, she ceased to require so much reassurance. Instead of a phone call from every hotel, an occasional call was sufficient; and now he was calling because he wanted to call and missed the closeness he felt with her. Sue and Art replaced a vicious cycle with a nurturing cycle. With each reciprocal demonstration of trust, they more fully sympathized with each other, and her insecurity fell away along with his resistance.

The breakthrough that occurred so dramatically for Sue and Art can be achieved by other couples with a concerted effort to move things off center. You might approach your partner and say, "You know, for some time I've been feeling that I'm not getting some things out of our marriage that are important to me. It occurred to me that if that's true for me, it's probably true for you, too. We've been doing things the same way for so long that each of us doesn't even know anymore what the other wants. Why don't we try telling each other what we'd like to see happen differently, and then we can both be more satisfied."

Next, you can each take four sheets of paper and make the following lists:

1. Changes you would like to make in yourself.
2. Changes you think your partner would like you to make.
3. Changes you would like your partner to make in himself/herself.
4. Changes you think your partner would like to make.

Then compare your lists. Are the changes you would like your partner to make the same as the ones your partner thinks you would like him or her to make, and vice versa? Are the changes you yourself would like to make the same as the ones your partner would like you to make, and vice versa? The answers can help you identify areas of agreement and disagreement, weak spots in your communications, and areas where you may not have realized that you both want the very same things. Couples often are amazed to find that both partners may want such changes as greater closeness and intimacy, better communication, more time together and shared activities, and more of a sense that each is the center of the other's life. Gradually, though, they have lost sight of this deeper harmony as each misunderstanding, accusation, attack, and counterattack has hardened the mortar in the walls of defense being erected between them.

ENDINGS

A relationship can end at any of the above stages, and so the ending phase overlaps with all the others. Any of the hypothetical situations we have discussed could turn into the final crisis of a relationship. Still, there are special issues that come up in such a crisis, some of which are discussed in Chapter 8. A person who is thinking of ending a relationship may attempt to conceal this intention from the partner, both to avoid hurting the partner and to keep her or his own options open. The partner, picking up mixed messages, tacitly conspires to disregard the threatening possibility of a breakup. However, enough evidence of disengagement comes through to put the partner in a state of anxiety—anxiety aroused by inconsistent signals of the other person's love.

If you feel anxious because you sense that your partner is thinking about breaking up with you, it is best to recognize the crisis at hand and bring it out into the open. To do this, you may need to overcome both your own resistance and your partner's. You don't want to hear the bad news, and your partner doesn't want to tell it to you. When you finally bring yourself to ask directly, your partner may deny his or her intentions. To bring clarity to the situation, try discussing openly your perception of your partner's uncertainty and how you feel about it. Talk about where you see the relationship going—what kind of commitment you want and what kind your partner wants. By raising these issues, you will be encouraging your partner to say what is on his or her mind.

If you show that you are strong enough to entertain the possibility of a breakup, your partner may feel comfortable about sharing her or his desire to leave. This in itself raises the intimacy level between the two of you—if you can listen and respond sympathetically rather than defensively. Then you can either intervene sooner to save the relationship (if possible) or know what you need to know to prepare for what is to come. Sometimes it seems that the greatest intimacy couples experience occurs around the end of the relationship, when, having given up the struggle, they finally feel that they can be open with each other. It is unfortunate that this could not happen sooner.

OVERCOMING YOUR OWN INSECURITY

Everyone feels a certain amount of insecurity. For everyone, there are some circumstances that arouse anxious feelings. A realistic goal is not to eliminate these painful feelings, but to reduce their frequency or intensity. Once the feelings are more bearable, a person can learn to give up self-defeating ways of avoiding them and develop useful strategies for coping with insecurity. These strategies, in turn, further reduce insecurity by inspiring self-confidence and expectations of success.

If feelings of insecurity keep you from having fulfilling romantic relationships, the recommendations that follow may help you reduce that obstacle at each of the four stages of a relationship.

BEGINNINGS

Feelings of insecurity can contribute to keeping you out of relationships altogether. It is another destructive cycle: you don't get involved because you feel anxious and not up to it, and then you feel even more anxious and unequal to the challenge because it's been so long since you've gotten involved. Since at this point you either do not have a partner or do not know your partner very well, it is your own past experience (rather than your partner's behavior) that is the primary source of the insecurity you feel.

Therefore, a major goal of therapy or self-help is to provide what are called *corrective emotional experiences.* These are experiences in which you take some unaccustomed risks, do things you may have been afraid to do before, but do them in a way that gives you a decent chance of a positive outcome. Some people may have an all-or-nothing view of relationships: they wish for total fulfillment, fear total rejection, and do nothing. Corrective experiences often are designed to bring about smaller successes and to encourage you to take pleasure in them. You can then build on these experiences to develop both greater confidence and greater realism in your approach to romance. There is no guarantee of a positive outcome on any one try, but the odds are more in your favor than before, and you will feel better about yourself for having tried. Although a therapist's support can be important in structuring such experiences and interpreting their outcomes, you can create corrective experiences for yourself by using any of the following suggestions that appeal to you.

Don't get hung up on unrealistic goals. If you approach every date with the idea that it has to turn into an ecstatic, all-consuming love affair, you lose out in three ways. First, you become uptight and anxious because so much is at stake. Second, most or all of your social encounters have to be accounted as failures when measured against your lofty goal. Third, you miss out on a variety of experiences which, besides being enjoyable in themselves, might be intermediate steps toward fulfilling love relationships.

You can have rewarding corrective experiences by setting more flexible goals for your contacts with people and by looking for relationships that will add different experiences to your life. Look around for someone you might like to get to know, without any particular agenda. Is there someone you know whom you might elevate to a new level of friendship? See if you can take some risks by creating more intimate, open relationships, and then see what positive effects may follow.

When it comes to romantic relationships, the combination of intimidating goals, fear of rejection, and a lack of positive experience can lead to inaction, so that a person never gets to test out the possibilities. A therapist may say to a client, "You're so afraid of rejection, you don't even know what it's like. Your assignment this week is to go out and get yourself rejected by three people." The therapist does not necessarily intend this to be taken literally. Rather, it is a dramatic statement that challenges the client's usual way of thinking. When the client is taken aback, the therapist can say, "Haven't you been kidding yourself by seeing rejection at every turn?" Literally or symbolically, rejection is transformed from a fear into a goal. It *is* a real accomplishment to be rejected rather than not even try to make contact. Of course, once you get out there and put yourself on the line, it is likely that not every approach will result in rejection. It does not matter whether you meet the goal of being rejected if you meet another goal, that of taking action and meeting people.

A man who benefited from this approach was Wayne, who was obsessively infatuated with an unattainable woman. He did not pursue other women as long as he could hold on to the fantasy of winning her affection, and to preserve his dream he never approached her either. His therapist encouraged him to go out with women with whom he was not in love, partly for practice and partly to have a range of positive social experiences. In this way he became more comfortable and confident with women, so that he could begin to approach women in whom he had a more serious interest. Thus, he created more than one possible romantic relationship, all of them more realistic than the one that obsessed him, each inoculating him against the dread of rejection by the others. This desensitization finally gave him the courage to approach his dream woman directly. She did reject him, but by then the prospect of other relationships had become real for him. At last he was able to loosen the grip of his obsession and move on to other, more gratifying relationships.

Show interest in people. We like people who seem to like us. If you show that you like people rather than looking for signs that you are liked in return, you *will* be liked. The most common reason for not being liked is the fear of not being liked, which causes people either to inhibit themselves or to show off in an effort to make people like them. To avoid these extremes, show some interest in a potential partner's activities, just as you want him or her to show interest in you. Draw the person out about the things that matter to him or her. Ask more than one question on the same topic. That will show your date that you want to hear more and that the first response did not dampen your interest. As she or he talks more and feels valued, she or he probably will become more curious about you and may pay you the same compliment in

return. If you are going to have a worthwhile relationship, each of you will
care about what is important to the other.

Anticipate and prepare for what you most fear. People generally are preoccupied
with preventing the disasters they fear will happen on a date, but this only
makes them more nervous. Instead of trying to prevent the things you most
fear, work out a strategy for coping with them if they *do* happen. You'll find
that you have resources you didn't know you had when you were using up your
energy worrying rather than planning. If you prepare yourself for the worst
eventualities, you will probably be less anxious and more relaxed going into
the situation. You will handle yourself better and enjoy yourself more.

This is not to endorse the magical belief many people have that if you dwell
on the worst, it won't happen. On the contrary, we recommend that you allow
for the possibility that the worst *may* happen and think about how you will
respond if it does. By reducing these feared calamities to more realistic,
manageable dimensions, you will be better able to cope with them, both
emotionally and practically.

Make use of pleasant associations. Some people reduce the anxiety they feel
before going on a date by recalling positive memories that put them in an
optimistic frame of mind. Think of a time in the past when you felt secure and
confident. In your imagination, put yourself into that setting. Try to feel your
body there, the way you were standing or sitting or lying down at the time,
until the sounds, colors, and other sensations from that occasion become
vivid. Let the feeling of security and confidence that you had then flow
through your body and your mind.

Next, imagine yourself going directly from that past situation to the date
you are anticipating. Or, if possible, try to bring the person you are going out
with into your memory of that happy occasion; make him or her a part of the
good feelings you recall. Imagine, as concretely as possible, how you might
interact with this person if you felt the way you did then. Do this as close as
possible to the time when you will be going out together; do it more than once
if you like. Then see if you can go into the date with those same positive
feelings: the confidence, the exuberance, the sense of being at peace.

Adopt a positive model. Think of someone you respect, someone you regard as
a model of success in life. Imagine how this self-confident person would
handle the date you are anticipating. Take some time to make up an elaborate
fantasy of this person out on a date with your prospective partner—what he or
she would say and do. Next, imagine yourself acting just like this person on
your first date with your prospective partner. Then go out and be this person

yourself. That may sound like a lot to ask; but remember, what mainly separates you from your successful model is different expectations. If you substitute his or her expectations for yours, you may find that you can fulfill them more easily than you would think.

Act as if your date is in love with you. If you are going out with a person for the first or second time, you generally do not know how that person feels about you. That uncertainty, especially when combined with past experiences of disapproval and rejection, can make you feel anxious and expect the worst. Instead, why not imagine the best? Go ahead, give yourself permission. Imagine how you would act if you knew that this person really, really liked you—indeed, was wildly infatuated with you. Imagine how you would respond if you knew that this person was just as hopeful as you of acceptance and approval. Go through the scene in your imagination before the date, so that you can visualize in detail how you will act with this person who is in love with you. Then try to *do* as much as possible of what you have rehearsed when you actually go out on the date. After all, your partner really may be infatuated with you. And even if your partner doesn't know that yet, sometimes you can tip the balance by acting as if that were so.

All of these fantasy exercises are ways of shedding old mental and emotional baggage, of changing habits based on negative expectations. You can use them to realize and create hopeful possibilities in the present instead of reacting to discouraging events in the past. Having prepared for a date in this positive spirit, you can do the same when it comes to interpreting what happened on a date.

Challenge negative interpretations. What makes an experience painful is not what objectively happens, but what you subjectively assume that it means— that is, the interpretation you give to those words or gestures of the partner. Do you interpret dating situations so as to see yourself as disliked and rejected? One woman said, "I went out with this guy, and he kept teasing me and joking with me. It seemed like he was putting me down. He just doesn't like me." But the man's joking might just as well be interpreted as a sign that he *did* like the woman, that he felt comfortable with her. His teasing might have been more accurately—and certainly more positively—seen as his attempt to make her feel at ease or to relieve his own anxiety. Maybe it was his way of getting on familiar terms with her.

Suppose a woman goes out with a man for the first time, and he brings her home early, saying, "Gee, I had a good time, but I'd better go. I have to get up early for work tomorrow." She feels anxious and upset, thinking, "He just wanted to get rid of me. He was bored with me. I guess he didn't find me very attractive." What if, instead, the man made sexual advances to her? Then she might think, "All he's interested in is sex!" Whatever happens, she interprets it negatively. This woman may as well not go out at all, since she has rejected herself already.

As in this example, feelings of anxiety, unworthiness, disappointment, and failure are linked to thoughts that usually are not accurate and may even be biased and irrational. They are beliefs, speculations, and interpretations, but not facts. The negative feelings come from those beliefs, not from the experience itself. What if the man was tired? What if he really did have to get up early for work? What if he acted as he did to show that he liked the woman and was not just looking for immediate sexual gratification? What if he was trying to act the way he thought *she* wanted? The woman would feel better if she believed any of these explanations. Would she be fooling herself? Happy people do, indeed, see the world through different eyes.

If you feel upset because of something a person did on a date with you, don't stop at the first explanation that comes into your mind. List three reasons why the person may have done what she or he did. Then take a look at your list. Have you mentioned any reasons that put you in a negative light? Have you included any that have nothing to do with you? If not, try to think of another explanation that has to do with other things in the person's life besides you. And how about some explanations that actually put you in a positive light, such as, "He's anxious because he's so interested in me"? Then see if you can estimate the probability that each explanation is the correct one.

Try always to think of two possible reasons for the things your partners do—one that reflects on you, and one that stems from other motives or concerns the partner may have. Then guess how likely each explanation is to be true. This exercise can help you break the habit of reading rejection into anything ambiguous that happens on a date.

Don't make rejection a self-fulfilling prophecy. "It's been three days, and I haven't heard from him (or her)," you sigh. True, and he or she hasn't heard from you, either. If your main concern is to protect yourself from anticipated rejection, you may miss the opportunity to show interest in your partner, which may be all you need to elicit reciprocal interest.

WHEN YOU ARE NOT YET COMMITTED

When you are feeling insecure in a dating relationship, and when the source of your insecurity does not clearly lie in your partner's behavior, the techniques described for reducing anxiety at the start of dating can be useful here as well. For example, if you are having a difficult discussion with your partner, put yourself in a positive frame of mind by remembering a time when you felt comfortable, contented, and in harmony with your surroundings. If you are jealous of someone with whom your partner associates, imagine how a self-confident friend would handle the situation, and then do likewise. Playing a new role—first in fantasy, and then with your partner—can open up new possibilities in a stalled relationship.

Similarly, the way you interpret your partner's behavior is just as crucial in an ongoing relationship as when you begin dating. Again, before you jump to the conclusion that your partner is putting you down, see if you can find a plausible explanation for his or her behavior that does not reflect badly on you. Always think of that second reason so that you won't feel rejected automatically—not to mention the third reason, the one that reflects well on you! Keep in mind that your partner cannot make you feel a certain way; he or she can say and do things, but you decide what it all means, which in turn affects the way you feel.

Discriminate between the present and the past. If you find yourself feeling anxious and defensive in your current relationship, and if you believe that your childhood traumas may be contributing to your insecurity, you might try making more conscious and explicit comparisons between the past and the present. For example, list the similarities and differences between your father or mother and your partner: How are they alike? How are they not alike? How did your father or mother make you feel? How does your partner make you feel? By bringing this association between the two men or women out into the light of day, you can examine it critically rather than continue acting as though your partner will behave as your parent once did.

Of course, if your partner *is* like your father or mother, then go back to the previous section, "Coping With Your Partner's Contribution to Your Insecurity." But if she or he is not, you can learn to act differently toward her or him. What would it mean to act differently? A helpful exercise is to prepare verbal pep talks that you can give to yourself at moments of stress—statements such as "That woman (or man) is not a threat to me. I know my partner loves me. I've got to be calm and not get upset and jump to conclusions." Through this kind of inner dialogue, you can instruct or remind yourself how to cope with difficult situations.

Take some risks to change what isn't working. If you are locked in an unproductive way of interacting with your partner, you may benefit greatly from stepping out of your accustomed role and trying something different. Doing something unfamiliar can feel awkward and even foolish; it can also be scary, since you may be giving up some immediate reassurance you are used to getting. In the long run, however, you stand to gain a greater feeling of security.

When we speak of taking risks, we usually mean *doing* something, taking some active step, such as asking someone out or initiating a dialogue with your partner. There are times, though, when you need to take the risk of *not* doing something. Charlotte, for example, was afraid she was driving her boyfriend away with her frequent requests that they do things together. She wanted to restrain herself from asking so much of him, but felt she could not live without the reassurance she was given when he responded to her requests. Her therapist encouraged her to look at the situation in a different way. "Your insecurity is denying you the very feedback you need from your partner to reduce your insecurity," he explained. "You keep asking him, 'Do you love me? Do you love me?' He keeps answering, 'Yes, yes,' but you don't really believe him; you think he's saying so only because you asked. You're not giving him the opportunity to offer freely what you could then take as real evidence that he cares for you. If you could get that deep assurance of his love, you probably wouldn't need to ask for reassurance so often."

An event was coming up to which Charlotte particularly hoped her boyfriend would invite her. On the advice of her therapist, she made this event into a test run. Her therapist showed her that she had much more to gain, and less to lose, by not asking her boyfriend to take her than by asking him. If she asked him, she risked driving him away; and even if he did agree to go with her, she still would not know whether he cared enough to ask her on his own. But if she waited to see whether he would invite her, either she would have a more meaningful demonstration of his love, or she would find out that he really did not feel very attached to her anyway. Viewed in that light, not asking him wasn't much of a risk. At worst, her eyes would be opened, and she would be free to go on to other relationships. Charlotte chose to wait, because then she would feel much better if he did invite her. She passed three days anxiously, but when he did invite her, she was elated. She began to feel more confident of his affection, which she no longer felt compelled to confirm by making small requests of him several times a week. What she had needed—and what she got from her therapist—was support both in seeing her choices clearly for what they were and in choosing the option that brought a delayed, but much larger, reward.

COMMITTED RELATIONSHIPS

In a long-term relationship, unfulfilling patterns can harden with time and because one or both partners lack options outside the relationship. A person may feel inhibited from asking for reassurance, shamed out of it by the partner. Difficult as it may be to break through this wall of noncommunication, the feelings and needs that are unexpressed will not go away. If you can identify and share your insecurities with your partner, you may be able to negotiate some compromises that will enable you to feel more secure. To do this, you need to be able to discuss the issue without blaming it on your partner. It is not always easy to decide when to acknowledge a problem as your own and when to bring up your partner's share of responsibility. Still, sometimes you can get better results by speaking of the problem as if it were your own and asking your partner to accommodate you.

Some people are reluctant to admit their feelings of insecurity for fear that doing so will give their partner ammunition to use against them later. This is not, however, always a realistic fear. Even if it is, you are better off in the long run challenging such intimidation than letting it silence you. If you take the risk of exposing your vulnerability and then it is used against you, make *that* behavior an issue by sharing your hurt feelings. In any event, if your partner belittles or ridicules you for expressing your feelings openly, then the problem between you is not just *your* insecurity. It is a problem large enough to be worth examining in couples' therapy, one that might prompt reconsideration of your choice of partner.

ENDINGS

How can you reassure yourself if you fear that your partner may leave you? If there is a reasonable basis for believing that your partner is pulling away, then the insecurity you feel is not the problem, for you have ample reason to feel insecure! In that case, turn back to "Endings" in the previous section, "Coping With Your Partner's Contribution to Your Insecurity." But what if your worries usually turn out to be unfounded? Then we really are talking *not* about a possible ending, but about feelings of insecurity that can come up at any point in a relationship. These are the feelings we have discussed throughout this section, "Overcoming Your Own Insecurity."

SOURCES OF SUPPORT

Overcoming insecurity involves trying unfamiliar things, accepting some discomfort, and risking disappointment, all while perhaps forgoing customary strategies for reducing anxiety. A professional counselor can do much to help you through these transitions—clarifying the choices you face, encouraging you at difficult moments, reminding you of your commitment when you seem to be falling back into old habits. You may also gain assistance from self-help support groups such as those listed in the Appendix. Although the ideas these groups have about insecure love may not always be scientifically based, just getting together with people who have similar problems can help alleviate your discomfort and strengthen your resolve.

To find a professional counselor, you can call your state psychological or psychiatric association or licensing board. National organizations such as the American Psychological Association, the American Psychiatric Association, the National Association of Social Workers, the American Board of Professional Psychology, and the National Register of Health Service Providers in Psychology (all in Washington, D.C.) can give you a list of approved providers in your area. Community mental health centers not only provide professional help, but can refer you to local support groups as well. Other sources of information about support groups in your community include the YM/YWCA and YM/YWHA, women's centers, women's health centers, rape and assault crisis centers, and local universities and public libraries. Many towns have an information and referral service or info-line listed at the front of the phone book. Some churches run divorce and separation support groups. If you cannot find a Parents Without Partners group in your area, you can contact the national office of this organization (listed in the Appendix).

The Appendix also includes a list of books from which you may gain additional insight. Some offer different perspectives on insecure love, any of which may be illuminating to you. Others teach relationship skills that may increase your confidence in relating to current or new partners. Still others focus on minimizing the effects of marital disruptions on children and raising children so that they will have a good chance to have secure, loving relationships.

POSTSCRIPT: THE NEXT GENERATION

A couple sits on the floor at opposite ends of the room in their marriage counselor's office, their eight-month-old baby between them. When the baby moves toward her father, her mother tenses up and moves slightly in the other direction. "I feel so disappointed when the baby does that; it's as if I've lost her," she says. "I love her so much I can't stand the thought that she might prefer my husband. Even when I'm alone with her it gets too intense sometimes if I'm with her too long, and I need to be away from her. Then as soon as she's gone I miss her all over again."

The baby's mother, Janet, grew up with two squabbling parents who "always put me in the middle, each one putting the other down." When her father came home drunk and beat her mother, Janet and her brothers had to sit on the couch, "screaming, but afraid to move." To deflect the anger and violence from herself, Janet became a clown who strove to amuse people and make them like her. Janet is married to a clinging, possessive man who, she says, "makes me feel stupid all the time. We compete over everything, and now we're competing for the baby's love." Janet's husband, who says that his mother made *him* feel stupid, expresses his insecurity by smothering Janet and their baby with love, which makes Janet feel on guard and suspicious. Both fearing a loss of affection, they act as rivals rather than as loving parents working together smoothly.

"I've got to learn to trust people," says Janet. "My husband has never given me a reason not to trust him, but I get suspicious of people and wonder what they want from me—mostly men, I think, because of my father." Janet recalls her father as cold and reprimanding; he refused to speak to her for a year after she went out with a boy he disapproved of. Janet has become more sympathetic toward her father after learning much more about his difficult childhood. This revelation has helped her understand his inability to reach out to her with a hug or say, "I love you." Meanwhile, Janet has difficulty showing affection toward her husband. Instead, she pours her affection into the baby, then withdraws when she feels especially vulnerable to rejection. Feeling unlovable, she wants to keep the baby on her "side." Thus we find the baby on the floor, her movements watched closely by a father and mother who cannot seem to recognize and express their love for each other.

Is there to be a third generation of anxiously attached people in this family? Will this baby grow up to be one of the unhappy individuals in our case studies? There are suggestions in recent research that children may develop attachment styles similar to their parents. Nonetheless, Janet may be able to start her child on a different path. Some people who were insecure in their relationships with their parents are able to create a secure emotional environment for their children. Apparently they do so by coming to terms with their bad experiences in childhood and getting involved in more positive relationships (what we referred to above as "corrective emotional experiences"). Janet and her husband still have the chance to achieve greater trust and mutual reassurance by using the techniques outlined earlier in this chapter. It is unfortunate that Janet did not have trusting relationships with men before she married, but she is now discarding the negative expectations about intimate relationships that she formed in childhood.

What does it mean for a person to have *positive* expectations about being loved? What would we want our children to expect from intimate relationships? We developed a questionnaire that measures expectations for love and affection. We asked participants to rate their expectations by placing a number from 0 ("highly improbable") to 8 ("highly probable") beside each of the following statements. We asked them to indicate not what they would *like* to have happen, but what they *expected* to happen. Participants were asked:

IN THE FUTURE, HOW STRONGLY DO YOU EXPECT...

1. to date attractive people who will give you a lot of attention and affection?
2. to be considered a most desirable date?
3. to be married to someone who unhesitatingly shows affection for you?
4. that someone you meet at a party will want to leave the party with you?
5. that someone you are introduced to at a party will make a date with you?
6. to be warmly received when you approach an attractive person for a date?
7. to have people of the opposite sex show real pleasure when you join them for group activities?
8. that a person of the opposite sex to whom you are introduced at a party will enjoy conversing with you?
9. that attractive people of the opposite sex will speak to you with a warm and friendly voice?
10. to marry someone who is very much in love with you?
11. to receive warm, receptive smiles from unfamiliar but attractive people of the opposite sex?

12. to be regarded as a best friend or confidante by several people of the opposite sex?

13. that after ten years of marriage, your spouse will love you as much as ever?

14. that the person you marry will be able to cheer you up when you are sad?

15. to be genuinely understood by a person of the opposite sex?

16. that people for whom you feel love will also love you?

Higher scores on this questionnaire indicate higher expectations for love and affection.

When this questionnaire was given to a group of male college students, it was found to be a valid indicator of confidence, self-esteem, and satisfaction in romantic relationships. Those who scored high on this scale were more comfortable and less anxious in dating situations than those who scored low. They dated more frequently and enjoyed dating more. When they awaited meeting an attractive woman in an experimental situation, they experienced more positive emotions and fewer negative ones. They were more likely to anticipate that the woman would find them attractive and interesting and would want to get acquainted with them. In addition, they had greater expectations of success in life generally.

Is there anything in the family backgrounds of those who have high expectations for love and affection that distinguishes them from those who score low? Our study identified one strikingly clear factor: greater parental acceptance. Those whose parents were involved with them in positive ways were more confident that they would find love and affection in romantic relationships.

Chapters 9 and 11 offer guidelines that may enable you as a parent to help your children toward secure relationships. Daughters whose parents were in harmony are less likely to be anxious about their own romantic involvements. When it comes to your relationships with your children and how you raise them, our specific findings differ for sons and daughters. However, the combination of love, warmth, acceptance, and firmness (as opposed to hostility, rejection, and either excessive control or laxity) represents a good bet for bringing up an emotionally secure child.

In line with this recommendation, some of the people we interviewed have expressed their determination to help their children avoid what they themselves experienced. One woman describes her success in avoiding the aloofness trap her parents fell into:

I can't remember my parents ever kissing. They rarely kissed or embraced us, and it wasn't really warm. To this day I have a hard time with hugging. When someone hugs me, unless it's someone I'm very close to, I just freeze. But with my son it's fine. Every night when he goes to bed I kiss him and say, "I love you." If I forget and walk out of the room, he'll yell, "Mom, hug, hug!" My son is very loving. When I drive him to school, he kisses me good-bye—unless there are a lot of kids there!

A man expresses similar sentiments:

My children's upbringing is the opposite of mine. I just wish I'd had what I feel I'm giving them. Words I never heard from my mother or father—"I love you"—my kids hear all the time from me. I've never laid a hand on my kids. I constantly let them know and show them that I love them. They always let me know they love me, too, and it's not just words. They know what love is; you can see that they do.

As you become more aware of the conflicts in your own childhood, you can appreciate your children more and be more sensitive to their needs. A woman who is dealing with these issues describes how she has gained immeasurable confidence in herself and looks forward to parenthood:

It's no fun growing up with a mother who's chronically depressed, as I did, so I felt I wanted to wait until I could be pretty sure I wouldn't be passing that on to my children. I had to separate what was my mother from what is me. I really am different from my mother. For one thing, I'm warm and affectionate and caring and loving in a demonstrative way. I've always been good with children—like the Pied Piper, actually. Kids love me. My other concern was consistency—whether I could be consistent with a child. By this point I feel confident that at least I can struggle with that like a normal person—the way everybody struggles with it.

WORKS CITED

IN TEXT

CHAPTER 1

Ainsworth, Mary D. S. "Infant-Mother Attachment." *American Psychologist* 34, 1979: pp. 932–937.

Bowlby, John. *Attachment and Loss: I. Attachment.* New York: Basic Books, 1969.

———. *Attachment and Loss: II. Separation.* New York: Basic Books, 1973.

———. *Attachment and Loss: III. Loss.* New York: Basic Books, 1980.

Hindy, Carl G. "Individual Differences in Three Facets of 'Lovesickness': Tendency Toward Anxious Romantic Attachments, Sexual Jealousy, and Heterosexual Depression." Doctoral dissertation, University of Connecticut, Storrs, CT, 1984. (*Dissertation Abstracts*, Order No. DA8508755.)

Hindy, Carl G., and Schwarz, J. Conrad. " 'Lovesickness' in Dating Relationships: An Attachment Perspective." Paper presented at the 93rd Annual Convention of the American Psychological Association, Los Angeles, CA, August 1985.

Lee, John A. "The Styles of Loving." *Psychology Today,* October 1974, pp. 43–51.

Ovid. *The Art of Love* (Rolfe Humphries, trans.). Bloomington: Indiana University Press, 1957.

Tennov, Dorothy. *Love and Limerence.* Briarcliff Manor, NY: Stein & Day, 1979.

CHAPTER 2

Hindy, Carl G. "Individual Differences in the Tendency Toward Anxious Romantic Attachments: Theoretical Considerations and Preliminary Scale Development." Unpublished master's thesis, University of Connecticut, Storrs, CT, 1983.

Hindy, Carl G., and Schwarz, J. Conrad. "Individual Differences in the Tendency Toward Anxious Romantic Attachments." Paper presented at the Second International Conference on Personal Relationships, Madison, WI, July 1984.

CHAPTER 5

Rotter, Julian B. *Social Learning and Clinical Psychology.* Englewood Cliffs, NJ: Prentice-Hall, 1954.

Rotter, Julian B. *The Development and Application of Social Learning Theory: Selected Papers.* New York: Praeger, 1982.

Waller, Willard. "The Rating and Dating Complex." *American Sociological Review* 2, 1937: pp. 727–734.

White, Gregory L. "Relative Involvement, Inadequacy, and Jealousy." *Alternative Lifestyles* 4 (3), August 1981: pp. 291–309.

CHAPTER 7

Chamblin, Minor H.; Hindy, Carl G.; and Mackaman, Shelley. "Jealousy: A Naturalistic Taxonomy of Provoking Situations and Behavioral Responses." Paper presented at the 32nd Annual Meeting of the Southeastern Psychological Association, March 27, 1986, Orlando, FL.

Earnest, Karen Derecho. "Jealousy Threat: Affect and Coping in Men and Women." Unpublished doctoral dissertation, University of Connecticut, Storrs, CT, 1988.

Freud, Sigmund. "Certain Neurotic Mechanisms in Jealousy, Paranoia, and Homosexuality." In *Collected Papers,* Vol. 2 (Joan Riviere, trans.). London: Hogarth, 1924.

Harrison, Yola; Chamblin, Minor H.; and Hindy, Carl G. "The Impact of Psychological Needs on Emotions in Jealousy Situations." Unpublished paper, University of North Florida, Jacksonville, FL, 1985.

Hupka, Ralph B. "Cultural Determinants of Jealousy." *Alternative Lifestyles* 4 (3), August 1981: pp. 310–356.

Janov, Arthur. *The Primal Scream.* New York: Dell, 1970.

Mosher, Donald L., and Tomkins, Sylvan S. "Scripting the Macho Man: Hypermasculine Socialization and Enculturation." *Journal of Sex Research* 25, 1988: pp. 60–84.

Reiss, Ira L. *Journey into Sexuality: An Exploratory Voyage.* Englewood Cliffs, NJ: Prentice-Hall, 1986.

Salovey, Peter, and Rodin, Judith. "The Heart of Jealousy: A Report on *Psychology Today*'s Jealousy and Envy Survey." *Psychology Today,* September 1985, pp. 22–25, 28–29.

White, Gregory L. "Comparison of Four Jealousy Scales." *Journal of Research in Personality* 18, 1984: pp. 115–130.

CHAPTER 8

Beck, Aaron T. *Love Is Never Enough: How Couples Can Overcome Misunderstandings, Resolve Conflicts, and Solve Relationship Problems Through Cognitive Therapy.* New York: Harper & Row, 1988.

Beck, Aaron T.; Rial, W. Y.; and Rickels, K. "Short Form of Depression Inventory: Cross-Validation." *Psychological Reports* 34, 1974: pp. 1184–1186.

Beck, Aaron T.; Rush, A. J.; Shaw, Brian F.; and Emery, Gary. *Cognitive Therapy of Depression.* New York: John Wiley and Sons, 1979.

Peele, Stanton, and Brodsky, Archie. *Love and Addiction.* New York: New American Library, 1976.

Scott, John Paul. "Critical Periods in Behavioral Development." *Science* 138, 1962: pp. 949–958.

Seligman, Martin E. P. *Helplessness: On Depression, Development, and Death.* San Francisco: W. H. Freeman & Co., 1975.

Vaughan, Diane. *Uncoupling: Turning Points in Intimate Relationships.* New York: Oxford University Press, 1986.

Weiner, Bernard. *Theories of Motivation: From Mechanism to Cognition.* Chicago: Rand McNally, 1972.

Weiss, Robert S. "The Emotional Impact of Marital Separation." In George Levinger and Oliver C. Moles, eds., *Divorce and Separation.* New York: Basic Books, 1979: pp. 201–210.

Weiss, Robert S. "Attachment in Adult Life." In Colin Murray Parkes and Joan Stevenson-Hinde, eds., *The Place of Attachment in Human Behavior.* New York: Basic Books, 1982: pp. 171–184.

Wickless, Cynthia, and Kirsch, Irving. "Cognitive Correlates of Anger, Anxiety, and Sadness." *Cognitive Therapy and Research* 12, 1988: pp. 367–377.

CHAPTER 9

Ainsworth, Mary D. S. (See references for Chapter 1 above.)

Bienvenu, Millard J., Sr. "Measurement of Marital Communication." *The Family Coordinator* 19, 1970: pp. 26–31.

Bowlby, John. (See references for Chapter 1 above.)

Locke, Harvey, and Wallace, Karl M. "Short Marital-Adjustment and Prediction Tests: Their Reliability and Validity." *Marriage and Family Living* 21, 1959: pp. 251–255.

Schaefer, Earl S. "Children's Report of Parental Behavior: An Inventory." *Child Development* 36, 1965: pp. 413–424.

Schwarz, J. Conrad. "Development and Validation of the Inter-Parental Conflict Scale"; "Development and Validation of the Inter-Parental Influence Scale." Unpublished manuscripts, University of Connecticut, Storrs, CT, 1988. Abstracted in John Touliatos, Barry F. Perlmutter, and Murray A. Straus, eds., *Handbook of Family Measurement Techniques.* Newbury Park, CA: Sage Publications, in press. Scale forms deposited with the National Auxiliary Publication Service (NAPS, c/o Microfiche Publications, 248 Hempstead Turnpike, West Hempstead, NY 11552).

Schwarz, J. Conrad. "Development and Validation of the Parental Competency Scale." Manuscript in preparation, University of Connecticut, Storrs, CT, 1989a. Scale available from Dr. J. Conrad Schwarz, University of Connecticut, Department of Psychology, U-20, 406 Babbidge Road, Storrs, CT 06269-1020.

Schwarz, J. Conrad. "Development and Validation of the Relationship with Mother and Father Scale: A Measure of Emotional Attachment and Coalition." Manuscript in preparation, University of Connecticut, Storrs, CT, 1989b. Scale available from Dr. J. Conrad Schwarz, University of Connecticut, Department of Psychology, U-20, 406 Babbidge Road, Storrs, CT 06269-1020.

Schwarz, J. Conrad, and Zuroff, David C. "Development and Validation of the Love

Inconsistency Scale." Unpublished manuscript, University of Connecticut, Storrs, CT, 1988. Abstracted in John Touliatos, Barry F. Perlmutter, and Murray A. Straus, eds., *Handbook of Family Measurement Techniques.* Newbury Park, CA: Sage Publications, in press. Scale forms deposited with the National Auxiliary Publication Service (NAPS, c/o Microfiche Publications, 248 Hempstead Turnpike, West Hempstead, NY 11552).

Weiss, Robert L., and Cerreto, Mary C. "The Marital Status Inventory: Development of a Measure of Dissolution Potential." *American Journal of Family Therapy* 8, 1980: pp. 80–85.

CHAPTER 10

Ainsworth, Mary D. S. (See references for Chapter 1 above.)

Bowlby, John. (See references for Chapter 1 above.)

Cohen, Keith N., and Clark, James A. "Transitional Object Attachments in Early Childhood and Personality Characteristics in Later Life." *Journal of Personality and Social Psychology* 46, 1984: pp. 106–111.

Gurtman, Michael B. "Heterosexual Trust: Theory and Measurement." Unpublished doctoral dissertation, University of Connecticut, Storrs, CT, 1979.

CHAPTER 11

Miller, Alice. *Prisoners of Childhood: How Narcissistic Parents Form and Deform the Emotional Lives of Their Gifted Children.* New York: Basic Books, 1981.

Schaefer, Earl S. (See references for Chapter 9 above.)

Schwarz, J. Conrad (1988). (See references for Chapter 9 above.)

Schwarz, J. Conrad (1989a). (See references for Chapter 9 above.)

Schwarz, J. Conrad (1989b). (See references for Chapter 9 above.)

Schwarz, J. Conrad, and Zuroff, David C. (See references for Chapter 9 above.)

Worell, Leonard, and Worell, Judith. *The Parent Behavior Form.* Manual in preparation. Available from Leonard Worell, Department of Psychology, University of Kentucky, Lexington, KY 40506.

CHAPTER 12

Hindy, Carl G. "Generalized Expectancies for Love and Affection in Heterosexual Dating Relationships." Paper presented at the 32nd Annual Meeting of the Southeastern Psychological Association, March 27, 1986, Orlando, FL.

Suggested

Reading

The Augustine Fellowship. *Sex and Love Addicts Anonymous.* Boston: The Augustine Fellowship, Sex and Love Addicts Anonymous, 1986.

Bach, George. *The Intimate Enemy: How to Fight Fair in Love and Marriage.* New York: Avon, 1981.

Bach, George, and Deutsch, Ronald M. *Pairing: How to Achieve Genuine Intimacy.* New York: Avon, 1971.

Barker, Robert L. *The Green-Eyed Marriage: Surviving Jealous Relationships.* New York: Free Press, 1987.

Bass, Ellen, and Davis, Laura. *The Courage to Heal: A Guide for Women Survivors of Child Sexual Abuse.* New York: Harper & Row, 1987.

Beck, Aaron T. *Love Is Never Enough: How Couples Can Overcome Misunderstandings, Resolve Conflicts, and Solve Relationship Problems Through Cognitive Therapy.* New York: Harper & Row, 1988.

Blotnick, Srully. *Otherwise Engaged: The Private Lives of Successful Career Women.* New York: Penguin, 1986.

Blumstein, Philip, and Schwartz, Pepper. *American Couples.* New York: William Morrow, 1983.

Botwin, Carol. *Men Who Can't Be Faithful.* New York: Warner Books, 1988.

Bowlby, John. *A Secure Base: Parent-Child Attachment and Healthy Human Development.* New York: Harper & Row, 1988.

Brame, Angela. *When Battered Women Kill.* New York: Free Press, 1987.

Branden, Nathaniel. *The Psychology of Romantic Love.* New York: Bantam, 1981.

Burns, David D. *Feeling Good: The New Mood Therapy.* New York: New American Library, 1981.

Burns, David D. *The Feeling Good Workbook: Using New Mood Therapy in Everyday Life.* New York: New American Library, 1989.

Burns, David D. *Intimate Connections: The New Clinically Tested Program for Overcoming Loneliness.* New York: William Morrow, 1985.

Carnes, Patrick. *Counseling the Sexual Addict.* Minneapolis: Compcare, 1986.

Carnes, Patrick. *Out of the Shadows: Understanding Sexual Addiction.* Minneapolis: Compcare, 1985.

Colgrove, Melba; Bloomfield, Harold H.; and McWilliams, Peter. *How to Survive the Loss of a Love.* New York: Bantam, 1982.

Cowan, Connell, and Kinder, Melvyn. *Smart Women, Foolish Choices.* New York: New American Library, 1986.

Cowan, Connell, and Kinder, Melvyn. *Women Men Love—Women Men Leave: Why Men Are Drawn to Women—What Makes Them Want to Stay.* New York: Crown, 1987.

Diamond, Jed. *Looking for Love in All the Wrong Places: Overcoming Romantic and Sexual Addictions.* New York: Putnam, 1988.

Dolesh, Daniel J., and Lehman, Sherelynn. *Love Me Love Me Not: How to Survive Infidelity.* New York: Paperjacks, 1987.

Dowling, Colette. *The Cinderella Complex: Women's Hidden Fear of Independence.* New York: Pocket Books, 1982.

Eichenbaum, Luise, and Orbach, Susie. *What Do Women Want: Exploding the Myth of Dependency.* New York: Berkley Books, 1984.

Ellis, Albert. *How to Stubbornly Refuse to Make Yourself Miserable About Anything—Yes, Anything.* Secaucus, NJ: Lyle Stuart, 1988.

Forward, Susan, and Torres, Joan. *Men Who Hate Women and the Women Who Love Them.* New York: Bantam, 1987.

Friday, Nancy. *Jealousy.* New York: Bantam, 1985.

Friday, Nancy. *My Mother/My Self.* New York: Dell, 1977.

Friday, Nancy. *My Secret Garden: Women's Sexual Fantasies.* New York: Pocket Books, 1982.

Friedman, Sonya. *A Hero Is More Than Just a Sandwich.* New York: Putnam, 1986.

Friedman, Sonya. *Men Are Just Desserts.* New York: Warner Books, 1983.

Friedman, Sonya. *Smart Cookies Don't Crumble: A Modern Woman's Guide to Living and Loving Her Own Life.* New York: Putnam, 1985.

Gardner, Richard A. *The Boys' and Girls' Book About Divorce.* New York: Bantam, 1970.

Gardner, Richard A. *The Parents' Book About Divorce.* New York: Doubleday, 1977.

Garner, Alan. *Conversationally Speaking: Tested New Ways to Increase Your Personal and Social Effectiveness.* New York: McGraw-Hill, 1981.

Ginott, Haim. *Between Parent and Child.* New York: Macmillan, 1965.

Ginott, Haim. *Between Parent and Teenager.* New York: Macmillan, 1969.

Glasser, William. *Reality Therapy.* New York: Harper & Row, 1965.

Golabuk, Philip. *Recovering From a Broken Heart.* New York: Harper & Row, 1987.

Goldstein, Sonja, and Solnit, Albert J. *Divorce and Your Child: Practical Suggestions for Parents.* New Haven, CT: Yale University Press, 1984.

Gordon, Barbara. *Jennifer Fever: Older Men, Younger Women.* New York: Harper & Row, 1988.

Gottman, John; Notarius, Cliff; Gonso, Jonni; and Markman, Howard. *A Couple's Guide to Communication.* Champaign, IL: Research Press, 1976.

Greenwald, Jerry A. *Creative Intimacy: How to Break the Patterns That Poison Your Relationships.* New York: Jove Publications, 1984.

Greif, Geoffrey L. *Single Fathers.* Lexington, MA: D.C. Heath, 1985.

Halpern, Howard M. *How to Break Your Addiction to a Person.* New York: Bantam, 1982.

Hazen, Barbara S. *Two Homes to Live in: A Child's Eye View of Divorce.* New York: Human Sciences Press, 1978.

Hoffman, Susanna. *Men Who Are Good for You, and Men Who Are Bad.* Berkeley, CA: Ten Speed Press, 1987.

Jakubowski, Patricia, and Lange, Arthur, J. *The Assertive Option: Your Rights and Responsibilities.* Champaign, IL: Research Press, 1978.

Johnson, Robert A. *We: Understanding the Psychology of Romantic Love.* New York: Harper & Row, 1985.

Kiev, Ari. *How to Keep Love Alive: Strategies for Using Conflict and Change to Make Love Grow.* New York: Harper & Row, 1981.

Kiley, Dan. *The Peter Pan Syndrome: Men Who Have Never Grown Up.* New York: Avon, 1984.

Kiley, Dan. *The Wendy Dilemma: When Women Stop Mothering Their Men.* New York: Avon, 1985.

Krantzler, Mel. *Creative Divorce: A New Opportunity for Personal Growth.* New York: M. Evans, 1974.

Krantzler, Mel. *Learning to Love Again.* New York: Harper & Row, 1987.

Leonard, Linda S. *On The Way to the Wedding: Transforming the Love Relationship.* Boston: Shambhala, 1985.

Lerner, Harriet G. *The Dance of Anger: A Woman's Guide to Changing the Patterns of Intimate Relationships.* New York: Harper & Row, 1986.

Lerner, Harriet G. *The Dance of Intimacy: A Woman's Guide to Courageous Acts of Change in Key Relationships.* New York: Harper & Row, 1989.

Levinson, Daniel J. *Seasons of a Man's Life.* New York: Knopf, 1978.

Marshall, Megan. *The Cost of Loving: Women and the New Fear of Intimacy.* New York: Putnam, 1984.

Miller, Jean B. *Toward a New Psychology of Women.* Second Edition. Boston: Beacon Press, 1986.

Money, John. *Love Maps.* New York: Irvington, 1986.

Naifeh, Steven, and Smith, Gregory W. *Why Can't Men Open Up?* New York: Warner Books, 1984.

Napier, Augustus Y. *The Fragile Bond: In Search of an Equal, Intimate, and Enduring Marriage.* New York: Harper & Row, 1988.

Nelsen, Jane. *Positive Discipline: A Warm, Practical, Step-by-Step Source Book for Parents and Teachers.* New York: Ballantine, 1977.

Norwood, Robin. *Women Who Love Too Much.* Los Angeles, CA: J. P. Tarcher, 1986.

Novak, William. *The Great American Man Shortage and What You Can Do About It.* New York: Bantam, 1983.

Patterson, Gerald R. *Families: Application of Social Learning to Family Life.* Champaign, IL: Research Press, 1971.

Patterson, Gerald R., and Forgatch, Marion S. *Parents and Adolescents Living Together—Part I: The Basics.* Eugene, OR: Castalia Publishing Company, 1987.

Paul, Jordan, and Paul, Margaret. *Do I Have to Give Up Me to Be Loved by You?* Minneapolis: Compcare, 1983.

Peele, Stanton, and Brodsky, Archie. *Love and Addiction.* New York: New American Library, 1976.

Person, Ethel Spector. *Dreams of Love and Fateful Encounters: The Power of Romantic Passion.* New York: Norton, 1988.

Richards, Arlene, and Willis, Irene. *How to Get It Together When Your Parents Are Coming Apart.* New York: Bantam, 1976.

Rosenstock, Harvey A.; Rosenstock, Judith D.; and Weiner, Janet. *Journey Through Divorce: Five Stages Toward Recovery.* New York: Human Sciences Press, 1988.

Rubin, Lillian. *Intimate Strangers: Men and Women Together.* New York: Harper & Row, 1983.

Russianoff, Penelope. *Why Do I Think I Am Nothing Without a Man?* New York: Bantam, 1983.

Safilios, Constantina R. *Love, Sex, and Sex Roles.* Englewood Cliffs, NJ: Prentice-Hall, 1977.

Scarf, Maggie. *Intimate Partners: Patterns in Love and Marriage.* New York: Random House, 1987.

Scarf, Maggie. *Unfinished Business: Pressure Points in the Lives of Women.* New York: Ballantine Books, 1980.

Schmidt, Jerry. *Help Yourself: A Guide to Self-Change.* Champaign, IL: Research Press, 1976.

Schneider, Jennifer P. *Back From Betrayal: Surviving His Affairs.* New York: Harper & Row, 1988.

Shain, Merle. *Hearts That We Broke Long Ago.* New York: Bantam, 1985.

Sheehy, Gail. *Passages.* New York: Bantam, 1977.

Sills, Judith. *How to Stop Looking for Someone Perfect and Find Someone to Love.* New York: Ballantine, 1985.

Sternberg, Robert J. *The Triangle of Love: Intimacy, Passion, Commitment.* New York: Harper & Row, 1988.

Strayhorn, Joseph M., Jr. *Talking It Out: A Guide to Effective Communication and Problem Solving.* Champaign, IL: Research Press, 1977.

Tafford, Abigail. *Crazy Time: Surviving Divorce.* New York: Bantam, 1984.

Tennov, Dorothy. *Love and Limerence.* Briarcliff Manor, NY: Stein & Day, 1979.

Vaughan, Diane. *Uncoupling: Turning Points in Intimate Relationships.* New York: Oxford University Press, 1986.

Viorst, Judith. *Necessary Losses.* New York: Fawcett, 1987.

Wallerstein, Judith S., and Kelly, Joan B. *Surviving the Breakup: How Children and Parents Cope With Divorce.* New York: Basic Books, 1980.

Wanderer, Zev, and Cabot, Tracy. *Letting Go: A Twelve-Week Personal Action Program to Overcome a Broken Heart.* New York: Dell, 1987.

Weiss, Robert S. *Marital Separation.* New York: Basic Books, 1975.

Woititz, Janet G. *Struggle for Intimacy.* Pompano Beach, FL: Health Communications, 1985.

Appendix

Organizations Providing Support in Coping With Anxiety, Insecurity, and Other Problems Related to Romantic Love

Adult Children of Alcoholics (ACA)
P.O. Box 3216
Torrance, California 90505

ACA offers self-help support groups for people aged 18 and over who grew up in alcoholic or other dysfunctional families.

Al-Anon Family Group Headquarters
1372 Broadway
New York, New York 10018

Al-Anon family groups act as a support system for relatives and friends of persons with alcohol problems.

Alcoholics Anonymous (AA)
P.O. Box 459
Grand Central Station
New York, New York 10163

AA runs group meetings for women and men. The meetings allow for sharing one's experience with others as a way to begin recovery from alcoholism.

The Augustine Fellowship
Sex and Love Addicts Anonymous (SLAA)
P.O. Box 119
New Town Branch
Boston, Massachusetts 02258

SLAA provides assistance to persons with unmanageable love and relationship problems. Group meetings attempt to identify and relieve unhealthy patterns of interacting in sexual and love relationships.

Batterers Anonymous
c/o Option House Outreach
3200 North E Street
San Bernardino, California 92405

Through weekly informational meetings, Batterers Anonymous offers help to men who abuse women, by providing positive alternatives to abusive behavior.

Co-Dependents Anonymous
P.O. Box 33577
Phoenix, Arizona 85067-3577

Co-Dependents Anonymous groups focus on changing unhealthy patterns of behavior (e.g., caretaking or being cared for, manipulating or being manipulated) formed in relationships with alcoholic and addicted persons, with the purpose of moving toward healthy relationships.

Co-Dependents of Sexual Addicts (COSA)
P.O. Box 14537
Minneapolis, Minnesota 55414

COSA serves as a support group for the families and friends of persons with sexual and love addictions. Member confidentiality is maintained.

National Association for Children of Alcoholics (NACoA)
31582 Coast Highway, Suite B
South Laguna, California 92677

NACoA is a clearinghouse for education and advocacy for people of all ages who have had alcoholic parents. It provides free packets of information and makes referrals to support groups such as Adult Children of Alcoholics, Al-Anon, and Co-Dependents Anonymous.

National Coalition Against Domestic Violence (NCADV)
1000 16th Street, N.W., Suite 303
Washington, D.C. 20036

NCADV provides information and referrals to women on issues of domestic violence. This group will provide assistance and help locate shelter for women who are experiencing domestic abuse.

Parents Without Partners, Inc. (PWP)
7910 Woodmont Avenue
Washington, D.C. 20014

PWP offers support groups, pertinent seminars, as well as opportunities to socialize, including meetings and parties, which are frequently held in members' homes.

Sex Addicts Anonymous (SAA)
P.O. Box 3038
Minneapolis, Minnesota 55403

SAA provides a support network for persons who compulsively repeat sexual behavior that is abusive, exploitative, and damaging to their home and work lives.

Sexaholics Anonymous (SA)
P.O. Box 300
Simi Valley, California 93062

SA helps individuals who are struggling with problems related to sex and love addiction.

Stepfamily Association of America
602 East Joppa Road
Baltimore, Maryland 21204

The national headquarters of the Stepfamily Association provides information about local chapters, which offer workshops, seminars, and support groups for members of combined families.

INDEX

About the

Authors

CARL G. HINDY, Ph.D., is a clinical psychologist in private practice in Nashua, New Hampshire, whose work focuses on love relationships and problems of attachment, separation, and loss. A Phi Beta Kappa graduate of Brandeis University, he received his M.A. and Ph.D. in clinical psychology from the University of Connecticut.

J. CONRAD SCHWARZ, Ph.D., Professor of Psychology at the University of Connecticut, Storrs, is also a clinical psychologist in private practice. He earned his bachelor's degree in psychology from Pennsylvania State University, where he was elected to Phi Beta Kappa, and his master's and doctoral degrees in clinical psychology from Ohio State University. Dr. Schwarz has been practicing psychotherapy and training clinical psychologists for more than twenty five years.

ARCHIE BRODSKY, a professional writer, is co-author of the pioneering classic *Love and Addiction,* as well as of other books in psychology and medicine, including *Medical Choices, Medical Chances* and *Diabetes: Caring for Your Emotions As Well As Your Health.* A Phi Beta Kappa graduate of the University of Pennsylvania, he is Senior Research Associate at the Program in Psychiatry and the Law, Massachusetts Mental Health Center, Harvard Medical School.